Learn Amazon SageMaker

A guide to building, training, and deploying machine
learning models for developers and data scientists

Julien Simon

BIRMINGHAM—MUMBAI

Learn Amazon SageMaker

Commissioning Editor: Sunith Shetty

Acquisition Editor: Ali Abidi

Senior Editor: David Sugarman

Content Development Editor: Joseph Sunil

Technical Editor: Manikandan Kurup

Copy Editor: Safis Editing

Project Coordinator: Aishwarya Mohan

Proofreader: Safis Editing

Indexer: Rekha Nair

Production Designer: Vijay Kamble

First published: August 2020

Production reference: 1260820

Published by Packt Publishing Ltd.
Livery Place
35 Livery Street
Birmingham
B3 2PB, UK.

ISBN 978-1-80020-891-9

www.packt.com

Dear reader, please accept my most sincere thanks for spending your hard-earned money on this book. I hope it will live up to your expectations, and help you grow as a Machine Learning professional.

Writing it is the conclusion of a process that started 40 years ago, when I opened a BASIC programming book for the Commodore VIC-20. Over the years, I've bought and read more technical books than I can remember, and writing one is a dream come true. I can only hope that traces of the undying brilliance found in the works of Donald Knuth, Brian Kernighan, Dennis Ritchie, Kirk McKusick, Richard Stevens, and Evi Nemeth somehow rubbed off on me during the years I spent reading them, but I very seriously doubt it.

First, I'd like to address my most sincere thanks to the Packt team, especially my editors Joseph Sunil and David Sugarman for their valuable feedback and advice. I never thought writing a book would be this painless. I would also like to thank my reviewers, particularly Javier Ramirez and Ricardo Sueiras, for helping me make this book better than it originally was.

I'd also like to thank the AWS service teams who work on Amazon SageMaker every day, and sometimes every night, to give our customers the best possible features and service quality. You are the unspoken heroes of this book, and I'm but your messenger. I hope I did you justice.

On a personal note, I'm forever indebted to my parents for their never-ending support, and for never pulling the literal plug on me when other kids were playing outside, or when the moon was already high the sky. Back then, I did take the road less traveled, and these long days and nights spent dissecting Commodores, Apple][s and Macs made all the difference.

My love also goes to my wife and children, who somehow kept the house calm enough during COVID-19 lockdown for me to write 13 chapters in 3 months, at my own amazement. Now, I promise I'll take more time to enjoy these sunny afternoons.

Finally, I want to dedicate this book to the memory of my uncle Guy Simon. Wherever he is now, I hope that he's proud of this Hobbit's adventures.

Packt.com

Subscribe to our online digital library for full access to over 7,000 books and videos, as well as industry leading tools to help you plan your personal development and advance your career. For more information, please visit our website.

Why subscribe?

- Spend less time learning and more time coding with practical eBooks and Videos from over 4,000 industry professionals

- Improve your learning with Skill Plans built especially for you

- Get a free eBook or video every month

- Fully searchable for easy access to vital information

- Copy and paste, print, and bookmark content

Did you know that Packt offers eBook versions of every book published, with PDF and ePub files available? You can upgrade to the eBook version at packt.com and as a print book customer, you are entitled to a discount on the eBook copy. Get in touch with us at customercare@packtpub.com for more details.

At www.packt.com, you can also read a collection of free technical articles, sign up for a range of free newsletters, and receive exclusive discounts and offers on Packt books and eBooks.

Foreword

If I had to pick a single source of frustration coming from the Machine Learning world, nowadays, without doubt I would mention the break necking speed at which everything around this domain evolves: algorithms, infrastructure, frameworks, best practices. By the time you experiment with a technique, a new method smashes the state-of-the-art. By the time you refactor that computer vision pipeline, your library of choice gets a major upgrade. Let alone all the headaches coming with shipping actual models to actual customers in production. Add debugging, scaling and monitoring to the list.

The way to cope with the ML madness can be summarized in two points: being up-to-date and having the right set of tools. This book covers both.

Once again, it is a matter of handling speed efficiently. You want to be on top of the latest advances in the field, in order to jump quickly from one technique to another. To do that effectively, though, you want to be using the right set of tools. Streamline your experimentation's pipelines, shorten the time from development to production, scale projects removing all the hassle of infrastructure maintenance, setup and updates. If you think this is what any Machine-Learning-oriented organization deserves, then AWS and SageMaker are what you are looking for, and this is the book you need to get up to speed.

Having worked with SageMaker myself, I can bring my testimony to the table. The completeness of the product is truly impressive: the team got your back for all the steps of the ML pipeline. From data ingestion by seamless integration with all the AWS storage solutions, to rapid prototyping within the familiar Jupyter notebooks. From automated data labelling, to automated model debugging. From hyper-parameter tuning and experiment handling, to the breadth of services supporting the deployment stage. Off-the-shelf Docker images, A/B testing, canary deployments capabilities, features' distribution shifts tracking. Just to name a few. SageMaker is a fully-fledged environment letting practitioners hit the ground running.

You still might wonder why you need Machine Learning at all. You have your rule-based systems in place. You master them inside out, and they are driving that nice uplift your company is currently enjoying. This is true. Thing is, it will not last forever.

Rules are good starting points, they are simple to debug, and provide tangible benefits almost immediately. They are not easy to adapt to a rapidly evolving market, though. Eventually, the initial uplift will start shrinking and the competitive advantage to fade out. That is when you realize you need to play smarter. The patterns a human spots in the data, the same that drove a rule-based approach in the first place, win in the short term. However, in the long run, you must increase the level of abstraction, and try removing the human touch from the workflow as much as possible. Welcome Machine Learning to the stage. The scale, efficiency, and financial gains reached by employing modern statistical learning strategies are almost limitless. The "almost" part of the story is generally driven by the technical debt slowing down Data Science projects. Which, once again, is why you imperatively need the right tools, SageMaker being one of those.

I still hear people pointing out that they are neither engineers nor scientists. They are analysts, more or less technical product managers. Business people to make it short. Do these individuals need to hear all the ML fuss? Yes, they do. Statistical learning is not only about building Netflix's recommendation engine from the ground up, or shipping Tesla's autonomous vehicles driving system. Those are impressive but still niche examples of the power of these techniques. It turns out that, as far as I am concerned, being able to build a model is a lot more impactful in a business context. First, because of the much higher number of professionals potentially involved. Second, because you do not necessarily build a model to blindly predict A given B. You might want to train an algorithm to model the interaction between A and B, their interdependencies, the process bridging them. In a nutshell, you train an algorithm to gain insights. This is what data-driven decision-making is all about, and what every moderately technical business person should pursue as a must. For this to happen, we need to democratize the access to Machine Learning, of course. Demystify the black box. Online learning resources are nowadays widely available to cover for the scientific part. What about the infrastructural side of the story instead? This is where AWS and SageMaker come to the rescue, bridging the gap between the product manager analyzing quarterly financial results, and the research scientist shipping self-flying drones. A single environment to win them all.

If I managed to tickle your curiosity enough, go ahead. Turn the page and let *Julien Simon* guide you through the wonderful world of Machine Learning with Amazon SageMaker.

Francesco Pochetti,

Senior Data Scientist at Mash & AWS ML Hero

Contributors

About the author

Julien Simon is a principal AI and machine learning developer advocate. He focuses on helping developers and enterprises to bring their ideas to life. He frequently speaks at conferences and blogs on AWS blogs and on Medium. Prior to joining AWS, Julien served for 10 years as CTO/VP of engineering in top-tier web start-ups where he led large software and ops teams in charge of thousands of servers worldwide. In the process, he fought his way through a wide range of technical, business, and procurement issues, which helped him gain a deep understanding of physical infrastructure, its limitations, and how cloud computing can help.

About the reviewers

Chaitanya Hazarey is a technical leader and machine learning architect with the AWS Machine Learning Product Management team. He helps customers design and build cloud native machine learning products. Driven to solve hard problems, he engages with partners and customers to modernize their machine learning stack and integrate with Amazon SageMaker, working together with the business and engineering teams to make products successful. He has a master's degree in computer science from USC, LA. He enjoys teaching at Amazon's Machine Learning University and his research interests include efficient training and inference techniques for deep learning algorithms.

Javier Ramirez is a Developer Advocate at AWS. He was previously head of engineering at Datatonic, an ML consultancy; cofounder and data engineer at Teowaki—a big data consultancy; CTO at ASPGems—a web development agency; and a Google Developer Expert in GCP for over 5 years. He has also cofounded Aprendoaprogramar and Utende in a career spanning over 20 years. He loves data, big and small, and he has extensive experience with SQL, NoSQL, graphs, in-memory databases, big data, and machine learning. He likes distributed, scalable, always-on systems. He has presented at events in over 20 countries, mentored dozens of start-ups, taught for 6 years at different universities, and trained hundreds of professionals on cloud, data engineering, and ML.

Packt is searching for authors like you

If you're interested in becoming an author for Packt, please visit `authors.packtpub.com` and apply today. We have worked with thousands of developers and tech professionals, just like you, to help them share their insight with the global tech community. You can make a general application, apply for a specific hot topic that we are recruiting an author for, or submit your own idea.

Table of Contents

Section 2:
Building and Training Models

3

AutoML with Amazon SageMaker Autopilot

4

Training Machine Learning Models

5

Training Computer Vision Models

6

Training Natural Language Processing Models

7

Extending Machine Learning Services Using Built-In Frameworks

8

Using Your Algorithms and Code

Section 3:
Diving Deeper on Training

9

Scaling Your Training Jobs

10
Advanced Training Techniques

Section 4:
Managing Models in Production

11
Deploying Machine Learning Models

12
Automating Machine Learning Workflows

13
Optimizing Prediction Cost and Performance

Other Books You May Enjoy

Index

Preface

Amazon SageMaker enables you to quickly build, train, and deploy **machine learning (ML)** models at scale, without managing any infrastructure. It helps you focus on the ML problem at hand and deploy high-quality models by removing the heavy lifting typically involved in each step of the ML process. This book is a comprehensive guide for data scientists and ML developers who want to learn the ins and outs of Amazon SageMaker.

You'll understand how to use various modules of SageMaker as a single toolset to solve the challenges faced in ML. As you progress, you'll cover features such as AutoML, built-in algorithms and frameworks, and the option for writing your own code and algorithms to build ML models. Later, the book will show you how to integrate Amazon SageMaker with popular deep learning libraries such as TensorFlow and PyTorch to increase the capabilities of existing models. You'll also learn to get the models to production faster with minimum effort and at a lower cost. Finally, you'll explore how to use Amazon SageMaker Debugger to analyze, detect, and highlight problems to understand the current model state and improve model accuracy.

By the end of this Amazon book, you'll be able to use Amazon SageMaker on the full spectrum of ML workflows, from experimentation, training, and monitoring, to scaling, deployment, and automation.

Who this book is for

This book is for software engineers, ML developers, data scientists, and AWS users who are new to using Amazon SageMaker and want to build high-quality ML models without worrying about infrastructure. Knowledge of the basics of AWS is required to grasp the concepts covered in this book more effectively. Some understanding of ML concepts and the Python programming language will also be beneficial.

What this book covers

Chapter 1, Getting Started with Amazon SageMaker, provides an overview of Amazon SageMaker, what its capabilities are, and how it helps solve many pain points faced by ML projects today.

Chapter 2, Handling Data Preparation Techniques, discusses data preparation options. Although this it isn't the core subject of the book, data preparation is a key topic in ML, and it should be covered at a high level.

Chapter 3, AutoML with Amazon SageMaker AutoPilot, shows you how to build, train, and optimize ML models automatically with Amazon SageMaker AutoPilot.

Chapter 4, Training Machine Learning Models, shows you how to build and train models using the collection of statistical ML algorithms built into Amazon SageMaker.

Chapter 5, Training Computer Vision Models, shows you how to build and train models using the collection of computer vision algorithms built into Amazon SageMaker.

Chapter 6, Training Natural Language Processing Models, shows you how to build and train models using the collection of natural language processing algorithms built into Amazon SageMaker.

Chapter 7, Extending Machine Learning Services Using Built-In Frameworks, shows you how to build and train ML models using the collection of built-in open source frameworks in Amazon SageMaker.

Chapter 8, Using Your Algorithms and Code, shows you how to build and train ML models using your own code on Amazon SageMaker, for example, R or custom Python.

Chapter 9, Scaling Your Training Jobs, shows you how to distribute training jobs to many managed instances, using either built-in algorithms or built-in frameworks.

Chapter 10, Advanced Training Techniques, shows you how to leverage advanced training in Amazon SageMaker.

Chapter 11, Deploying Machine Learning Models, shows you how to deploy ML models in a variety of configurations.

Chapter 12, Automating Deployment Tasks, shows you how to automate the deployment of ML models on Amazon SageMaker.

Chapter 13, Optimizing Cost and Performance, shows you how to optimize model deployments, both from an infrastructure perspective and from a cost perspective.

To get the most out of this book

You will need a functional AWS account to run everything.

If you are using the digital version of this book, we advise you to type the code yourself or access the code via the GitHub repository (link available in the next section). Doing so will help you avoid any potential errors related to the copying and pasting of code.

Download the example code files

You can download the example code files for this book from your account at www.packt.com. If you purchased this book elsewhere, you can visit www.packtpub.com/support and register to have the files emailed directly to you.

You can download the code files by following these steps:

1. Log in or register at www.packt.com.
2. Select the **Support** tab.
3. Click on **Code Downloads**.
4. Enter the name of the book in the **Search** box and follow the onscreen instructions.

Once the file is downloaded, please make sure that you unzip or extract the folder using the latest version of:

- WinRAR/7-Zip for Windows
- Zipeg/iZip/UnRarX for Mac
- 7-Zip/PeaZip for Linux

The code bundle for the book is also hosted on GitHub at https://github.com/PacktPublishing/Learn-Amazon-SageMaker. In case there's an update to the code, it will be updated on the existing GitHub repository.

We also have other code bundles from our rich catalog of books and videos available at https://github.com/PacktPublishing/. Check them out!

Download the color images

We also provide a PDF file that has color images of the screenshots/diagrams used in this book. You can download it here: https://static.packt-cdn.com/downloads/9781800208919_ColorImages.pdf.

Conventions used

There are a number of text conventions used throughout this book.

`Code in text`: Indicates code words in text, database table names, folder names, filenames, file extensions, pathnames, dummy URLs, user input, and Twitter handles. Here is an example: "You can use the `describe-spot-price-history` API to collect this information programmatically."

A block of code is set as follows:

```
od = sagemaker.estimator.Estimator(
    container,
    role,
    train_instance_count=2,
    train_instance_type='ml.p3.2xlarge',
    train_use_spot_instances=True,
    train_max_run=3600,                    # 1 hours
    train_max_wait=7200,                   # 2 hour
    output_path=s3_output)
```

When we wish to draw your attention to a particular part of a code block, the relevant lines or items are set in bold:

```
[<sagemaker.model_monitor.model_monitoring.MonitoringExecution
at 0x7fdd1d55a6d8>,
<sagemaker.model_monitor.model_monitoring.MonitoringExecution
at 0x7fdd1d581630>,
<sagemaker.model_monitor.model_monitoring.MonitoringExecution
at 0x7fdce4b1c860>]
```

Bold: Indicates a new term, an important word, or words that you see on screen. For example, words in menus or dialog boxes appear in the text like this. Here is an example: "We can find more information about our monitoring job in the SageMaker console, in the **Processing jobs** section."

> **Tips or important notes**
> Appear like this.

Get in touch

Feedback from our readers is always welcome.

General feedback: If you have questions about any aspect of this book, mention the book title in the subject of your message and email us at customercare@packtpub.com.

Errata: Although we have taken every care to ensure the accuracy of our content, mistakes do happen. If you have found a mistake in this book, we would be grateful if you would report this to us. Please visit www.packtpub.com/support/errata, selecting your book, clicking on the Errata Submission Form link, and entering the details.

Piracy: If you come across any illegal copies of our works in any form on the internet, we would be grateful if you would provide us with the location address or website name. Please contact us at copyright@packt.com with a link to the material.

If you are interested in becoming an author: If there is a topic that you have expertise in, and you are interested in either writing or contributing to a book, please visit authors.packtpub.com.

Reviews

Please leave a review. Once you have read and used this book, why not leave a review on the site that you purchased it from? Potential readers can then see and use your unbiased opinion to make purchase decisions, we at Packt can understand what you think about our products, and our authors can see your feedback on their book. Thank you!

For more information about Packt, please visit packt.com.

Section 1: Introduction to Amazon SageMaker

The objective of this section is to introduce you to the key concepts, help you download supporting data, and introduce you to example scenarios and use cases.

This section comprises the following chapters:

- *Chapter 1, Getting Started with Amazon SageMaker*
- *Chapter 2, Handling Data Preparation Techniques*

1

Introduction to Amazon SageMaker

Machine learning (**ML**) practitioners use a large collection of tools in the course of their projects: open source libraries, deep learning frameworks, and more. In addition, they often have to write their own tools for automation and orchestration. Managing these tools and their underlying infrastructure is time-consuming and error-prone.

This is the very problem that Amazon SageMaker was designed to address (`https://aws.amazon.com/sagemaker/`). Amazon SageMaker is a fully managed service that helps you quickly build and deploy ML models. Whether you're just beginning with ML or you're an experienced practitioner, you'll find SageMaker features to improve the agility of your workflows, as well as the performance of your models. You'll be able to focus 100% on the ML problem at hand, without spending any time installing, managing, and scaling ML tools and infrastructure.

In this first chapter, we're going to learn what the main capabilities of SageMaker are, how they help solve pain points faced by ML practitioners, and how to set up SageMaker:

- Exploring the capabilities of Amazon SageMaker
- Demonstrating the strengths of Amazon SageMaker

- Setting up Amazon SageMaker on your local machine
- Setting up an Amazon SageMaker notebook instance
- Setting up Amazon SageMaker Studio

Technical requirements

You will need an AWS account to run the examples included in this chapter. If you haven't got one already, please point your browser to `https://aws.amazon.com/getting-started/` to learn about AWS and its core concepts, and to create an AWS account. You should also familiarize yourself with the AWS Free Tier (`https://aws.amazon.com/free/`), which lets you use many AWS services for free within certain usage limits.

You will need to install and configure the AWS Command-line Interface (CLI) for your account (`https://aws.amazon.com/cli/`).

You will need a working Python 3.x environment. Be careful not to use Python 2.7, as it is no longer maintained. Installing the Anaconda distribution (`https://www.anaconda.com/`) is not mandatory but is strongly encouraged as it includes many projects that we will need (Jupyter, `pandas`, `numpy`, and more).

Code examples included in the book are available on GitHub at `https://github.com/PacktPublishing/Learn-Amazon-SageMaker`. You will need to install a Git client to access them (`https://git-scm.com/`).

Exploring the capabilities of Amazon SageMaker

Amazon SageMaker was launched at AWS re:Invent 2017. Since then, a lot of new features have been added: you can see the full (and ever-growing) list at `https://aws.amazon.com/about-aws/whats-new/machine-learning`.

In this section, you'll learn about the main capabilities of Amazon SageMaker and their purpose. Don't worry, we'll dive deep on each of them in later chapters. We will also talk about the SageMaker **Application Programming Interfaces** (**APIs**), and the **Software Development Kits** (**SDKs**) that implement them.

The main capabilities of Amazon SageMaker

At the core of Amazon SageMaker is the ability to build, train, optimize, and deploy models on fully managed infrastructure, and at any scale. This lets you focus on studying and solving the ML problem at hand, instead of spending time and resources on building and managing infrastructure. Simply put, you can go from building to training to deploying more quickly. Let's zoom in on each step and highlight relevant SageMaker capabilities.

Building

Amazon SageMaker provides you with two development environments:

- **Notebook instances**: Fully managed Amazon EC2 instances that come preinstalled with the most popular tools and libraries: Jupyter, Anaconda, and so on.
- **Amazon SageMaker Studio**: A full-fledged integrated development environment for ML projects.

When it comes to experimenting with algorithms, you can choose from the following:

- A collection of 17 **built-in algorithms** for ML and deep learning, already implemented and optimized to run efficiently on AWS. No ML code to write!
- A collection of built-in open source frameworks (**TensorFlow**, **PyTorch**, **Apache MXNet**, **scikit-learn**, and more), where you simply bring your own code.
- Your own code running in your own container: custom Python, R, C++, Java, and so on.
- Algorithms and pretrained models from AWS Marketplace for ML (https://aws.amazon.com/marketplace/solutions/machine-learning).

In addition, **Amazon SageMaker Autopilot** uses AutoML to automatically build, train, and optimize models without the need to write a single line of ML code.

Amazon SageMaker also includes two major capabilities that help with building and preparing datasets:

- **Amazon SageMaker Ground Truth**: Annotate datasets at any scale. Workflows for popular use cases are built in (image detection, entity extraction, and more), and you can implement your own. Annotation jobs can be distributed to workers that belong to private, third-party, or public workforces.

- **Amazon SageMaker Processing**: Run data processing and model evaluation batch jobs, using either scikit-learn or Spark.

Training

As mentioned earlier, Amazon SageMaker takes care of provisioning and managing your training infrastructure. You'll never spend any time managing servers, and you'll be able to focus on ML. On top of this, SageMaker brings advanced capabilities such as the following:

- **Managed storage** using either Amazon S3, Amazon EFS, or Amazon FSx for Lustre depending on your performance requirements.

- **Managed spot training**, using Amazon EC2 Spot instances for training in order to reduce costs by up to 80%.

- **Distributed training** automatically distributes large-scale training jobs on a cluster of managed instances

- **Pipe mode** streams infinitely large datasets from Amazon S3 to the training instances, saving the need to copy data around.

- **Automatic model tuning** runs hyperparameter optimization in order to deliver high-accuracy models more quickly.

- **Amazon SageMaker Experiments** easily tracks, organizes, and compares all your SageMaker jobs.

- **Amazon SageMaker Debugger** captures the internal model state during training, inspects it to observe how the model learns, and detects unwanted conditions that hurt accuracy.

Deploying

Just as with training, Amazon SageMaker takes care of all your deployment infrastructure, and brings a slew of additional features:

- **Real-time endpoints**: This creates an HTTPS API that serves predictions from your model. As you would expect, autoscaling is available.

- **Batch transform**: This uses a model to predict data in batch mode.

- Infrastructure monitoring with **Amazon CloudWatch**: This helps you to view real-time metrics and keep track of infrastructure performance.

- **Amazon SageMaker Model Monitor**: This captures data sent to an endpoint, and compares it with a baseline to identify and alert on data quality issues (missing features, data drift, and more).

- **Amazon SageMaker Neo**: This compiles models for a specific hardware architecture, including embedded platforms, and deploys an optimized version using a lightweight runtime.

- **Amazon Elastic Inference**: This adds fractional GPU acceleration to CPU-based instances in order to find the best cost/performance ratio for your prediction infrastructure.

The Amazon SageMaker API

Just like all other AWS services, Amazon SageMaker is driven by APIs that are implemented in the language SDKs supported by AWS (`https://aws.amazon.com/tools/`). In addition, a dedicated Python SDK, aka the 'SageMaker SDK,' is also available. Let's look at both, and discuss their respective benefits.

The AWS language SDKs

Language SDKs implement service-specific APIs for all AWS services: S3, EC2, and so on. Of course, they also include SageMaker APIs, which are documented at `https://docs.aws.amazon.com/sagemaker/latest/dg/api-and-sdk-reference.html`.

When it comes to data science and ML, Python is the most popular language, so let's take a look at the SageMaker APIs available in `boto3`, the AWS SDK for the Python language (`https://boto3.amazonaws.com/v1/documentation/api/latest/reference/services/sagemaker.html`). These APIs are quite low level and verbose: for example, `create_training_job()` has a lot of JSON parameters that don't look very obvious. You can see some of them in the next screenshot. You may think that this doesn't look very appealing for everyday ML experimentation… and I would totally agree!

```python
response = client.create_training_job(
    TrainingJobName='string',
    HyperParameters={
        'string': 'string'
    },
    AlgorithmSpecification={
        'TrainingImage': 'string',
        'AlgorithmName': 'string',
        'TrainingInputMode': 'Pipe'|'File',
        'MetricDefinitions': [
            {
                'Name': 'string',
                'Regex': 'string'
            },
        ],
        'EnableSageMakerMetricsTimeSeries': True|False
    },
    RoleArn='string',
    InputDataConfig=[
        {
            'ChannelName': 'string',
            'DataSource': {
                'S3DataSource': {
                    'S3DataType': 'ManifestFile'|'S3Prefix'|'AugmentedManifestFil
                    'S3Uri': 'string',
                    'S3DataDistributionType': 'FullyReplicated'|'ShardedByS3Key',
                    'AttributeNames': [
                        'string',
                    ]
                },
                'FileSystemDataSource': {
                    'FileSystemId': 'string',
                    'FileSystemAccessMode': 'rw'|'ro',
                    'FileSystemType': 'EFS'|'FSxLustre',
                    'DirectoryPath': 'string'
                }
```

Figure 1.1 A partial view of the create_training_job() API in boto3

Indeed, these service-level APIs are not meant to be used for experimentation in notebooks. Their purpose is automation, through either bespoke scripts or Infrastructure-as-Code tools such as AWS CloudFormation (`https://aws.amazon.com/cloudformation`) and Terraform (`https://terraform.io`). Your DevOps team will use them to manage production, where they do need full control over each possible parameter.

So, what should you use for experimentation? You should use the Amazon SageMaker SDK.

The Amazon SageMaker SDK

The Amazon SageMaker SDK (`https://github.com/aws/sagemaker-python-sdk`) is a Python SDK specific to Amazon SageMaker. You can find its documentation at `https://sagemaker.readthedocs.io/en/stable/`.

> **Note:**
>
> The code examples in this book are based on the first release of the SageMaker SDK v2, released in August 2020. For the sake of completeness, and to help you migrate your own notebooks, the companion GitHub repository includes examples for SDK v1 and v2.

Here, the abstraction level is much higher: the SDK contains objects for models, estimators, models, predictors, and so on. We're definitely back into ML territory.

For instance, this SDK makes it extremely easy and comfortable to fire up a training job (one line of code) and to deploy a model (one line of code). Infrastructure concerns are abstracted away, and we can focus on ML instead. Here's an example. Don't worry about the details for now:

```
# Configure the training job
my_estimator = TensorFlow(
    'my_script.py',
    role=my_sageMaker_role,
    instance_type='ml.p3.2xlarge',
    instance_count=1,
    framework_version='2.1.0')
# Train the model
my_estimator.fit('s3://my_bucket/my_training_data/')
```

```
# Deploy the model to an HTTPS endpoint
my_predictor = my_estimator.deploy(
    initial_instance_count=1,
    instance_type='ml.c5.2xlarge')
```

Now that we know a little more about Amazon SageMaker, let's see how it helps typical customers make their ML workflows more agile and more efficient.

Demonstrating the strengths of Amazon SageMaker

Alice and Bob are both passionate, hardworking people who try their best to build great ML solutions. Unfortunately, a lot of things stand in their way and slow them down.

In this section, let's look at the challenges that they face in their daily projects, and how Amazon SageMaker could help them be more productive.

Solving Alice's problems

Alice has a PhD and works in a large public research lab. She's a trained data scientist, with a strong background in math and statistics. She spends her time on large scientific projects involving bulky datasets. Alice generally doesn't know much about IT and infrastructure, and she honestly doesn't care at all for these topics. Her focus is on advancing her research, and publishing papers.

For her daily work, she can rely on her own powerful (but expensive) desktop workstation. She enjoys the fact that she can work on her own, but she can only experiment with a fraction of her dataset if she wants to keep training times reasonable.

She tries to maintain the software configuration of her machine herself, as IT doesn't know much about the esoteric tools she uses. When something goes wrong, she wastes precious hours fixing it, and that's frustrating.

When Alice wants to run large experiments, she has to use remote servers hosted in the computing centre: a farm of very powerful multi-GPU servers, connected to a petabyte of network-attached storage. Of course, she has to share these servers with other researchers. Every week, the team leads meet and try to prioritize projects and workloads: this is never easy, and decisions often need to be escalated to the lab director.

Let's see how SageMaker and cloud computing can help Alice.

Launching an inexpensive SageMaker notebook instance in minutes, Alice could start running some sample notebooks, and she would quickly become familiar with the service, as it's based on the same tools she already uses. Scaling up, she then could train her own model on a cluster of powerful GPU instances, created on demand with just a couple of lines of code. That's more computing power than she would have ever managed using in the computing centre, and she wouldn't have to set up anything!

Thanks to the automatic model tuning feature in SageMaker, Alice would also be able to significantly improve the accuracy of her models in just a few hours of parallel optimization. Again, doing this with her previous setup would have been impossible due to the lack of computing resources. Deploying models would be equally straightforward: adapting a couple of lines of code found in a sample notebook, Alice would use the batch transform feature to predict her test dataset, again spending no time at all worrying about tools or infrastructure.

Last but not least, keeping track of her expenses would be easy: the AWS console would tell her how much she's spent, which would be less than expected thanks to the on-demand nature of SageMaker infrastructure!

Solving Bob's problems

Bob is a DevOps engineer, and he's in charge of a large training cluster shared by a team of data scientists. They can start their distributed jobs in seconds, and it's just simpler for Bob to manage a single cluster. Auto Scaling is set up, but capacity planning is still needed to find the right amount of EC2 instances and to optimize the cost using the right mix of Reserved, Spot, and On-Demand instances. Bob has a weekly meeting with the team to make sure they'll have enough instances… and they also ping him on Slack when they need extra capacity on the fly. Bob tries to automatically reduce capacity at night and on weekends when the cluster is less busy, but he's quite sure they're spending too much anyway. Oh, well.

Once models have been trained and validated, Bob uses **Continuous Integration and Continuous Deployment (CI/CD)** to deploy them automatically to the production Docker cluster. Bob maintains bespoke containers for training and prediction: libraries, dependencies, and in-house tools. That takes a bit of time, but he enjoys doing it. He just hopes that no one will ask him to do PyTorch and Apache MXNet too.

Let's see how Bob could use SageMaker to improve his ML workflows.

As SageMaker is based on Docker containers, Bob could get rid of his bespoke containers and use their built-in counterparts. Migrating the training workloads to SageMaker would be pretty easy. This would help Bob get rid of his training cluster, and let every data scientist train completely on demand instead. With Managed Spot Training, Bob could certainly optimize training costs even more.

The data science team would quickly adopt advanced features like distributed training, Pipe mode, and automatic model tuning. This would save them a lot of time, and the team would no longer have to maintain the kludgy code they have written to implement similar features.

Of course, Alice and Bob are fictional characters. Yet, I keep meeting many customers who share some (and sometimes all) of their pain points. That may be your case too, so please let me get you started with Amazon SageMaker.

Setting up Amazon SageMaker on your local machine

A common misconception is that you can't use SageMaker outside of the AWS cloud. Obviously, it is a cloud-based service, and its most appealing capabilities require cloud infrastructure to run. However, many developers like to set up their development environment their own way, and SageMaker lets them do that: in this section, you will learn how to install the SageMaker SDK on your local machine or on a local server. In later chapters, you'll learn how to train and deploy models locally.

It's good practice to isolate Python environments in order to avoid dependency hell. Let's see how we can achieve this using two popular projects: `virtualenv` (https://virtualenv.pypa.io) and Anaconda (https://www.anaconda.com/).

Installing the SageMaker SDK with virtualenv

If you've never worked with `virtualenv` before, please read this tutorial before proceeding – https://packaging.python.org/guides/installing-using-pip-and-virtual-environments/:

1. First, let's create a new environment named `sagemaker`, and activate it:

```
$ mkdir workdir
$ cd workdir
$ python3 -m venv sagemaker
$ source sagemaker/bin/activate
```

2. Now, let's install `boto3`, the SageMaker SDK, and the `pandas` library (`https://pandas.pydata.org/`), which is also required:

    ```
    $ pip install boto3 sagemaker pandas
    ```

3. Now, let's quickly check that we can import these SDKs in Python:

    ```
    $ python3
    Python 3.7.4 (default, Aug 13 2019, 15:17:50)
    >>> import boto3
    >>> import sagemaker
    >>> print(boto3.__version__)
    1.12.39
    >>> print(sagemaker.__version__)
    1.55.3
    >>> exit
    ```

The installation looks fine. Your own versions will certainly be newer and that's fine. Now, let's run a quick test with a local Jupyter server (`https://jupyter.org/`). If Jupyter isn't installed on your machine, you can find instructions at `https://jupyter.org/install`:

1. First, let's create a Jupyter kernel based on our virtual environment:

    ```
    $ pip install ipykernel
    $ python3 -m ipykernel install --user --name=sagemaker
    ```

2. Then, we can launch Jupyter:

    ```
    $ jupyter notebook
    ```

3. Creating a new notebook, we can see that the `sagemaker` kernel is available, so let's select it in the **New** menu, as seen in the following screenshot:

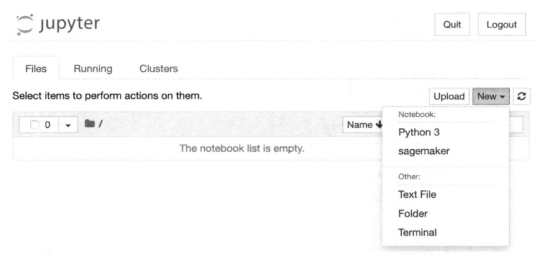

Figure 1.2 Creating a new notebook

4. Finally, we can check that the SDKs are available, by importing them and printing their version, as shown in the following screenshot:

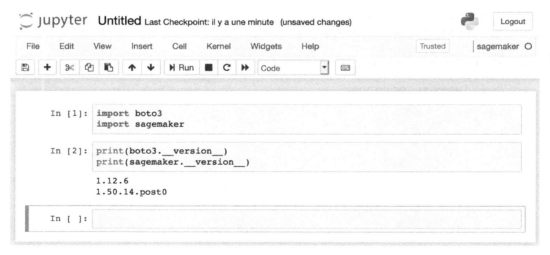

Figure 1.3 Checking the SDK version

This completes the installation with `virtualenv`. Don't forget to terminate Jupyter, and to deactivate your `virtualenv`:

```
$ deactivate
```

Installing the SageMaker SDK with Anaconda

Anaconda includes a package manager named `conda` that lets you create and manage isolated environments. If you've never worked with `conda` before, you should do the following first:

- Install Anaconda: `https://docs.anaconda.com/anaconda/install/`
- Read this tutorial: `https://docs.conda.io/projects/conda/en/latest/user-guide/getting-started.html`

Perform the following steps to install the Sagemaker SDK with conda:

1. Let's create and activate a new `conda` environment named `conda-sagemaker`:

    ```
    $ conda create -y -n conda-sagemaker
    $ conda activate conda-sagemaker
    ```

2. Then, we install `pandas`, `boto3,` and the SageMaker SDK. The latter has to be installed with `pip`, as it's not available as a `conda` package:

    ```
    $ conda install -y boto3 pandas
    $ pip install sagemaker
    ```

3. Now, let's add Jupyter and its dependencies to the environment, and create a new kernel:

    ```
    $ conda install -y jupyter ipykernel
    $ python3 -m ipykernel install --user --name conda-sagemaker
    ```

4. Then, we can launch Jupyter, and check that the `conda-sagemaker` kernel is present in the **New** menu, as is visible in the next screenshot:

```
$ jupyter notebook
```

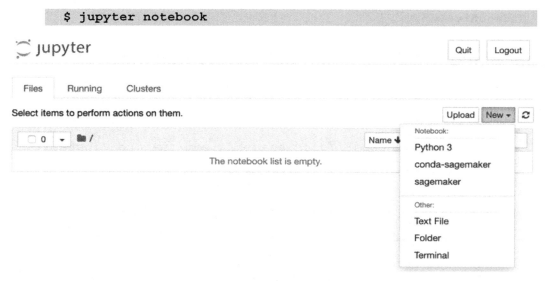

Figure 1.4 Creating a new conda environment

5. As shown in the following screenshot, we can create a notebook using this kernel, and check that the SDKs are imported correctly:

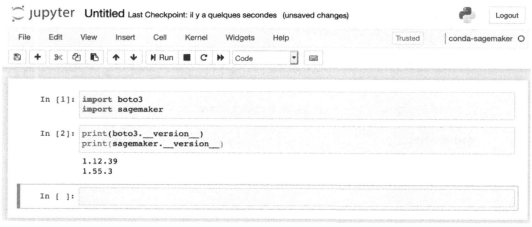

Figure 1.5 Checking the SDK version

This completes the installation with `conda`. Whether you'd rather use it over `virtualenv` is largely a matter of personal preference. You can definitely run all notebooks in this book and build your own projects with one or the other.

A word about AWS permissions

Amazon Identity and Access Management (IAM) enables you to manage access to AWS services and resources securely (https://aws.amazon.com/iam). Of course, this applies to Amazon SageMaker as well, and you need to make sure that your AWS user has sufficient permissions to invoke the SageMaker API.

> **Note:**
> If you're not familiar with IAM at all, please read the following documentation: https://docs.aws.amazon.com/IAM/latest/UserGuide/introduction.html

You can run a quick test by using the AWS CLI on one of the SageMaker APIs, for example, `list-endpoints`. I'm using the `eu-west-1` region here, but feel free to use the region that is nearest to you:

```
$ aws sagemaker list-endpoints --region eu-west-1
{
    "Endpoints": []
}
```

If you get an error message complaining about insufficient permissions, you need to update the IAM role attached to your AWS user.

If you own the AWS account in question, you can easily do this yourself in the IAM console, by adding the `AmazonSageMakerFullAccess` managed policy to your role. Note that this policy is extremely permissive: this is fine for a development account, but certainly not for a production account.

If you work with an account where you don't have administrative rights (such as a company-provided account), please contact your IT administrator to add SageMaker permissions to your AWS account.

For more information on SageMaker permissions, please refer to the documentation: https://docs.aws.amazon.com/sagemaker/latest/dg/security-iam.html.

Setting up an Amazon SageMaker notebook instance

Experimentation is a key part of the ML process. Developers and data scientists use a collection of open source tools and libraries for data exploration and processing, and of course, to evaluate candidate algorithms. Installing and maintaining these tools takes a fair amount of time, which would probably be better spent on studying the ML problem itself!

In order to solve this problem, Amazon SageMaker makes it easy to fire up a **notebook instance** in minutes. A notebook instance is a fully managed Amazon EC2 instance that comes preinstalled with the most popular tools and libraries: Jupyter, Anaconda (and its conda package manager), numpy, pandas, deep learning frameworks, and even NVIDIA GPU drivers.

> **Note:**
> If you're not familiar with S3 at all, please read the following documentation:
> https://docs.aws.amazon.com/AmazonS3/latest/dev/
> Welcome.html

Let's create one such instance using the AWS Console (https://console.aws.amazon.com/sagemaker/):

1. In the **Notebook** section of the left-hand vertical menu, click on **Notebook instances**, as shown in the next screenshot:

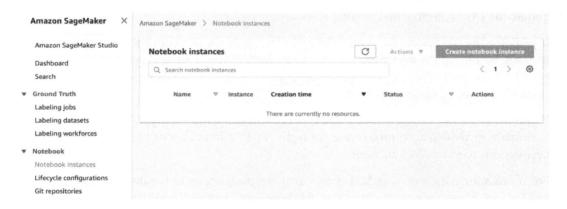

Figure 1.6 Creating a notebook instance

> **Note:**
> The AWS console is a living thing. By the time you're reading this, some screens may have been updated. Also, you may notice small differences from one region to the next, as some features or instance types are not available there.

2. Then, click on **Create notebook instance**. In the **Notebook instance settings** box, we need to enter a name, and select an instance type: as you can see in the drop-down list, SageMaker lets us pick from a very wide range of instance types. As you would expect, pricing varies according to the instance size, so please make sure you familiarize yourself with instance features and costs (`https://aws.amazon.com/sagemaker/pricing/`).

3. We'll stick to `ml.t2.medium` for now. As a matter of fact, it's an excellent default choice if your notebooks only invoke SageMaker APIs that create fully managed infrastructure for training and deployment – no need for anything larger. If your workflow requires local data processing and model training, then feel free to scale up as needed.

We can ignore Elastic Inference for now, it will be covered in *Chapter 13, Optimizing Prediction Cost and Performance*. Thus, your setup screen should look like the following screenshot:

Create notebook instance

Amazon SageMaker provides pre-built fully managed notebook instances that run Jupyter notebooks. The notebook instances include example code for common model training and hosting exercises. Learn more ⤴

Notebook instance settings

Notebook instance name

| first-notebook-instance |

Maximum of 63 alphanumeric characters. Can include hyphens (-), but not spaces. Must be unique within your account in an AWS Region.

Notebook instance type

| ml.t2.medium ▼ |

Elastic Inference **Learn more** ⤴

| none ▼ |

Figure 1.7 Creating a notebook instance

4. As you can see in the following screenshot, we could optionally apply a lifecycle configuration, a script that runs either when a notebook instance is created or restarted, in order to install additional libraries, clone repositories, and so on. We could also add additional storage (the default is set to 5 GB):

Figure 1.8 Creating a notebook instance

5. In the **Permissions and encryption** section, we need to create an Amazon IAM role for the notebook instance: it will allow it to access storage in Amazon S3, to create Amazon SageMaker infrastructure, and so on.

Select **Create a new role**, which opens the following screen:

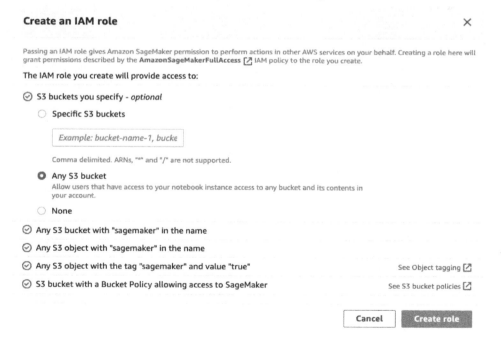

Figure 1.9 Creating an IAM role

The only decision we have to make here is whether we want to allow our notebook instance to access specific Amazon S3 buckets. Let's select **Any S3 bucket** and click on **Create role**. This is the most flexible setting for development and testing, but we'd want to apply much stricter settings for production. Of course, we can edit this role later on in the IAM console, or create a new one.

Optionally, we can disable root access to the notebook instance, which helps lock down its configuration. We can also enable storage encryption using **Amazon Key Management Service** (`https://aws.amazon.com/kms`). Both features are extremely important in high-security environments, but we won't enable them here.

Once you've completed this step, your screen should look like this, although the name of the role will be different:

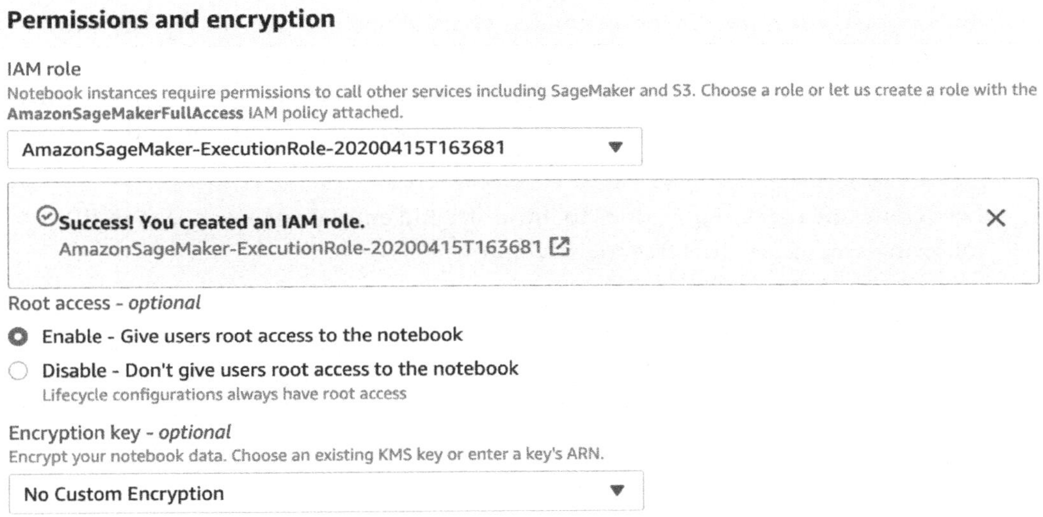

Permissions and encryption

IAM role
Notebook instances require permissions to call other services including SageMaker and S3. Choose a role or let us create a role with the **AmazonSageMakerFullAccess** IAM policy attached.

> AmazonSageMaker-ExecutionRole-20200415T163681 ▼

> ⊘**Success! You created an IAM role.**   ✕
> AmazonSageMaker-ExecutionRole-20200415T163681 ↗

Root access - *optional*
🔘 Enable - Give users root access to the notebook
⚪ Disable - Don't give users root access to the notebook
    Lifecycle configurations always have root access

Encryption key - *optional*
Encrypt your notebook data. Choose an existing KMS key or enter a key's ARN.

> No Custom Encryption ▼

Figure 1.10 Creating an IAM role

6. As shown in the following screenshot, the optional **Network** section lets you pick the **Amazon Virtual Private Cloud (VPC)** where the instance will be launched. This is useful when you need tight control over network flows from and to the instance, for example, to deny it access to the internet. Let's not use this feature here:

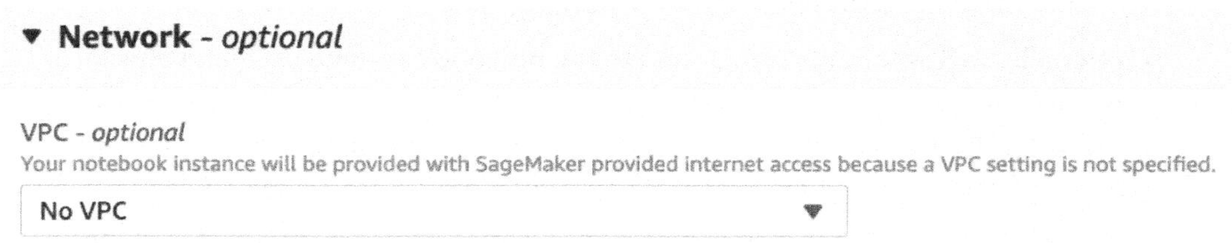

▼ **Network** - *optional*

VPC - *optional*
Your notebook instance will be provided with SageMaker provided internet access because a VPC setting is not specified.

No VPC	▼

Figure 1.11 Setting the VPC

7. The optional **Git repositories** section lets you add one or more **Git** repositories that will be automatically cloned on the notebook instance when it's first created. You can select any public Git repository, or select one from a list of repositories that you previously defined in Amazon SageMaker: the latter can be done under **Git repositories** in the **Notebook** section of the left-hand vertical menu.

Let's clone one of my repositories to illustrate, and enter its name as seen in the following screenshot. Feel free to use your own!

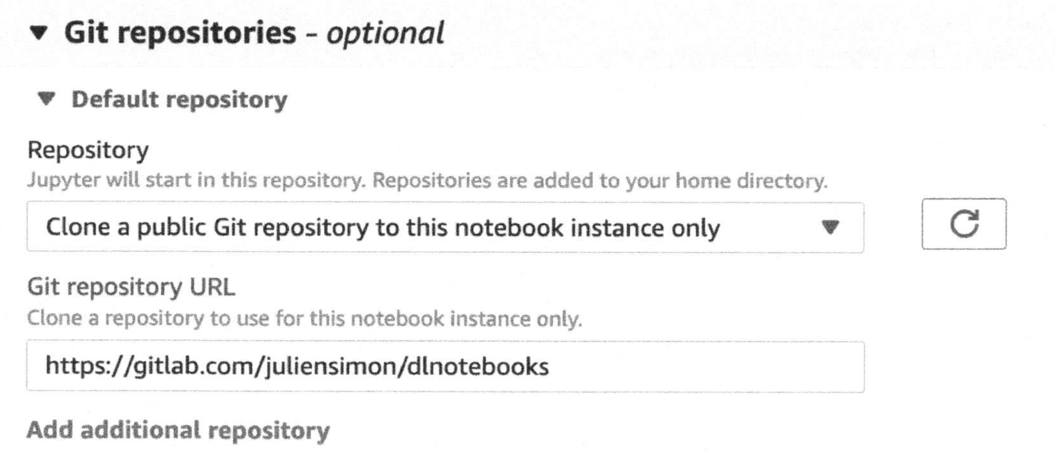

▼ **Git repositories** - *optional*

▼ **Default repository**

Repository
Jupyter will start in this repository. Repositories are added to your home directory.

Clone a public Git repository to this notebook instance only	▼		C

Git repository URL
Clone a repository to use for this notebook instance only.

https://gitlab.com/juliensimon/dlnotebooks

Add additional repository

Figure 1.12 Setting Git repositories

8. Last but not least, the optional **Tags** section lets us tag notebook instances. It's always good practice to tag AWS resources, as this makes it much easier to manage them later on. Let's add a couple of tags.

9. As shown in the following screenshot, let's click on **Create notebook instance**:

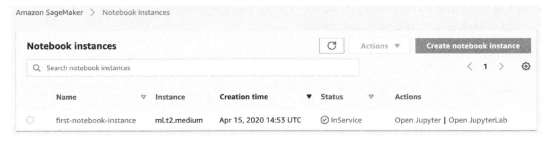

Figure 1.13 Setting tags

Under the hood, SageMaker fires up a fully managed Amazon EC2 instance, using an **Amazon Machine Image (AMI)** preinstalled with Jupyter, Anaconda, deep learning libraries, and so on. Don't look for it in the EC2 console, you won't see it.

10. Five to ten minutes later, the instance is in service, as shown in the following screenshot. Let's click on **Open JupyterLab**:

Figure 1.14 Opening a notebook instance

We'll jump straight into **Jupyter Lab**. As shown in the following screenshot, we see in the left-hand panel that the repository has been cloned. In the **Launcher** panel, we see the many conda environments that are readily available for **TensorFlow**, **PyTorch**, **Apache MXNet**, and more:

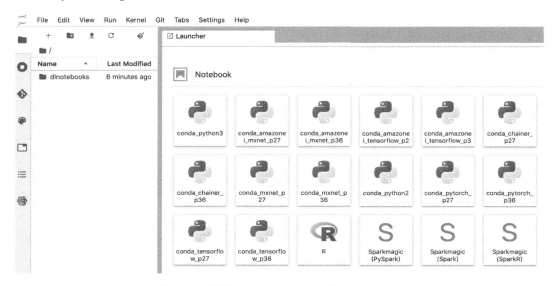

Figure 1.15 Notebook instance welcome screen

The rest is vanilla Jupyter, and you can get to work right away!

Coming back to the AWS console, we see that we can stop, start, and delete a notebook instance, as shown in the next screenshot:

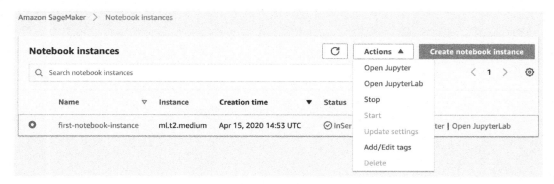

Figure 1.16 Stopping a notebook instance

Stopping a notebook instance is identical to stopping an Amazon EC2 instance: storage is persisted until the instance is started again.

When a notebook instance is stopped, you can then delete it: the storage will be destroyed, and you won't be charged for anything any longer.

If you're going to use this instance to run the examples in this book, I'd recommend stopping it and restarting it. This will save you the trouble of recreating it again and again, your work will be preserved, and the costs will really be minimal.

Setting up Amazon SageMaker Studio

Amazon SageMaker Studio goes one step further in integrating the ML tools you need from experimentation to production. At its core is an integrated development environment based on Jupyter that makes it instantly familiar.

In addition, SageMaker Studio is integrated with other SageMaker capabilities, such as SageMaker Experiments to track and compare all jobs, SageMaker Autopilot to automatically create ML models, and more. A lot of operations can be achieved in just a few clicks, without having to write any code.

SageMaker Studio also further simplifies infrastructure management. You won't have to create notebook instances: SageMaker Studio provides you with compute environments that are readily available to run your notebooks.

> **Note:**
> This section requires basic knowledge of Amazon VPC and Amazon IAM. If you're not familiar with them at all, please read the following documentation:
> a) `https://docs.aws.amazon.com/vpc/latest/userguide/what-is-amazon-vpc.html`
> b) `https://docs.aws.amazon.com/IAM/latest/UserGuide/introduction.html`

Onboarding to Amazon SageMaker Studio

You can access SageMaker Studio using any of these three options:

1. **Use the quick start procedure**: This is the easiest option for individual accounts, and we'll walk through it in the following paragraphs.

2. **Use AWS Single Sign-On (SSO)**: If your company has an SSO application set up, this is probably the best option. You can learn more about SSO onboarding at `https://docs.aws.amazon.com/sagemaker/latest/dg/onboard-sso-users.html`. Please contact your IT administrator for details.

3. **Use Amazon IAM**: If your company doesn't use SSO, this is probably the best option. You can learn more about SSO onboarding at `https://docs.aws.amazon.com/sagemaker/latest/dg/onboard-iam.html`. Again, please contact your IT administrator for details.

Onboarding with the quick start procedure

Perform the following steps to access the SageMaker Studio with the quick start procedure:

1. First, open the AWS Console in one of the regions where Amazon SageMaker Studio is available, for example, `https://us-east-2.console.aws.amazon.com/sagemaker/`.

2. As shown in the following screenshot, the left-hand vertical panel has a link to **SageMaker Studio**:

Figure 1.17 Opening SageMaker Studio

3. Clicking on this link opens the onboarding screen, and you can see its first section in the next screenshot:

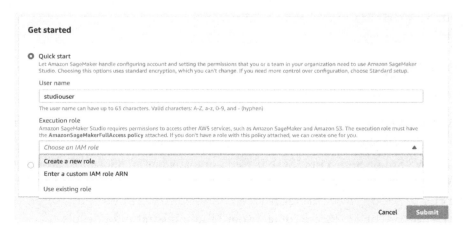

Figure 1.18 Running Quick start

4. Let's select **Quick start**. Then, we enter the username we'd like to use to log into SageMaker Studio, and we create a new IAM role as shown in the preceding screenshot. This opens the following screen:

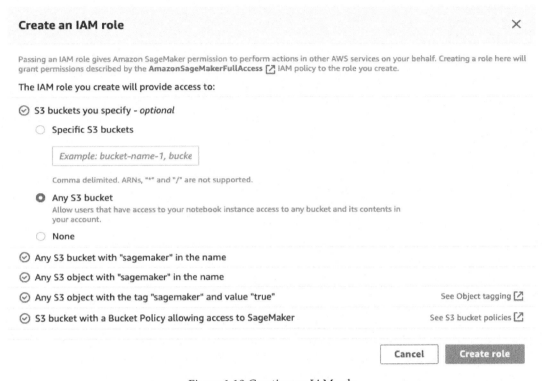

Figure 1.19 Creating an IAM role

The only decision we have to make here is whether we want to allow our notebook instance to access specific Amazon S3 buckets. Let's select **Any S3 bucket** and click on **Create role**. This is the most flexible setting for development and testing, but we'd want to apply much stricter settings for production. Of course, we can edit this role later on in the IAM console, or create a new one.

5. Once we've clicked on **Create role**, we're back to the previous screen, where we just have to click on **Submit** to launch the onboarding procedure. Depending on your account setup, you may get an extra screen asking you to select a VPC and a subnet. I'd recommend selecting any subnet in your default VPC.

6. A few minutes later, SageMaker Studio is in service, as shown in the following screenshot. We could add extra users if we needed to, but for now, let's just click on **Open Studio**:

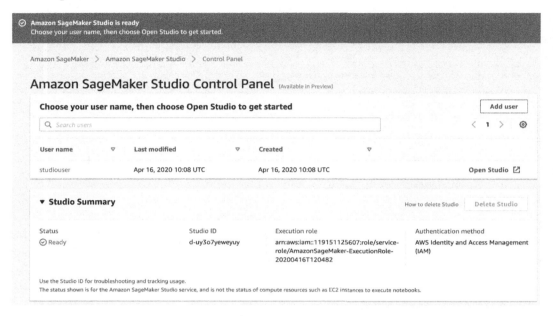

Figure 1.20 Launching SageMaker Studio

Don't worry if this takes a few more minutes, as SageMaker Studio needs to complete the first-run setup of your environment. As shown in the following screenshot, SageMaker Studio opens, and we see the familiar JupyterLab layout:

> **Note:**
>
> SageMaker Studio is a living thing. By the time you're reading this, some screens may have been updated. Also, you may notice small differences from one region to the next, as some features or instance types are not available everywhere.

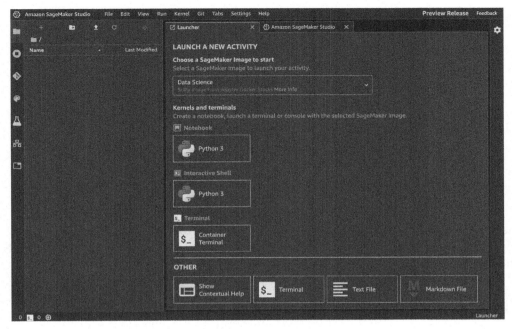

Figure 1.21 SageMaker Studio welcome screen

7. We can immediately create our first notebook. In the **Launcher** tab, let's select **Data Science**, and click on **Notebook – Python 3**.

8. This opens a notebook, as is visible in the following screenshot. We first check that SDKs are readily available. If this is the first time you've launched the **Data Science** image, please wait for a couple of minutes for the environment to start:

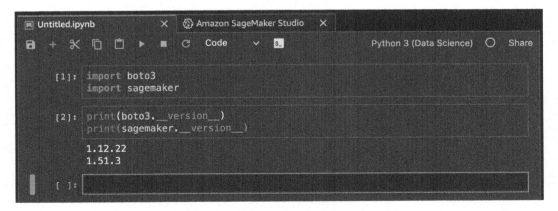

Figure 1.22 Checking the SDK version

9. When we're done working with SageMaker Studio, all we have to do is close the browser tab. If we want to resume working, we just have to go back to the SageMaker console, and click on **Open Studio**.

Now that we've completed this exercise, let's review what we learned in this chapter.

Summary

In this chapter, you discovered the main capabilities of Amazon SageMaker, and how they help solve your ML pain points. By providing you with managed infrastructure and pre-installed tools, SageMaker lets you focus on the ML problem itself. Thus, you can go more quickly from experimenting with models to deploying them in production.

Then, you learned how to set up Amazon SageMaker on your local machine, on a notebook instance, and on Amazon SageMaker Studio. The latter is a managed ML IDE where many other SageMaker capabilities are just a few clicks away.

In the next chapter, we'll see how you can use Amazon SageMaker and other AWS services to prepare your datasets for training.

2
Handling Data Preparation Techniques

Data is the starting point of any machine learning project, and it takes lots of work to turn data into a dataset that can be used to train a model. That work typically involves annotating datasets, running bespoke scripts to preprocess them, and saving processed versions for later use. As you can guess, doing all this work manually, or building tools to automate it, is not an exciting prospect for machine learning teams.

In this chapter, you will learn about AWS services that help you build and process data. We'll first cover **Amazon SageMaker Ground Truth**, a capability of Amazon SageMaker that helps you quickly build accurate training datasets. Then, we'll talk about **Amazon SageMaker Processing**, another capability that helps you run your data processing workloads, such as feature engineering, data validation, model evaluation, and model interpretation. Finally, we'll discuss other AWS services that may help with data analytics: **Amazon Elastic Map Reduce**, **AWS Glue**, and **Amazon Athena**:

- Discovering Amazon SageMaker Ground Truth
- Exploring Amazon SageMaker Processing
- Processing data with other AWS services

Technical requirements

You will need an AWS account to run examples included in this chapter. If you haven't got one already, please point your browser at https://aws.amazon.com/getting-started/ to create one. You should also familiarize yourself with the AWS Free Tier (https://aws.amazon.com/free/), which lets you use many AWS services for free within certain usage limits.

You will need to install and to configure the AWS **Command-Line Interface (CLI)** for your account (https://aws.amazon.com/cli/).

You will need a working Python 3.x environment. Be careful not to use Python 2.7, as it is no longer maintained. Installing the Anaconda distribution (https://www.anaconda.com/) is not mandatory, but strongly encouraged as it includes many projects that we will need (Jupyter, pandas, numpy, and more).

Code examples included in the book are available on GitHub at https://github.com/PacktPublishing/Learn-Amazon-SageMaker. You will need to install a Git client to access them (https://git-scm.com/).

Discovering Amazon SageMaker Ground Truth

Added to Amazon SageMaker in late 2018, Amazon SageMaker Ground Truth helps you quickly build accurate training datasets. Machine learning practitioners can distribute labeling work to public and private workforces of human labelers. Labelers can be productive immediately, thanks to built-in workflows and graphical interfaces for common image, video, and text tasks. In addition, Ground Truth can enable automatic labeling, a technique that trains a machine learning model able to label data without additional human intervention.

In this section, you'll learn how to use Ground Truth to label images and text.

Using workforces

The first step in using Ground Truth is to create a workforce, a group of workers in charge of labeling data samples.

Let's head out to the SageMaker console: in the left-hand vertical menu, we click on **Ground Truth**, then on **Labeling workforces**. Three types of workforces are available: **Amazon Mechanical Turk**, **Vendor**, and **Private**. Let's discuss what they are, and when you should use them.

Amazon Mechanical Turk

Amazon Mechanical Turk (`https://www.mturk.com/`) makes it easy to break down large batch jobs into small work units that can be processed by a distributed workforce.

With Mechanical Turk, you can enroll tens or even hundreds of thousands of workers located across the globe. This is a great option when you need to label extremely large datasets. For example, think about a dataset for autonomous driving, made up of 1000 hours of video: each frame would need to be processed in order to identify other vehicles, pedestrians, road signs, and more. If you wanted to annotate every single frame, you'd be looking at 1,000 hours x 3,600 seconds x 24 frames per second = **86.4 million images**! Clearly, you would have to scale out your labeling workforce to get the job done, and Mechanical Turk lets you do that.

Vendor workforce

As scalable as Mechanical Turk is, sometimes you need more control on who data is shared with, and on the quality of annotations, particularly if additional domain knowledge is required.

For this purpose, AWS has vetted a number of data labeling companies, which have integrated Ground Truth in their workflows. You can find the list of companies on **AWS Marketplace** (`https://aws.amazon.com/marketplace/`), under **Machine Learning | Data Labeling Services | Amazon SageMaker Ground Truth Services**.

Private workforce

Sometimes, data can't be processed by third parties. Maybe it's just too sensitive, or maybe it requires expert knowledge that only your company's employees have. In this case, you can create a private workforce, made up of well-identified individuals that will access and label your data.

Creating a private workforce

Creating a private workforce is the quickest and simplest option. Let's see how it's done:

1. Starting from the **Labeling workforces** entry in the SageMaker console, we select the **Private** tab, as seen in the following screenshot. Then, we click on **Create private team**:

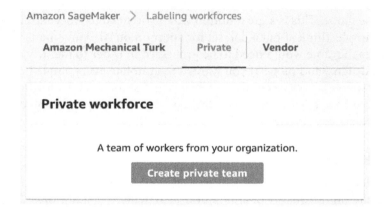

Figure 2.1 – Creating a private workforce

2. We give the team a name, then we have to decide whether we're going to invite workers by email, or whether we're going to import users that belong to an existing **Amazon Cognito** group.

    Amazon Cognito (`https://aws.amazon.com/cognito/`) is a managed service that lets you build and manage user directories at any scale. Cognito supports both social identity providers (Google, Facebook, and Amazon), and enterprise identity providers (Microsoft Active Directory, SAML).

    This makes a lot of sense in an enterprise context, but let's keep things simple and use email instead. Here, I will use some sample email addresses: please make sure to use your own, otherwise you won't be able to join the team!

3.   Then, we need to enter an organization name, and more importantly a contact email that workers can use for questions and feedback on the labeling job. These conversations are extremely important in order to fine-tune labeling instructions, pinpoint problematic data samples, and more.

4.   Optionally, we can set up notifications with **Amazon Simple Notification Service** (`https://aws.amazon.com/sns/`), to let workers know that they have work to do.

5.   The screen should look like in the following screenshot. Then, we click on **Create private team**:

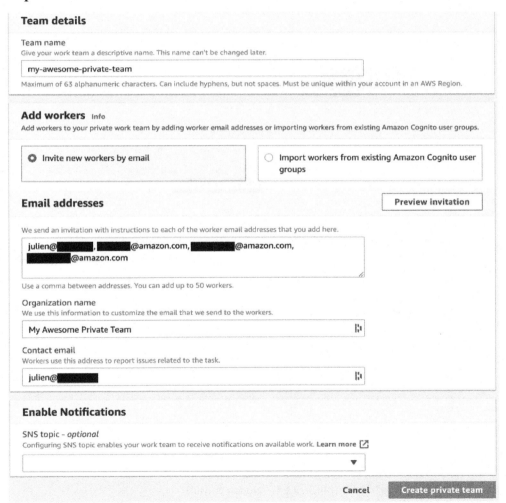

Figure 2.2 – Setting up a private workforce

6. A few seconds later, the team has been set up. Invitations have been sent to workers, requesting that they join the workforce by logging in to a specific URL. The invitation email looks like that shown in the following screenshot:

You're invited by My Awesome Private Team to work on a labeling project.

You're invited to work on a labeling project.

You will need this user name and temporary password to log in the first time.

User name: ███████████

Temporary password: ███████████

Open the link below to log in:

https://8rj5pzrz3j.labeling.eu-west-1.sagemaker.aws

After you log in with your temporary password, you are required to create a new one. If you have any questions, please contact ███████████

Figure 2.3 – Email invitation

7. Clicking on the link opens a login window. Once we've logged in and defined a new password, we're taken to a new screen showing available jobs, as in the following screenshot. As we haven't defined one yet, it's obviously empty:

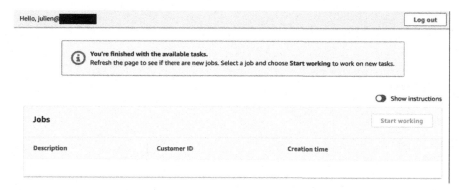

Figure 2.4 – Worker console

Let's keep our workers busy and create an image labeling job.

Uploading data for labeling

As you would expect, Amazon SageMaker Ground Truth uses Amazon S3 to store datasets:

1. Using the AWS CLI, we create an S3 bucket hosted in the same region we're running SageMaker in. Bucket names are globally unique, so please make sure to pick your own unique name when you create the bucket. Use the following code:

   ```
   $ aws s3 mb s3://sagemaker-book --region eu-west-1
   ```

2. Then, we copy the cat images located in the chapter2 folder of our GitHub repository as follows:

   ```
   $ aws s3 cp --recursive cat/ s3://sagemaker-book/
   chapter2/cat/
   ```

Now that we have some data waiting to be labeled, let's create a labeling job.

Creating a labeling job

As you would expect, we need to define the location of the data, what type of task we want to label it for, and what our instructions are:

1. In the left-hand vertical menu of the SageMaker console, we click on **Ground Truth**, then on **Labeling jobs**, then on the **Create labeling job** button.

2. First, we give the job a name, say my-cat-job. Then, we define the location of the data in S3. Ground Truth expects a **manifest file**: a manifest file is a **JSON** file that lets you filter which objects need to be labeled, and which ones should be left out. Once the job is complete, a new file, called the augmented manifest, will contain labeling information, and we'll be able to use this to feed data to training jobs.

3.   Then, we define the location and the type of our input data, just like in the following screenshot:

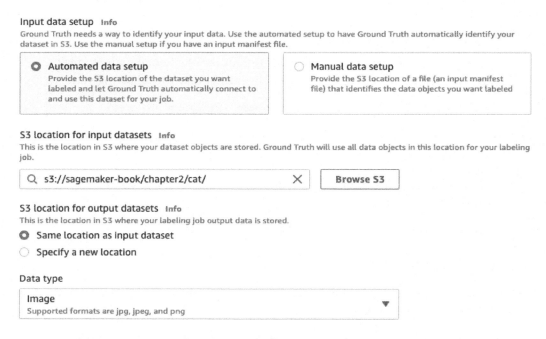

Input data setup Info

Ground Truth needs a way to identify your input data. Use the automated setup to have Ground Truth automatically identify your dataset in S3. Use the manual setup if you have an input manifest file.

⦿ **Automated data setup**
   Provide the S3 location of the dataset you want labeled and let Ground Truth automatically connect to and use this dataset for your job.

◯ **Manual data setup**
   Provide the S3 location of a file (an input manifest file) that identifies the data objects you want labeled

S3 location for input datasets Info

This is the location in S3 where your dataset objects are stored. Ground Truth will use all data objects in this location for your labeling job.

🔍 s3://sagemaker-book/chapter2/cat/   ✕   **Browse S3**

S3 location for output datasets Info

This is the location in S3 where your labeling job output data is stored.

⦿ Same location as input dataset

◯ Specify a new location

Data type

Image
Supported formats are jpg, jpeg, and png   ▼

Figure 2.5 – Configuring input data

4.   As is visible in the next screenshot, we select the IAM role that we created for SageMaker in the first chapter (your name will be different), and we then click on the **Complete data setup** button to validate this section:

IAM Role Info

Provide the ID or ARN for your own AWS KMS encryption key for Amazon SageMaker to access your S3 bucket. Choose a role or let us create a role with the **AmazonSageMakerFullAccess** IAM policy attached.

AmazonSageMaker-ExecutionRole-20200501T145026   ▼

Use this button to process and complete your input data setup.

   Complete data setup

⊘ Input data connection successful View more details

Figure 2.6 – Validating input data

Clicking on **View more details**, you can learn about what is happening under the hood. SageMaker Ground Truth crawls your data in S3 and creates a JSON file called the **manifest file**. You can go and download it from S3 if you're curious. This file points at your objects in S3 (images, text files, and so on).

5. Optionally, we could decide to work either with the full manifest, a random sample, or a filtered subset based on a **SQL** query. We could also provide an **Amazon KMS** key to encrypt the output of the job. Let's stick to the defaults here.

6. The **Task type** section asks us what kind of job we'd like to run. Please take a minute to explore the different task categories that are available (text, image, video, point cloud, and custom). You'll see that SageMaker Ground Truth can help you with the following tasks:

a) **Text classification**

b) **Named entity recognition**

c) **Image classification**: Categorizing images in specific classes

d) **Object detection**: Locating and labeling objects in images with bounding boxes

e) **Semantic segmentation**: Locating and labeling objects in images with pixel-level precision

f) **Video clip classification**: Categorizing videos in specific classes

g) **Multi-frame video object detection and tracking**

h) **3D point clouds**: Locating and labeling objects in 3D data, such as LIDAR data for autonomous driving

i) **Custom user-defined tasks**

As shown in the next screenshot, let's select the **Image** task category and the **Semantic segmentation** task, and then click **Next**:

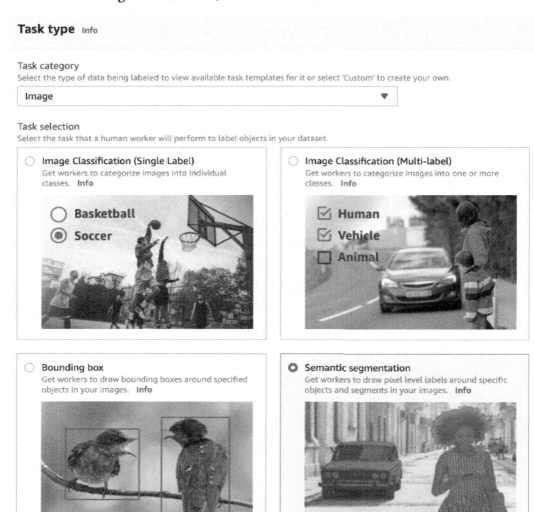

Figure 2.7 – Selecting a task type

7. On the next screen, visible in the following screenshot, we first select our private team of workers:

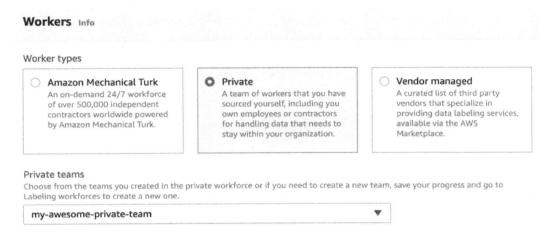

Workers Info

Worker types

○ **Amazon Mechanical Turk**
An on-demand 24/7 workforce of over 500,000 independent contractors worldwide powered by Amazon Mechanical Turk.

● **Private**
A team of workers that you have sourced yourself, including you own employees or contractors for handling data that needs to stay within your organization.

○ **Vendor managed**
A curated list of third party vendors that specialize in providing data labeling services, available via the AWS Marketplace.

Private teams
Choose from the teams you created in the private workforce or if you need to create a new team, save your progress and go to Labeling workforces to create a new one.

my-awesome-private-team   ▼

Figure 2.8 – Selecting a team type

8. If we had a lot of samples (say, tens of thousands or more), we should consider enabling **automated data labeling**, as this feature would reduce both the duration and the cost of the labeling job. Indeed, as workers would start labeling data samples, SageMaker Ground Truth would train a machine learning model on these samples. It would use them as a dataset for a supervised learning problem. With enough worker-labeled data, this model would pretty quickly be able to match and exceed human accuracy, at which point it would replace workers and label the rest of the dataset. If you'd like to know more about this feature, please read the documentation at https://docs.aws.amazon.com/sagemaker/latest/dg/sms-automated-labeling.html.

9. The last step in configuring our training job is to enter instructions for the workers. This is an important step, especially if your job is distributed to third-party workers. The better our instructions, the higher the quality of the annotations. Here, let's explain what the job is about, and enter a `cat` label for workers to apply.

    In a real-life scenario, you should add detailed instructions, provide sample images for good and bad examples, explain what your expectations are, and so on. The following screenshot shows what our instructions look like:

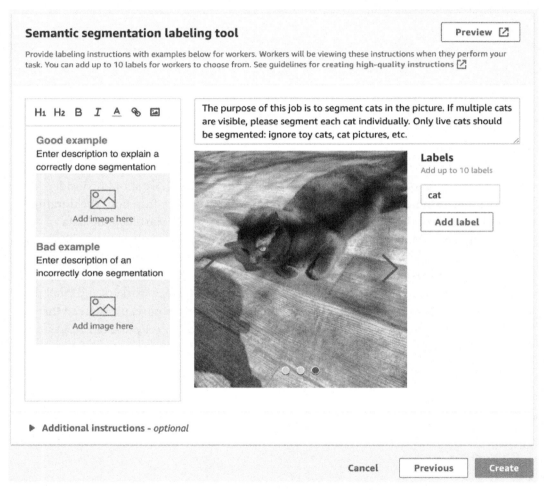

Figure 2.9 – Setting up instructions

10. Once we're done with instructions, we click on **Create** to launch the labeling job. After a few minutes, the job is ready to be distributed to workers.

Labeling images

Logging in to the worker URL, we can see from the screen shown in the following screenshot that we have work to do:

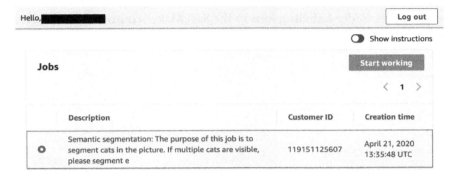

Figure 2.10 – Worker console

1. Clicking on **Start working** opens a new window, visible in the next picture. It displays instructions as well as a first image to work on:

Figure 2.11 – Labeling images

2. Using the graphical tools in the toolbar, and especially the auto-segment tool, we can very quickly produce high-quality annotations. Please take a few minutes to practice, and you'll be able to do the same in no time.

3. Once we're done with the three images, the job is complete, and we can visualize the labeled images under **Labeling jobs** in the SageMaker console. Your screen should look like the following screenshot:

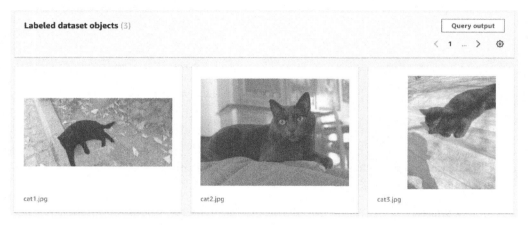

Figure 2.12 – Labeled images

More importantly, we can find labeling information in the S3 output location.

In particular, the **augmented manifest** (`output/my-cat-job/manifests/ output/output.manifest`) contains annotation information on each data sample, such as the classes present in the image, and a link to the segmentation mask:

```
{"source-ref":"s3://sagemaker-book/chapter2/cat/cat1.
jpg",
"my-cat-job-ref":"s3://sagemaker-book/chapter2/cat/
output/my-cat-job/annotations/consolidated-annotation/
output/0_2020-04-21T13:48:00.091190.png","my-cat-job-
ref-metadata":{"internal-color-map":{"0":{"class-
name":"BACKGROUND","hex-color":"#ffffff","confide
nce":0.8054600000000001},"1":{"class-name":"cat","hex-
color":"#2ca02c","confidence":0.8054600000000001},
"type":"groundtruth/semantic-segmentation","human-
annotated":"yes","creation-date":"2020-04-
21T13:48:00.562419","job-name":"labeling-job/my-cat-
job"}}
```

Yes, that's quite a mouthful! Don't worry though: in *Chapter 5, Training Computer Vision Models*, we'll see how we can feed this information directly to the built-in computer vision algorithms implemented in Amazon SageMaker. Of course, we could also parse this information, and convert it for whatever framework we use to train our computer vision model.

As you can see, SageMaker Ground Truth makes it easy to label image datasets. You just need to upload your data to S3 and create a workforce. Ground Truth will then distribute the work automatically, and store the results in S3.

We just saw how to label images, but what about text tasks? Well, they're equally easy to set up and run. Let's go through an example.

Labeling text

This is a quick example of labeling text for named entity recognition. The dataset is made up of text fragments from one of my blog posts, where we'd like to label all AWS service names. These are available in our GitHub repository:

```
$ cat ner/1.txt
With great power come great responsibility. The second you
create AWS resources, you're responsible for them: security of
course, but also cost and scaling. This makes monitoring and
alerting all the more important, which is why we built services
like Amazon CloudWatch, AWS Config and AWS Systems Manager.
```

We will start labeling text using the following steps:

1. First, let's upload text fragments to S3 with the following line of code:

    ```
    $ aws s3 cp --recursive ner/ s3://sagemaker-book/
    chapter2/ner/
    ```

2.   Just like in the previous example, we configure a text labeling job, set up input data, and select an IAM role, as shown in the following screenshot:

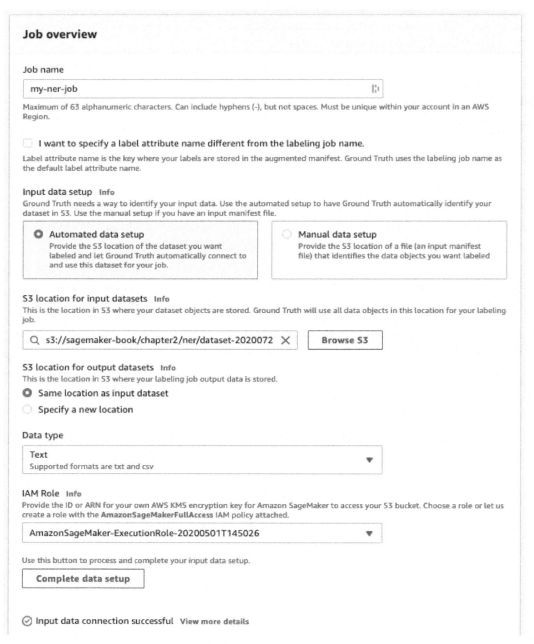

Figure 2.13 – Creating a text labeling job

3. Then, we select **Text** as the category, and **Named entity recognition** as the task.

4. On the next screen, shown in the following screenshot, we simply select our private team again, add a label, and enter instructions:

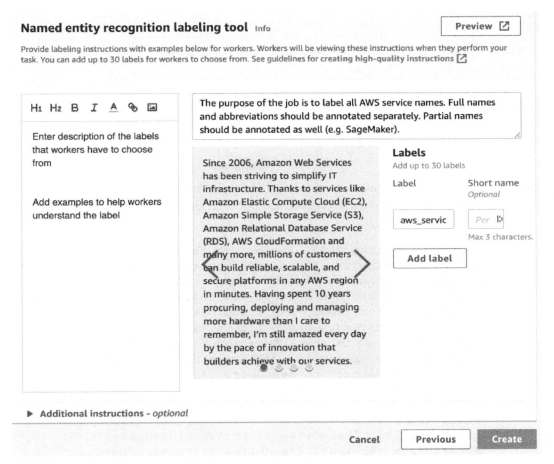

Figure 2.14 – Setting up instructions

5. Once the job is ready, we log in to the worker console and start labeling. You can see a labeled example in the following screenshot:

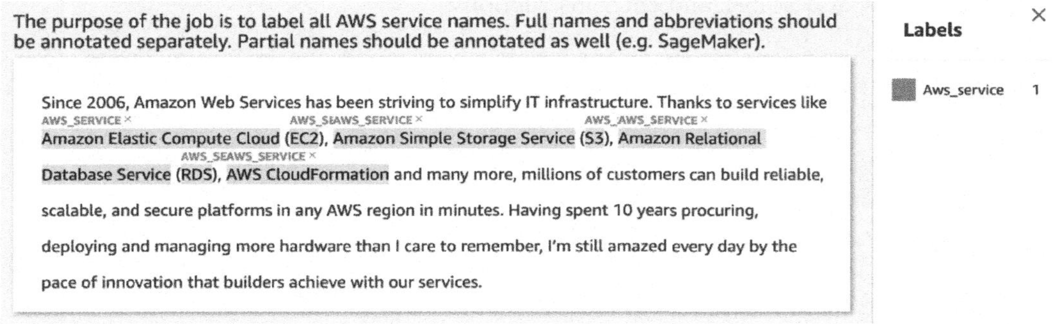

The purpose of the job is to label all AWS service names. Full names and abbreviations should be annotated separately. Partial names should be annotated as well (e.g. SageMaker).

Since 2006, Amazon Web Services has been striving to simplify IT infrastructure. Thanks to services like Amazon Elastic Compute Cloud (EC2), Amazon Simple Storage Service (S3), Amazon Relational Database Service (RDS), AWS CloudFormation and many more, millions of customers can build reliable, scalable, and secure platforms in any AWS region in minutes. Having spent 10 years procuring, deploying and managing more hardware than I care to remember, I'm still amazed every day by the pace of innovation that builders achieve with our services.

Labels

Aws_service   1

Figure 2.15 – Labeling text

6. We're done quickly, and we can find the labeling information in our S3 bucket. Here's what we find for the preceding text: for each entity, we get a start offset, an end offset, and a label:

```
{"source": "Since 2006, Amazon Web Services has been
striving to simplify IT infrastructure. Thanks to
services like Amazon Elastic Compute Cloud (EC2),
Amazon Simple Storage Service (S3), Amazon Relational
Database Service (RDS), AWS CloudFormation and many more,
millions of customers can build reliable, scalable, and
secure platforms in any AWS region in minutes. Having
spent 10 years procuring, deploying and managing more
hardware than I care to remember, I'm still amazed
every day by the pace of innovation that builders achieve
with our services.","my-ner-job": {"annotations":
{"entities":[{"endOffset":133,"startOffset":105,"label":
"aws_service"}, {"endOffset":138,"startOffset":135,
"label":"aws_service"},{"endOffset":170,"startOffset":
141,"label":"aws_service"}, {"endOffset":174,
"startOffset":172,"label":"aws_service"}, {"endOffset":
211,"startOffset":177,"label":"aws_service"},
{"endOffset":216,"startOffset":213,"label":
"aws_service"}, {"endOffset":237,"startOffset":
219,"label":"aws_service"}], "labels":[{"label":
"aws_service"}]}}, "my-ner-job-metadata": {"entities":
[{"confidence":0.12},{"confidence":0.08},{"confidence":
0.13},{"confidence":0.07},{"confidence":0.14},
{"confidence":0.08},{"confidence":0.1}],"job-name":
"labeling-job/my-ner-job","type":"groundtruth/text-span",
```

```
"creation-date":"2020-04-21T14:32:36.573013",
"human-annotated":"yes"}}
```

Amazon SageMaker Ground Truth really makes it easy to label datasets at scale. It has many nice features including job chaining and custom workflows, which I encourage you to explore at `https://docs.aws.amazon.com/sagemaker/latest/dg/sms.html`.

Next, we're going to learn about Amazon SageMaker Processing, and you can easily use it to process any dataset using your own code.

Exploring Amazon SageMaker Processing

Collecting and labeling data samples is only the first step in preparing a dataset. Indeed, it's very likely that you'll have to pre-process your dataset in order to do the following, for example:

- Convert it to the input format expected by the machine learning algorithm you're using.
- Rescale or normalize numerical features.
- Engineer higher-level features, for example, one-hot encoding.
- Clean and tokenize text for natural language processing applications.
- And more!

Once training is complete, you may want to run additional jobs to post-process the predicted data and to evaluate your model on different datasets.

In this section, you'll learn about Amazon SageMaker Processing, a SageMaker capability that helps you run batch jobs related to your machine learning project.

Discovering the Amazon SageMaker Processing API

The Amazon SageMaker Processing API is part of the SageMaker SDK, which we already installed in *Chapter 1, Introducing Amazon SageMaker*. Its documentation is available at `https://sagemaker.readthedocs.io`.

SageMaker Processing provides you with a built-in Docker container that can run Python batch jobs written with **scikit-learn** (`https://scikit-learn.org`). You can also use your own container if you'd like. Logs are available in **Amazon CloudWatch Logs** in the `/aws/sagemaker/ProcessingJobs` log group.

Let's first see how we can use scikit-learn and SageMaker Processing to prepare a dataset for training.

> **Note:**
>
> You can run this example, and all future examples, either on your local machine, on a Notebook instance, or in SageMaker Studio. Please make sure to enable the appropriate `conda` or `virtualenv` environment, as explained in *Chapter 1, Getting Started with Amazon SageMaker*.
>
> For the rest of the book, I also recommend that you follow along and run the code available in the companion GitHub repository. Every effort has been made to check all code samples present in the text. However, for those of you who have an electronic version, copying and pasting may have unpredictable results: formatting issues, weird quotes, and so on.

Processing a dataset with scikit-learn

Here's the high-level process:

- Upload your unprocessed dataset to Amazon S3.
- Write a script with scikit-learn in order to load the dataset, process it, and save the processed features and labels.
- Run this script with SageMaker Processing on managed infrastructure.

Uploading the dataset to Amazon S3

First, we need a dataset. We'll use the direct marketing dataset published by S. Moro, P. Cortez, and P. Rita in "A Data-Driven Approach to Predict the Success of Bank Telemarketing", Decision Support Systems, Elsevier, 62:22-31, June 2014.

This dataset describes a binary classification problem: will a customer accept a marketing offer, yes or no? It contains a little more than 41,000 labeled customer samples. Let's dive in:

1. Creating a new Jupyter notebook, let's first download and extract the dataset:

```sh
%%sh
apt-get -y install unzip       # Only needed in SageMaker
Studio
wget -N https://sagemaker-sample-data-us-west-2.s3-us-
west-2.amazonaws.com/autopilot/direct_marketing/bank-
additional.zip
unzip -o bank-additional.zip
```

2. Then, we load it with `pandas`:

```python
import pandas as pd
data = pd.read_csv('./bank-additional/bank-additional-
full.csv')
print(data.shape)
(41188, 21)
```

3. Now, let's display the first five lines:

```python
data[:5]
```

This prints out the table visible in the following figure:

	age	job	marital	education	default	housing	loan	contact	month	day_of_week	duration	campaign	pdays	previous	poutcome
0	56	housemaid	married	basic.4y	no	no	no	telephone	may	mon	261	1	999	0	nonexistent
1	57	services	married	high.school	unknown	no	no	telephone	may	mon	149	1	999	0	nonexistent
2	37	services	married	high.school	no	yes	no	telephone	may	mon	226	1	999	0	nonexistent
3	40	admin.	married	basic.6y	no	no	no	telephone	may	mon	151	1	999	0	nonexistent
4	56	services	married	high.school	no	no	yes	telephone	may	mon	307	1	999	0	nonexistent

Figure 2.16 – Viewing the dataset

Scrolling to the right, we can see a column named **y**, storing the labels.

4. Now, let's upload the dataset to Amazon S3. We'll use a default bucket automatically created by SageMaker in the region we're running in. We'll just add a prefix to keep things nice and tidy:

```
import sagemaker
prefix = 'sagemaker/DEMO-smprocessing/input'
input_data = sagemaker.Session().upload_data(path='./
bank-additional/bank-additional-full.csv', key_
prefix=prefix)
```

Writing a processing script with scikit-learn

As SageMaker Processing takes care of all infrastructure concerns, we can focus on the script itself. We don't have to worry about Amazon S3 either: SageMaker Processing will automatically copy the input dataset from S3 into the container, and the processed datasets from the container to S3.

Container paths are provided when we configure the job itself. Here's what we'll use:

- The input dataset: /opt/ml/processing/input
- The processed training set: /opt/ml/processing/train
- The processed test set: /opt/ml/processing/test

In our Jupyter environment, let's start writing a new Python file named preprocessing.py. As you would expect, this script will load the dataset, perform basic feature engineering, and save the processed dataset:

1. First, we read our single command-line parameter with the argparse library (https://docs.python.org/3/library/argparse.html): the ratio for the training and test datasets. The actual value will be passed to the script by the SageMaker Processing SDK:

```
import argparse
parser = argparse.ArgumentParser()
parser.add_argument('--train-test-split-ratio',
                    type=float, default=0.3)
args, _ = parser.parse_known_args()
print('Received arguments {}'.format(args))
split_ratio = args.train_test_split_ratio
```

2. We load the input dataset using `pandas`. At startup, SageMaker Processing automatically copied it from S3 to a user-defined location inside the container; here, it is `/opt/ml/processing/input`:

```
import os
import pandas as pd
input_data_path = os.path.join('/opt/ml/processing/
input', 'bank-additional-full.csv')
df = pd.read_csv(input_data_path)
```

3. Then, we remove any line with missing values, as well as duplicate lines:

```
df.dropna(inplace=True)
df.drop_duplicates(inplace=True)
```

4. Then, we count negative and positive samples, and display the class ratio. This will tell us how unbalanced the dataset is:

```
one_class = df[df['y']=='yes']
one_class_count = one_class.shape[0]
zero_class = df[df['y']=='no']
zero_class_count = zero_class.shape[0]
zero_to_one_ratio = zero_class_count/one_class_count
print("Ratio: %.2f" % zero_to_one_ratio)
```

5. Looking at the dataset, we can see a column named `pdays`, telling us how long ago a customer has been contacted. Some lines have a `999` value, and that looks pretty suspicious: indeed, this is a placeholder value meaning that a customer has never been contacted. To help the model understand this assumption, let's add a new column stating it explicitly:

```
import numpy as np
df['no_previous_contact'] = np.where(df['pdays'] == 999,
1, 0)
```

6. In the `job` column, we can see three categories (`student`, `retired`, and `unemployed`) that should probably be grouped to indicate that these customers don't have a full-time job. Let's add another column:

```
df['not_working'] = np.where(np.in1d(df['job'],
['student', 'retired', 'unemployed']), 1, 0)
```

7. Now, let's split the dataset into training and test sets. Scikit-learn has a convenient API for this, and we set the split ratio according to a command-line argument passed to the script:

```
from sklearn.model_selection import train_test_split
X_train, X_test, y_train, y_test = train_test_split(
        df.drop('y', axis=1),
        df['y'],
        test_size=split_ratio, random_state=0)
```

8. The next step is to scale numerical features and to one-hot encode the categorical features. We'll use `StandardScaler` for the former, and `OneHotEncoder` for the latter:

```
from sklearn.compose import make_column_transformer
from sklearn.preprocessing import
StandardScaler,OneHotEncoder
preprocess = make_column_transformer(
   (['age', 'duration', 'campaign', 'pdays', 'previous'],
   StandardScaler()),
   (['job', 'marital', 'education', 'default', 'housing',
    'loan','contact', 'month', 'day_of_week',
    'poutcome'],
   OneHotEncoder(sparse=False))
)
```

9. Then, we process the training and test datasets:

```
train_features = preprocess.fit_transform(X_train)
test_features = preprocess.transform(X_test)
```

10. Finally, we save the processed datasets, separating the features and labels. They're saved to user-defined locations in the container, and SageMaker Processing will automatically copy the files to S3 before terminating the job:

```
train_features_output_path = os.path.join('/opt/ml/
processing/train', 'train_features.csv')
train_labels_output_path = os.path.join('/opt/ml/
processing/train', 'train_labels.csv')
test_features_output_path = os.path.join('/opt/ml/
processing/test', 'test_features.csv')
test_labels_output_path = os.path.join('/opt/ml/
processing/test', 'test_labels.csv')
```

```
pd.DataFrame(train_features).to_csv(train_features_
output_path, header=False, index=False)
pd.DataFrame(test_features).to_csv(test_features_output_
path, header=False, index=False)
```
```
y_train.to_csv(train_labels_output_path, header=False,
index=False)
y_test.to_csv(test_labels_output_path, header=False,
index=False)
```

That's it. As you can see, this code is vanilla scikit-learn, so it shouldn't be difficult to adapt your own scripts for SageMaker Processing. Now let's see how we can actually run this.

Running a processing script

Coming back to our Jupyter notebook, we use the `SKLearnProcessor` object from the SageMaker SDK to configure the processing job:

1. First, we define which version of scikit-learn we want to use, and what our infrastructure requirements are. Here, we go for an `ml.m5.xlarge` instance, an all-round good choice:

```
from sagemaker.sklearn.processing import SKLearnProcessor
```
```
sklearn_processor = SKLearnProcessor(
    framework_version='0.20.0',
    role=sagemaker.get_execution_role(),
    instance_type='ml.m5.xlarge',
    instance_count=1)
```

2. Then, we simply launch the job, passing the name of the script, the dataset input path in S3, the user-defined dataset paths inside the SageMaker Processing environment, and the command-line arguments:

```
from sagemaker.processing import ProcessingInput,
ProcessingOutput
```
```
sklearn_processor.run(
    code='preprocessing.py',
    inputs=[ProcessingInput(
        source=input_data,    # Our data in S3
        destination='/opt/ml/processing/input')
    ],
    outputs=[
        ProcessingOutput(
            source='/opt/ml/processing/train',
            output_name='train_data'),
```

```
        ProcessingOutput(
            source='/opt/ml/processing/test',
            output_name='test_data'
            )
    ],
    arguments=['--train-test-split-ratio', '0.2']
)
```

As the job starts, SageMaker automatically provisions a managed `ml.m5.xlarge` instance, pulls the appropriate container to it, and runs our script inside the container. Once the job is complete, the instance is terminated, and we only pay for the amount of time we used it. There is zero infrastructure management, and we'll never leave idle instances running for no reason.

3. After a few minutes, the job is complete, and we can see the output of the script as follows:

```
Received arguments Namespace(train_test_split_ratio=0.2)
Reading input data from /opt/ml/processing/input/bank-
additional-full.csv
Positive samples: 4639
Negative samples: 36537
Ratio: 7.88
Splitting data into train and test sets with ratio 0.2
Running preprocessing and feature engineering
transformations
Train data shape after preprocessing: (32940, 58)
Test data shape after preprocessing: (8236, 58)
Saving training features to /opt/ml/processing/train/
train_features.csv
Saving test features to /opt/ml/processing/test/test_
features.csv
Saving training labels to /opt/ml/processing/train/train_
labels.csv
Saving test labels to /opt/ml/processing/test/test_
labels.csv
```

The following screenshot shows the log in CloudWatch:

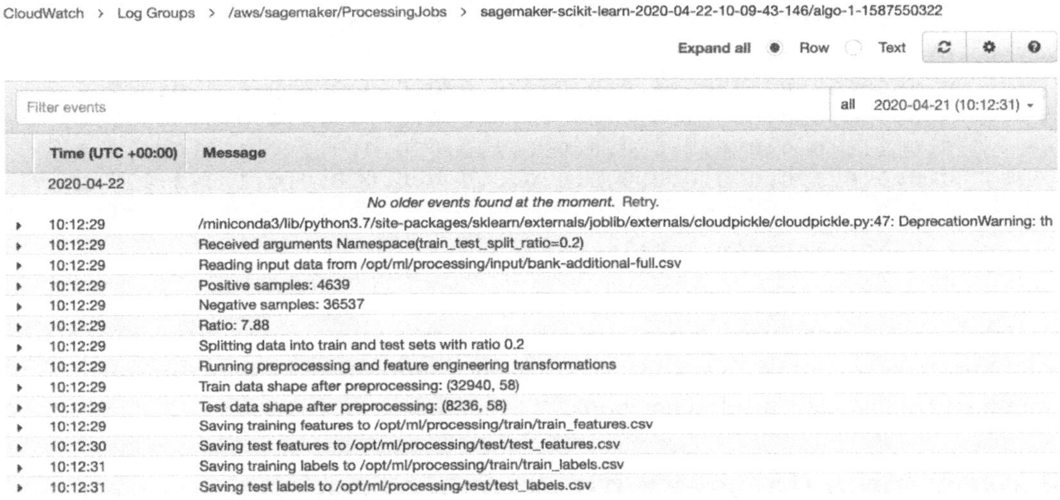

CloudWatch > Log Groups > /aws/sagemaker/ProcessingJobs > sagemaker-scikit-learn-2020-04-22-10-09-43-146/algo-1-1587550322

Expand all ● Row ○ Text   🔄 ⚙ ❓

| Filter events | | all   2020-04-21 (10:12:31) ▾ |

Time (UTC +00:00)	Message
2020-04-22	
	No older events found at the moment. Retry.
▸ 10:12:29	/miniconda3/lib/python3.7/site-packages/sklearn/externals/joblib/externals/cloudpickle/cloudpickle.py:47: DeprecationWarning: th
▸ 10:12:29	Received arguments Namespace(train_test_split_ratio=0.2)
▸ 10:12:29	Reading input data from /opt/ml/processing/input/bank-additional-full.csv
▸ 10:12:29	Positive samples: 4639
▸ 10:12:29	Negative samples: 36537
▸ 10:12:29	Ratio: 7.88
▸ 10:12:29	Splitting data into train and test sets with ratio 0.2
▸ 10:12:29	Running preprocessing and feature engineering transformations
▸ 10:12:29	Train data shape after preprocessing: (32940, 58)
▸ 10:12:29	Test data shape after preprocessing: (8236, 58)
▸ 10:12:29	Saving training features to /opt/ml/processing/train/train_features.csv
▸ 10:12:30	Saving test features to /opt/ml/processing/test/test_features.csv
▸ 10:12:31	Saving training labels to /opt/ml/processing/train/train_labels.csv
▸ 10:12:31	Saving test labels to /opt/ml/processing/test/test_labels.csv

Figure 2.17 – Viewing the log in CloudWatch Logs

4. Finally, we can describe the job and see the location of the processed datasets:

```
preprocessing_job_description =
    sklearn_processor.jobs[-1].describe()
output_config =
    preprocessing_job_description['ProcessingOutputConfig']
for output in output_config['Outputs']:
    print(output['S3Output']['S3Uri'])
```

This results in the following output:

```
s3://sagemaker-eu-west-1-123456789012/sagemaker-scikit-
learn-2020-04-22-10-09-43-146/output/train_data
```

```
s3://sagemaker-eu-west-1-123456789012/sagemaker-scikit-
learn-2020-04-22-10-09-43-146/output/test_data
```

In a terminal, we can use the AWS CLI to fetch the processed training set located at the preceding path, and take a look at the first sample and label:

```
$ aws s3 cp s3://sagemaker-eu-west-1-123456789012/
sagemaker-scikit-learn-2020-04-22-09-45-05-711/output/
train_data/train_features.csv .
```

```
$ aws s3 cp s3://sagemaker-eu-west-1-123456789012/
sagemaker-scikit-learn-2020-04-22-09-45-05-711/output/
```

```
train_data/train_labels.csv .
$ head -1 train_features.csv
0.09604515376959515,-0.6572847857673993,-
0.20595554104907898,0.19603112301129622,-
0.35090125695736246,0.0,0.0,0.0,0.0,0.0,0.0,0.0,0.0,0.0,
1.0,0.0,0.0,0.0,1.0,0.0,0.0,0.0,0.0,0.0,0.0,0.0,0.0,1.0,
0.0,1.0,0.0,0.0,1.0,0.0,0.0,1.0,0.0,0.0,0.0,1.0,0.0,0.0,
0.0,0.0,1.0,0.0,0.0,0.0,0.0,0.0,0.0,0.0,0.0,1.0,0.0,0.0,
1.0,0.0
$ head -1 train_labels.csv
no
```

Now that the dataset has been processed with our own code, we could use it to train a machine learning model. In real life, we would also automate these steps instead of running them manually inside a notebook.

Processing a dataset with your own code

In the previous example, we used a built-in container to run our scikit-learn code. SageMaker Processing also makes it possible to use your own container. Here's the high-level process:

1. Upload your dataset to Amazon S3.

2. Write a processing script with your language and library of choice: load the dataset, process it, and save the processed features and labels.

3. Define a Docker container that contains your script and its dependencies. As you would expect, the processing script should be the entry point of the container.

4. Build the container and push it to **Amazon ECR** (https://aws.amazon.com/ecr/), AWS' Docker registry service.

5. Using your container, run your script on the infrastructure managed by Amazon SageMaker.

Here are some additional resources if you'd like to explore SageMaker Processing:

- A primer on Amazon ECR: https://docs.aws.amazon.com/AmazonECR/latest/userguide/what-is-ecr.html

- Documentation on building your own container: https://docs.aws.amazon.com/sagemaker/latest/dg/build-your-own-processing-container.html

- A full example based on **Spark MLlib**: `https://github.com/awslabs/ amazon-sagemaker-examples/tree/master/sagemaker_ processing/feature_transformation_with_sagemaker_ processing`.

- Additional notebooks: `https://github.com/awslabs/amazon- sagemaker-examples/tree/master/sagemaker_processing`.

As you can see, SageMaker Processing makes it really easy to run data processing jobs. You can focus on writing and running your script, without having to worry about provisioning and managing infrastructure.

Processing data with other AWS services

Over the years, AWS has built many analytics services (`https://aws.amazon.com/ big-data/`). Depending on your technical environment, you could pick one or the other to process data for your machine learning workflows.

In this section, you'll learn about three services that are popular choices for analytics workloads, why they make sense in a machine learning context, and how to get started with them:

- **Amazon Elastic Map Reduce (EMR)**

- **AWS Glue**

- **Amazon Athena**

Amazon Elastic Map Reduce

Launched in 2009, Amazon Elastic Map Reduce, aka Amazon EMR, started as a managed environment for Apache Hadoop applications (`https://aws.amazon.com/ emr/`). Over the years, the service has added support for plenty of additional projects, such as **Spark**, **Hive**, **HBase**, **Flink**, and more. With additional features like EMRFS, an implementation of HDFS backed by Amazon S3, EMR is a prime contender for data processing at scale. You can learn more about EMR at `https://docs.aws.amazon. com/emr/`.

When it comes to processing machine learning data, Spark is a very popular choice thanks to its speed and its extensive feature engineering capabilities (`https://spark. apache.org/docs/latest/ml-features`). As SageMaker also supports Spark, this creates interesting opportunities to combine the two services.

Running a local Spark notebook

Notebook instances can run **PySpark** code locally for fast experimentation. This is as easy as selecting the Python3 kernel, and writing PySpark code. The following screenshot shows a code snippet where we load samples from the MNIST dataset in **libsvm** format. You can find the full example at https://github.com/awslabs/amazon-sagemaker-examples/tree/master/sagemaker-spark:

Figure 2.18 – Running a PySpark notebook

A local notebook is fine for experimenting at a small scale. For larger workloads, you'll certainly want to train on an EMR cluster.

Running a notebook backed by an Amazon EMR cluster

Notebook instances support **SparkMagic** kernels for Spark, PySpark, and SparkR (`https://github.com/jupyter-incubator/sparkmagic`). This makes it possible to connect a Jupyter notebook running on a Notebook instance to an Amazon EMR cluster, an interesting combination if you need to perform interactive exploration and processing at scale.

The setup procedure is documented in detail in this AWS blog post: `https://aws.amazon.com/blogs/machine-learning/build-amazon-sagemaker-notebooks-backed-by-spark-in-amazon-emr/`.

Processing data with Spark, training the model with Amazon SageMaker

We haven't talked about training models with SageMaker yet (we'll start doing that in the following chapters). When we get there, we'll discuss why this is a powerful combination compared to running everything on EMR.

AWS Glue

AWS Glue is a managed ETL service (`https://aws.amazon.com/glue/`). Thanks to Glue, you can easily clean your data, enrich it, convert it to a different format, and so on. Glue is not only a processing service: it also includes a metadata repository where you can define data sources (aka the **Glue Data Catalog**), a crawler service to fetch data from these sources, a scheduler that handles jobs and retries, and workflows to run everything smoothly. To top it off, Glue can also work with on-premise data sources.

AWS Glue works best with structured and semi-structured data. The service is built on top of Spark, giving you the option to use both built-in transforms and the Spark transforms in Python or Scala. Based on the transforms that you define on your data, Glue can automatically generate Spark scripts. Of course, you can customize them if needed, and you can also deploy your own scripts.

If you like the expressivity of Spark but don't want to manage EMR clusters, AWS Glue is a very interesting option. As it's based on popular languages and frameworks, you should quickly feel comfortable with it.

You can learn more about Glue at `https://docs.aws.amazon.com/glue/`, and you'll also find code samples at `https://github.com/aws-samples/aws-glue-samples`.

Amazon Athena

Amazon Athena is a serverless analytics service that lets you easily query Amazon S3 at scale, using only standard **SQL** (`https://aws.amazon.com/athena/`). There is zero infrastructure to manage, and you pay only for the queries that you run. Athena is based on Presto (`https://prestodb.io`).

Athena is extremely easy to use: just define the S3 bucket in which your data lives, apply a schema definition, and run your SQL queries! In most cases, you will get results in seconds. Once again, this doesn't require any infrastructure provisioning. All you need is some data in S3 and some SQL queries. Athena can also run federated queries, allowing you to query and join data located across different backends (Amazon DynamoDB, Apache Hbase, JDBC-compliant sources, and more).

If you're working with structured and semi-structured datasets stored in S3, and if SQL queries are sufficient to process these datasets, Athena should be the first service that you try. You'll be amazed at how productive Athena makes you, and how inexpensive it is. Mark my words.

You can learn more about Athena at `https://docs.aws.amazon.com/athena/`, and you'll also find code samples at `https://github.com/aws-samples/aws-glue-samples`.

Summary

In this chapter, you learned how Amazon SageMaker Ground Truth helps you build highly accurate training datasets using image and text labeling workflows. We'll see in *Chapter 5, Training Computer Vision Models*, how to use image datasets labeled with Ground Truth.

Then, you learned about Amazon SageMaker Processing, a capability that helps you run your own data processing workloads on managed infrastructure: feature engineering, data validation, model evaluation, and so on.

Finally, we discussed three other AWS services (Amazon EMR, AWS Glue, and Amazon Athena), and how they could fit into your analytics and machine learning workflows.

In the next chapter, we'll start training models using the built-in machine learning models of Amazon SageMaker.

Section 2: Building and Training Models

In this section, you will understand how to build and train machine learning models with Amazon SageMaker. This part covers AutoML, built-in algorithms, built-in frameworks, and helps you design your own code. Using notebooks based on the SageMaker SDK, it will explain how to read training data, how to set up training jobs, how to define training parameters, and how to train on fully managed infrastructure.

This section comprises the following chapters:

- *Chapter 3, AutoML with Amazon SageMaker AutoPilot*
- *Chapter 4, Training Machine Learning Models*
- *Chapter 5, Training Computer Vision Models*
- *Chapter 6, Training Natural Language Processing Models*
- *Chapter 7, Extending Machine Learning Services Using Built-In Frameworks*
- *Chapter 8, Using Your Algorithms and Code*

3
AutoML with Amazon SageMaker Autopilot

In the previous chapter, you learned how Amazon SageMaker helps you build and prepare datasets. In a typical machine learning project, the next step would be to start experimenting with algorithms in order to find an early fit and get a sense of the predictive power you could expect from the model.

Whether you work with statistical machine learning or deep learning, three options are available when it comes to selecting an algorithm:

- Write your own, or customize an existing one. This only makes sense if you have strong skills in statistics and computer science, if you're quite sure that you can do better than well-tuned, off-the-shelf algorithms, and if you're given enough time to work on the project. Let's face it, these conditions are rarely met.

- Use a built-in algorithm implemented in one of your favorite libraries, such as **Linear Regression** or **XGBoost**. For deep learning problems, this includes pretrained models available in **TensorFlow**, **PyTorch**, and so on. This option saves you the trouble of writing machine learning code. Instead, it lets you focus on feature engineering and model optimization.

- Use **AutoML**, a rising technique that lets you automatically build, train, and optimize machine learning models.

In this chapter, you will learn about **Amazon SageMaker Autopilot**, an AutoML capability part of Amazon SageMaker. We'll see how to use it in Amazon SageMaker Studio, without writing a single line of code, and also how to use it with the Amazon SageMaker SDK:

- Discovering Amazon SageMaker Autopilot

- Using Amazon SageMaker Autopilot in SageMaker Studio

- Using Amazon SageMaker Autopilot with the SageMaker SDK

- Diving deep on Amazon SageMaker Autopilot

Technical requirements

You will need an AWS account to run examples included in this chapter. If you haven't got one already, please point your browser at `https://aws.amazon.com/getting-started/` to create it. You should also familiarize yourself with the AWS Free Tier (`https://aws.amazon.com/free/`), which lets you use many AWS services for free within certain usage limits.

You will need to install and configure the AWS **Command-Line Interface** (**CLI**) for your account (`https://aws.amazon.com/cli/`).

You will need a working Python 3.x environment. Be careful not to use Python 2.7, as it is no longer maintained. Installing the Anaconda distribution (`https://www.anaconda.com/`) is not mandatory, but is strongly encouraged as it includes many projects that we will need (Jupyter, `pandas`, `numpy`, and more).

Code examples included in the book are available on GitHub at `https://github.com/PacktPublishing/Learn-Amazon-SageMaker`. You will need to install a Git client to access them (`https://git-scm.com/`).

Discovering Amazon SageMaker Autopilot

Added to Amazon SageMaker in late 2019, **Amazon SageMaker Autopilot** is an AutoML capability that takes care of all machine learning steps for you. You only need to upload a columnar dataset to an Amazon S3 bucket, and define the column you want the model to learn (the **target attribute**). Then, you simply launch an Autopilot job, with either a few clicks in the SageMaker Studio GUI, or a couple of lines of code with the SageMaker SDK.

The simplicity of SageMaker Autopilot doesn't come at the expense of transparency and control. You can see how your models are built, and you can keep experimenting to refine results. In that respect, SageMaker Autopilot should appeal to new and seasoned practitioners alike.

In this section, you'll learn about the different steps of a SageMaker Autopilot job, and how they contribute to delivering high-quality models:

- Analyzing data
- Feature engineering
- Model tuning

Let's start by seeing how SageMaker Autopilot analyzes data.

Analyzing data

This step is first responsible for understanding what type of machine learning problem we're trying to solve. SageMaker Autopilot currently supports **linear regression**, **binary classification**, and **multi-class classification**.

> **Note:**
> A frequent question is "how much data is needed to build such models?". This is a surprisingly difficult question. The answer—if there is one—depends on many factors, such as the number of features and their quality. As a basic rule of thumb, some practitioners recommend having 10-100 times more samples than features. In any case, I'd advise you to collect no fewer than hundreds of samples (for each class, if you're building a classification model). Thousands or tens of thousands are better, especially if you have more features. For statistical machine learning, there is rarely a need for millions of samples, so start with what you have, analyze the results, and iterate before going on a data collection rampage!

By analyzing the distribution of the target attribute, SageMaker Autopilot can easily figure out which one is the right one. For instance, if the target attribute has only two values (say, yes and no), it's pretty likely that you're trying to build a binary classification model.

Then, SageMaker Autopilot computes statistics on the dataset and on individual columns: the number of unique values, the mean, median, and so on. Machine learning practitioners very often do this in order to get a first feel for the data, and it's nice to see it automated. In addition, SageMaker Autopilot generates a Jupyter notebook, the **data exploration notebook**, to present these statistics in a user-friendly way.

Once SageMaker Autopilot has analyzed the dataset, it builds ten **candidate pipelines** that will be used to train candidate models. A pipeline is a combination of the following:

- A data processing job, in charge of feature engineering. As you can guess, this job runs on **Amazon SageMaker Processing**, which we studied in *Chapter 2, Handling Data Preparation Techniques*.

- A training job, running on the processed dataset. The algorithm is selected automatically by SageMaker Autopilot based on the problem type.

Next, let's see how Autopilot can be used in feature engineering.

Feature engineering

This step is responsible for preprocessing the input dataset according to the pipelines defined during data analysis.

The ten candidate pipelines are fully documented in another auto-generated notebook, the **candidate generation notebook**. This notebook isn't just descriptive: you can actually run its cells, and manually reproduce the steps performed by SageMaker Autopilot. This level of transparency and control is extremely important, as it lets you understand exactly how the model was built. Thus, you're able to verify that it performs the way it should, and you're able to explain it to your stakeholders. Also, you can use the notebook as a starting point for additional optimization and tweaking if you're so inclined.

Lastly, let's take a look at model tuning in Autopilot.

Model tuning

This step is responsible for training and tuning models according to the pipelines defined during data analysis. For each pipeline, SageMaker Autopilot will launch an **automatic model tuning** job (we'll cover this topic in detail in a later chapter). In a nutshell, each tuning job will use **hyperparameter optimization** to train a large number of increasingly accurate models on the processed dataset. As usual, all of this happens on managed infrastructure.

Once the model tuning is complete, you can view the model information and metrics in Amazon SageMaker Studio, build visualizations, and so on. You can do the same programmatically with the **Amazon SageMaker Experiments** SDK.

Finally, you can deploy your model of choice just like any other SageMaker model using either the SageMaker Studio GUI or the SageMaker SDK.

Now that we understand the different steps of an Autopilot job, let's run a job in SageMaker Studio.

Using SageMaker Autopilot in SageMaker Studio

We will build a model using only SageMaker Studio. We won't write a line of machine learning code, so get ready for zero-code AI.

In this section, you'll learn how to do the following:

- Launch a SageMaker Autopilot job in SageMaker Studio.
- Monitor the different steps of the job.
- Visualize models and compare their properties.

Launching a job

First, we need a dataset. We'll reuse the direct marketing dataset used in *Chapter 2, Handling Data Preparation Techniques*. This dataset describes a binary classification problem: will a customer accept a marketing offer, yes or no? It contains a little more than 41,000 labeled customer samples. Let's dive in:

1. Let's open SageMaker Studio, and create a new **Python 3 notebook** using the **Data Science** kernel, as shown in the following screenshot:

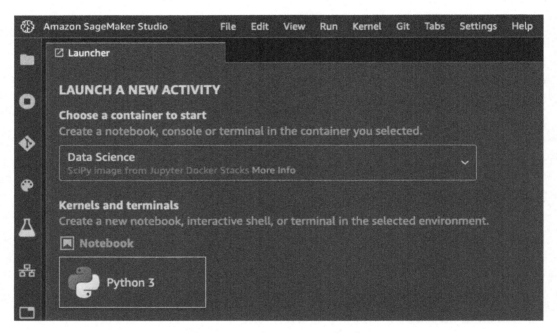

Figure 3.1 – Creating a notebook

2. Now, let's download and extract the dataset as follows:

```
%%sh
apt-get -y install unzip
wget -N https://sagemaker-sample-data-us-west-2.s3-us-
west-2.amazonaws.com/autopilot/direct_marketing/bank-
additional.zip
unzip -o bank-additional.zip
```

3. In *Chapter 2, Handling Data Preparation Techniques*, we ran a feature engineering script with Amazon SageMaker Processing. We will do no such thing here: we simply upload the dataset as is to S3, into the **default bucket** created by SageMaker:

```
import sagemaker
prefix = 'sagemaker/DEMO-autopilot/input'
sess   = sagemaker.Session()
uri = sess.upload_data(path="./bank-additional/bank-
additional-full.csv", key_prefix=prefix)
print(uri)
```

The dataset will be available in S3 at the following location:

```
s3://sagemaker-us-east-2-123456789012/sagemaker/DEMO-
autopilot/input/bank-additional-full.csv
```

4. Now, we click on the flask icon in the left-hand vertical icon bar. This opens the **Experiments** tab, and we click on the **Create Experiment** button to create a new Autopilot job.

5. The next screen is where we configure the job. As shown in the following screenshot, we first give it the name of `my-first-autopilot-job`:

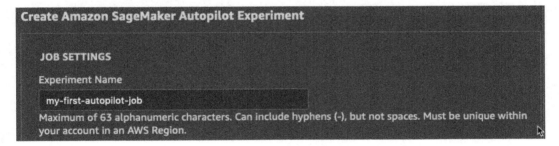

Figure 3.2 – Creating an Autopilot Experiment

We set the location of the input dataset using the path returned in *step 3*. As is visible in the following screenshot, we can either browse S3 buckets or enter the S3 location directly:

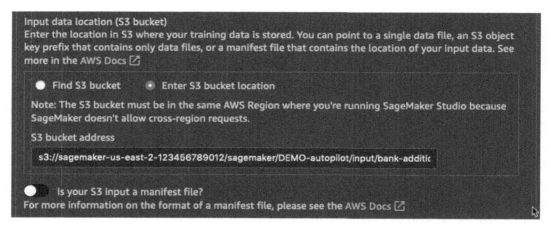

Figure 3.3 – Defining the input location

6. The next step is to define the name of the **target attribute**, as shown in the following screenshot. The column storing the yes or no label is called y:

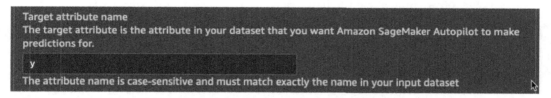

Figure 3.4 – Defining the target attribute

As shown in the following screenshot, we set the output location where job artifacts will be copied to: s3://sagemaker-us-east-2-123456789012/ sagemaker/DEMO-autopilot/output/:

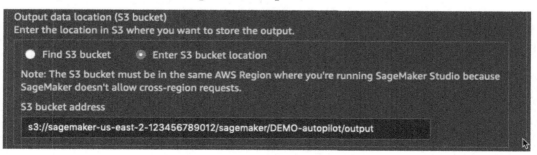

Figure 3.5 – Defining the output location

7. We set the type of job we want to train, as shown in the next screenshot. Here, we select **Auto** in order to let SageMaker Autopilot figure out the problem type. Alternatively, we could select **Binary classification**, and pick either the **Accuracy** (the default setting) or the **F1** metric:

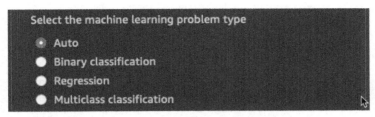

Figure 3.6 – Setting the problem type

8. Finally, we decide whether we want to run a full job, or simply generate notebooks. We'll go with the former, as shown in the following screenshot. The latter would be a good option if we wanted to train and tweak the parameters manually:

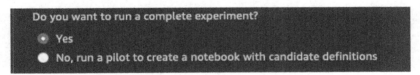

Figure 3.7 – Running a complete experiment

9. Optionally, in the **Advanced Settings** section, we would change the IAM role, set an encryption key for job artifacts, and define the VPC where we'd like to launch job instances. Let's keep default values here.

10. The job setup is complete: all it took was this one screen. Then, we click on **Create Experiment**, and off it goes!

Monitoring a job

Once the job is launched, it goes through the three steps that we already discussed, which should take around 5 hours to complete. The new experiment is listed in the **Experiments** tab, and we can right-click **Describe AutoML Job** to describe its current status. This opens the following screen, where we can see the progress of the job:

1. As expected, the job starts by analyzing data, as highlighted in the following screenshot:

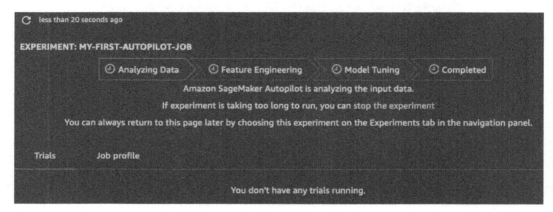

Figure 3.8 – Viewing job progress

2. About 10 minutes later, the data analysis is complete, and the job moves on to feature engineering. As shown in the next screenshot, we can also see new two buttons in the top-right corner, pointing at the **candidate generation** and **data exploration** notebooks; don't worry, we'll take a deeper look at both later in the chapter:

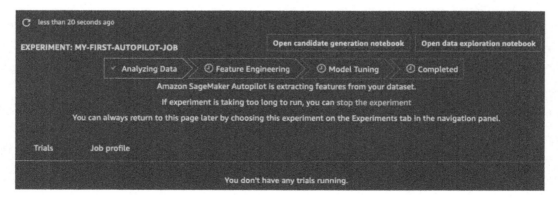

Figure 3.9 – Viewing job progress

3.   Once feature engineering is complete, the job then moves on the model tuning. As visible in the following picture, we see the first models being trained in the **Trials** tab. A trial is the name Amazon SageMaker Experiments uses for a collection of related jobs, such as processing jobs, batch transform jobs, training jobs, and so on:

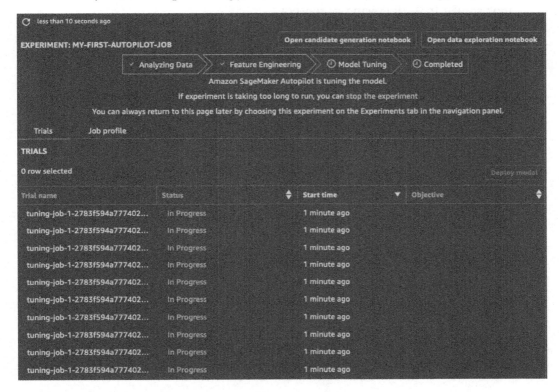

Figure 3.10 – Viewing tuning jobs

4. At first, we see ten tuning jobs, corresponding to the ten candidate pipelines. Once a job is complete, we can see its **Objective**, that is to say, the metric that the job tried to optimize (in this case, it's the validation accuracy). We can sort jobs based on this metric, and the best tuning job so far is highlighted with a star. Your screen should look similar to the following screenshot:

Figure 3.11 – Viewing results

5. If we select a job and right-click **Open in trial details**, we can see plenty of additional information, such as the other jobs that belong to the same trial. In the following screenshot, we also see the actual algorithm that was used for training (**XGBoost**) along with its hyperparameter values:

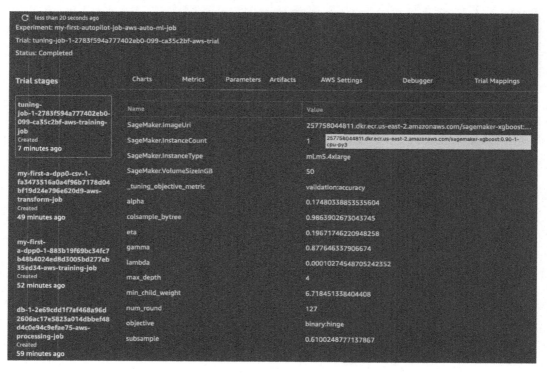

Figure 3.12 – Examining a job

6. After several hours, the SageMaker Autopilot job is complete. 500 jobs have been trained. This is a default value that can be changed in the SageMaker API.

At this point, we could simply deploy the top job, but instead, let's compare the top ten ones using the visualization tools built into SageMaker Studio.

Comparing jobs

A single SageMaker Autopilot job trains hundreds of jobs. Over time, you may end up with tens of thousands of jobs, and you may wish to compare their properties. Let's see how:

1. Going to the **Experiments** tab on the left, we locate our job and right-click **Open in trial component list**, as visible in the following screenshot:

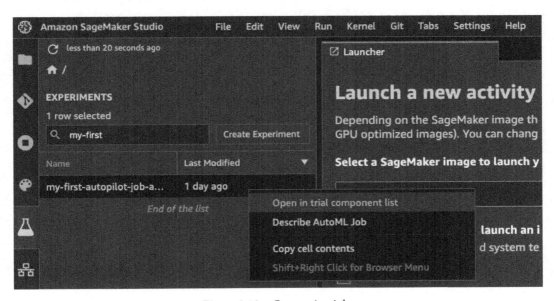

Figure 3.13 – Comparing jobs

2. This opens the **Trial Component List**, as shown in the following screenshot.

    We open the **Table Properties** panel on the right by clicking on the icon
    representing a cog. In the **Metrics** section, we tick the **ObjectiveMetric** box. In the
    Type filter section, we only tick **Training job**. In the main panel, we sort jobs by
    descending objective metric by clicking on the arrow. We hold *Shift* and click the
    top ten jobs to select them. Then, we click on the **Add chart** button:

Figure 3.14 – Comparing jobs

3. This opens the **Trial Component Chart** tab, as visible in the screenshot that follows.
    Click inside the chart box at the bottom to open the **Chart properties** panel on
    the right:

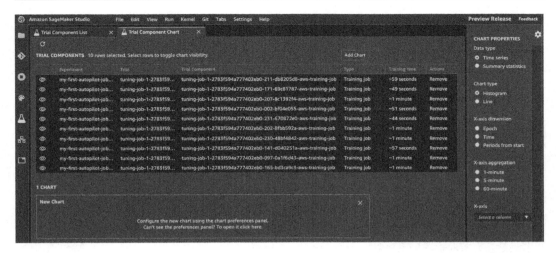

Figure 3.15 – Comparing jobs

As our training jobs are very short (about a minute), there won't be enough data for **Time series** charts, so let's select **Summary statistics** instead. We're going to build a **scatter plot**, putting the maximum training accuracy and validation accuracy in perspective, as shown in the following screenshot. We also color data points with our trial names:

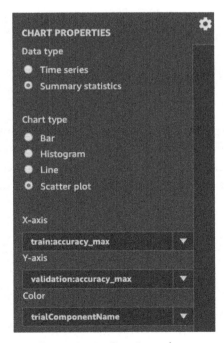

Figure 3.16 – Creating a chart

4. Zooming in on the following chart, we can quickly visualize our jobs and their respective metrics. We could build additional charts showing the impact of certain hyperparameters on accuracy. This would help us shortlist a few models for further testing. Maybe we would end up considering several of them for ensemble prediction:

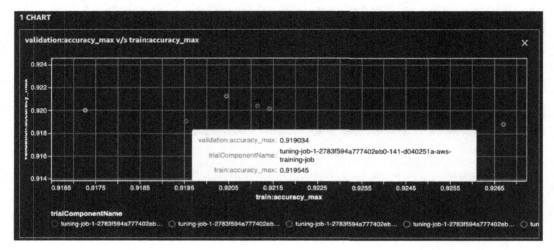

Figure 3.17 – Plotting accuracies

The next step is to deploy a model and start testing it.

Deploying and invoking a model

The SageMaker Studio GUI makes it extremely easy to deploy a model. Let's see how:

1. Going back to the **Experiments** tab, we right-click the name of our experiment and select **Describe AutoML Job**. This opens the list of training jobs. Making sure that they're sorted by descending objective, we select the best one (it's highlighted with a star), as shown in the screenshot that follows, and then we click on the **Deploy model** button:

Figure 3.18 – Deploying a model

2. On the screen shown in the following screenshot, we just give the endpoint name and leave all other settings as is. The model will be deployed on a real-time HTTPS endpoint backed by an `ml.m5.xlarge` instance:

Deploy model

REQUIRED SETTINGS

Endpoint name

my-first-autopilot-endpoint

Maximum of 63 alphanumeric characters. Can include hyphens (-), but not spaces. Must be unique within your account in an AWS Region.

Instance type   Instance count

ml.m5.xlarge   ▼   1

Data capture
SageMaker Studio will save prediction requests and responses from the endpoint to an Amazon S3 location specified below

☐ Save prediction requests

☐ Save prediction responses

Deploy model

Figure 3.19 – Deploying a model

3. Heading to the **Endpoints** section in the left-hand vertical panel, we can see the endpoint being created. As shown in the following screenshot, it will initially be in the **Creating** state. After a few minutes, it will be **In service**:

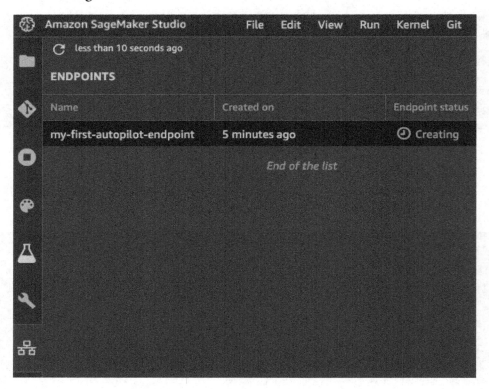

Figure 3.20 – Creating an endpoint

4. Moving to a Jupyter notebook (we can reuse the one we wrote to download the dataset), we define the name of the endpoint, and a sample to predict. Here, I'm using the first line of the dataset:

```
ep_name = 'my-first-autopilot-endpoint'
sample =
'56,housemaid,married,basic.4y,no,no,no,telephone,
may,mon,261,1,999,0,nonexistent,1.1,93.994,-36.4,4.857,
5191.0'
```

5. We create a `boto3` client for the SageMaker runtime. This runtime contains a single API, `invoke_endpoint` (`https://boto3.amazonaws.com/v1/documentation/api/latest/reference/services/sagemaker-runtime.html`). This makes it efficient to embed in client applications that just need to invoke models:

```
import boto3
sm_rt = boto3.Session().client('runtime.sagemaker')
```

6. We send the sample to the endpoint, also passing the input and output content types:

```
response = sm_rt.invoke_endpoint(EndpointName=ep_name,
                                 ContentType='text/csv',
                                 Accept='text/csv',
                                 Body=sample)
```

7. We decode the prediction and print it – this customer is not likely to accept the offer:

```
response = response['Body'].read().decode("utf-8")
print(response)
```

This sample is predicted as a `no`:

```
no
```

8. When we're done testing the endpoint, we should delete it to avoid unnecessary charges. We can do this with the `delete_endpoint` API in `boto3` (`https://boto3.amazonaws.com/v1/documentation/api/latest/reference/services/sagemaker.html#SageMaker.Client.delete_endpoint`):

```
sm = boto3.Session().client('sagemaker')
sm.delete_endpoint(EndpointName=ep_name)
```

Congratulations, you've successfully built, trained, and deployed your first machine learning model on Amazon SageMaker. That was pretty simple, wasn't it? The only code we wrote was to download the dataset and to predict with our model.

Using the **SageMaker Studio** GUI is a great way to quickly experiment with a new dataset, and also to let less technical users build models on their own. Now, let's see how we can use SageMaker Autopilot programmatically with the **SageMaker SDK**.

Using the SageMaker Autopilot SDK

The Amazon SageMaker SDK includes a simple API for SageMaker Autopilot. You can find its documentation at `https://sagemaker.readthedocs.io/en/stable/automl.html`.

In this section, you'll learn how to use this API to train a model on the same dataset as in the previous section.

Launching a job

The SageMaker SDK makes it extremely easy to launch an Autopilot job – just upload your data in S3, and call a single API! Let's see how:

1. First, we import the SageMaker SDK:

    ```
    import sagemaker
    sess = sagemaker.Session()
    ```

2. Then, we download the dataset:

    ```
    %%sh
    wget -N https://sagemaker-sample-data-us-west-2.s3-us-
    west-2.amazonaws.com/autopilot/direct_marketing/bank-
    additional.zip
    unzip -o bank-additional.zip
    ```

3. Next, we upload the dataset to S3:

    ```
    bucket = sess.default_bucket()
    prefix = 'sagemaker/DEMO-automl-dm'
    s3_input_data = upload_data(path="./bank-additional/bank-
    additional-full.csv", key_prefix=prefix+'input')
    ```

4. We then configure the AutoML job, which only takes one line of code. We define the **target attribute** (remember, that column is named y), and where to store training artifacts. Optionally, we can also set a maximum run time for the job, a maximum run time per job, or reduce the number of candidate models that will be tuned. Please note that restricting the job's duration too much is likely to impact its accuracy. For development purposes, this isn't a problem, so let's cap our job at one hour, or 250 tuning jobs (whichever limit it hits first):

    ```
    from sagemaker.automl.automl import AutoML
    auto_ml_job = AutoML(
    ```

```
        role = sagemaker.get_execution_role(),
        sagemaker_session = sess,
        target_attribute_name = 'y',
        output_path =
        's3://{}/{}/output'.format(bucket,prefix),
        max_runtime_per_training_job_in_seconds = 600,
        max_candidates = 250,
        total_job_runtime_in_seconds = 3600
    )
```

5. Next, we launch the Autopilot job, passing it the location of the training set. We turn logs off (who wants to read hundreds of tuning logs?), and we set the call to non-blocking, as we'd like to query the job status in the next cells:

```
auto_ml_job.fit(inputs=s3_input_data, logs=False,
wait=False)
```

The job starts right away. Now let's see how we can monitor its status.

Monitoring a job

While the job is running, we can use the `describe_auto_ml_job()` API to monitor its progress:

1. For example, the following code will check the job's status every 30 seconds until the data analysis step completes:

```
from time import sleep
job = auto_ml_job.describe_auto_ml_job()
job_status = job['AutoMLJobStatus']
job_sec_status = job['AutoMLJobSecondaryStatus']
if job_status not in ('Stopped', 'Failed'):
    while job_status in ('InProgress') and job_sec_status
    in ('AnalyzingData'):
        sleep(30)
        job = auto_ml_job.describe_auto_ml_job()
        job_status = job['AutoMLJobStatus']
        job_sec_status = job['AutoMLJobSecondaryStatus']
        print (job_status, job_sec_status)
```

2. Once the data analysis is complete, the two auto-generated notebooks are available. We can find their location using the same API:

```
job = auto_ml_job.describe_auto_ml_job()
job_candidate_notebook = job['AutoMLJobArtifacts']
['CandidateDefinitionNotebookLocation']
job_data_notebook = job['AutoMLJobArtifacts']
['DataExplorationNotebookLocation']
print(job_candidate_notebook)
print(job_data_notebook)
```

This prints out the S3 paths for the two notebooks:

```
s3://sagemaker-us-east-2-123456789012/sagemaker/
DEMO-automl-dm/output/automl-2020-04-24-14-21-16-938/
sagemaker-automl-candidates/pr-1-a99cb56acb5945d695
c0e74afe8ffe3ddaebafa94f394655ac973432d1/notebooks/
SageMakerAutopilotCandidateDefinitionNotebook.ipynb
```

```
s3://sagemaker-us-east-2-123456789012/sagemaker/
DEMO-automl-dm/output/automl-2020-04-24-14-21-16-938/
sagemaker-automl-candidates/pr-1-a99cb56acb5945d695
c0e74afe8ffe3ddaebafa94f394655ac973432d1/notebooks/
SageMakerAutopilotDataExplorationNotebook.ipynb
```

3. Using the AWS CLI, we can copy the two notebooks locally. We'll take a look at them later in this chapter:

```
%%sh -s $job_candidate_notebook $job_data_notebook
aws s3 cp $1 .
aws s3 cp $2 .
```

4. While the feature engineering runs, we can wait for completion using the same code snippet as the preceding, looping while job_sec_status is equal to FeatureEngineering.

5. Once the feature engineering is complete, the model tuning starts. While it's running, we can use the **Amazon SageMaker Experiments SDK** to keep track of jobs. We'll cover SageMaker Experiments in detail in a later chapter, but here, the code is simple enough to give you a sneak peek! All it takes is to pass the experiment name to the `ExperimentAnalytics` object. Then, we can retrieve information on all tuning jobs so far in a `pandas` DataFrame. From then on, it's business as usual, and we can easily display the number of jobs that have already run, and the top 5 jobs so far:

```
import pandas as pd
from sagemaker.analytics import ExperimentAnalytics
exp = ExperimentAnalytics(
    sagemaker_session=sess,
    experiment_name=job['AutoMLJobName'] +
                    '-aws-auto-ml-job'
)
df = exp.dataframe()
print("Number of jobs: ", len(df))
df = pd.concat([df['ObjectiveMetric - Max'],
df.drop(['ObjectiveMetric - Max'], axis=1)], axis=1)
df.sort_values('ObjectiveMetric - Max', ascending=0)[:5]
```

This `pandas` code outputs the following table:

Number of jobs:	109		
	ObjectiveMetric - Max	TrialComponentName	DisplayName
35	0.918594	tuning-job-1-57d7f377bfe54b40b1-050-b8c34b30-a...	tuning-job-1-57d7f377bfe54b40b1-050-b8c34b30-a...
43	0.917700	tuning-job-1-57d7f377bfe54b40b1-045-20ddd705-a...	tuning-job-1-57d7f377bfe54b40b1-045-20ddd705-a...
21	0.917316	tuning-job-1-57d7f377bfe54b40b1-065-2d7d46ad-a...	tuning-job-1-57d7f377bfe54b40b1-065-2d7d46ad-a...
17	0.916933	tuning-job-1-57d7f377bfe54b40b1-071-a0ce585e-a...	tuning-job-1-57d7f377bfe54b40b1-071-a0ce585e-a...
49	0.915911	tuning-job-1-57d7f377bfe54b40b1-039-024a3819-a...	tuning-job-1-57d7f377bfe54b40b1-039-024a3819-a...

Figure 3.21 – Viewing jobs

6. Once the model tuning is complete, we can very easily find the best candidate:

```
job_best_candidate = auto_ml_job.best_candidate()
print(job_best_candidate['CandidateName'])
print(job_best_candidate['FinalAutoMLJobObjectiveMetric'])
```

This prints out the name of the best tuning job, along with its validation accuracy:

```
tuning-job-1-57d7f377bfe54b40b1-030-c4f27053
{'MetricName': 'validation:accuracy', 'Value':
0.9197599935531616}
```

Then, we can deploy and test the model using the SageMaker SDK. We've covered a lot of ground already, so let's save that for future chapters, where we'll revisit this example.

Cleaning up

SageMaker Autopilot creates many underlying artifacts such as dataset splits, pre-processing scripts, pre-processed datasets, models, and so on. If you'd like to clean up completely, the following code snippet will do that. Of course, you could also use the AWS CLI:

```
import boto3
job_outputs_prefix = '{}/output/{}'.format(prefix,
job['AutoMLJobName'])
s3_bucket = boto3.resource('s3').Bucket(bucket)
s3_bucket.objects.filter(Prefix=job_outputs_prefix).delete()
```

Now that we know how to train models using both the SageMaker Studio GUI and the SageMaker SDK, let's take a look under the hood. Engineers like to understand how things really work, right?

Diving deep on SageMaker Autopilot

In this section, we're going to learn in detail how SageMaker Autopilot processes data and trains models. If this feels too advanced for now, you're welcome to skip this material. You can always revisit it later once you've gained more experience with the service.

First, let's look at the artifacts that SageMaker Autopilot produces.

The job artifacts

Listing our S3 bucket confirms the existence of many different artifacts:

```
$ aws s3 ls s3://sagemaker-us-east-2-123456789012/sagemaker/
DEMO-autopilot/output/my-first-autopilot-job/
```

We can see many new prefixes. Let's figure out what's what:

```
PRE data-processor-models/
PRE preprocessed-data/
PRE sagemaker-automl-candidates/
PRE transformed-data/
PRE tuning/
```

The `preprocessed-data/tuning_data` prefix contains the training and validation splits generated from the input dataset. Each split is further broken into small CSV chunks:

- The `sagemaker-automl-candidates` prefix contains ten data preprocessing scripts (`dpp[0-9].py`), one for each pipeline. It also contains the code to train them (`trainer.py`) on the input dataset, and the code to process the input dataset with each one of the ten resulting models (`sagemaker_serve.py`).

- The `data-processor-models` prefix contains the ten data processing models trained by the `dpp` scripts.

- The `transformed-data` prefix contains the ten processed versions of the training and validation splits.

- The `sagemaker-automl-candidates` prefix contains the two auto-generated notebooks.

- Finally, the `tuning` prefix contains the actual models trained during the **Model Tuning** step.

The following diagram summarizes the relationship between these artifacts:

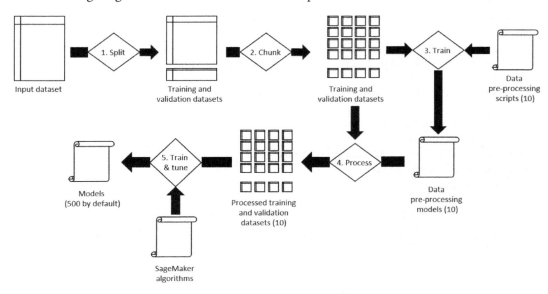

Figure 3.22 – Summing up the Autopilot process

In the next sections, we'll take a look at the two **auto-generated notebooks**, which are one of the most important features in SageMaker Autopilot.

The Data Exploration notebook

This notebook is available in Amazon S3 once the data analysis step is complete.

The first section, seen in the following screenshot, simply displays a sample of the dataset:

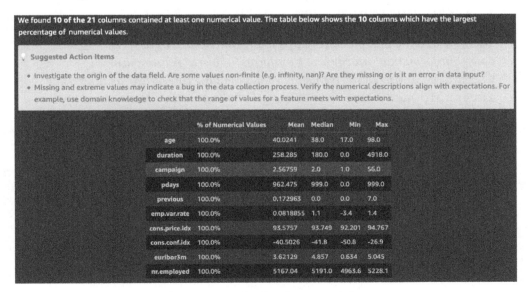

Dataset Sample

The following table is a random sample of **10** rows from the training dataset. For ease of presentation, we are only showing **20 of the 21** columns of the dataset.

Suggested Action Items

- Verify the input headers correctly align with the columns of the dataset sample. If they are incorrect, update the header names of your input dataset in Amazon Simple Storage Service (Amazon S3).

	age	job	marital	education	default	housing	loan	contact	month	day_of_week	...	campaign	pdays	previous	poutcome
0	45	blue-collar	married	high.school	no	no	no	telephone	jun	wed	...	4	999	0	nonexistent
1	46	management	married	university.degree	no	yes	no	telephone	may	fri	...	5	999	0	nonexistent
2	39	admin.	married	university.degree	no	no	no	cellular	may	tue	...	7	999	0	nonexistent
3	25	student	single	high.school	no	yes	no	cellular	apr	wed	...	1	999	0	nonexistent
4	38	services	divorced	high.school	no	no	no	cellular	jul	thu	...	1	999	0	nonexistent
5	33	technician	married	university.degree	no	yes	no	telephone	may	thu	...	3	999	1	failure
6	47	management	married	high.school	no	no	yes	cellular	apr	fri	...	1	999	1	failure
7	48	technician	married	high.school	unknown	yes	no	telephone	may	fri	...	3	999	0	nonexistent
8	33	services	married	university.degree	no	unknown	unknown	telephone	may	thu	...	1	999	0	nonexistent
9	28	blue-collar	single	basic.9y	no	no	no	telephone	jun	tue	...	1	999	0	nonexistent

Figure 3.23 – Viewing dataset statistics

Shown in the following screenshot, the second section focuses on column analysis: percentages of missing values, counts of unique values, and descriptive statistics. For instance, it appears that the pdays field has both a maximum value and a median of 999, which looks suspicious. As explained in the previous chapter, 999 is indeed a placeholder value meaning that a customer has never been contacted before:

We found **10 of the 21** columns contained at least one numerical value. The table below shows the **10** columns which have the largest percentage of numerical values.

Suggested Action Items

- Investigate the origin of the data field. Are some values non-finite (e.g. infinity, nan)? Are they missing or is it an error in data input?
- Missing and extreme values may indicate a bug in the data collection process. Verify the numerical descriptions align with expectations. For example, use domain knowledge to check that the range of values for a feature meets with expectations.

	% of Numerical Values	Mean	Median	Min	Max
age	100.0%	40.0241	38.0	17.0	98.0
duration	100.0%	258.285	180.0	0.0	4918.0
campaign	100.0%	2.56759	2.0	1.0	56.0
pdays	100.0%	962.475	999.0	0.0	999.0
previous	100.0%	0.172963	0.0	0.0	7.0
emp.var.rate	100.0%	0.0818855	1.1	-3.4	1.4
cons.price.idx	100.0%	93.5757	93.749	92.201	94.767
cons.conf.idx	100.0%	-40.5026	-41.8	-50.8	-26.9
euribor3m	100.0%	3.62129	4.857	0.634	5.045
nr.employed	100.0%	5167.04	5191.0	4963.6	5228.1

Figure 3.24 – Viewing dataset statistics

As you can see, this notebook saves us the trouble of computing these statistics ourselves, and we can use them to quickly check that the dataset is what we expect.

Now, let's look at the second notebook. As you will see, it's extremely insightful!

The Candidate Generation notebook

This notebook contains the definition of the ten candidate pipelines, and how they're trained. This is a **runnable notebook**, and advanced practitioners can use it to replay the AutoML process, and keep refining their experiment. Please note that this is totally optional! It's perfectly OK to deploy the top model directly and start testing it.

Having said that, let's run one of the pipelines manually:

1. We open the notebook and save a read-write copy by clicking on the **Import notebook** link in the top-right corner.

2. Then, we run the cells in the **SageMaker Setup** section to import all required artifacts and parameters.

3. Moving to the **Candidate Pipelines** section, we create a runner object that will launch jobs for selected candidate pipelines:

```
from sagemaker_automl import AutoMLInteractiveRunner,
AutoMLLocalCandidate
```
```
automl_interactive_runner =
AutoMLInteractiveRunner(AUTOML_LOCAL_RUN_CONFIG)
```

4. Then, we add the first pipeline (dpp0). The notebook tells us: "*This data transformation strategy first transforms 'numeric' features using* RobustImputer *(converts missing values to nan), 'categorical' features using* ThresholdOneHotEncoder. *It merges all the generated features and applies* RobustStandardScaler. *The transformed data will be used to tune a xgboost model.*" We just need to run the following cell to add it:

```
automl_interactive_runner.select_candidate(
    {"data_transformer": {
        "name": "dpp0",
        ...
    }
)
```

If you're curious about the implementation of `RobustImputer` or `ThresholdOneHotEncoder`, hyperlinks take you to the appropriate source file in the `sagemaker_sklearn_extension` module (`https://github.com/aws/sagemaker-scikit-learn-extension/`).

This way, you can understand exactly how data has been processed. As these objects are based on scikit-learn objects, they should quickly look very familiar. For instance, we can see that `RobustImputer` is built on top of `sklearn.impute.SimpleImputer`, with added functionality. Likewise, `ThresholdOneHotEncoder` is an extension of `sklearn.preprocessing.OneHotEncoder`.

5. Taking a quick look at other pipelines, we see different processing strategies and algorithms. You should see the **Linear Learner** algorithm used in some pipelines: it's one of the **built-in algorithms** in SageMaker, and we'll cover it in the next chapter.

6. Scrolling down, we get to the **Selected Candidates** section, where we can indeed confirm that we have only selected the first pipeline:

```
automl_interactive_runner.display_candidates()
```

This is visible in the result here:

Candidate Name	Algorithm	Feature Transformer
dpp0-xgboost	xgboost	dpp0.py

This also tells us that data will be processed by the `dpp0.py` script, and that the model will be trained using the XGBoost algorithm.

7. Clicking on the **dpp0** hyperlink opens the script. As expected, we see that it builds a scikit-learn transformer pipeline (not to be confused with the SageMaker pipeline composed of preprocessing and training jobs). Missing values are imputed in the numerical features, and the categorical features are one-hot encoded. Then, all features are scaled and the labels are encoded:

```
numeric_processors = Pipeline(
    steps=[('robustimputer',
           RobustImputer(strategy='constant',
                         fill_values=nan))]
)
categorical_processors = Pipeline(
    steps=[('thresholdonehotencoder',
```

```
                ThresholdOneHotEncoder(threshold=301))]
    )
column_transformer = ColumnTransformer(
    transformers=[
        ('numeric_processing', numeric_processors, numeric),
        ('categorical_processing', categorical_processors,
         categorical)]
    )
```

```
return Pipeline(steps=[
    ('column_transformer', column_transformer),
    ('robuststandardscaler', RobustStandardScaler())]
    )
```

8. Back in the notebook, we launch this script in the **Run Data Transformation Steps** section:

```
automl_interactive_runner.fit_data_transformers(parallel_
jobs=7)
```

9. This creates two sequential SageMaker jobs, and their artifacts are stored in a new prefix created for the notebook run:

```
$ aws s3 ls s3://sagemaker-us-east-2-123456789012/
sagemaker/DEMO-autopilot/output/my-first-autopilot-job/
my-first-a-notebook-run-24-13-17-22/
```

The first job trains the dpp0 transformers on the input dataset.

The second job processes the input dataset with the resulting model. For the record, this job uses the SageMaker **Batch Transform** feature, which will be covered in a later chapter.

Going back to SageMaker Studio, let's find out more about these two jobs. Starting from the **Experiments** tab on the left (the flask icon, remember?), we select **Unassigned trial components**, and we see our two jobs there: my-first-a-notebook-run-24-13-17-22-dpp0-train-24-13-38-38-aws-training-job and my-first-a-notebook-run-24-13-17-22-dpp0-transform-24-13-38-38-aws-transform-job.

10. Double-clicking a job name opens the **Describe Trial Component** window, as shown in the following screenshot. It tells us everything there is to know about the job: the parameters, location of artifacts, and more:

Figure 3.25 – Describing a trial

Once data processing is complete, the notebook proceeds with **automatic model tuning** and **model deployment**. We haven't yet discussed these topics, so let's stop there for now. I encourage you to go through the rest of the notebook once you're comfortable with them.

Summary

As you can see, Amazon SageMaker Autopilot makes it easy to build, train, and optimize machine learning models for beginners and advanced users alike.

In this chapter, you learned about the different steps of an Autopilot job, and what they mean from a machine learning perspective. You also learned how to use both the SageMaker Studio GUI and the SageMaker SDK to build a classification model with minimal coding. Then, we dived deep on the auto-generated notebooks, which give you full control and transparency over the modeling processing. In particular, you learned how to run the Candidate Generation notebook manually, in order to replay all steps involved.

In the next chapter, you will learn how to use the built-in algorithms in Amazon SageMaker to train models for a variety of machine learning problems.

4

Training Machine Learning Models

In the previous chapter, you learned how Amazon SageMaker Autopilot makes it easy to build, train, and optimize models automatically, without writing a line of machine learning code.

For problem types that are not supported by SageMaker Autopilot, the next best option is to use one of the algorithms already implemented in SageMaker, and to train it on your dataset. These algorithms are referred to as **built-in algorithms**, and they cover many typical machine learning problems, from classification to time series to anomaly detection.

In this chapter, you will learn about built-in algorithms for supervised and unsupervised learning, what type of problems you can solve with them, and how to use them with the SageMaker SDK:

- Discovering the built-in algorithms in Amazon SageMaker
- Training and deploying models with built-in algorithms
- Using the SageMaker SDK with built-in algorithms
- Working with more built-in algorithms

Technical requirements

You will need an AWS account to run the examples included in this chapter. If you don't already have one, please point your browser to https://aws.amazon.com/getting-started/ to create it. You should also familiarize yourself with the AWS Free Tier (https://aws.amazon.com/free/), which lets you use many AWS services for free within certain usage limits.

You will need to install and to configure the AWS command-line interface for your account (https://aws.amazon.com/cli/).

You will need a working Python 3.x environment. Be careful not to use Python 2.7, as it is no longer maintained. Installing the Anaconda distribution (https://www.anaconda.com/) is not mandatory, but strongly encouraged as it includes many projects that we will need (Jupyter, pandas, numpy, and more).

Code examples included in the book are available on GitHub at https://github.com/PacktPublishing/Learn-Amazon-SageMaker. You will need to install a Git client to access them (https://git-scm.com/).

Discovering the built-in algorithms in Amazon SageMaker

Built-in algorithms are machine learning algorithms implemented, and in some cases invented, by Amazon (https://docs.aws.amazon.com/sagemaker/latest/dg/algos.html). They let you quickly train and deploy your own models without writing a line of machine learning code. Indeed, since the training and prediction algorithm is readily available, you don't have to worry about implementing it, and you can focus on the machine learning problem at hand. As usual, with SageMaker, infrastructure is fully managed, saving you even more time.

In this section, you'll learn about the built-in algorithms for traditional machine learning problems. Algorithms for computer vision and natural language processing will be covered in the next two chapters.

Supervised learning

Supervised learning focuses on problems that require a labeled dataset, such as regression, or classification:

- **Linear Learner** builds linear models to solve regression problems, as well as classification problems (binary or multi-class).

- **Factorization Machines** builds linear models to solve regression problems, as well as classification problems (binary or multi-class). Factorization machines are a generalization of linear models, and they're a good fit for high dimension sparse datasets, such as user-item interaction matrices in recommendation problems.

- **K-nearest neighbors (KNN)** builds non-parametric models for regression and classification problems.

- **XGBoost** builds models for regression, classification, and ranking problems. XGBoost is possibly the most widely used machine algorithm used today, and SageMaker uses the open source implementation available at `https://github.com/dmlc/xgboost`.

- **DeepAR** builds forecasting models for multivariate time series. DeepAR is an Amazon-invented algorithm based on **Recurrent Neural Networks,** and you can read more about it at `https://arxiv.org/abs/1704.04110`.

- **Object2Vec** learns low-dimension embeddings from general-purpose high dimensional objects. Object2Vec is an Amazon-invented algorithm.

Unsupervised learning

Unsupervised learning doesn't require a labeled dataset, and includes problems such as clustering or anomaly detection:

- **K-means** builds clustering models. SageMaker uses a modified version of the web-scale k-means clustering algorithm (`https://www.eecs.tufts.edu/~dsculley/papers/fastkmeans.pdf`).

- **Principal Component Analysis (PCA)** builds dimensionality reduction models.

- **Random Cut Forest** builds anomaly detection models.

- **IP Insights** builds models to identify usage patterns for IPv4 addresses. This comes in handy for monitoring, cybersecurity, and so on.

We'll cover some of these algorithms in detail in the rest of this chapter.

A word about scalability

Before we dive into training and deploying models with the algorithms, you may wonder why you should use them instead of their counterparts in well-known libraries such as `scikit-learn` and `R`.

First, these algorithms have been implemented and tuned by Amazon teams, who are not exactly newcomers to machine learning! A lot of effort has been put into making sure that these algorithms run as fast as possible on AWS infrastructure, no matter what type of instance you use. In addition, many of these algorithms support **distributed training** out of the box, letting you split model training across a cluster of fully managed instances.

Thanks to this, benchmarks indicate that these algorithms are generally 10x better than competing implementations. In many cases, they are also much more cost effective. You can learn more about this at the following links:

- AWS Tel Aviv Summit 2018: "*Speed Up Your Machine Learning Workflows with Built-In Algorithms*": `https://www.youtube.com/watch?v=IeIUr78OrE0`
- "*Elastic Machine Learning Algorithms in Amazon*", Liberty et al., SIGMOD'20: SageMaker: `https://dl.acm.org/doi/abs/10.1145/3318464.3386126`

Of course, these algorithms benefit from all the features present in SageMaker, as you will find out by the end of the book.

Training and deploying models with built-in algorithms

Amazon SageMaker lets you train and deploy models in many different configurations. Although it encourages best practices, it is a modular service that lets you do things your own way.

In this section, we first look at a typical end-to-end workflow, where we use SageMaker from data upload all the way to model deployment. Then, we discuss alternative workflows, and how you can cherry pick the features that you need. Finally, we will take a look under the hood, and see what happens from an infrastructure perspective when we train and deploy.

Understanding the end-to-end workflow

Let's look at a typical SageMaker workflow. You'll see it again and again in our examples, as well as in the AWS notebooks available on GitHub (`https://github.com/awslabs/amazon-sagemaker-examples/`):

1. **Make your dataset available in Amazon S3**: In most examples, we'll download a dataset from the internet, or load a local copy. However, in real life, your raw dataset would probably already be in S3, and you would prepare it using one of the services discussed in *Chapter 2, Handling Data Preparation Tasks*: splitting it for training and validation, engineering features, and so on. In any case, the dataset must be in a format that the algorithm understands, such as CSV and `protobuf`.

2. **Configure the training job**: This is where you select the algorithm that you want to train with, set hyperparameters, and define infrastructure requirements for the training job.

3. **Launch the training job**: This is where we pass it the location of your dataset in S3. Training takes place on managed infrastructure, created and provisioned automatically according to your requirements. Once training is complete, the **model artifact** is saved in S3. Training infrastructure is terminated automatically, and you only pay for what you actually used.

4. **Deploy the model**: You can deploy a model either on a **real-time HTTPS endpoint** for live prediction, or for **batch transform**. Again, you simply need to define infrastructure requirements.

5. **Predict data**: Either invoking a real-time endpoint or a batch transformer. As you would expect, infrastructure is managed here too. For production, you would also monitor the quality of data and predictions.

6. **Clean up!**: This involves taking the endpoint down, to avoid unnecessary charges.

Understanding this workflow is critical in being productive with Amazon SageMaker. Fortunately, the SageMaker SDK has simple APIs that closely match these steps, so you shouldn't be confused about which one to use, and when to use it.

Before we start looking at the SDK, let's consider alternative workflows that could make sense in your business and technical environments.

Using alternative workflows

Amazon SageMaker is a modular service that lets you work your way. Let's first consider a workflow where you would train on SageMaker and deploy on your own server, whatever the reasons may be.

Exporting a model

Steps 1-3 would be the same as in the previous example, and then you would do the following:

1. Download the training artifact from S3, which is materialized as a `model.tar.gz` file.

2. Extract the model stored in the artifact.

3. On your own server, load the model with the appropriate machine learning library:

    a) **For XGBoost models**: Use one of the implementations available at `https://xgboost.ai/`.

    b) **For BlazingText models**: Use the `fastText` implementation available at `https://fasttext.cc/`.

    c) **For all other models**: Use **Apache MXNet** (`https://mxnet.apache.org/`).

Importing a model

Now, let's see how you could import an existing model and deploy it on SageMaker:

1. Package your model in a model artifact (`model.tar.gz`).

2. Upload the artifact to an S3 bucket.

3. Register the artifact as a SageMaker model.

4. Deploy the model and predict, just like in the previous *steps 4* and *5*.

This is just a quick look. We'll run full examples for both workflows in *Chapter 11, Managing Models in Production*.

Using fully managed infrastructure

All SageMaker jobs run on managed infrastructure. Let's take a look under the hood, and see what happens when we train and deploy models.

Packaging algorithms in Docker containers

All SageMaker algorithms must be packaged in **Docker** containers. Don't worry, you don't need to know much about Docker in order to use SageMaker. If you're not familiar with it, I would recommend going through this tutorial to understand key concepts and tools: `https://docs.docker.com/get-started/`. It's always good to know a little more than actually required!

As you would expect, built-in algorithms are pre-packaged, and containers are readily available for training and deployment. They are hosted in **Amazon Elastic Container Registry (ECR)**, AWS' Docker registry service (`https://aws.amazon.com/ecr/`). As ECR is a region-based service, you will find a collection of containers in each region where SageMaker is available.

You can find the list of built-in algorithm containers at `https://docs.aws.amazon.com/sagemaker/latest/dg/sagemaker-algo-docker-registry-paths.html`. For instance, the name of the container for the Linear Learner algorithm in the eu-west-1 region is `438346466558.dkr.ecr.eu-west-1.amazonaws.com/linear-learner:latest`. These containers can only be pulled to SageMaker managed instances, so you won't be able to run them on your local machine.

Now let's look at the underlying infrastructure.

Creating the training infrastructure

When you launch a training job, SageMaker fires up infrastructure according to your requirements (instance type and instance count).

Once a training instance is in service, it pulls the appropriate training container from ECR. Hyperparameters are applied to the algorithm, which also receives the location of your dataset. By default, the algorithm then copies the full dataset from S3, and starts training. If distributed training is configured, SageMaker automatically distributes dataset batches to the different instances in the cluster.

Once training is complete, the model is packaged in a model artifact saved in S3. Then, the training infrastructure is shut down automatically. Logs are available in **Amazon CloudWatch Logs**. Last but not least, you're only charged for the exact amount of training time.

Creating the prediction infrastructure

When you launch a deployment job, SageMaker once again creates infrastructure according to your requirements.

Let's focus on real-time endpoints for now, and not on batch transform.

Once an endpoint instance is in service, it pulls the appropriate prediction container from ECR, and loads your model from S3. Then, the HTTPS endpoint is provisioned, and is ready for prediction within minutes.

If you configured the endpoint with several instances, load balancing and high availability are set up automatically. If you configured **Auto Scaling**, this is applied as well.

As you would expect, an endpoint stays up until it's deleted explicitly, either in the AWS Console or with a SageMaker API call. In the meantime, you will be charged for the endpoint, so **please make sure to delete endpoints that you don't need!**

Now that we understand the big picture, let's start looking at the SageMaker SDK, and how we can use it to train and deploy models.

Using the SageMaker SDK with built-in algorithms

Being familiar with the SageMaker SDK is important to making the most of SageMaker. You can find its documentation at `https://sagemaker.readthedocs.io`.

Walking through a simple example is the best way to get started. In this section, we'll use the Linear Learner algorithm to train a regression model on the Boston Housing dataset. We'll proceed very slowly, leaving no stone unturned. Once again, these concepts are essential, so please take your time, and make sure you understand every step fully.

> **Note:**
> Reminder: I recommend that you follow along and run the code available in the companion GitHub repository. Every effort has been made to check all code samples present in the text. However, for those of you who have an electronic version, copying and pasting may have unpredictable results: formatting issues, weird quotes, and so on.

Preparing data

Built-in algorithms expect the dataset to be in a certain format, such as **CSV**, **protobuf**, or **libsvm**. Supported formats are listed in the algorithm documentation. For instance, Linear Learner supports CSV and recordIO-wrapped protobuf (`https://docs.aws.amazon.com/sagemaker/latest/dg/linear-learner.html#ll-input_output`).

Our input dataset is already in the repository in CSV format, so let's use that. Dataset preparation will be extremely simple, and we'll run it manually:

1. Using `pandas`, we load the CSV dataset with pandas:

```
import pandas as pd
dataset = pd.read_csv('housing.csv')
```

2. Then, we print the shape of the dataset:

```
print(dataset.shape)
```

It contains 506 samples and 13 columns:

```
(506, 13)
```

3. Now, we display the first 5 lines of the dataset:

```
dataset[:5]
```

This prints out the table visible in the following diagram. For each house, we see 12 features, and a target attribute (medv) set to the median value of the house in thousands of dollars:

	crim	zn	indus	chas	nox	age	rm	dis	rad	tax	ptratio	lstat	medv
0	0.00632	18.0	2.31	0	0.538	6.575	65.2	4.0900	1	296.0	15.3	4.98	24.0
1	0.02731	0.0	7.07	0	0.469	6.421	78.9	4.9671	2	242.0	17.8	9.14	21.6
2	0.02729	0.0	7.07	0	0.469	7.185	61.1	4.9671	2	242.0	17.8	4.03	34.7
3	0.03237	0.0	2.18	0	0.458	6.998	45.8	6.0622	3	222.0	18.7	2.94	33.4
4	0.06905	0.0	2.18	0	0.458	7.147	54.2	6.0622	3	222.0	18.7	5.33	36.2

Figure 4.1 – Viewing the dataset

4. Reading the algorithm documentation (https://docs.aws.amazon.com/sagemaker/latest/dg/cdf-training.html), we see that *Amazon SageMaker requires that a CSV file doesn't have a header record and that the target variable is in the first column.* Accordingly, we move the medv column to the front of the dataframe:

```
dataset = pd.concat([dataset['medv'],
                     dataset.drop(['medv'], axis=1)],
                    axis=1)
```

5. A bit of scikit-learn magic helps split the dataframe up into two parts: 90% for training, and 10% for validation:

```
from sklearn.model_selection import train_test_split
training_dataset, validation_dataset = train_test_
split(dataset, test_size=0.1)
```

6. We save these two splits to individual CSV files, without either an index or a header:

```
training_dataset.to_csv('training_dataset.csv',
                        index=False, header=False)
```

```
validation_dataset.to_csv('validation_dataset.csv',
                          index=False, header=False)
```

7. We now need to upload these two files to S3. We could use any bucket, and here we'll use the default bucket conveniently created by SageMaker in the region we're running in. We can find its name with the `sagemaker.Session.default_bucket()` API:

```
import sagemaker
sess = sagemaker.Session()
bucket = sess.default_bucket()
```

8. Finally, we use the `sagemaker.Session.upload_data()` API to upload the two **CSV** files to the default bucket. Here, the training and validation datasets are made of a single file each, but we could upload multiple files if needed. For this reason, **we must upload the datasets under different S3 prefixes**, so that their files won't be mixed up:

```
prefix = 'boston-housing'
training_data_path = sess.upload_data(
    path='training_dataset.csv',
    key_prefix=prefix + '/input/training')
validation_data_path = sess.upload_data(
    path='validation_dataset.csv',
    key_prefix=prefix + '/input/validation')
print(training_data_path)
print(validation_data_path)
```

The two S3 paths look like this. Of course, the account number in the default bucket name will be different:

```
s3://sagemaker-eu-west-1-123456789012/boston-housing/
input/training/training_dataset.csv
```

```
s3://sagemaker-eu-west-1-123456789012/boston-housing/
input/validation/validation_dataset.csv
```

Now that data is ready in S3, we can configure the training job.

Configuring a training job

The `Estimator` object (`sagemaker.estimator.Estimator`) is the cornerstone of model training. It lets you select the appropriate algorithm, define your training infrastructure requirements, and more.

The SageMaker SDK also includes algorithm-specific estimators, such as `sagemaker.LinearLearner` or `sagemaker.PCA`. I generally find them less flexible than the generic estimator (no CSV support, for one thing), and I don't recommend using them. Using the `Estimator` object also lets you reuse your code across examples, as we will see in the next sections:

1. Earlier in this chapter, we learned that SageMaker algorithms are packaged in Docker containers. Using `boto3` and the `image_uris.retrieve()` API, we can easily find the name of the Linear Learner algorithm in the region we're running:

    ```
    import boto3
    from sagemaker import image_uris

    region = boto3.Session().region_name
    container = image_uris.retrieve('linear-learner', region)
    ```

2. Now that we know the name of the container, we can configure our training job with the `Estimator` object. In addition to the container name, we also pass the IAM role that SageMaker instances will use, the instance type and instance count to use for training, as well as the output location for the model. `Estimator` will generate a training job automatically, and we could also set our own prefix with the `base_job_name` parameter:

    ```
    from sagemaker.estimator import Estimator

    ll_estimator = Estimator(
        container,
        role=sagemaker.get_execution_role(),
        instance_count=1,
        instance_type='ml.m5.large',
        output_path='s3://{}/{}/output'.format(bucket,
                                               prefix))
    ```

SageMaker supports plenty of different instance types, with some differences across AWS regions. You can find the full list at `https://docs.aws.amazon.com/sagemaker/latest/dg/instance-types-az.html`.

Which one should we use here? Looking at the Linear Learner documentation (`https://docs.aws.amazon.com/sagemaker/latest/dg/linear-learner.html#ll-instances`), we see that *you can train the Linear Learner algorithm on single- or multi-machine CPU and GPU instances*. Here, we're working with a tiny dataset, so let's select the smallest training instance available in our region: `ml.m5.large`.

Checking the pricing page (`https://aws.amazon.com/sagemaker/pricing/`), we see that this instance costs $0.15 per hour in the eu-west-1 region (the one I'm using for this job).

3. Next, we have to set **hyperparameters**. This step is possibly one of the most obscure and most difficult parts of any machine learning project. Here's my tried and tested advice: read the algorithm documentation, stick to mandatory parameters only unless you really know what you're doing, and quickly check optional parameters for default values that could clash with your dataset. In *Chapter 10, Advanced Training Techniques*, we'll see how to solve hyperparameter selection with **Automatic Model Tuning**.

    Let's look at the documentation, and see which hyperparameters are mandatory (`https://docs.aws.amazon.com/sagemaker/latest/dg/ll_hyperparameters.html`). As it turns out, there is only one: `predictor_type`. It defines the type of problem that Linear Learner is training on (regression, binary classification, or multiclass classification).

    Taking a deeper look, we see that the default value for `mini_batch_size` is 1000: this isn't going to work well with our 506-sample dataset, so let's set it to 32. We also learn that the `normalize_data` parameter is set to true by default, which makes it unnecessary to normalize data ourselves:

    ```
    ll_estimator.set_hyperparameters(
        predictor_type='regressor',
        mini_batch_size=32)
    ```

4. Now, let's define the data channels: a channel is a named source of data passed to a SageMaker estimator. All built-in algorithms need at least a train channel, and many also accept additional channels for validation and testing. Here, we have two channels, which both provide data in CSV format. The `TrainingInput()` API lets us define their location, their format, whether they are compressed, and so on:

    ```
    training_data_channel = sagemaker.TrainingInput(
        s3_data=training_data_path,
        content_type='text/csv')
    ```

```
validation_data_channel = sagemaker.TrainingInput(
    s3_data=validation_data_path,
    content_type='text/csv')
```

By default, data served by a channel will be fully copied to each training instance, which is fine for small datasets. We'll study alternatives in *Chapter 10, Advanced Training Techniques*.

5. Everything is now ready for training, so let's launch our job.

Launching a training job

All it takes is one line of code:

1. We simply pass a Python dictionary containing the two channels to the fit() API:

```
l1_estimator.fit({'train': training_data_channel,
                  'validation': validation_data_channel})
```

Immediately, the training job starts:

```
Starting - Starting the training job.
```

2. As soon as the job is launched, it appears in the SageMaker console in the **Training jobs** section, and in the **Experiments** tab of SageMaker Studio. There, you can see all job metadata: the location of the dataset, hyperparameters, and more.

3. The training log is visible in the notebook, and it's also stored in Amazon CloudWatch Logs, under the /aws/sagemaker/TrainingJobs prefix.

    Here are the first few lines, showing the infrastructure being provisioned, as explained earlier in the *Using fully managed infrastructure* section:

```
Starting - Starting the training job...
Starting - Launching requested ML instances......
Starting - Preparing the instances for training...
Downloading - Downloading input data...
Training - Training image download completed.
```

4. At the end of the training log, we see information on the **mean square error** (MSE) and loss metrics:

```
#quality_metric: host=algo-1, validation mse
<loss>=13.7226685169
#quality_metric: host=algo-1, validation absolute_loss
<loss>=2.86944983987
```

5. Once training is complete, the model is copied automatically to S3, and SageMaker tells us how long the job took:

```
Uploading - Uploading generated training model
Completed - Training job completed
Training seconds: 49
Billable seconds: 49
```

We mentioned earlier than the cost for an `ml.m5.large` instance is $0.15 per hour. As we trained for 49 seconds, this job cost us (49/3600)*0.15= $0.002, one fifth of a penny. Any time spent setting up infrastructure ourselves would have certainly cost more!

6. Looking at the output location in our S3 bucket, we see the model artifact:

```
%%bash -s "$ll_estimator.output_path"
aws s3 ls --recursive $1
```

You should see the model artifact: `model.tar.gz`

We'll see in *Chapter 11, Deploying Machine Learning Models*, what's inside that artifact, and how to deploy the model outside of SageMaker. For now, let's deploy it to a real-time endpoint.

Deploying a model

This is my favorite part in SageMaker; we only need one line of code to deploy a model to an **HTTPS endpoint**:

1. It's good practice to create identifiable and unique endpoint names. We could also let SageMaker create one for us during deployment:

```
from time import strftime, gmtime
timestamp = strftime('%d-%H-%M-%S', gmtime())
endpoint_name = 'linear-learner-demo-'+timestamp
print(endpoint_name)
```

Here, the endpoint name is `linear-learner-demo-29-08-37-25`.

2. We deploy the model using the `deploy()` API. As this is a test endpoint, we use the smallest endpoint instance available, `ml.t2.medium`. In the eu-west-1 region, this will only cost us $0.07 per hour:

```
ll_predictor = ll_estimator.deploy(
    endpoint_name=endpoint_name,
    initial_instance_count=1,
    instance_type='ml.t2.medium')
```

While the endpoint is created, we can see it in the **Endpoints** section of the SageMaker console, and in the **Endpoints** tab of SageMaker Studio.

3. A few minutes later, the endpoint is in service. We can use the `predict()` API to send it a CSV sample for prediction. We set content type and serialization accordingly: built-in functions are available, and we use them as is:

```
ll_predictor.content_type = 'text/csv'
ll_predictor.serializer =
    sagemaker.serializers.CSVSerializer()
ll_predictor.deserializer =
    sagemaker.deserializers.CSVDeserializer()
test_sample = '0.00632,18.00,2.310,0,0.5380,6.5750,65.20,
4.0900,1,296.0,15.30,4.98'
response = ll_predictor.predict(test_sample)
print(response)
```

The prediction output tells us that this house should cost $30,173:

```
[['{"predictions": [{"score": 30.17342185974121}]}']]
```

We can also predict multiple samples at a time:

```
test_samples = [
'0.00632,18.00,2.310,0,0.5380,6.5750,65.20,4.0900,1,296.0
,15.30,4.98',
'0.02731,0.00,7.070,0,0.4690,6.4210,78.90,4.9671,2,242.0,
17.80,9.14']
response = ll_predictor.predict(test_samples)
print(response)
```

Now the prediction output is as follows:

```
[['{"predictions": [{"score": 30.413358688354492}',
'{"score": 24.884408950805664}]}']]
```

When we're done working with the endpoint, **we shouldn't forget to delete it to avoid unnecessary charges**.

Cleaning up

Deleting an endpoint is as simple as calling the `delete_endpoint()` API:

```
ll_predictor.delete_endpoint()
```

At the risk of repeating myself, the topics covered in this section are extremely important, so please make sure you're completely familiar with them, as we'll constantly use them in the rest of the book. Please spend some time reading the service and SDK documentation as well:

- `https://docs.aws.amazon.com/sagemaker/latest/dg/algos.html`
- `https://sagemaker.readthedocs.io`

Now let's explore other built-in algorithms. You'll see that the workflow and the code are very similar!

Working with more built-in algorithms

In the rest of this chapter, we will run more examples with built-in algorithms, both in supervised and unsupervised mode. This will help you become very familiar with the SageMaker SDK, and learn how to solve actual machine learning problems. The following list shows some of these algorithms:

- Classification with XGBoost
- Recommendation with Factorization Machines
- Dimensionality reduction with PCA
- Anomaly detection with Random Cut Forest

Classification with XGBoost

Let's train a model on the Boston Housing dataset with the **XGBoost** algorithm (`https://github.com/dmlc/xgboost`). As we will see in *Chapter 7, Using Built-in Frameworks*, SageMaker also supports XGBoost scripts:

1. We reuse the dataset preparation steps from the previous examples.

2. We find the name of the XGBoost container. As several versions are supported, we select the latest one (1.0-1 at the time of writing):

```
import boto3
from sagemaker import image_uris
```

```
region = boto3.Session().region_name
container = image_uris.retrieve('xgboost', region,
                                version='latest')
```

3. We configure the `Estimator` function. The code is strictly identical to the one used with `LinearLearner`:

```
xgb_estimator = Estimator(
    container,
    role=sagemaker.get_execution_role(),
    instance_count=1,
    instance_type='ml.m5.large',
    output_path='s3://{}/{}/output'.format(bucket,
                                           prefix))
```

4. Taking a look at the hyperparameters (`https://docs.aws.amazon.com/sagemaker/latest/dg/xgboost_hyperparameters.html`), we see that the only required one is `num_round`. As it's not obvious which value to set, we'll go for a large value, and we'll also define the `early_stopping_rounds` parameter in order to avoid overfitting. Of course, we need to set the objective for a regression problem:

```
xgb_estimator.set_hyperparameters(
    objective='reg:linear',
    num_round=200,
    early_stopping_rounds=10)
```

5. We define the training input, just like in the previous example:

```
training_data_channel = sagemaker.TrainingInput(
    s3_data=training_data_path,
    content_type='text/csv')
validation_data_channel = sagemaker.TrainingInput(
    s3_data=validation_data_path,
    content_type='text/csv')
```

6. We then launch the training job:

```
xgb_estimator.fit({'train': training_data_channel,
                   'validation': validation_data_channel})
```

7. The job only ran for 22 rounds, meaning that **early stopping** was triggered. Looking at the training log, we see that round #12 was actually the best one, with a **root mean square error** (RMSE) of 2.43126:

```
[12]#011train-rmse:1.25702#011validation-rmse:2.43126
<output removed>
[22]#011train-rmse:0.722193#011validation-rmse:2.43355
```

8. Deploying still takes one line of code:

```
from time import strftime, gmtime

timestamp = strftime('%d-%H-%M-%S', gmtime())
endpoint_name = 'xgb-demo'+'-'+timestamp

xgb_predictor = xgb_estimator.deploy(
    endpoint_name=endpoint_name,
    initial_instance_count=1,
    instance_type='ml.t2.medium')
```

9. Once the model is deployed, we used the `predict()` API again to send it a CSV sample:

```
test_sample = '0.00632,18.00,2.310,0,0.5380,6.5750,65.20,
4.0900,1,296.0,15.30,4.98'

xgb_predictor.content_type = 'text/csv'
xgb_predictor.serializer =
    sagemaker.serializers.CSVSerializer()
xgb_predictor.deserializer =
    sagemaker.deserializers.CSVDeserializer()

response = xgb_predictor.predict(test_sample)

print(response)
```

The result tells us that this house should cost $23,754.

```
[['23.73023223876953']]
```

10. Finally, we delete the endpoint when we're done:

```
xgb_predictor.delete_endpoint()
```

As you can see, the SageMaker workflow is pretty simple, and makes it easy to experiment quickly with different algorithms without having to rewrite all your code.

Let's move on to the Factorization Machines algorithm. In the process, we will learn about the highly efficient recordIO-wrapped protobuf format.

Recommendation with Factorization Machines

Factorization Machines is a generalization of linear models (`https://www.csie.ntu.edu.tw/~b97053/paper/Rendle2010FM.pdf`). They're well-suited for high dimension sparse datasets, such as user-item interaction matrices for recommendation.

In this example, we're going to train a recommendation model based on the **MovieLens** dataset (`https://grouplens.org/datasets/movielens/`).

The dataset exists in several versions. To minimize training times, we'll use the 100k version. It contains 100,000 ratings (integer values from 1 to 5) assigned by 943 users to 1,682 movies. The dataset is already split for training and validation.

As you know by now, training and deploying with SageMaker is very simple. Most of the code will be identical to the two previous examples, which is great! This lets us focus on understanding and preparing data.

Understanding sparse datasets

Imagine building a matrix to store this dataset. It would have 943 lines (one per user) and 1,682 columns (one per movie). Cells would store the ratings. The following diagram shows a basic example:

	Movie 1	Movie 2	Movie 3	Movie 4	Movie 5	Movie 6
User 1		2		4	5	
User 2	3	1	4			4
User 3		2	3			
User 4		2			5	

Figure 4.2 – Sparse matrix

Hence, the matrix would have 943*1,682=1,586,126 cells. However, as only 100,000 ratings are present, 93.69% of cells would be empty. Storing our dataset this way would be extremely inefficient. It would needlessly consume RAM, storage, and network bandwidth to store and transfer lots of zero values!

In fact, things are much worse, as the algorithm expects the input dataset to look like in the following diagram:

User 1	User 2	User 3	User 4	Movie 1	Movie 2	Movie 3	Movie 4	Movie 5	Movie 6	Ratings
1					1					2
1							1			4
1								1		5
	1			1						3
	1				1					1
	1					1				4
	1								1	4
		1			1					2
		1				1				3
			1		1					2
			1					1		5

Figure 4.3 – Sparse matrix

Why do we need to store data this way? The answer is simple: Factorization Machines is a **supervised learning** algorithm, so we need to train it on labeled samples.

Looking at the preceding diagram, we see that each line represents a movie review. The matrix on the left stores its one-hot encoded features (users and movies), and the vector on the right stores its label. For instance, the last line tells us that user 4 has given movie 5 a "5" rating.

The size of this matrix is 100,000 lines by 2,625 columns (943 movies plus 1,682 movies). The total number of cells is 262,500,000, which are only 0.076% full (200,000 / 262,500,000). If we used a 32-bit value for each cell, we would need almost a gigabyte of memory to store this matrix. This is horribly inefficient, but still manageable.

Just for fun, let's do the same exercise for the largest version of MovieLens, which has 25 million ratings, 62,000 movies and 162,000 users. The matrix would have 25 million lines and 224,000 columns, for a total of 5,600,000,000,000 cells. Yes, that's 5.6 trillion cells, and although they would be 99.999% empty, we would still need over 20 terabytes of RAM to store them. Ouch. If that's not bad enough, consider recommendation models with millions of users and products: the numbers are mind-boggling!

Instead of using a plain matrix, we'll use a **sparse matrix**, a data structure specifically designed and optimized for sparse datasets. Scipy has exactly the object we need, named lil_matrix (https://docs.scipy.org/doc/scipy/reference/generated/scipy.sparse.lil_matrix.html). This will help us to get rid of all these nasty zeros.

Understanding protobuf and RecordIO

So how will we pass this sparse matrix to the SageMaker algorithm? As you would expect, we're going to serialize the object, and store it in S3. We're not going to use Python serialization, however. Instead, we're going to use protobuf (https://developers. google.com/protocol-buffers/), a popular and efficient serialization mechanism.

In addition, we're going to store the protobuf-encoded data in a record format called **RecordIO** (https://mxnet.apache.org/api/faq/recordio/). Our dataset will be stored as a sequence of records in a single file. This has the following benefits:

- A single file is easier to move around: who wants to deal with thousands of individual files that can get lost or corrupted?

- A sequential file is faster to read, which makes the training process more efficient.

- A sequence of records is easy to split for distributed training.

Don't worry if you're not familiar with protobuf and RecordIO. The SageMaker SDK includes utility functions that hide their complexity.

Building a Factorization Machines model on MovieLens

We will begin building the model using the following steps:

1. In a Jupyter notebook, we first download and extract the MovieLens dataset:

```
%%sh
wget http://files.grouplens.org/datasets/movielens/
ml-100k.zip
unzip ml-100k.zip
```

2. As the dataset is ordered by user ID, we shuffle it as a precaution. Then, we take a look at the first few lines:

```
%cd ml-100k
!shuf ua.base -o ua.base.shuffled
!head -5 ua.base.shuffled
```

We see four columns: the user ID, the movie ID, the rating, and a timestamp (which we'll ignore in our model):

```
378   43    3     880056609
919   558   5     875372988
90    285   5     891383687
249   245   2     879571999
416   64    5     893212929
```

3. We define sizing constants:

```
num_users = 943
num_movies = 1682
num_features = num_users+num_movies
num_ratings_train = 90570
num_ratings_test = 9430
```

4. Now, let's write a function to load a dataset into a sparse matrix. Based on the previous explanation, we go through the dataset line by line. In the X matrix, we set the appropriate user and movie columns to 1. We also store the rating in the Y vector:

```
import csv
import numpy as np
from scipy.sparse import lil_matrix
def loadDataset(filename, lines, columns):
    X = lil_matrix((lines, columns)).astype('float32')
    Y = []
    line=0
    with open(filename,'r') as f:
        samples=csv.reader(f,delimiter='\t')
        for userId,movieId,rating,timestamp in samples:
            X[line,int(userId)-1] = 1
            X[line,int(num_users)+int(movieId)-1] = 1
            Y.append(int(rating))
            line=line+1
    Y=np.array(Y).astype('float32')
    return X,Y
```

5. We then process the training and test datasets:

```
X_train, Y_train = loadDataset('ua.base.shuffled',
                               num_ratings_train,
                               num_features)
X_test, Y_test = loadDataset('ua.test',
                             num_ratings_test,
                             num_features)
```

6. We check that the shapes are what we expect:

```
print(X_train.shape)
print(Y_train.shape)
print(X_test.shape)
print(Y_test.shape)
```

This displays the dataset shapes:

```
(90570, 2625)
(90570,)
(9430, 2625)
(9430,)
```

7. Now, let's write a function that converts a dataset to the RecordIO-wrapped `protobuf`, and uploads it to an S3 bucket. We first create an in-memory binary stream with `io.BytesIO()`. Then, we use the life-saving `write_spmatrix_to_sparse_tensor()` function to write the sample matrix and the label vector to that buffer in `protobuf` format. Finally, we use `boto3` to upload the buffer to S3:

```
import io, boto3
import sagemaker.amazon.common as smac
def writeDatasetToProtobuf(X, Y, bucket, prefix, key):
    buf = io.BytesIO()
    smac.write_spmatrix_to_sparse_tensor(buf, X, Y)
    buf.seek(0)
    obj = '{}/{}'.format(prefix, key)

    boto3.resource('s3').Bucket(bucket).Object(obj).
    upload_fileobj(buf)

    return 's3://{}/{}'.format(bucket,obj)
```

Had our data been stored in a `numpy` array instead of `lilmatrix`, we would have used the `write_numpy_to_dense_tensor()` function instead. It has the same effect.

8. We apply this function to both datasets, and we store their S3 paths:

```
import sagemaker
bucket = sagemaker.Session().default_bucket()
prefix = 'fm-movielens'
train_key    = 'train.protobuf'
train_prefix = '{}/{}'.format(prefix, 'train')
test_key     = 'test.protobuf'
test_prefix  = '{}/{}'.format(prefix, 'test')
```

```
output_prefix  = 's3://{}/{}/output'.format(bucket,
                                             prefix)
```

```
train_data = writeDatasetToProtobuf(X_train, Y_train,
            bucket, train_prefix, train_key)
```

```
test_data  = writeDatasetToProtobuf(X_test, Y_test,
            bucket, test_prefix, test_key)
```

9. Taking a look at the S3 bucket in a terminal, we see that the training dataset only takes 5.5 MB. The combination of sparse matrix, protobuf, and RecordIO has paid off:

```
$ aws s3 ls s3://sagemaker-eu-west-1-123456789012/
fm-movielens/train/train.protobuf
5796480 train.protobuf
```

10. What comes next is SageMaker business as usual. We find the name of the Factorization Machines container, configure the Estimator function, and set the hyperparameters:

```
from sagemaker import image_uris
region=boto3.Session().region_name
container=image_uris.retrieve('factorization-machines',
region)
fm=sagemaker.estimator.Estimator(
    container,
    role=sagemaker.get_execution_role(),
    instance_count=1,
    instance_type='ml.c5.xlarge',
    output_path=output_prefix)
fm.set_hyperparameters(
    feature_dim=num_features,
    predictor_type='regressor',
    num_factors=64,
    epochs=10)
```

Looking at the documentation (https://docs.aws.amazon.com/ sagemaker/latest/dg/fact-machines-hyperparameters.html), we see that the required hyperparameters are feature_dim, predictor_type, and num_factors. The default setting for epochs is 1, which feels a little low, so we use 10 instead.

11. We then launch the training job. Did you notice that we didn't configure training inputs? We're simply passing the location of the two `protobuf` files. As `protobuf` is the default format for Factorization Machines (as well as other built-in algorithms), we can save a step:

```
fm.fit({'train': train_data, 'test': test_data})
```

12. Once the job is over, we deploy the model to a real-time endpoint:

```
endpoint_name = 'fm-movielens-100k'
fm_predictor = fm.deploy(
    endpoint_name=endpoint_name,
    instance_type='ml.t2.medium',
    initial_instance_count=1)
```

13. We'll now send samples to the endpoint in JSON format (https://docs.aws.amazon.com/sagemaker/latest/dg/fact-machines.html#fm-inputoutput). For this purpose, we write a custom serializer to convert input data to JSON. The default JSON deserializer will be used automatically since we set the content type to `'application/json'`:

```
import json
def fm_serializer(data):
    js = {'instances': []}
    for row in data:
        js['instances'].append({'features':
                                row.tolist()})
    return json.dumps(js)
fm_predictor.content_type = 'application/json'
fm_predictor.serializer = fm_serializer
```

14. We send the first three samples of the test set for prediction:

```
result = fm_predictor.predict(X_test[:3].toarray())
print(result)
```

The prediction looks like this:

```
{'predictions': [{'score': 3.3772034645080566}, {'score':
3.4299235343933105}, {'score': 3.6053106784820557}]}
```

15. Using this model, we could fill all the empty cells in the recommendation matrix. For each user, we would simply predict the score of all movies, and store say the top 50 movies. That information would be stored in a backend, and the corresponding metadata (title, genre, and so on) would be displayed to the user in a frontend application.

16. Finally, we delete the endpoint:

```
fm_predictor.delete_endpoint()
```

So far, we've only used supervised learning algorithms. In the next section, we'll move on to unsupervised learning with Principal Component Analysis.

Using Principal Component Analysis

Principal Component Analysis (PCA) is a dimension reductionality algorithm. It's often applied as a preliminary step before regression or classification. Let's use it on the `protobuf` dataset built in the Factorization Machines example. Its 2,625 columns are a good candidate for dimensionality reduction! We will use PCA by observing the following steps:

1. Starting from the processed dataset, we configure the `Estimator` for PCA. By now, you should (almost) be able to do this with your eyes closed:

```
import boto3
from sagemaker import image_uris

region = boto3.Session().region_name
container = image_uris.retrieve('pca', region)

pca = sagemaker.estimator.Estimator(
    container=container,
    role=sagemaker.get_execution_role(),
    instance_count=1,
    instance_type='ml.c5.xlarge',
    output_path=output_prefix)
```

2. We then set the hyperparameters. The required ones are the initial number of features, the number of principal components to compute, and the batch size:

```
pca.set_hyperparameters(feature_dim=num_features,
                        num_components=64,
                        mini_batch_size=1024)
```

3. We train and deploy the model:

```
pca.fit({'train': train_data, 'test': test_data})

pca_predictor = pca.deploy(
    endpoint_name='pca-movielens-100k',
    instance_type='ml.t2.medium',
    initial_instance_count=1)
```

4. Then, we predict the first test sample, using the same serialization code as in the previous example:

```
import json
def pca_serializer(data):
    js = {'instances': []}
    for row in data:
        js['instances'].append({'features':
                                row.tolist()})
    return json.dumps(js)
pca_predictor.content_type = 'application/json'
pca_predictor.serializer = pca_serializer
result = pca_predictor.predict(X_test[0].toarray())
print(result)
```

This prints out the 64 principal components of the test sample. In real life, we typically would process the dataset with this model, save the results, and use them to train a regression model:

```
{'projections': [{'projection': [-0.008711372502148151,
0.0019895541481673717, 0.002355781616643071,
0.012406938709318638, -0.0069608548656105995,
-0.009556426666676998, <output removed>]}]}
```

Don't forget to delete the endpoint when you're done. Then, let's run one more unsupervised learning example to conclude this chapter!

Detecting anomalies with Random Cut Forest

Random Cut Forest (**RCF**) is an unsupervised learning algorithm for anomaly detection (`https://proceedings.mlr.press/v48/guha16.pdf`). We're going to apply it to a subset of the household electric power consumption dataset (`https://archive.ics.uci.edu/ml/`), available in the GitHub repository for this book. The data has been aggregated hourly over a period of little less than a year (just under 8,000 values):

1. In a Jupyter notebook, we load the dataset with `pandas`, and we display the first few lines:

```
import pandas as pd
df = pd.read_csv('item-demand-time.csv', dtype = object,
names=['timestamp','value','client'])
df.head(3)
```

As shown in the following screenshot, the dataset has three columns: an hourly timestamp, the power consumption value (in kilowatt-hours), and the client ID:

	timestamp	value	client
0	2014-01-01 01:00:00	38.34991708126038	client_12
1	2014-01-01 02:00:00	33.5820895522388	client_12
2	2014-01-01 03:00:00	34.41127694859037	client_12

Figure 4.4 – Viewing the columns

2. Using `matplotlib`, we plot the dataset to get a quick idea of what it looks like:

```
import matplotlib
import matplotlib.pyplot as plt
df.value=pd.to_numeric(df.value)
df_plot=df.pivot(index='timestamp',columns='item',
                 values='value')
df_plot.plot(figsize=(40,10))
```

The plot is shown in the following diagram. We see three time series corresponding to three different clients:

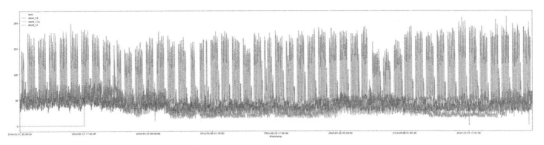

Figure 4.5 – Viewing the dataset

3. There are two issues with this dataset. First, it contains several time series: RCF can only train a model on a single series. Second, RCF requires **integer values**. Let's solve both problem with `pandas`: we only keep the `"client_12"` time series, we multiply its values by 100, and cast them to the integer type:

```
df = df[df['item']=='client_12']
df = df.drop(['item', 'timestamp'], axis=1)
df.value *= 100
df.value = df.value.astype('int32')
df.head()
```

The following diagram shows the first lines of the transformed dataset:

	value
0	3834
1	3358
2	3441

Figure 4.6 – The values of the first lines

4. We plot it again to check that it looks like expected. Note the large drop right after step 2,000, highlighted by a box in the following diagram. This is clearly an anomaly, and hopefully our model will catch it:

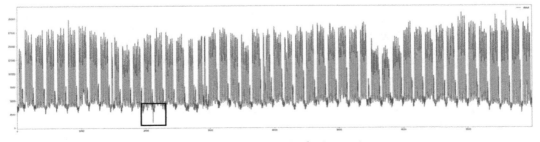

Figure 4.7 – Viewing a single time series

5. As in the previous examples, we save the dataset to a CSV file, which we upload to S3:

```
import boto3
import sagemaker

sess = sagemaker.Session()
bucket = sess.default_bucket()
prefix = 'electricity'

df.to_csv('electricity.csv', index=False, header=False)

training_data_path = sess.upload_data(
                        path='electricity.csv',
                        key_prefix=prefix +
                                    '/input/training')
```

6. Then, we define the **training channel**. There are a couple of quirks that we haven't met before. SageMaker generally doesn't have many of these, and reading the documentation goes a long way in pinpointing them (https://docs.aws.amazon.com/sagemaker/latest/dg/randomcutforest.html).

    First, the **content type** must state that data is not labeled. The reason for this is that RCF can accept an optional test channel where anomalies are labeled (`label_size=1`). Even though the training channel never has labels, we still need to tell RCF. Second, the only **distribution policy** supported in RCF is `ShardedByS3Key`. This policy splits the dataset across the different instances in the training cluster, instead of sending them a full copy. We won't run distributed training here, but we need to set that policy nonetheless:

```
training_data_channel =
    sagemaker.TrainingInput(
        s3_data=training_data_path,
        content_type='text/csv;label_size=0',
        distribution='ShardedByS3Key')
rcf_data = {'train': training_data_channel}
```

7. The rest is business as usual: train and deploy! Once again, we reuse the code for the previous examples, and it's almost unchanged:

```
from sagemaker.estimator import Estimator
from sagemaker import image_uris

role = sagemaker.get_execution_role()
region = boto3.Session().region_name
container = image_uris.retrieve('randomcutforest',
                                    region)
```

```
rcf_estimator = Estimator(container,
    role=role,
    instance_count=1,
    instance_type='ml.m5.large',
    output_path='s3://{}/{}/output'.format(bucket,
                                        prefix))
```

```
rcf_estimator.set_hyperparameters(feature_dim=1)
rcf_estimator.fit(rcf_data)
```

```
endpoint_name = 'rcf-demo'
rcf_predictor = rcf_estimator.deploy(
    endpoint_name=endpoint_name,
    initial_instance_count=1,
    instance_type='ml.t2.medium')
```

8. After a few minutes, the model is deployed. We convert the input time series to a Python list, and we send it to the endpoint for prediction. We use CSV and JSON, respectively, for serialization and deserialization:

```
rcf_predictor.content_type = 'text/csv'
rcf_predictor.serializer =
    sagemaker.serializers.CSVSerializer()
```

```
rcf_predictor.deserializer =
    sagemaker.deserializers.JSONDeserializer()
```

```
values = df['value'].astype('str').tolist()
response = rcf_predictor.predict(values)
print(response)
```

The response contains the anomaly score for each value in the time series. It looks like this:

```
{'scores': [{'score': 1.0868037776}, {'score':
1.5307718138}, {'score': 1.4208102841} …
```

9. We then convert this response to a Python list, and we then compute its mean and its standard deviation:

```
from statistics import mean,stdev
```

```
scores = []
for s in response['scores']:
    scores.append(s['score'])
```

```
score_mean = mean(scores)
score_std = stdev(scores)
```

10. We plot a subset of the time series and the corresponding scores. Let's focus on the [2000-2500] interval, as this is where we saw a large drop. We also plot a line representing the mean plus three standard deviations (99.7% of the score distribution): any score largely exceeding the line is likely to be an anomaly:

```
df[2000:2500].plot(figsize=(40,10))
plt.figure(figsize=(40,10))
plt.plot(scores[2000:2500])
plt.autoscale(tight=True)
plt.axhline(y=score_mean+3*score_std, color='red')
plt.show()
```

The drop is clearly visible in the following plot:

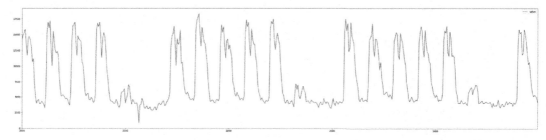

Figure 4.8 – Zooming in on an anomaly

As you can see on the following score plot, its score is sky high! Beyond a doubt, this value is an anomaly:

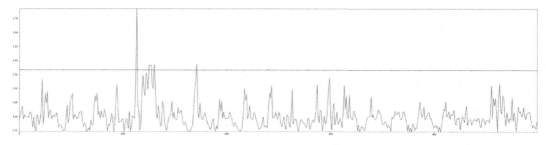

Figure 4.9 – Viewing anomaly scores

Exploring other intervals of the time series, we could certainly find more. Who said machine learning wasn't fun?

11. Finally, we delete the endpoint:

```
rcf_predictor.delete_endpoint()
```

Having gone through five complete examples, you should now be familiar with built-in algorithms, the SageMaker workflow, and the SDK. To fully master these topics, I would recommend experimenting with your datasets, and running the additional examples available at `https://github.com/awslabs/amazon-sagemaker-examples/tree/master/introduction_to_amazon_algorithms`.

Summary

As you can see, built-in algorithms are a great way to quickly train and deploy models without having to write any machine learning code.

In this chapter, you learned about the SageMaker workflow, and how to implement it with a handful of APIs from the SageMaker SDK, without ever worrying about infrastructure.

You learned how to work with data in CSV and RecordIO-wrapped protobuf format, the latter being the preferred format for large-scale training on bulky datasets. You also learned how to build models with important algorithms for supervised and unsupervised learning: Linear Learner, XGBoost, Factorization Machines, PCA, and Random Cut Forest.

In the next chapter, you will learn how to use additional built-in algorithms to build computer vision models.

5
Training Computer Vision Models

In the previous chapter, you learned how to use SageMaker's built-in algorithms for traditional machine learning problems including classification, regression, and anomaly detection. We saw that these algorithms work well on tabular data, such as CSV files. However, they are not well suited for image datasets, and they generally perform very poorly on **computer vision (CV)** tasks.

For a few years now, CV has taken the world by storm, and not a month goes by without a new breakthrough in extracting patterns from images and videos. In this chapter, you will learn about three built-in algorithms designed specifically for CV tasks. We'll discuss the types of problems that you can solve with them. We'll also spend a lot of time explaining how to prepare image datasets, as this crucial topic is often inexplicably overlooked. Of course, we'll train and deploy models too.

This chapter covers the following topics:

- Discovering the CV built-in algorithms in Amazon SageMaker
- Preparing image datasets
- Using the CV built-in algorithms: **image classification**, **object detection**, and **semantic segmentation**.

Technical requirements

You will need an AWS account to run the examples included in this chapter. If you haven't got one already, please point your browser to https://aws.amazon.com/getting-started/ to create it. You should also familiarize yourself with the AWS Free Tier (https://aws.amazon.com/free/), which lets you use many AWS services for free within certain usage limits.

You will need to install and configure the AWS **Command-Line Interface** (**CLI**) for your account (https://aws.amazon.com/cli/).

You will need a working Python 3.x environment. Be careful not to use Python 2.7, as it is no longer maintained. Installing the Anaconda distribution (https://www.anaconda.com/) is not mandatory, but strongly encouraged, as it includes many projects that we will need (Jupyter, pandas, numpy, and more).

The code examples included in the book are available on GitHub at https://github.com/PacktPublishing/Learn-Amazon-SageMaker. You will need to install a Git client to access them (https://git-scm.com/).

Discovering the CV built-in algorithms in Amazon SageMaker

SageMaker includes three CV algorithms, based on proven deep learning networks. In this section, you'll learn about these algorithms, what kind of problems they can help you solve, and what their training scenarios are:

- **Image classification** assigns one or more labels to an image.
- **Object detection** detects and classifies objects in an image.
- **Semantic segmentation** assigns every pixel of an image to a specific class.

Discovering the image classification algorithm

Starting from an input image, the **image classification** algorithm predicts a probability for each class present in the training dataset. This algorithm is based on the **ResNet** convolutional neural network (https://arxiv.org/abs/1512.03385). Published in 2015, **ResNet** won the ILSVRC classification task that same year (http://www.image-net.org/challenges/LSVRC/). Since then, it has become a popular and versatile choice for image classification.

Many hyperparameters can be set, including the depth of the network, which can range from 18 to 200 layers. In general, the more layers the network has, the better it will learn, at the expense of increased training times.

Please note that the **image classification** algorithm supports both **single-label** and **multi-label** classification. We will focus on single-label classification in this chapter. Working with several labels is very similar, and you'll find a complete example at `https://github.com/awslabs/amazon-sagemaker-examples/blob/master/introduction_to_amazon_algorithms/imageclassification_mscoco_multi_label/`.

Discovering the object detection algorithm

Starting from an input image, the **object detection** algorithm predicts both the class and the location of each object in the image. Of course, the algorithm can only detect object classes present in the training dataset. The location of each object is defined by a set of four coordinates, called a **bounding box**.

This algorithm is based on the **Single Shot MultiBox Detector** (**SSD**) architecture (`https://arxiv.org/abs/1512.02325`). For classification, you can pick from two base networks: **VGG-16** (`https://arxiv.org/abs/1409.1556`) or **ResNet-50**.

The following output shows an example of object detection (source: `https://www.dressagechien.net/wp-content/uploads/2017/11/chien-et-velo.jpg`):

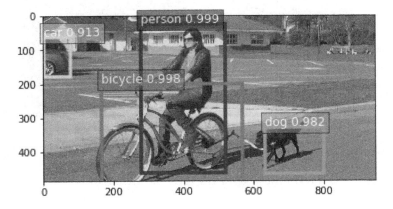

Figure 5.1 – Test image

Discovering the semantic segmentation algorithm

Starting from an input image, the **semantic segmentation** algorithm predicts the class of every pixel of the image. This is a much harder problem than image classification (which only considers the full image) or object detection (which only focuses on specific parts of the image). Using the probabilities contained in a prediction, it's possible to build **segmentation masks** that cover specific objects in the picture.

Three neural networks may be used for segmentation:

- **Fully Convolutional Networks (FCNs)**: https://arxiv.org/abs/1411.4038

- **Pyramid Scene Parsing (PSP)**: https://arxiv.org/abs/1612.01105

- **DeepLab** v3: https://arxiv.org/abs/1706.05587

The encoder network is **ResNet**, with either 50 or 101 layers.

The following output shows the result of segmenting the previous image. We see the segmentation masks, and each class is assigned a unique color; the background is black, and so on:

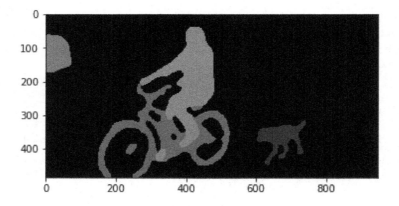

Figure 5.2 – Segmented test image

Now let's see how we can train these algorithms on our own data.

Training with CV algorithms

All three algorithms are based on **supervised learning**, so our starting point will be a labeled dataset. Of course, the nature of these labels will be different for each algorithm:

- Class labels for **image classification**
- Bounding boxes and class labels for **object detection**
- Segmentation masks and class labels for **semantic segmentation**

Annotating image datasets is a lot of work. If you need to build your own dataset, **Amazon SageMaker Ground Truth** can definitely help, and we studied it in *Chapter 2, Handling Data Preparation Tasks*. Later in this chapter, we'll show you how to use image datasets labeled with Ground Truth.

When it comes to packaging datasets, the use of **RecordIO** files is strongly recommended (`https://mxnet.apache.org/api/faq/recordio`). Packaging images in a small number of record-structured files makes it much easier to move datasets around and to split them for distributed training. Having said that, you can also train on individual image files if you prefer.

Once your dataset is ready in S3, you need to decide whether you'd like to train from scratch, or whether you'd like to start from a pretrained network.

Training from scratch is fine if you have plenty of data, and if you're convinced that there's value in building a specific model with it. However, this will take a lot of time, possibly hundreds of epochs, and hyperparameter selection will be absolutely critical in getting good results.

Using a pretrained network is generally the better option, even if you have lots of data. Thanks to **transfer learning**, you can start from a model trained on a huge collection of images (think millions), and fine-tune it on your data and classes. Training will be much shorter, and you will get models with higher accuracy rates quicker.

Given the complexity of the models and the size of datasets, training with CPU instances is simply not an option. We'll use GPU instances for all examples.

Last but not least, all three algorithms are based on **Apache MXNet**. This lets you export their models outside of SageMaker, and deploy them anywhere you like.

In the next sections, we're going to zoom in on image datasets, and how to prepare them for training.

Preparing image datasets

Input formats are more complex for image datasets than for tabular datasets, and we need to get them exactly right. The CV algorithms in SageMaker support three input formats:

- Image files
- **RecordIO** files
- Augmented manifests built by **SageMaker Ground Truth**

In this section, you'll learn how to prepare datasets in these different formats. To the best of my knowledge, this topic has rarely been addressed in such detail. Get ready to learn a lot!

Working with image files

This is the simplest format, and it's supported by all three algorithms. Let's see how to use it with the **image classification** algorithm.

Converting an image classification dataset to image format

A dataset in image format has to be stored in S3. Images don't need to be sorted in any way, and you simply could store all of them in the same bucket.

Images are described in a **list file**, a text file containing a line per image. For **image classification**, three columns are present: the unique identifier of the image, its class label, and its path. Here is an example:

```
1023    5    prefix/image2753.jpg
38      6    another_prefix/image72.jpg
983     2    yet_another_prefix/image863.jpg
```

The first line tells us that image2753.jpg belongs to class 5, and has been assigned ID 1023.

You need a list file for each channel, so you would need one for the training dataset, one for the validation dataset, and so on. You can either write bespoke code to generate them, or you can use a simple program that is part of **Apache MXNet**. This program is called im2rec, and it's available in Python and C++. We'll use the Python version.

Let's use the "Dogs vs. Cats" dataset available on **Kaggle** (`https://www.kaggle.com/c/dogs-vs-cats`). This dataset is 812 MB. Unsurprisingly, it contains two classes: dogs and cats. It's already split for training and testing (25,000 and 12,500 images, respectively). Here's how we can use it:

1. We create a **Kaggle** account, accept the rules of the "Dogs vs. Cats" competition, and install the `kaggle` CLI (`https://github.com/Kaggle/kaggle-api`).

2. In a Terminal, we download and extract the training dataset (you can ignore the test set, which is only needed for the competition). I recommend doing this on a Notebook instance or an EC2 instance instead of your local machine, as we'll later sync the processed dataset to S3:

```
$ kaggle competitions download -c dogs-vs-cats
$ unzip dogs-vs-cats.zip
$ unzip train.zip
```

3. Dog and cat images are mixed up in the same folder. We create a subfolder for each class, and move the appropriate images there:

```
$ cd train
$ mkdir dog cat
$ find . -name 'dog.*' -exec mv {} dog \;
$ find . -name 'cat.*' -exec mv {} cat \;
```

4. We'll need validation images, so let's move 1,250 random dog images and 1,250 random cat images to specific directories. I'm using `bash` scripting here, but feel free to use any tool you like:

```
$ mkdir -p val/dog val/cat
$ ls dog | sort -R | tail -1250 | while read file;
do mv dog/$file val/dog; done
$ ls cat | sort -R | tail -1250 | while read file;
do mv cat/$file val/cat; done
```

5. We move the remaining 22,500 images to the training folder:

```
$ mkdir train
$ mv dog cat train
```

6. Our dataset now looks like this:

```
$ du -h
33M        ./val/dog
28M        ./val/cat
60M        ./val
289M       ./train/dog
248M       ./train/cat
537M       ./train
597M       .
```

7. We download the im2rec tool from GitHub (https://github.com/apache/incubator-mxnet/blob/master/tools/im2rec.py). It requires two dependencies, Apache MXNet and OpenCV, which we install as follows:

```
$ wget https://raw.githubusercontent.com/apache/
incubator-mxnet/master/tools/im2rec.py
$ pip install mxnet opencv-python
```

8. We run im2rec to build two list files, one for training data and one for validation data:

```
$ python3 im2rec.py --list --recursive dogscats-train
train
$ python3 im2rec.py --list --recursive dogscats-val val
```

This creates the dogscats-train.lst and dogscats-val.lst files. Their three columns are a unique image identifier, the class label (0 for cats, 1 for dogs), and the image path, as follows:

```
3197 0.000000      cat/cat.1625.jpg
15084 1.000000     dog/dog.12322.jpg
1479 0.000000      cat/cat.11328.jpg
5262 0.000000      cat/cat.3484.jpg
20714 1.000000     dog/dog.6140.jpg
```

9. We move the list files to specific directories. This is required because they will be passed to the estimator as two new channels, train_lst and validation_lst:

```
$ mkdir train_lst val_lst
$ mv dogscats-train.lst train_lst
$ mv dogscats-val.lst val_lst
```

10. The dataset now looks like this:

```
$ du -h
33M        ./val/dog
28M        ./val/cat
60M        ./val
700K       ./train_lst
80K        ./val_lst
289M       ./train/dog
248M       ./train/cat
537M       ./train
597M       .
```

11. Finally, we sync this folder to the SageMaker default bucket for future use. Please make sure to only sync the four folders, and nothing else:

```
$ aws s3 sync .
  s3://sagemaker-eu-west-1-123456789012/dogscats-images/
input/
```

Now, let's move on to using the image format with the object detection algorithms.

Converting detection datasets to image format

The general principle is identical. We need to build a file tree representing the four channels: train, validation, train_annotation, and validation_annotation.

The main difference lies in how labeling information is stored. Instead of list files, we need to build JSON files.

Here's an example of a fictitious picture in an object detection dataset. For each object in the picture, we define the coordinates of the top-left corner of its bounding box, its height, and its width. We also define the class identifier, which points to a category array that also stores class names:

```
{
    "file": " my-prefix/my-picture.jpg",
    "image_size": [{"width": 512,"height": 512,"depth": 3}],
    "annotations": [
        {
          "class_id": 1,
          "left": 67, "top": 121, "width": 61, "height": 128
        },
        {
```

```
        "class_id": 5,
        "left": 324, "top": 134, "width": 112, "height": 267
      }
   ],
   "categories": [
      { "class_id": 1, "name": "pizza" },
      { "class_id": 5, "name": "beer" }
   ]
}
```

We would need to do this for every picture in the dataset, building a JSON file for the training set and one for the validation set.

Finally, let's see how to use the image format with the semantic segmentation algorithm.

Converting segmentation datasets to image format

Image format is the only format supported by the image segmentation algorithm.

This time, we need to build a file tree representing the four channels: `train`, `validation`, `train_annotation`, and `validation_annotation`. The first two channels contain the source images, and the last two contain the segmentation mask images.

File naming is critical in matching an image to its mask: the source image and the mask image must have the same name in their respective channels. Here's an example:

```
├── train
│   ├── image001.png
│   ├── image007.png
│   └── image042.png
├── train_annotation
│   ├── image001.png
│   ├── image007.png
│   └── image042.png
├── validation
│   ├── image059.png
│   ├── image062.png
│   └── image078.png
└── validation_annotation
    ├── image059.png
    ├── image062.png
    └── image078.png
```

You can see sample pictures in the following figure. The source image on the left would go to the `train` folder and the mask picture on the right would go to the `train_annotation` folder. They should have the same name, so that the algorithm could match them.

Figure 5.3 – Sample image from the Pascal VOC dataset

One clever feature of this format is how it matches class identifiers to mask colors. Mask images are PNG files with a 256-color palette. Each class in the dataset is assigned a specific entry in the color palette. These colors are the ones you see in masks for objects belonging to that class.

If your labeling tool or your existing dataset don't support this PNG feature, you can add your own color mapping file. Please refer to the AWS documentation for details: `https://docs.aws.amazon.com/sagemaker/latest/dg/semantic-segmentation.html`

Now, let's prepare the **Pascal VOC** dataset. This dataset is frequently used to benchmark object detection and semantic segmentation models (`http://host.robots.ox.ac.uk/pascal/VOC/`):

1. We first download and extract the 2012 version of the dataset. Again, I recommend using an AWS-hosted instance to speed up network transfers:

```
$ wget http://host.robots.ox.ac.uk/pascal/VOC/voc2012/
VOCtrainval_11-May-2012.tar
$ tar xvf VOCtrainval_11-May-2012.tar
```

2. We create a work directory where we'll build the four channels:

```
$ mkdir s3_data
$ cd s3_data
$ mkdir train validation train_annotation validation_
annotation
```

3. Using the list of training files defined in the dataset, we copy the corresponding images to the `train` folder. I'm using `bash` scripting here; feel free to use your tool of choice:

```
$ for file in `cat ../VOCdevkit/VOC2012/ImageSets/
Segmentation/train.txt | xargs`; do cp ../VOCdevkit/
VOC2012/JPEGImages/$file".jpg" train; done
```

4. We then do the same for the validation images, training masks, and validation masks:

```
$ for file in `cat ../VOCdevkit/VOC2012/ImageSets/
Segmentation/val.txt | xargs`; do cp ../VOCdevkit/
VOC2012/JPEGImages/$file".jpg" validation; done
```

```
$ for file in `cat ../VOCdevkit/VOC2012/ImageSets/
Segmentation/train.txt | xargs`; do cp ../VOCdevkit/
VOC2012/SegmentationClass/$file".png" train_annotation;
done
```

```
$ for file in `cat ../VOCdevkit/VOC2012/ImageSets/
Segmentation/val.txt | xargs`; do cp ../VOCdevkit/
VOC2012/SegmentationClass/$file".png" validation_
annotation; done
```

5. We check that we have the same number of images in the two training channels, and in the two validation channels:

```
$ for dir in train train_annotation validation
validation_annotation; do find $dir -type f | wc -l; done
```

We see 1,464 training files and masks, and 1,449 validation files and masks. We're all set:

```
1464
1464
1449
1449
```

6. The last step is to sync the file tree to S3 for later use. Again, please make sure to sync only the four folders:

```
$ aws s3 sync . s3://sagemaker-eu-west-1-123456789012/
pascalvoc-segmentation/input/
```

We know how to prepare classification, detection, and segmentation datasets in image format. This is a critical step, and you have to get things exactly right.

Still, I'm sure that you found the steps in this section a little painful. So did I! Now imagine doing the same with millions of images. That doesn't sound very exciting, does it?

We need an easier way to prepare image datasets. Let's see how we can simplify dataset preparation with **RecordIO** files.

Working with RecordIO files

RecordIO files are easier to move around. It's much more efficient for an algorithm to read a large sequential file than to read lots of tiny files stored at random disk locations.

Converting an Image Classification dataset to RecordIO

Let's convert the "Dogs vs. Cats" dataset to RecordIO:

1. Starting from a freshly extracted copy of the dataset, we move the images to the appropriate class folder:

```
$ cd train
$ mkdir dog cat
$ find . -name 'dog.*' -exec mv {} dog \;
$ find . -name 'cat.*' -exec mv {} cat \;
```

2. We run `im2rec` to generate list files for the training dataset (90%) and the validation dataset (10%). There's no need to split the dataset ourselves!

```
$ python3 im2rec.py --list --recursive --train-ratio 0.9
dogscats .
```

3. We run `im2rec` once more to generate the RecordIO files:

```
$ python3 im2rec.py --num-thread 8 dogscats .
```

This creates four new files: two RecordIO files (.rec) containing the packed images, and two index files (.idx) containing the offsets of these images inside the record files:

```
$ ls dogscats*
dogscats_train.idx dogscats_train.lst dogscats_train.rec
dogscats_val.idx dogscats_val.lst dogscats_val.rec
```

4. Let's store the RecordIO files in S3, as we'll use them later:

```
$ aws s3 cp dogscats_train.rec s3://sagemaker-eu-
west-1-123456789012/dogscats/input/train/
```

```
$ aws s3 cp dogscats_val.rec s3://sagemaker-eu-
west-1-123456789012/dogscats/input/validation/
```

This was much simpler, wasn't it? im2rec has additional options to resize images and more. It can also break the dataset into several chunks, a useful technique for **Pipe Mode** and **Distributed Training**. We'll study them in *Chapter 10, Advanced Training Techniques*.

Now, let's move on to using RecordIO files for object detection.

Converting an object detection dataset to RecordIO

The process is very similar. A major difference is the format of list files. Instead of dealing only with class labels, we also need to store bounding boxes.

Let's see what this means for the Pascal VOC dataset. The following image is taken from the dataset:

Figure 5.4 – Sample image from the Pascal VOC dataset

It contains three chairs. The labeling information is stored in an individual **XML** file, shown in a slightly abbreviated form:

```
<annotation>
        <folder>VOC2007</folder>
        <filename>003988.jpg</filename>
        . . .
        <object>
                <name>chair</name>
                <pose>Unspecified</pose>
                <truncated>1</truncated>
                <difficult>0</difficult>
                <bndbox>
                     <xmin>1</xmin>
                     <ymin>222</ymin>
                     <xmax>117</xmax>
                     <ymax>336</ymax>
                </bndbox>
        </object>
        <object>
                <name>chair</name>
                <pose>Unspecified</pose>
                <truncated>1</truncated>
                <difficult>1</difficult>
                <bndbox>
                     <xmin>429</xmin>
                     <ymin>216</ymin>
                     <xmax>448</xmax>
                     <ymax>297</ymax>
                </bndbox>
        </object>
        <object>
                <name>chair</name>
                <pose>Unspecified</pose>
                <truncated>0</truncated>
                <difficult>1</difficult>
                <bndbox>
                     <xmin>281</xmin>
                     <ymin>149</ymin>
                     <xmax>317</xmax>
                     <ymax>211</ymax>
```

```
                        </bndbox>
            </object>
    </annotation>
```

Converting this to a list file entry should look like this:

```
9404 2 6  8.0000  0.0022  0.6607  0.2612  1.0000  0.0000 8.0000
0.9576  0.6429  1.0000  0.8839  1.0000 8.0000  0.6272  0.4435
0.7076  0.6280  1.0000 VOC2007/JPEGImages/003988.jpg
```

Let's decode each column:

- 9404 is a unique image identifier.

- 2 is the number of columns containing header information, including this one.

- 6 is the number of columns for labeling information. These six columns are the class identifier, the four bounding-box coordinates, and a flag telling us whether the object is difficult to see (we won't use it).

- The following is for the first object:

  a) 8 is the class identifier. Here, 8 is the chair class.

  b) 0.0022 0.6607 0.2612 1.0000 are the relative coordinates of the **bounding box** with respect to the height and width of the image.

  c) 0 means that the object is not difficult.

- For the second object, we have the following:

  a) 8 is the class identifier.

  b) 0.9576 0.6429 1.0000 0.8839 are the coordinates of the second object.

  c) 1 means that the object is difficult.

- The third object has the following:

  a) 8 is the class identifier.

  b) 0.6272 0.4435 0.7076 0.628 are the coordinates of the third object.

  c) 1 means that the object is difficult.

- VOC2007/JPEGImages/003988.jpg is the path to the image.

So how do we convert thousands of XML files into a couple of list files? Unless you enjoy writing parsers, this isn't a very exciting task.

Fortunately, our work has been cut out for us. Apache MXNet includes a Python script, prepare_dataset.py, that will handle this task. Let's see how it works:

1. For the next steps, you will need an Apache MXNet environment with at least 10 GB of storage. Here, I'm using a **Notebook instance** with the mxnet_p36 kernel, storing and processing data in /tmp. You could work locally too, provided that you install MXNet and its dependencies:

```
$ source activate mxnet_p36
$ cd /tmp
```

2. Download the 2007 and 2012 Pascal VOC datasets with wget, and extract them with tar in the same directory:

http://host.robots.ox.ac.uk/pascal/VOC/voc2012/VOCtrainval_11-May-2012.tar
http://host.robots.ox.ac.uk/pascal/VOC/voc2007/VOCtrainval_06-Nov-2007.tar
http://host.robots.ox.ac.uk/pascal/VOC/voc2007/VOCtest_06-Nov-2007.tar

3. Clone the Apache MXNet repository (https://github.com/apache/incubator-mxnet/):

```
$ git clone --single-branch --branch v1.4.x https://
github.com/apache/incubator-mxnet
```

4. Run the prepare_dataset.py script to build our training dataset, merging the training and validation sets of the 2007 and 2012 versions:

```
$ python3 incubator-mxnet/example/ssd/tools/prepare_
dataset.py --dataset pascal --year 2007,2012 --set
trainval --root VOCdevkit --target VOCdevkit/train.lst
```

5. Run it again to generate our validation dataset, using the test set of the 2007 version:

```
$ python3 incubator-mxnet/example/ssd/tools/prepare_
dataset.py --dataset pascal --year 2007 --set test --root
VOCdevkit --target VOCdevkit/val.lst
```

6. In the `VOCdevkit` directory, we see the files generated by the script. Feel free to take a look at the list files; they should have the format presented previously:

```
train.idx  train.lst  train.rec  val.idx  val.lst  val.
rec  VOC2007  VOC2012
```

7. Let's store the RecordIO files in S3 as we'll use them later:

```
$ aws s3 cp train.rec s3://sagemaker-eu-
west-1-123456789012/pascalvoc/input/train/
```

```
$ aws s3 cp val.rec s3://sagemaker-eu-
west-1-123456789012/pascalvoc/input/validation/
```

The `prepare_dataset.py` script has really made things simple here. It also supports the **COCO** dataset (`http://cocodataset.org`), and the workflow is extremely similar.

What about converting other public datasets? Well, your mileage may vary. You'll find more information at the following links:

- `https://gluon-cv.mxnet.io/build/examples_datasets/index.html`

- `https://github.com/apache/incubator-mxnet/tree/master/example`

RecordIO is definitely a step forward. Still, when working with custom datasets, it's very likely that you'll have to write your own list file generator. That's not a huge deal, but it's extra work.

Datasets labeled with **Amazon SageMaker Ground Truth** solve these problems altogether. Let's see how this works!

Working with SageMaker Ground Truth files

In *Chapter 2, Handling Data Preparation Techniques*, you learned about SageMaker Ground Truth workflows and their outcome, an **augmented manifest** file. This file is in **JSON Lines** format: each JSON object describes a specific annotation.

Here's an example from the semantic segmentation job we ran in *Chapter 2, Handling Data Preparation Techniques* (the story is the same for other task types). We see the paths to the source image and the segmentation mask, as well as color map information telling us how to match mask colors to classes:

```
{"source-ref":"s3://julien-sagemaker-book/chapter2/cat/
cat1.jpg",
"my-cat-job-ref":"s3://julien-sagemaker-book/chapter2/
cat/output/my-cat-job/annotations/consolidated-
annotation/output/0_2020-04-21T13:48:00.091190.png",
"my-cat-job-ref-metadata":{
   "internal-color-map":{
    "0":{"class-name":"BACKGROUND","hex-color": "#ffffff",
        "confidence": 0.8054600000000001},
    "1":{"class-name":"cat","hex-color": "#2ca02c",
        "confidence":0.8054600000000001}
},
"type":"groundtruth/semantic-segmentation",
"human-annotated":"yes",
"creation-date":"2020-04-21T13:48:00.562419",
"job-name":"labeling-job/my-cat-job"}}
```

The following images are the ones referenced in the preceding JSON document:

Figure 5.5 – Source image and segmented image

This is exactly what we would need to train our model. In fact, we can pass the augmented manifest to the SageMaker `Estimator` as is. No data processing is required whatsoever.

To use an **augmented manifest** pointing at labeled images in S3, we would simply pass its location and the name of the JSON attributes (highlighted in the previous example):

```
training_data_channel = sagemaker.s3_input(
    s3_data=augmented_manifest_file_path,
    s3_data_type='AugmentedManifestFile',
    attribute_names=['source-ref', 'my-job-cat-ref'])
```

That's it! This is much simpler than anything we've seen before.

You can find more examples of using SageMaker Ground Truth at `https://github.com/awslabs/amazon-sagemaker-examples/tree/master/ground_truth_labeling_jobs`.

Now that we know how to prepare image datasets for training, let's put the CV algorithms to work.

Using the built-in CV algorithms

In this section, we're going to train and deploy models with all three algorithms using public image datasets. We will cover both training from scratch and transfer learning.

Training an image classification model

In this first example, let's use the image classification algorithm to build a model classifying the "Dogs vs. Cats" dataset that we prepared in a previous section. We'll first train using image format, and then using RecordIO format.

Training in image format

We will begin training using the following steps:

1. In a Jupyter notebook, we define the appropriate data paths:

```python
import sagemaker

session = sagemaker.Session()
bucket = session.default_bucket()
prefix = 'dogscats-images'

s3_train_path =
    's3://{}/{}/input/train/'.format(bucket, prefix)
s3_val_path =
    's3://{}/{}/input/val/'.format(bucket, prefix)

s3_train_lst_path =
    's3://{}/{}/input/train_lst/'.format(bucket, prefix)
s3_val_lst_path =
    's3://{}/{}/input/val_lst/'.format(bucket, prefix)

s3_output = 's3://{}/{}/output/'.format(bucket, prefix)
```

2. We configure the `Estimator` for the image classification algorithm:

```
from sagemaker import image_uris

region_name = session.boto_region_name
container = image_uris.retrieve('image-classification',
                                region)

role = sagemaker.get_execution_role()

ic = sagemaker.estimator.Estimator(container,
            role=role,
            instance_count=1,
            instance_type='ml.p2.xlarge',
            output_path=s3_output)
```

We use a GPU instance called `ml.p2.xlarge`, which is a cost-effective option that packs more than enough punch for this dataset ($1.361/hour in `eu-west-1`). If you want significantly faster training, I recommend using `ml.p3.2xlarge` instead ($4.627/hour).

3. What about hyperparameters? (`https://docs.aws.amazon.com/sagemaker/latest/dg/IC-Hyperparameter.html`). We set the number of classes (2) and the number of training samples (22,500). Since we're working with the image format, we need to resize images explicitly, setting the smallest dimension to 224 pixels. As we have enough data, we decide to train from scratch. In order to keep the training time low, we settle for an 18-layer **ResNet** model, and we train only for 10 epochs:

```
ic.set_hyperparameters(num_layers=18,
                       use_pretrained_model=0,
                       num_classes=2,
                       num_training_samples=22500,
                       resize=224,
                       mini_batch_size=128,
                       epochs=10)
```

4. We define the four channels, setting their content type to `application/x-image`:

```
from sagemaker import TrainingInput

train_data = TrainingInput (
    s3_train_path,
    distribution='FullyReplicated',
    content_type='application/x-image',
    s3_data_type='S3Prefix')
```

```
val_data = TrainingInput (
    s3_val_path,
    distribution='FullyReplicated',
    content_type='application/x-image',
    s3_data_type='S3Prefix')
train_lst_data = TrainingInput (
    s3_train_lst_path,
    distribution='FullyReplicated',
    content_type='application/x-image',
    s3_data_type='S3Prefix')
val_lst_data = TrainingInput (
    s3_val_lst_path,
    distribution='FullyReplicated',
    content_type='application/x-image',
    s3_data_type='S3Prefix')
s3_channels = {'train': train_data,
               'validation': val_data,
               'train_lst': train_lst_data,
               'validation_lst': val_lst_data}
```

5. We launch the training job as follows:

```
ic.fit(inputs=s3_channels)
```

In the training log, we see that data download takes about 2.5 minutes. Surprise, surprise: we also see that the algorithm builds RecordIO files before training. This step lasts about 1.5 minutes:

```
Searching for .lst files in /opt/ml/input/data/train_lst.
Creating record files for dogscats-train.lst
Done creating record files...
Searching for .lst files in /opt/ml/input/data/
validation_lst.
Creating record files for dogscats-val.lst
Done creating record files...
```

6. As the training starts, we see that an epoch takes approximately 2.5 minutes:

```
Epoch[0] Time cost=150.029
Epoch[0] Validation-accuracy=0.678906
```

7. The job lasts 20 minutes in total, and delivers a validation accuracy of **92.3%** (hopefully, you see something similar). This is pretty good considering that we haven't even tweaked the hyperparameters yet.

8. We then deploy the model on a small CPU instance as follows:

```
ic_predictor = ic.deploy(initial_instance_count=1,
                         instance_type='ml.t2.medium')
```

9. We download the following test image and send it for prediction in `application/x-image` format.

Figure 5.6 – Test picture

We'll use the following code to apply predictions on the image:

```
!wget -O /tmp/test.jpg https://upload.wikimedia.org/
wikipedia/commons/b/b7/LabradorWeaving.jpg
```

```
with open('test.jpg', 'rb') as f:
    payload = f.read()
    payload = bytearray(payload)
```

```
ic_predictor.content_type = 'application/x-image'

result = ic_predictor.predict(payload)
print(result)
```

According to our model, this image is a dog, with 96.2% confidence:

```
b'[0.03780071064829826, 0.9621992707252502]'
```

10. When we're done, we delete the endpoint as follows:

```
ic_predictor.delete_endpoint()
```

Now let's run the same training job with the dataset in RecordIO format.

Training in RecordIO format

The only difference is how we define the input channels. We only need two channels this time in order to serve the RecordIO files we uploaded to S3. Accordingly, the content type is set to `application/x-recordio`:

```
from sagemaker import TrainingInput
prefix = 'dogscats'
s3_train_path=
    's3://{}/{}/input/train/'.format(bucket, prefix)
s3_val_path=
    's3://{}/{}/input/validation/'.format(bucket, prefix)
train_data = TrainingInput(
    s3_train_path,
    distribution='FullyReplicated',
    content_type='application/x-recordio',
    s3_data_type='S3Prefix')
validation_data = TrainingInput(
    s3_val_path,
    distribution='FullyReplicated',
    content_type='application/x-recordio',
    s3_data_type='S3Prefix')
```

Training again, we see that data download now takes 1.5 minutes, and that the file generation step has disappeared. In addition, an epoch now lasts 142 seconds, an 8% improvement. Although it's difficult to draw any conclusion from a single run, using RecordIO datasets will generally save you time and money, even when training on a single instance.

The "Dogs vs. Cats" dataset has over 10,000 samples per class, which is more than enough to train from scratch. Now, let's try a dataset where that's not the case.

Fine-tuning an image classification model

Please consider the **Caltech-256** dataset, a popular public dataset of 15,240 images in 256 classes, plus a clutter class (http://www.vision.caltech.edu/Image_Datasets/Caltech256/). Browsing the image categories, we see that all classes have a small number of samples. For instance, the duck class only has 60 images: it's doubtful that a deep learning algorithm, no matter how sophisticated, could extract the unique visual features of ducks with that little data.

In such cases, training from scratch is simply not an option. Instead, we will use a technique called **transfer learning**, where we start from a network that has already been trained on a very large and diverse image dataset. **ImageNet** (http://www.image-net.org/) is probably the most popular choice for pretraining, with 1,000 classes and millions of images.

The pretrained network has already learned how to extract patterns from complex images. Assuming that the images in our dataset are similar enough to those in the pretraining dataset, our model should be able to inherit that knowledge. Training for only a few more epochs on our dataset, we should be able to **fine-tune** the pretrained model on our data and classes.

Let's see how we can easily do this with SageMaker. In fact, we'll reuse the code for the previous example with minimal changes. Let's get into it:

1. We download the Caltech-256 in RecordIO format. (If you'd like, you could download it in its original format, and convert it as shown in the previous example: practice makes perfect!):

```
%%sh
wget http://data.mxnet.io/data/caltech-256/caltech-256-
60-train.rec
wget http://data.mxnet.io/data/caltech-256/caltech-256-
60-val.rec
```

2. We upload the dataset to S3:

```
import sagemaker
session = sagemaker.Session()
bucket = session.default_bucket()
prefix = 'caltech256/'
s3_train_path = session.upload_data(
    path='caltech-256-60-train.rec',
    bucket=bucket, key_prefix=prefix+'input/train')
s3_val_path = session.upload_data(
```

```
            path='caltech-256-60-val.rec',
            bucket=bucket, key_prefix=prefix+'input/validation')
```

3. We configure the `Estimator` function for the image classification algorithm. The code is strictly identical to *step 3* in the previous example.

4. We use **ResNet-50** this time, as it should be able to cope with the complexity of our images. Of course, we set `use_pretrained_network` to 1. The final fully connected layer of the pretrained network will be resized to the number of classes present in our dataset, and its weights will be assigned random values.

    We set the correct number of classes (256+1) and training samples as follows:

```
ic.set_hyperparameters(num_layers=50,
                       use_pretrained_model=1,
                       num_classes=257,
                       num_training_samples=15240,
                       learning_rate=0.001,
                       epochs=10)
```

    Since we're fine-tuning, we only train for 10 epochs, with a smaller learning rate of 0.001.

5. We configure channels and we launch the training job. The code is strictly identical to *step 5* in the previous example.

6. After 10 epochs, we see the metric in the training log as follows:

```
Epoch[9] Validation-accuracy=0.838278
```

    This is quite good for just a few minutes of training. Even with enough data, it would have taken much longer to get that result from scratch.

7. To deploy and test the model, we would reuse *steps 7-9* in the previous example.

As you can see, transfer learning is a very powerful technique. It can deliver excellent results, even when you have little data. You will also train for fewer epochs, saving time and money in the process.

Now, let's move on to the next algorithm, **object detection**.

Training an object detection model

In this example, we'll use the object detection algorithm to build a model on the Pascal VOC dataset that we prepared in a previous section:

1. We start by defining data paths:

```
import sagemaker

session = sagemaker.Session()
bucket = session.default_bucket()

prefix = 'pascalvoc'

s3_train_data = 's3://{}/{}/input/train'.format(bucket,
prefix)

s3_validation_data = 's3://{}/{}/input/validation'.
format(bucket, prefix)

s3_output_location = 's3://{}/{}/output'.format(bucket,
prefix)
```

2. We select the object detection algorithm:

```
from sagemaker import image_uris

region = sess.boto_region_name
container = image_uris.retrieve('object-detection',
region)
```

3. We configure the `Estimator` function. We'll use `ml.p3.2xlarge` this time, because of the increased complexity of the algorithm:

```
od = sagemaker.estimator.Estimator(
        container,
        sagemaker.get_execution_role(),
        instance_count=1,
        instance_type='ml.p3.2xlarge',
        output_path=s3_output_location)
```

4. We set the required hyperparameters. We select a pretrained ResNet-50 network for the base network. We set the number of classes and training samples. We settle on 30 epochs, which should be enough to start seeing results:

```
od.set_hyperparameters(base_network='resnet-50',
                       use_pretrained_model=1,
                       num_classes=20,
                       num_training_samples=16551,
                       epochs=30)
```

5. We then configure the two channels, and we launch the training job:

```
from sagemaker.session import TrainingInput
train_data = TrainingInput (
        s3_train_data,
        distribution='FullyReplicated',
        content_type='application/x-recordio',
        s3_data_type='S3Prefix')
validation_data = TrainingInput (
        s3_validation_data,
        distribution='FullyReplicated',
        content_type='application/x-recordio',
        s3_data_type='S3Prefix')
data_channels = {'train': train_data,
                 'validation': validation_data}
od.fit(inputs=data_channels)
```

6. Training lasts for 2 hours. This is a pretty heavy model! We get a **mean average precision (mAP) metric** of 0.494. Looking at the SageMaker console, we can see it graphed over time in the **Training jobs** section, as shown in the following plot taken from CloudWatch. We should definitely have trained some more, but we should be able to test the model already:

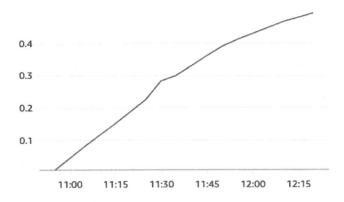

Figure 5.7 – Validation accuracy

7. We deploy the model to a CPU instance:

```
od_predictor = od.deploy(initial_instance_count = 1,
                         instance_type = 'ml.c5.2xlarge')
```

8. We download a test image, and send it for prediction as a byte array. The content type is set to image/jpeg:

```
import json
!wget -O test.jpg https://upload.wikimedia.org/wikipedia/
commons/6/67/Chin_Village.jpg
with open(file_name, 'rb') as image:
    f = image.read()
    b = bytearray(f)
od_predictor.content_type = 'image/jpeg'
results = od_predictor.predict(b)
response = json.loads(results)
print(response)
```

9. The response contains a list of predictions. Each individual prediction contains a class identifier, the confidence score, and the relative coordinates of the bounding box. Here are the first predictions in the response:

```
{'prediction':
[[14.0, 0.7515302300453186, 0.39770469069480896,
0.37605002522468567, 0.5998836755752563, 1.0],
[14.0, 0.6490200161933899, 0.8020403385162354,
0.2027685046195984, 0.9918708801269531,
0.8575668931007385]
```

Using this information, we could plot the bounding boxes on the source image. For the sake of brevity, I will not include the code here, but you'll find it in the GitHub repository for this book. The following output shows the result:

Figure 5.8 – Test image

10. When we're done, we delete the endpoint as follows:

```
od_predictor.delete_endpoint()
```

This concludes our exploration of object detection. We have one more algorithm to go: **semantic segmentation**.

Training a semantic segmentation model

In this example, we'll use the semantic segmentation algorithm to build a model on the Pascal VOC dataset that we prepared in a previous section:

1. As usual, we define the data paths, as follows:

```
import sagemaker

session = sagemaker.Session()
bucket = sess.default_bucket()
prefix = 'pascalvoc-segmentation'

s3_train_data = 's3://{}/{}/input/train'.format(bucket,
prefix)

s3_validation_data = 's3://{}/{}/input/validation'.
format(bucket, prefix)

s3_train_annotation_data = 's3://{}/{}/input/train_
annotation'.format(bucket, prefix)

s3_validation_annotation_data = 's3://{}/{}/input/
validation_annotation'.format(bucket, prefix)

s3_output_location =
's3://{}/{}/output'.format(bucket, prefix)
```

2. We select the semantic segmentation algorithm, and we configure the
    `Estimator` function:

```
from sagemaker import image_uris

container = image_uris.retrieve('semantic-segmentation',
region)

seg = sagemaker.estimator.Estimator(
        container,
        sagemaker.get_execution_role(),
        instance_count = 1,
        instance_type = 'ml.p3.2xlarge',
        output_path = s3_output_location)
```

3. We define the required hyperparameters. We select a pretrained ResNet-50 network
    for the base network, and a pretrained **FCN** for detection. We set the number
    of classes and training samples. Again, we settle on 30 epochs, which should be
    enough to start seeing results:

```
seg.set_hyperparameters(backbone='resnet-50',
                        algorithm='fcn',
                        use_pretrained_model=True,
```

```
                  num_classes=21,
                  num_training_samples=1464,
                  epochs=30)
```

4. We configure the four channels, setting the content type to image/jpeg for source images, and image/png for mask images. Then, we launch the training job:

```
from sagemaker import TrainingInput

train_data = TrainingInput(
             s3_train_data,
             distribution='FullyReplicated',
             content_type='image/jpeg',
             s3_data_type='S3Prefix')

validation_data = TrainingInput(
             s3_validation_data,
             distribution='FullyReplicated',
             content_type='image/jpeg',
             s3_data_type='S3Prefix')

train_annotation = TrainingInput(
             s3_train_annotation_data,
             distribution='FullyReplicated',
             content_type='image/png',
             s3_data_type='S3Prefix')

validation_annotation = TrainingInput(
             s3_validation_annotation_data,
             distribution='FullyReplicated',
             content_type='image/png',
             s3_data_type='S3Prefix')

data_channels = {
  'train': train_data,
  'validation': validation_data,
  'train_annotation': train_annotation,
  'validation_annotation':validation_annotation
}

seg.fit(inputs=data_channels)
```

5. Training lasts about 40 minutes. We get a **mean intersection-over-union metric (mIOU)** of 0.49, as shown in the following plot taken from CloudWatch:

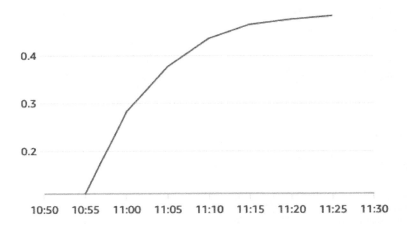

Figure 5.9 – Validation mIOU

6. We deploy the model to a CPU instance:

```
seg_predictor = seg.deploy(initial_instance_count=1,
                           instance_type='ml.c5.2xlarge')
```

7. Once the endpoint is in service, we grab a test image, and we send it for prediction as a byte array with the appropriate content type:

```
!wget -O test.jpg https://upload.wikimedia.org/wikipedia/
commons/e/ea/SilverMorgan.jpg
filename = 'test.jpg'
seg_predictor.content_type = 'image/jpeg'
seg_predictor.accept = 'image/png'
with open(filename, 'rb') as image:
    img = image.read()
    img = bytearray(img)
response = seg_predictor.predict(img)
```

8. Using the **Python Imaging Library** (**PIL**), we process the response mask and display it:

```
import PIL
from PIL import Image
import numpy as np
import io

num_classes = 21
mask = np.array(Image.open(io.BytesIO(response)))
plt.imshow(mask, vmin=0, vmax=num_classes-1,
cmap='gray_r')
plt.show()
```

The following images show the source image and the predicted mask. This result is promising, and would improve with more training:

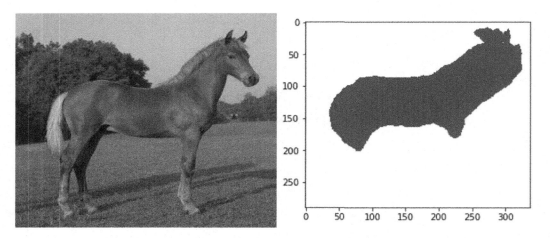

Figure 5.10 – Test image and segmented test image

9. Predicting again with the protobuf `accept` type, we receive class probabilities for all the pixels in the source image. The response is a protobuf buffer, which we save to a binary file:

```
seg_predictor.content_type = 'image/jpeg'
seg_predictor.accept = 'application/x-protobuf'
response = seg_predictor.predict(img)

results_file = 'results.rec'
with open(results_file, 'wb') as f:
    f.write(response)
```

10. The buffer contains two tensors: one with the shape of the probability tensor, and one with the actual probabilities. We load them using **Apache MXNet** and print their shape as follows:

```
from sagemaker.amazon.record_pb2 import Record
import mxnet as mx

rec = Record()
recordio = mx.recordio.MXRecordIO(results_file, 'r')
protobuf = rec.ParseFromString(recordio.read())

shape = list(rec.features["shape"].int32_tensor.values)
values = list(rec.features["target"].float32_tensor.
values)

print(shape.shape)
print(values.shape)
```

The output is as follows:

```
[1, 21, 289, 337]
2045253
```

This tells us that the `values` tensor describes one image of size 289x337, where each pixel is assigned 21 probabilities, one for each of the Pascal VOC classes. You can check that 289*337*21=2,045,253.

11. Knowing that, we can now reshape the `values` tensor, retrieve the 21 probabilities for the (0,0) pixel, and print the class identifier with the highest probability:

```
mask = np.reshape(np.array(values), shape)
pixel_probs = mask[0,:,0,0]
print(pixel_probs)
print(np.argmax(pixel_probs))
```

Here is the output:

```
[9.68291104e-01 3.72813665e-04 8.14868137e-04
1.22414716e-03

 4.57380433e-04 9.95167647e-04 4.29908326e-03
7.52388616e-04

 1.46311778e-03 2.03254796e-03 9.60668200e-04
1.51833100e-03

 9.39570891e-04 1.49350625e-03 1.51627266e-03
3.63648031e-03

 2.17934581e-03 7.69103528e-04 3.05095245e-03
2.10589729e-03
```

```
   1.12741732e-03]
 0
```

The highest probability is at index 0: the predicted class for pixel (0,0) is class 0, the background class.

12. When we're done, we delete the endpoint as follows:

```
seg_predictor.delete_endpoint()
```

Summary

As you can see, these three algorithms make it easy to train CV models. Even with default hyperparameters, we get good results pretty quickly. Still, we start feeling the need to scale our training jobs. Don't worry: once the relevant features have been covered in future chapters, we'll revisit some of our CV examples and we'll scale them radically!

In this chapter, you learned about the image classification, object detection, and semantic segmentation algorithms. You also learned how to prepare datasets in image, RecordIO, and SageMaker Ground Truth formats. Labeling and preparing data is a critical step that takes a lot of work, and we covered it in great detail. Finally, you learned how to use the SageMaker SDK to train and deploy models with the three algorithms, as well as how to interpret results.

In the next chapter, you will learn how to use built-in algorithms for natural language processing.

6
Training Natural Language Processing Models

In the previous chapter, you learned how to use SageMaker's built-in algorithms for **Computer Vision (CV)** to solve problems including image classification, object detection, and semantic segmentation.

Natural Language Processing (NLP) is another very promising field in machine learning. Indeed, NLP algorithms have proven very effective in modeling language and extracting context from unstructured text. Thanks to this, applications such as search, translation, and chatbots are now commonplace.

In this chapter, you will learn about built-in algorithms designed specifically for NLP tasks. We'll discuss the types of problems that you can solve with them. As in the previous chapter, we'll also cover in great detail how to prepare real-life datasets such as Amazon customer reviews. Of course, we'll train and deploy models too. We will cover all of this under the following topics:

- Discovering the NLP algorithms in Amazon SageMaker

- Preparing natural language datasets

- Using the built-in CV algorithms of **BlazingText**, **Latent Dirichlet Allocation**, and **Neural Topic Model**

Technical requirements

You will need an AWS account to run the examples included in this chapter. If you haven't got one already, please point your browser to `https://aws.amazon.com/getting-started/` to create it. You should also familiarize yourself with the AWS Free Tier (`https://aws.amazon.com/free/`), which lets you use many AWS services for free within certain usage limits.

You will need to install and configure the AWS **Command-Line Interface (CLI)** for your account (`https://aws.amazon.com/cli/`).

You will need a working Python 3.x environment. Be careful to not use Python 2.7, as it is no longer maintained. Installing the Anaconda distribution (`https://www.anaconda.com/`) is not mandatory, but strongly encouraged, as it includes many projects that we will need (Jupyter, `pandas`, `numpy`, and more).

The code examples included in the book are available on GitHub at `https://github.com/PacktPublishing/Learn-Amazon-SageMaker`. You will need to install a Git client to access them (`https://git-scm.com/`).

Discovering the NLP built-in algorithms in Amazon SageMaker

SageMaker includes four NLP algorithms, enabling supervised and unsupervised learning scenarios. In this section, you'll learn about these algorithms, what kind of problems they solve, and what their training scenarios are:

- **BlazingText** builds text classification models (supervised learning) or computes word vectors (unsupervised learning). **BlazingText** is an Amazon-invented algorithm.

- **Latent Dirichlet Allocation** (**LDA**) builds unsupervised learning models that group a collection of text documents into topics. This technique is called **topic modeling**.

- **Neural Topic Model** (**NTM**) is another **topic modeling** algorithm based on neural networks, and it gives you more insight into how topics are built.

- **Sequence-to-sequence** (**seq2seq**) builds deep learning models predicting a sequence of output tokens from a sequence of input tokens.

Discovering the BlazingText algorithm

The BlazingText algorithm was invented by Amazon. You can read more about it at `https://www.researchgate.net/publication/320760204_BlazingText_Scaling_and_Accelerating_Word2Vec_using_Multiple_GPUs`. BlazingText is an evolution of **FastText**, a library for efficient text classification and representation learning developed by Facebook (`https://fasttext.cc`).

It lets you train text classification models, as well as compute **word vectors**. Also called **embeddings**, **word vectors** are the cornerstone of many NLP tasks, such as finding word similarities, word analogies, and so on. **Word2Vec** is one of the leading algorithms to compute these vectors (`https://arxiv.org/abs/1301.3781`), and it's the one BlazingText implements.

The main improvement of BlazingText is its ability to train on GPU instances, where as FastText only supports CPU instances.

The speed gain is significant, and this is where its name comes from: "blazing" is faster than "fast"! If you're curious about benchmarks, you'll certainly enjoy this blog post: `https://aws.amazon.com/blogs/machine-learning/amazon-sagemaker-blazingtext-parallelizing-word2vec-on-multiple-cpus-or-gpus/`.

Finally, BlazingText is fully compatible with FastText. Models can be very easily exported and tested, as you will see later in the chapter.

Discovering the LDA algorithm

This unsupervised learning algorithm uses a generative technique, named **topic modeling**, to identify topics present in a large collection of text documents. It was first applied to machine learning in 2003 (`http://jmlr.csail.mit.edu/papers/v3/blei03a.html`).

Please note that LDA is not a classification algorithm. You pass it the number of topics to build, not the list of topics you expect. To paraphrase Forrest Gump: *"Topic modeling is like a box of chocolates, you never know what you're gonna get."*

LDA assumes that every text document in the collection was generated from several latent (meaning "hidden") topics. A topic is represented by a word probability distribution. For each word present in the collection of documents, this distribution gives the probability that the word appears in documents generated by this topic. For example, in a "finance" topic, the distribution would yield high probabilities for words such as "revenue", "quarter", or "earnings", and low probabilities for "ballista" or "platypus" (or so I should think).

Topic distributions are not considered independently. They are represented by a **Dirichlet distribution**, a multivariate generalization of univariate distributions (`https://en.wikipedia.org/wiki/Dirichlet_distribution`). This mathematical object gives the algorithm its name.

Given the number of words in the vocabulary and the number of latent topics, the purpose of the LDA algorithm is to build a model that is as close as possible to an ideal Dirichlet distribution. In other words, it will try to group words so that distributions are as well formed as possible, and match the specified number of topics.

Training data needs to be carefully prepared. Each document needs to be converted to a **bag of words** representation: each word is replaced by a pair of integers, representing a unique word identifier and the word count in the document. The resulting dataset can be saved either to **CSV** format, or to **RecordIO-wrapped protobuf** format, a technique we already studied with **Factorization machines** in *Chapter 4, Training Machine Learning Models*.

Once the model has been trained, we can score any document, and get a score per topic. The expectation is that documents containing similar words should have similar scores, making it possible to identify their top topics.

Discovering the NTM algorithm

NTM is another algorithm for topic modeling. It was invented by Amazon, and you can read more about it at `https://arxiv.org/abs/1511.06038`. This blog post also sums up the key elements of the paper:

`https://aws.amazon.com/blogs/machine-learning/amazon-sagemaker-neural-topic-model-now-supports-auxiliary-vocabulary-channel-new-topic-evaluation-metrics-and-training-subsampling/`

As with LDA, documents need to be converted to a bag-of-words representation, and the dataset can be saved either to CSV or to RecordIO-wrapped protobuf format.

For training, NTM uses a completely different approach based on neural networks, and more precisely, on an encoder architecture (`https://en.wikipedia.org/wiki/Autoencoder`). In true deep learning fashion, the encoder trains on mini-batches of documents. It tries to learn their latent features by adjusting network parameters through backpropagation and optimization.

Unlike LDA, NTM can tell us which words are the most impactful in each topic. It also gives us two per-topic metrics, **Word Embedding Topic Coherence** and **Topic Uniqueness**:

- WETC tells us how semantically close the topic words are. This value is between 0 and 1, the higher the better. It's computed using the **cosine similarity** (`https://en.wikipedia.org/wiki/Cosine_similarity`) of the corresponding word vectors in a pretrained GloVe model (another algorithm similar to Word2Vec).
- TU tells us how unique the topic is, that is to say, whether its words are found in other topics or not. Again, the value is between 0 and 1, and the higher the score, the more unique the topic is.

Once the model has been trained, we can score documents, and get a score per topic.

Discovering the seq2seq algorithm

The **seq2seq** algorithm is based on **Long Short-Term Memory** (**LSTM**) neural networks (`https://arxiv.org/abs/1409.3215`). As its name implies, seq2seq can be trained to map one sequence of tokens to another. Its main application is machine translation, training on large bilingual corpuses of text, such as the **Workshop on Statistical Machine Translation** (**WMT**) datasets (`http://www.statmt.org/wmt20/`).

In addition to the implementation available in SageMaker, AWS has also packaged the **AWS Sockeye** (`https://github.com/awslabs/sockeye`) algorithm into an open source project, which also includes tools for dataset preparation.

I won't cover seq2seq in this chapter. It would take too many pages to get into the appropriate level of detail, and there's no point in just repeating what's already available in the Sockeye documentation.

You can find a seq2seq example in the notebook available at `https://github.com/ awslabs/amazon-sagemaker-examples/tree/master/introduction_to_ amazon_algorithms/seq2seq_translation_en-de`. Unfortunately, it uses the low-level `boto3` API – which we will cover in *Chapter 12, Automating Machine Learning Workflows*. Still, it's a valuable read, and you won't have much trouble figuring things out.

Training with NLP algorithms

Just like for CV algorithms, training is the easy part, especially with the SageMaker SDK. By now, you should be familiar with the workflow and the APIs, and we'll keep using them in this chapter.

Preparing data for NLP algorithms is another story. First, real-life datasets are generally pretty bulky. In this chapter, we'll work with millions of samples and hundreds of millions of words. Of course, they need to be cleaned, processed, and converted to the format expected by the algorithm.

As we go through the chapter, we'll use the following techniques:

- Loading and cleaning data with the `pandas` library (`https://pandas. pydata.org`)

- Removing stop words and lemmatizing with the **Natural Language Toolkit** (**NLTK**) library (`https://www.nltk.org`)

- Tokenizing with the `spacy` library (`https://spacy.io/`)

- Building vocabularies and generating bag-of-words representations with the `gensim` library (`https://radimrehurek.com/gensim/`)

- Running data processing jobs with **Amazon SageMaker Processing**, which we studied in *Chapter 2, Handling Data Preparation Techniques*

Granted, this isn't an NLP book, and we won't go extremely far into processing data. Still, this will be quite fun, and hopefully an opportunity to learn about popular open source tools for NLP.

Preparing natural language datasets

For the CV algorithms in the previous chapter, data preparation focused on the technical format required for the dataset (**Image** format, **RecordIO**, or **augmented manifest**). The images themselves weren't processed.

Things are quite different for NLP algorithms. Text needs to be heavily processed, converted, and saved in the right format. In most learning resources, these steps are abbreviated or even ignored. Data is already "automagically" ready for training, leaving the reader frustrated and sometimes dumbfounded on how to prepare their own datasets.

No such thing here! In this section, you'll learn how to prepare NLP datasets in different formats. Once again, get ready to learn a lot!

Let's start with preparing data for BlazingText.

Preparing data for classification with BlazingText

BlazingText expects labeled input data in the same format as FastText:

- A plain text file, with one sample per line.
- Each line has two fields:

   a) A label in the form of `__label__LABELNAME__`

   b) The text itself, formed into space-separated tokens (words and punctuations)

Let's get to work and prepare a customer review dataset for sentiment analysis (positive, neutral, or negative). We'll use the **Amazon Reviews** dataset available at `https://s3.amazonaws.com/amazon-reviews-pds/readme.html`. That should be more than enough real-life data.

Before starting, please make sure that you have enough storage space. Here, I'm using a notebook instance with 10 GB of storage. I've also picked a C5 instance type to run processing steps faster:

1. Let's download the camera reviews:

```
%%sh
aws s3 cp s3://amazon-reviews-pds/tsv/amazon_reviews_us_
Camera_v1_00.tsv.gz /tmp
```

2. We load the data with `pandas`, ignoring any line that causes an error. We also drop any line with missing values:

```
data = pd.read_csv(
    '/tmp/amazon_reviews_us_Camera_v1_00.tsv.gz',
    sep='\t', compression='gzip',
    error_bad_lines=False, dtype='str')
data.dropna(inplace=True)
```

3. We print the data shape and the column names:

```
print(data.shape)
print(data.columns)
```

This gives us the following output:

```
(1800755, 15)
Index(['marketplace','customer_id','review_id','product_
id','product_parent', 'product_title','product_category',
'star_rating','helpful_votes','total_votes','vine',
'verified_purchase','review_headline','review_body',
'review_date'], dtype='object')
```

4. 1.8 million lines! We keep 100,000, which is enough for our purpose. We also drop all columns except `star_rating` and `review_body`:

```
data = data[:100000]
data = data[['star_rating', 'review_body']]
```

5. Based on star ratings, we add a new column named `label`, with labels in the proper format. You have to love how `pandas` makes this so simple. Then, we drop the `star_rating` column:

```
data['label'] = data.star_rating.map({
    '1': '__label__negative__',
    '2': '__label__negative__',
    '3': '__label__neutral__',
    '4': '__label__positive__',
    '5': '__label__positive__'})
data = data.drop(['star_rating'], axis=1)
```

6. BlazingText expect labels at the beginning of each line, so we move the label column to the front:

```
data = data[['label', 'review_body']]
```

7. Data should now look like in the following figure:

	label	review_body
0	__label__positive__	ok
1	__label__positive__	Perfect, even sturdier than the original!
2	__label__negative__	If the words, "Cheap Chinese Junk" com...
3	__label__positive__	Exactly what I wanted and expected. Perfect fo...
4	__label__positive__	I will look past the fact that they tricked me...

Figure 6.1 – Viewing the dataset

8. BlazingText expects space-separated tokens: each word and each punctuation sign must be space-separated from the next. Let's use the handy `punkt` tokenizer from the `nltk` library. Depending on the instance type you're using, this could take a couple of minutes:

```
!pip -q install nltk

import nltk
nltk.download('punkt')
data['review_body'] = data['review_body'].apply(nltk.
word_tokenize)
```

9. We join tokens into a single string, which we also convert to lower case:

```
data['review_body'] =
data.apply(lambda row: " ".join(row['review_body']).
lower(), axis=1)
```

10. The data should now look like that in the following figure. Notice that all the tokens are correctly space-separated:

	label	review_body
0	__label__positive__	ok
1	__label__positive__	perfect , even sturdier than the original !
2	__label__negative__	if the words , & # 34 ; cheap chinese junk & #...
3	__label__positive__	exactly what i wanted and expected . perfect f...
4	__label__positive__	i will look past the fact that they tricked me...

Figure 6.2 – Viewing the tokenized dataset

11. Finally, we split the dataset for training (95%) and validation (5%), and we save both splits as plain text files:

```
from sklearn.model_selection import train_test_split
training, validation = train_test_split(data, test_
size=0.05)
np.savetxt('/tmp/training.txt', training.values,
fmt='%s')
np.savetxt('/tmp/validation.txt', validation.values,
fmt='%s')
```

12. If you open one of the files, you should see plenty of lines similar to this one:

```
__label__neutral__ really works for me , especially on
the streets of europe . wished it was less expensive
though . the rain cover at the base really works . the
padding which comes in contact with your back though will
suffocate & make your back sweaty .
```

Data preparation wasn't too bad, was it? Still, tokenization ran for a minute or two. Now, imagine running it on millions of samples. Sure, you could fire up a larger **Notebook instance** or use a larger environment in **SageMaker Studio**. You'd also pay more for as long as you're using it, which would probably be wasteful if only this one step required that extra computing muscle. In addition, imagine having to run the same script on many other datasets. Do you want to do this manually again and again, waiting 20 minutes every time and hoping Jupyter doesn't crash? Certainly not, I should think!

You already know the answer to both problems. It's **Amazon SageMaker Processing**, which we studied in *Chapter 2, Handling Data Preparation Techniques*. You should have the best of both worlds, using the smallest and least expensive environment possible for experimentation, and running on-demand jobs when you need more resources. Day in, day out, you'll save money and get the job done faster.

Let's move this processing code to SageMaker Processing.

Preparing data for classification with BlazingText, version 2

We've covered this in detail in *Chapter 2, Handling Data Preparation Techniques*, so I'll go faster this time:

1. We upload the dataset to S3:

```
import sagemaker

session = sagemaker.Session()
prefix = 'amazon-reviews-camera'

input_data = session.upload_data(
    path='/tmp/amazon_reviews_us_Camera_v1_00.tsv.gz',
    key_prefix=prefix)
```

2. We define the processor:

```
from sagemaker.sklearn.processing import SKLearnProcessor

sklearn_processor = SKLearnProcessor(
    framework_version='0.20.0',
    role= sagemaker.get_execution_role(),
    instance_type='ml.c5.2xlarge',
    instance_count=1)
```

3. We run the processing job, passing the processing script and its arguments:

```
from sagemaker.processing import ProcessingInput,
ProcessingOutput

sklearn_processor.run(
    code='preprocessing.py',
    inputs=[
        ProcessingInput(
            source=input_data,
            destination='/opt/ml/processing/input')
    ],
```

```
        outputs=[
            ProcessingOutput(
                output_name='train_data',
                source='/opt/ml/processing/train'),
            ProcessingOutput(
                output_name='validation_data',
                source='/opt/ml/processing/validation')
        ],
        arguments=[
            '--filename',
                'amazon_reviews_us_Camera_v1_00.tsv.gz',
            '--num-reviews', '100000',
            '--split-ratio', '0.05'
        ]
    )
```

4. The abbreviated preprocessing script is as follows. The full version is in the GitHub repository for the book. We first install the `nltk` package:

```
import argparse, os, subprocess, sys
import pandas as pd
import numpy as np
from sklearn.model_selection import train_test_split
def install(package):
    subprocess.call([sys.executable, "-m", "pip",
                     "install", package])
if __name__=='__main__':
    install('nltk')
    import nltk
```

5. We read the command-line arguments:

```
parser = argparse.ArgumentParser()
parser.add_argument('--filename', type=str)
parser.add_argument('--num-reviews', type=int)
parser.add_argument('--split-ratio', type=float,
                    default=0.1)
args, _ = parser.parse_known_args()
filename = args.filename
num_reviews = args.num_reviews
split_ratio = args.split_ratio
```

6. We read the input dataset and process it as follows:

```
input_data_path =
os.path.join('/opt/ml/processing/input', filename)

data = pd.read_csv(input_data_path, sep='\t',
        compression='gzip', error_bad_lines=False,
        dtype='str')

# Process data
. . .
```

7. Finally, we split it for training and validation, and save it to two text files:

```
training, validation = train_test_split(
                       data, test_size=split_ratio)

training_output_path = os.path.join('
                       /opt/ml/processing/train',
                       'training.txt')

validation_output_path = os.path.join(
                       /opt/ml/processing/validation',
                       'validation. txt')

np.savetxt(training_output_path,
        training.values, fmt='%s')

np.savetxt(validation_output_path,
        validation.values, fmt='%s')
```

As you can see, it doesn't take much to convert manual processing code to a SageMaker Processing job. You can actually reuse most of the code too, as it deals with generic topics such as command-line arguments, inputs, and outputs. The only trick is using `subprocess.call` to install dependencies inside the processing container.

Equipped with this script, you can now process data at scale as often as you want, without having to run and manage long-lasting notebooks.

Now, let's prepare data for the other BlazingText scenario: word vectors!

Preparing data for word vectors with BlazingText

BlazingText lets you compute word vectors easily and at scale. It expects input data in the following format:

- A plain text file, with one sample per line.

- Each sample must have space-separated tokens (words and punctuations).

Let's process the same dataset as in the previous section:

1. We'll need the `spacy` library, so let's install it along with its English language model:

```
%%sh
pip -q install spacy
python -m spacy download en
```

2. We load the data with `pandas`, ignoring any line that causes an error. We also drop any line with missing values. We should have more than enough data anyway:

```
data = pd.read_csv(
    '/tmp/amazon_reviews_us_Camera_v1_00.tsv.gz',
    sep='\t', compression='gzip',
    error_bad_lines=False, dtype='str')
data.dropna(inplace=True)
```

3. We keep 100,000 lines, and we also drop all columns except `review_body`:

```
data = data[:100000]
data = data[['review_body']]
```

We write a function to tokenize reviews with `spacy`, and we apply it to the `DataFrame`. This step should be noticeably faster than `nltk` tokenization in the previous example, as `spacy` is based on `Cython` (`https://cython.org`):

```
import spacy
spacy_nlp = spacy.load('en')
def tokenize(text):
    tokens = spacy_nlp.tokenizer(text)
    tokens = [ t.text for t in tokens ]
    return " ".join(tokens).lower()
data['review_body'] = data['review_body'].apply(tokenize)
```

4. The data should now look like that in the following figure:

	review_body
0	ok
1	perfect , even sturdier than the original !
2	if the words , & # 34;cheap chinese junk&#34 ;...
3	exactly what i wanted and expected . perfect f...
4	i will look past the fact that they tricked me...

Figure 6.3 – Viewing the tokenized dataset

5. Finally, we save the reviews to a plain text file:

```
import numpy as np
np.savetxt('/tmp/training.txt', data.values, fmt='%s')
```

6. Opening this file, you should see one tokenized review per line:

```
Ok
perfect , even sturdier than the original !
```

Here too, we should really be running these steps using SageMaker Processing. You'll find the corresponding notebook and preprocessing script in the GitHub repository for the book.

Now, let's prepare data for the LDA and NTM algorithms.

Preparing data for topic modeling with LDA and NTM

In this example, we will use the **Million News Headlines** dataset (https://doi.org/10.7910/DVN/SYBGZL), which is also available in the GitHub repository. As the name implies, it contains a million news headlines from Australian news source ABC. Unlike product reviews, headlines are very short sentences. Building a topic model should be an interesting challenge!

Tokenizing data

As you would expect, both algorithms require a tokenized dataset:

1. We'll need the `nltk` and the `gensim` libraries, so let's install them:

```
%%sh
pip -q install nltk gensim
```

2. Once we've downloaded the dataset, we load it entirely with `pandas`:

```
num_lines = 1000000

data = pd.read_csv('abcnews-date-text.csv.gz',
                   compression='gzip',
                   error_bad_lines=False,
                   dtype='str', nrows=num_lines)
```

3. The data should look like that in the following figure:

	publish_date	headline_text
0	20030219	aba decides against community broadcasting lic...
1	20030219	act fire witnesses must be aware of defamation
2	20030219	a g calls for infrastructure protection summit
3	20030219	air nz staff in aust strike for pay rise
4	20030219	air nz strike to affect australian travellers

Figure 6.4 – Viewing the tokenized dataset

4. It's sorted by date, and we shuffle it as a precaution. We then drop the date column:

```
data = data.sample(frac=1)
data = data.drop(['publish_date'], axis=1)
```

5. We write a function to clean up and process the headlines. First, we get rid of all punctuation signs and digits. Using `nltk`, we also remove stop words, namely words that are extremely common and don't add any context, such as `this`, `any`, and so on. In order to reduce the vocabulary size while keeping the context, we could apply either **stemming** or **lemmatisation**, two popular NLP techniques (https://nlp.stanford.edu/IR-book/html/htmledition/stemming-and-lemmatization-1.html).

Let's go with the latter here. Depending on your instance type, this could run for several minutes:

```
import string
import nltk
from nltk.corpus import stopwords
#from nltk.stem.snowball import SnowballStemmer
from nltk.stem import WordNetLemmatizer

nltk.download('stopwords')
stop_words = stopwords.words('english')

#stemmer = SnowballStemmer("english")
wnl = WordNetLemmatizer()

def process_text(text):
    for p in string.punctuation:
        text = text.replace(p, '')
        text = ''.join([c for c in text if not
                        c.isdigit()])
        text = text.lower().split()
        text = [w for w in text if not w in stop_words]
        #text = [stemmer.stem(w) for w in text]
        text = [wnl.lemmatize(w) for w in text]
        return text
data['headline_text'] = data['headline_text'].
apply(process_text)
```

6. Once processed, the data should look like that in the following figure:

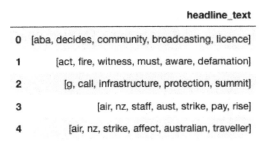

	headline_text
0	[aba, decides, community, broadcasting, licence]
1	[act, fire, witness, must, aware, defamation]
2	[g, call, infrastructure, protection, summit]
3	[air, nz, staff, aust, strike, pay, rise]
4	[air, nz, strike, affect, australian, traveller]

Figure 6.5 – Viewing the lemmatized dataset

Now that reviews have been tokenized, we need to convert them to a bag-of-words representation, replacing each word with a unique integer identifier and its frequency count.

Converting data to bag of words

We will convert the reviews into a bag of words using the following steps:

1. The `gensim` library has exactly what we need! We build a **dictionary**, the list of all words present in the document collection:

```
from gensim import corpora
dictionary = corpora.Dictionary(data['headline_text'])
print(dictionary)
```

The dictionary looks like this:

```
Dictionary(83131 unique tokens: ['aba', 'broadcasting',
'community', 'decides', 'licence']...)
```

This number feels very high. If we have too many dimensions, training will be very long, and the algorithm may have trouble fitting the data. For example, NTM is based on a neural network architecture. The input layer will be sized based on the number of tokens, so we need to keep them reasonably low. It will speed up training, and help the encoder learn a manageable number of latent features.

2. We could go back and clean headlines some more. Instead, we use a `gensim` function that removes extreme words, outlier words that are either extremely rare or extremely frequent. Then, taking a bold bet, we decide to restrict the vocabulary to the top 512 remaining words. Yes, that's less than 1%:

```
dictionary.filter_extremes(keep_n=512)
```

3. We write the vocabulary to a text file. Not only does this help us check what the top words are, but we'll also pass this file to the NTM algorithm as an extra **channel**. You'll see why this is important when we train the model:

```
with open('vocab.txt', 'w') as f:
    for index in range(0,len(dictionary)):
        f.write(dictionary.get(index)+'\n')
```

4. We use the dictionary to build a bag of words for each headline. It's stored in a new column called `tokens`. When we're done, we drop the text review:

```
data['tokens'] = data.apply(lambda row: dictionary.
doc2bow(row['headline_text']), axis=1)
data = data.drop(['headline_text'], axis=1)
```

5. The data should now look like that in the following figure:

	tokens
774398	[(0, 1), (1, 1), (2, 1), (3, 1), (4, 1)]
189893	[(5, 1), (6, 1), (7, 1)]
628809	[(8, 1), (9, 1)]
693184	[(10, 1)]
31959	[(11, 1), (12, 1), (13, 1), (14, 1), (15, 1)]

Figure 6.6 – Viewing the bag-of-words dataset

As you can see, each word has been replaced with its unique identifier and its frequency count in the review. For instance, the last line tells us that word #11 is present once, word #12 is present once, and so on.

Data processing is now complete. The last step is to save it to the appropriate input format.

Saving input data

NTM and LDA expect data in either the CSV format, or the RecordIO-wrapped protobuf format. Just like for the **Factorization matrix** example in *Chapter 4, Training Machine Learning Models*, the data we're working with is quite sparse. Any given review only contains a small number of words from the vocabulary. As CSV is a dense format, we would end up with a huge amount of zero-frequency words. Not a good idea!

Once again, we'll use `lil_matrix`, a **sparse matrix** object available in `SciPy`. It will have as many lines as we have reviews and as many columns as we have words in the dictionary:

1. We create the sparse matrix as follows:

```
from scipy.sparse import lil_matrix
num_lines = data.shape[0]
num_columns = len(dictionary)
token_matrix = lil_matrix((num_lines,num_columns))
                    .astype('float32')
```

2. We write a function to add a headline to the matrix. For each token, we simply write its frequency in the appropriate column:

```
def add_row_to_matrix(line, row):
    for token_id, token_count in row['tokens']:
        token_matrix[line, token_id] = token_count
    return
```

3. We then iterate over headlines and add them to the matrix. Quick note: we can't use row index values, as they might be larger than the number of lines:

```
line = 0
for _, row in data.iterrows():
    add_row_to_matrix(line, row)
    line+=1
```

4. The last step is to write this matrix into a memory buffer in `protobuf` format and upload it to S3 for future use:

```
import io, boto3
import sagemaker
import sagemaker.amazon.common as smac

buf = io.BytesIO()
smac.write_spmatrix_to_sparse_tensor(buf, token_matrix,
None)
buf.seek(0)

bucket = sagemaker.Session().default_bucket()
prefix = 'headlines-lda-ntm'
train_key = 'reviews.protobuf'
obj = '{}/{}'.format(prefix, train_key))

s3 = boto3.resource('s3')
s3.Bucket(bucket).Object(obj).upload_fileobj(buf)
s3_train_path = 's3://{}/{}'.format(bucket,obj)
```

5. Building the (1000000, 512) matrix takes a few minutes. Once it's been uploaded to S3, we can see that it's only 42 MB. Lil' matrix indeed:

```
$ aws s3 ls s3://sagemaker-eu-west-1-123456789012/amazon-
reviews-ntm/training.protobuf
43884300 training.protobuf
```

This concludes data preparation for LDA and NTM. Now, let's see how we can use text datasets prepared with **SageMaker Ground Truth**.

Using datasets labeled with SageMaker Ground Truth

As discussed in *Chapter 2, Handling Data Preparation Techniques*, SageMaker Ground Truth supports text classification tasks. We could definitely use their output to build a dataset for FastText or BlazingText.

First, I ran a quick text classification job on a few sentences, applying one of two labels: "aws_service" if the sentence mentions an AWS service, "no_aws_service" if it doesn't.

Once the job is complete, I can fetch the **augmented manifest** from S3. It's in **JSON Lines** format, and here's one of its entries:

```
{"source":"With great power come great responsibility. The
second you create AWS resources, you're responsible for them:
security of course, but also cost and scaling. This makes
monitoring and alerting all the more important, which is
why we built services like Amazon CloudWatch, AWS Config and
AWS Systems Manager.","my-text-classification-job":0,"my-
text-classification-job-metadata":{"confidence":0.84,"
job-name":"labeling-job/my-text-classification-job","class-
name":"aws_service","human-annotated":"yes","creation-
date":"2020-05-11T12:44:50.620065","type":"groundtruth/text-
classification"}}
```

Shall we write a bit of Python code to put this in BlazingText format? Of course!

1. We load the augmented manifest directly from S3:

```
import pandas as pd

bucket = 'sagemaker-book'
prefix = 'chapter2/classif/output/my-text-classification-
job/manifests/output'
manifest = 's3://{}/{}/output.manifest'.format(bucket,
prefix)

data = pd.read_json(manifest, lines=True)
```

The data looks like that in the following figure:

my-text-classification-job	my-text-classification-job-metadata	source
0	0 {'confidence': 0.84, 'job-name': 'labeling-job...	Since 2006, Amazon Web Services has been striv...
1	0 {'confidence': 0.84, 'job-name': 'labeling-job...	With great power come great responsibility. Th...
2	1 {'confidence': 0.56, 'job-name': 'labeling-job...	Still, customers told us that their operations...
3	0 {'confidence': 0.84, 'job-name': 'labeling-job...	We got to work, and today we're very happy to ...

Figure 6.7 – Viewing the labeled dataset

2. The label is buried in the "`my-text-classification-job-metadata`" column. We extract it into a new column:

```
def get_label(metadata):
    return metadata['class-name']
data['label'] =
data['my-text-classification-job-metadata'].apply(get_
label)
data = data[['label', 'source']]
```

The data now looks like that in the following figure. From then on, we can apply tokenization, and so on. That was easy, wasn't it?

	label	source
0	aws_service	Since 2006, Amazon Web Services has been striv...
1	aws_service	With great power come great responsibility. Th...
2	no_aws_service	Still, customers told us that their operations...
3	aws_service	We got to work, and today we're very happy to ...

Figure 6.8 – Viewing the processed dataset

Now let's build NLP models!

Using the built-in algorithms for NLP

In this section, we're going to train and deploy models with BlazingText, LDA, and NTM. Of course, we'll use the datasets prepared in the previous section.

Classifying text with BlazingText

BlazingText makes it extremely easy to build a text classification model, especially if you have no NLP skills. Let's see how:

1. We upload the training and validation datasets to S3. Alternatively, we could use the output paths returned by a SageMaker Processing job:

```
import boto3, sagemaker
session = sagemaker.Session()
bucket = session.default_bucket()
prefix = 'amazon-reviews'
s3_train_path = session.upload_data(path='/tmp/training.
txt', bucket=bucket, key_prefix=prefix+'/input/train')
```

```
s3_val_path = session.upload_data(path='/tmp/validation.
txt', bucket=bucket, key_prefix=prefix+'/input/
validation')
```

```
s3_output = 's3://{}/{}/output/'.format(bucket, prefix)
```

2. We configure the `Estimator` function for BlazingText:

```
from sagemaker import image_uris

region_name = boto3.Session().region_name
container = image_uris.retrieve('blazingtext', region)
```

```
bt = sagemaker.estimator.Estimator(container,
    sagemaker.get_execution_role(),
    instance_count=1,
    instance_type='ml.g4dn.xlarge',
    output_path=s3_output)
```

3. We set a single hyperparameter, telling BlazingText to train in supervised mode:

```
bt.set_hyperparameters(mode='supervised')
```

4. We define channels, setting the content type to `text/plain`, and then we launch the training:

```
from sagemaker import TrainingInput
```

```
train_data = TrainingInput (s3_train_path,
distribution='FullyReplicated', content_type='text/
plain', s3_data_type='S3Prefix')
```

```
validation_data = TrainingInput (s3_val_path,
distribution='FullyReplicated', content_type='text/
plain',
s3_data_type='S3Prefix')
```

```
s3_channels = {'train': train_data,
               'validation': validation_data}
```

```
bt.fit(inputs=s3_channels)
```

5. We get a validation accuracy close to 88%, which is quite good in the absence of any hyperparameter tweaking. We then deploy the model to a small CPU instance:

```
bt_predictor = bt.deploy(initial_instance_count=1,
                         instance_type='ml.t2.medium')
```

6. Once the endpoint is up, we send three tokenized samples for prediction, asking for all three labels:

```
import json

sentences = ['This is a bad camera it doesnt work at all
, i want a refund  . ' , 'The camera works , the pictures
are decent quality, nothing special to say about it . ' ,
'Very happy to have bought this , exactly what I needed .
']

payload = {"instances":sentences, "configuration":{"k":
3}}

bt_predictor.content_type = 'application/json'

response = bt_predictor.predict(json.dumps(payload))
```

7. Printing the response, we see that the three samples were correctly categorized. It's interesting to see that the second review is neutral/positive. Indeed, it doesn't include any negative words:

```
[{'prob': [0.9758228063583374, 0.023583529517054558,
0.0006236258195713162], 'label': ['__label__negative__',
'__label__neutral__', '__label__positive__']},
{'prob': [0.5177792906761169, 0.2864232063293457,
0.19582746922969818], 'label': ['__label__neutral__', '__
label__positive__', '__label__negative__']},
{'prob': [0.9997835755348206, 0.000205090589588508,
4.133415131946094e-05], 'label': ['__label__positive__',
'__label__neutral__', '__label__negative__']}]
```

8. As usual, we delete the endpoint once we're done:

```
bt_predictor.delete_endpoint()
```

Now, let's train BlazingText to compute word vectors.

Computing word vectors with BlazingText

The code is almost identical to the previous example, with only two differences. First, there is only one channel, containing training data. Second, we need to set BlazingText to unsupervised learning mode.

BlazingText supports the training modes implemented in Word2Vec: **skipgram** and **continuous bag of words (cbow)**. It adds a third mode, **batch_skipgram**, for faster distributed training. It also supports **subword embeddings**, a technique that makes it possible to return a word vector for words that are misspelled or not part of the vocabulary.

Let's go for skipgram with subword embeddings. We leave the dimension of vectors unchanged (the default is 100):

```
bt.set_hyperparameters(mode='skipgram', subwords=True)
```

Unlike other algorithms, there is nothing to deploy here. The model artifact is in S3 and can be used for downstream NLP applications.

Speaking of which, BlazingText is compatible with FastText, so how about trying to load the models we just trained in FastText?

Using BlazingText models with FastText

First, we need to compile FastText, which is extremely simple. You can even do it on a Notebook instance without having to install anything:

```
$ git clone https://github.com/facebookresearch/fastText.git
$ cd fastText
$ make
```

Let's first try our classification model.

Using a BlazingText classification model with FastText

We will try the model using the following steps:

1. We copy the model artifact from S3 and extract it as follows:

    ```
    $ aws s3 ls s3://sagemaker-eu-west-1-123456789012/amazon-
    reviews/output/JOB_NAME/output/model.tar.gz .
    $ tar xvfz model.tar.gz
    ```

2. We load model.bin with FastText:

    ```
    $ fasttext predict model.bin -
    ```

3. We predict samples and view their top class as follows:

```
This is a bad camera it doesnt work at all , i want a
refund  .
__label__negative__

The camera works , the pictures are decent quality,
nothing special to say about it .
__label__neutral__

Very happy to have bought this , exactly what I needed
__label__positive__
```

We exit with *Ctrl + C*. Now, let's explore our vectors.

Using BlazingText word vectors with FastText

We will now use FastText with the vectors as follows:

1. We copy the model artifact from S3, and we extract it:

```
$ aws s3 ls s3://sagemaker-eu-west-1-123456789012/amazon-
reviews-word2vec/output/JOB_NAME/output/model.tar.gz .
$ tar xvfz model.tar.gz
```

2. We can explore word similarities. For example, let's look for words that are closest to `telephoto`. This could help us improve how we handle search queries or how we recommend similar products:

```
$ fasttext nn vectors.bin
Query word? Telephoto
telephotos 0.951023
75-300mm 0.79659
55-300mm 0.788019
18-300mm 0.782396
. . .
```

3. We can also look for analogies. For example, let's ask our model the following question: what's the Canon equivalent for the Nikon D3300 camera?

```
$ fasttext analogies vectors.bin
Query triplet (A - B + C)? nikon d3300 canon
xsi 0.748873
700d 0.744358
100d 0.735871
```

According to our model, you should consider the XSI and 700d cameras!

As you can see, word vectors are amazing and BlazingText makes it easy to compute them at any scale. Now, let's move on to topic modeling, another fascinating subject.

Modeling topics with LDA

In a previous section, we prepared a million news headlines, and we're now going to use them for topic modeling with LDA:

1. By loading the process from the dataset in S3, we define the useful paths:

```
import sagemaker

session = sagemaker.Session()
bucket = session.default_bucket()
prefix = reviews-lda-ntm'
train_key = 'reviews.protobuf'

obj = '{}/{}'.format(prefix, train_key)
s3_train_path = 's3://{}/{}'.format(bucket,obj)
s3_output = 's3://{}/{}/output/'.format(bucket, prefix)
```

2. We configure the `Estimator` function:

```
from sagemaker import image_uris

region_name = boto3.Session().region_name
container = image_uris.retrieve('lda', region)


lda = sagemaker.estimator.Estimator(container,
        role = sagemaker.get_execution_role(),
        instance_count=1,
        instance_type='ml.c5.2xlarge',
        output_path=s3_output)
```

3. We set hyperparameters: how many topics we want to build (10), how many dimensions the problem has (the vocabulary size), and how many samples we're training on. Optionally, we can set a parameter named `alpha0`. According to the documentation: "*Small values are more likely to generate sparse topic mixtures and large values (greater than 1.0) produce more uniform mixtures*". Let's set it to 0.1 and hope that the algorithm can indeed build well-identified topics:

```
lda.set_hyperparameters(num_topics=5,
    feature_dim=len(dictionary),
    mini_batch_size=num_lines,
    alpha0=0.1)
```

4. We launch training. As RecordIO is the default format expected by the algorithm, we don't need to define channels:

```
lda.fit(inputs={'train': s3_train_path})
```

5. Once training is complete, we deploy to a small CPU instance:

```
lda_predictor = lda.deploy(initial_instance_count=1,
                           instance_type='ml.t2.medium')
```

6. Before we send samples for prediction, we need to process them just like we processed the training set. We write a function that takes care of this: building a sparse matrix, filling it with bags of words, and saving to an in-memory protobuf buffer:

```
def process_samples(samples, dictionary):
    num_lines = len(samples)
    num_columns = len(dictionary)
    sample_matrix = lil_matrix((num_lines,
                     num_columns)).astype('float32')

    for line in range(0, num_lines):
        s = samples[line]
        s = process_text(s)
        s = dictionary.doc2bow(s)
        for token_id, token_count in s:
            sample_matrix[line, token_id] = token_count
        line+=1

    buf = io.BytesIO()
    smac.write_spmatrix_to_sparse_tensor(buf,
                                         sample_matrix,
                                         None)
    buf.seek(0)
    return buf
```

Please note that we need the dictionary here. This is why the corresponding SageMaker Processing job saved a pickled version of it, which we could later unpickle and use.

7. Then, we define a Python array containing five headlines, named `samples`. These are real headlines I copied from the ABC news website at `https://www.abc.net.au/news/`:

```
samples = [ "Major tariffs expected to end Australian
barley trade to China", "Satellite imagery sparks more
speculation on North Korean leader Kim Jong-un", "Fifty
trains out of service as fault forces Adelaide passengers
to 'pack like sardines", "Germany's Bundesliga plans its
return from lockdown as football world watches", "All AFL
players to face COVID-19 testing before training resumes"
]
```

8. Let's process and predict them:

```
lda_predictor.content_type = 'application/x-recordio-
protobuf'
```

```
response = lda_predictor.predict(
          process_samples(samples, dictionary))
print(response)
```

9. The response contains a score vector for each review (extra decimals have been removed for brevity). Each vector reflects a mix of topics, with a score per topic. All scores add up to 1:

```
{'predictions': [
{'topic_mixture': [0,0.22,0.54,0.23,0,0,0,0,0,0]},
{'topic_mixture': [0.51,0.49,0,0,0,0,0,0,0,0]}, {'topic_
mixture': [0.38,0,0.22,0,0.40,0,0,0,0,0]}, {'topic_
mixture': [0.38,0.62,0,0,0,0,0,0,0,0]}, {'topic_mixture':
[0,0.75,0,0,0,0,0,0.25,0,0]}]}
```

10. This isn't easy to read. Let's print the top topic and its score:

```
import numpy as np
```

```
vecs = [r['topic_mixture'] for r in
response['predictions']]
```

```
for v in vecs:
    top_topic = np.argmax(v)
    print("topic %s, %2.2f" % (top_topic, v[top_topic]))
```

This prints out the following result:

```
topic 2, 0.54
topic 0, 0.51
topic 4, 0.40
topic 1, 0.62
topic 1, 0.75
```

11. As usual, we delete the endpoint once we're done:

```
lda_predictor.delete_endpoint()
```

Interpreting LDA results is not easy, so let's be careful here. No wishful thinking!

- We see that each headline has a definite topic, which is good news. Apparently, LDA was able to identify solid topics, maybe thanks to the low `alpha0` value.

- The top topics for unrelated headlines are different, which is promising.

- The last two headlines are both about sports and their top topic is the same, which is another good sign.

- All five reviews scored zero on topics 5, 6, 8, and 9. This probably means that other topics have been built, and we would need to run more examples to discover them.

Is this a successful model? Probably. Can we be confident that topic 0 is about world affairs, topic 1 about sports, and topic 2 about commerce? Not until we've predicted a few thousand more reviews and checked that related headlines are assigned to the same topic.

As mentioned at the beginning of the chapter, LDA is not a classification algorithm. It has a mind of its own and it may build totally unexpected topics. Maybe it will group headlines according to sentiment or city names. It all depends on the distribution of these words inside the document collection.

Wouldn't it be nice if we could see which words "weigh" more in a certain topic? That would certainly help us understand topics a little better. Enter NTM!

Modeling topics with NTM

This example is very similar to the previous one. We'll just highlight the differences, and you'll find a full example in the GitHub repository for the book. Let's get into it:

1. We upload the **vocabulary file** to S3:

```
s3_auxiliary_path = session.upload_data(path='vocab.txt',
key_prefix=prefix + '/input/auxiliary')
```

2. We select the NTM algorithm:

```
from sagemaker import image_uris
region_name = boto3.Session().region_name
container = image_uris.retrieve('ntm', region)
```

3. Once we've configured the `Estimator`, we set the hyperparameters:

```
ntm.set_hyperparameters(num_topics=10,
                        feature_dim=len(dictionary),
                        optimizer='adam',
                        mini_batch_size=256,
                        num_patience_epochs=10)
```

4. We launch training, passing the vocabulary file in the `auxiliary` channel:

```
ntm.fit(inputs={'train': s3_training_path,
                'auxiliary': s3_auxiliary_path})
```

When training is complete, we see plenty of information in the training log. First, we see the average WETC and TU scores for the 10 topics:

```
(num_topics:10) [wetc 0.42, tu 0.86]
```

These are decent results. Topic unicity is high, and the semantic distance between topic words is average.

For each topic, we see its WETC and TU scores, as well as its top words, that is to say, the words that have the highest probability of appearing in documents associated with this topic.

- Let's look at each one in detail and try to put names to topics:

- Topic 0 is pretty obvious, I think. Almost all words are related to crime, so let's call it `crime`:

```
[0.51, 0.84] stabbing charged guilty pleads murder fatal
man assault bail jailed alleged shooting arrested teen
girl accused boy car found crash
```

- The following topic, topic 1, is a little fuzzier. How about `legal`?

```
[0.36, 0.85] seeker asylum climate live front hears
change export carbon tax court wind challenge told
accused rule legal face stand boat
```

- Topic 2 is about accidents and fires. Let's call it `disaster`:

```
[0.39, 0.78] seeker crew hour asylum cause damage truck
country firefighter blaze crash warning ta plane near
highway accident one fire fatal
```

- Topic 3 is obvious: `sports`. The TU score is the highest, showing that sports articles use a very specific vocabulary found nowhere else:

```
[0.54, 0.93] cup world v league one match win title final
star live victory england day nrl miss beat team afl
player
```

- Topic 4 is a strange mix of weather information and natural resources. It has the lowest WETC and the lowest TU scores too. Let's call it `unknown1`:

```
[0.35, 0.77] coast korea gold north east central pleads
west south guilty queensland found qld rain beach cyclone
northern nuclear crop mine
```

- Topic 5 is about world affairs, it seems. Let's call it `international`:

```
[0.38, 0.88] iraq troop bomb trade korea nuclear kill
soldier iraqi blast pm president china pakistan howard
visit pacific u abc anti
```

- Topic 6 feels like local news, as it contains abbreviations for Australian regions: `qld` is Queensland, `ta` is Tasmania, `nsw` is New South Wales, and so on. Let's call it `local`:

```
[0.25, 0.88] news hour country rural national abc ta
sport vic abuse sa nsw weather nt club qld award business
```

- Topic 7 is a no-brainer: `finance`. It has the highest WETC score, showing that its words are closely related from a semantic point of view. Topic unicity is also very high, and we would probably see the same for domain-specific topics on medicine or engineering:

```
[0.62, 0.90] share dollar rise rate market fall profit
price interest toll record export bank despite drop loss
post high strong trade
```

- Topic 8 is about politics, with a bit of crime thrown in. Some people would say that's actually the same thing. As we already have a `crime` topic, we'll name this one `politics`:

```
[0.41, 0.90] issue election vote league hunt interest
poll parliament gun investigate opposition raid arrest
police candidate victoria house northern crime rate
```

- Topic 9 is another mixed bag. It's hard to say whether it's about farming or missing people! Let's go with `unknown2`:

```
[0.37, 0.84] missing search crop body found wind rain
continues speaks john drought farm farmer smith pacific
crew river find mark tourist
```

All things considered, that's a pretty good model: 8 clear topics out of 10.

Let's define our list of topics and run our sample headlines through the model after deploying it:

```
topics = ['crime','legal','disaster','sports','unknown1',
          'international','local','finance','politics',
          'unknown2']
samples = [ "Major tariffs expected to end Australian barley
trade to China", "US woman wanted over fatal crash asks for
release after coronavirus halts extradition", "Fifty trains out
of service as fault forces Adelaide passengers to 'pack like
sardines", "Germany's Bundesliga plans its return from lockdown
as football world watches", "All AFL players to face COVID-19
testing before training resumes" ]
```

We use the following function to print the top three topics and their score:

```
import numpy as np
for r in response['predictions']:
    sorted_indexes = np.argsort(r['topic_weights']).tolist()
    sorted_indexes.reverse()
    top_topics = [topics[i] for i in sorted_indexes]
    top_weights = [r['topic_weights'][i]
                    for i in sorted_indexes]

    pairs = list(zip(top_topics, top_weights))
    print(pairs[:3])
```

Here's the output:

```
[('finance', 0.30),('international', 0.22),('sports', 0.09)]
[('unknown1', 0.19),('legal', 0.15),('politics', 0.14)]
[('crime', 0.32), ('legal', 0.18), ('international', 0.09)]
[('sports', 0.28),('unknown1', 0.09),('unknown2', 0.08)]
[('sports', 0.27),('disaster', 0.12),('crime', 0.11)]
```

Headlines 0, 2, 3, and 4 are right on target. That's not surprising given how strong these topics are.

Headline 1 scores very high on the topic we called legal. Maybe Adelaide passengers should sue the train company? Seriously, we would need to find other matching headlines to get a better sense of what the topic is really about.

As you can see, NTM makes it easier to understand what topics are about. We could improve the model by processing the vocabulary file, adding or removing specific words to influence topics, increase the number of topics, fiddle with alpha0, and so on. My intuition tells me that we should really see a weather topic in there. Please experiment and see if you want make it appear.

If you'd like to run another example, you'll find interesting techniques in this notebook:

https://github.com/awslabs/amazon-sagemaker-examples/
blob/master/introduction_to_applying_machine_learning/
ntm_20newsgroups_topic_modeling/ntm_20newsgroups_topic_model.
ipynb

Summary

NLP is a very exciting topic. It's also a difficult one because of the complexity of language in general, and due to how much processing is required to build datasets. Having said that, the built-in algorithms in SageMaker will help you get good results out of the box. Training and deploying models are straightforward processes, which leaves you more time to explore, understand, and prepare data.

In this chapter, you learned about the BlazingText, LDA, and NTM algorithms. You also learned how to process datasets using popular open source tools such as nltk, spacy, and gensim, and how to save them in the appropriate format. Finally, you learned how to use the SageMaker SDK to train and deploy models with all three algorithms, as well as how to interpret the results. This concludes our exploration of built-in algorithms.

In the next chapter, you will learn how to use built-in machine learning frameworks such as **scikit-learn**, **TensorFlow**, **PyTorch**, and **Apache MXNet**.

7

Extending Machine Learning Services Using Built-In Frameworks

In the last three chapters, you learned how to use built-in algorithms to train and deploy models, without having to write a line of machine learning code. However, these algorithms don't cover the full spectrum of machine learning problems. In a lot of cases, you'll need to write your own code. Thankfully, several open source frameworks make this reasonably easy.

In this chapter, you will learn how to train and deploy models with the most popular open source frameworks for machine learning and deep learning. We will cover the following topics:

- Discovering the built-in frameworks in Amazon SageMaker
- Running your framework code on Amazon SageMaker
- Using the built-in frameworks
- Let's get started!

Technical requirements

You will need an AWS account to run the examples included in this chapter. If you haven't got one already, please point your browser to https://aws.amazon.com/getting-started/ to create one. You should also familiarize yourself with the AWS Free Tier (https://aws.amazon.com/free/), which lets you use many AWS services for free within certain usage limits.

You will need to install and configure the AWS Command-Line Interface for your account (https://aws.amazon.com/cli/).

You will need a working Python 3.x environment. Be careful not to use Python 2.7, as it is no longer maintained. Installing the Anaconda distribution (https://www.anaconda.com/) is not mandatory, but strongly encouraged, as it includes many projects that we will need (Jupyter, pandas, numpy, and more).

You will need a working Docker installation. You can find installation instructions and the necessary documentation at https://docs.docker.com.

The code examples included in the book are available on GitHub at https://github.com/PacktPublishing/Learn-Amazon-SageMaker. You will need to install a Git client to access them (https://git-scm.com/).

Discovering the built-in frameworks in Amazon SageMaker

SageMaker lets you train and deploy your models with all major machine learning and deep learning frameworks:

- **Scikit-Learn** is undoubtedly the most widely used open source library for machine learning. If you're new to this topic, start here: `https://scikit-learn.org`.

- **XGBoost** is an extremely popular and versatile open source algorithm for regression, classification, and ranking problems (`https://xgboost.ai`). It's also available as a built-in algorithm, as presented in *Chapter 4, Training Machine Learning Models*. Using it in framework mode will give us more flexibility.

- **TensorFlow** is the #1 open source library for deep learning (`https://www.tensorflow.org`). SageMaker supports both the 1.x and 2.x versions, as well as the lovable **Keras** API (`https://keras.io`).

- **PyTorch** is another highly popular open source library for deep learning (`https://pytorch.org`). Researchers in particular enjoy its flexibility.

- **Apache MXNet** is an interesting challenger for deep learning. Natively implemented in C++, it's often faster and more scalable than its competitors. Its **Gluon** API brings rich toolkits for computer vision (`https://gluon-cv.mxnet.io`), natural language processing (`https://gluon-nlp.mxnet.io`), and time series data (`https://gluon-ts.mxnet.io`).

- **Chainer** is another worthy challenger for deep learning (`https://chainer.org`).

- **Reinforcement learning**: SageMaker supports several major frameworks, such as **Intel Coach** and **Ray RLib**. I won't discuss this topic here as this could take up another book!

- SageMaker also provides a **Spark** SDK, which lets you train and deploy models directly from your Spark application using either **PySpark** or **Scala** (`https://github.com/aws/sagemaker-spark`).

You'll find plenty of examples of all of these at `https://github.com/awslabs/amazon-sagemaker-examples/tree/master/sagemaker-python-sdk`.

In this chapter, we'll focus on the most popular ones: XGBoost, Scikit-Learn, TensorFlow, PyTorch, and Spark.

The best way to get started is to run an initial simple example. As you will see, the workflow is the same as for built-in algorithms. We'll highlight a few differences along the way, which we'll dive into later in this chapter.

Running a first example

In this example, we'll build a binary classification model with the XGBoost built-in framework. We'll use our own training script based on the `xgboost.XGBClassifier` object by using the Direct Marketing dataset, which we already used in *Chapter 3, AutoML with Amazon SageMaker Autopilot*:

1. First, download and extract the dataset:

```
%%sh
wget -N https://sagemaker-sample-data-us-west-2.s3-us-
west-2.amazonaws.com/autopilot/direct_marketing/bank-
additional.zip
unzip -o bank-additional.zip
```

2. Import the SageMaker SDK and define an S3 prefix for the job:

```
import sagemaker

sess   = sagemaker.Session()
bucket = sess.default_bucket()
prefix = 'xgboost-direct-marketing'
```

3. Load the dataset and apply very basic processing (as it's not our focus here). Simply one-hot encode the categorical features, move the labels to the first column (an XGBoost requirement), shuffle the dataset, split it for training and validation, and save the results in two separate CSV files:

```
import pandas as pd
import numpy as np
from sklearn.model_selection import train_test_split

data = pd.read_csv('./bank-additional/bank-additional-
full.csv')

data = pd.get_dummies(data)
data = data.drop(['y_no'], axis=1)
data = pd.concat([data['y_yes'],
                  data.drop(['y_yes'], axis=1)], axis=1)

data = data.sample(frac=1, random_state=123)
train_data, val_data = train_test_split(data,
                                        test_size=0.05)
```

```
train_data.to_csv('training.csv', index=False,
                   header=True)
val_data.to_csv('validation.csv', index=False,
                   header=True)
```

4. Upload the two files to S3. Since CSV is the default format for XGBoost, we don't need to define `s3_input` objects:

```
training = sess.upload_data(path='training.csv',
            key_prefix=prefix + "/training")
validation = sess.upload_data(path="validation.csv",
            key_prefix=prefix + "/validation")
output    = 's3://{}/{}/output/'.format(bucket,prefix)
```

5. Define an estimator for the training job. Of course, we could use the generic `Estimator` object and pass the name of the XGBoost container hosted in **Amazon ECR**. Instead, we will use the `XGBoost` object, which automatically selects the right container:

```
from sagemaker.xgboost import XGBoost
xgb_estimator = XGBoost(
    role= sagemaker.get_execution_role(),
    entry_point='xgb-dm.py',
    instance_count=1,
    instance_type='ml.m5.large',
    framework_version='1.0-1',
    py_version='py3',
    output_path=output,
    hyperparameters={'max-depth': 5,'eval-metric': 'auc'}
)
```

Several parameters are familiar here: the role, the infrastructure requirements, and the output path. What about the other ones? `Entry_point` is the path of our training script (available in the GitHub repository for this book). `Hyperparameters` are passed to it. We also have to select a `framework_version`; this is the version of XGBoost that we want to use. Finally, `py_version` lets us select Python 3, which is the only version supported by the SageMaker SDK v2.

6. We train as usual, passing the two channels:

```
xgb_estimator.fit({'training':training,
                   'validation':validation})
```

7. We also deploy as usual, creating a unique endpoint name:

```
import time

xgb_endpoint_name =
    prefix+time.strftime("%Y-%m-%d-%H-%M-%S",
    time.gmtime())

xgb_predictor = xgb_estimator.deploy(
    endpoint_name=xgb_endpoint_name,
    initial_instance_count=1,
    instance_type='ml.t2.medium')
```

Then, load a few samples from the validation set and send them for prediction in CSV format. The response contains a score between 0 and 1 for each sample:

```
payload = val_data[:10].drop(['y_yes'], axis=1)
payload = payload.to_csv(header=False,
            index=False).rstrip('\n')

xgb_predictor.content_type = 'text/csv'
xgb_predictor.serializer =
    sagemaker.serializers.CSVSerializer()
xgb_predictor.deserializer =
    sagemaker.deserializers.CSVDeserializer()

response = xgb_predictor.predict(payload)
print(response)
```

This prints out the following probabilities:

```
[['0.07206538'], ['0.02661967'], ['0.16043524'],
['4.026455e-05'], ['0.0002120432'], ['0.52123886'],
['0.50755614'], ['0.00015006188'], ['3.1439096e-05'],
['9.7614546e-05']]
```

8. When we're done, we delete the endpoint:

```
xgb_predictor.delete_endpoint()
```

We used XGBoost here, but the workflow would be identical for another framework. This standard way of training and deploying makes it really easy to switch from built-in algorithms to frameworks or from one framework to the next.

The points that we need to focus on here are as follows:

- **Framework containers**: What are they? Can we see how they're built? Can we customize them? Can we use them to train on our local machine?

- **Training**: How does a SageMaker training script differ from vanilla framework code? How does it receive hyperparameters? How should it read input data? Where should it save the model?

- **Deploying**: How is the model deployed? Should the script provide some code for this? What's the input format for prediction?

- **Managing dependencies**: Can we add additional source files besides the `entry_point` script? Can we add libraries for training and deployment?

- All these questions will be answered now!

Working with framework containers

SageMaker contains a training and prediction container for each built-in framework and are updated regularly to their latest versions. Deep learning frameworks have separate containers for CPU and GPU instances. All these containers are collectively known as **deep learning containers** (`https://aws.amazon.com/machine-learning/containers`).

As we saw in the previous example, this lets you simply bring your own code without having to maintain bespoke containers. In most cases, you won't need to look any further, and you can happily forget that these containers even exist.

If you're curious or if you have custom requirements, you'll be happy to learn that the code for these containers is open source:

- **Scikit-learn**: `https://github.com/aws/sagemaker-scikit-learn-container`

- **XGBoost**: `https://github.com/aws/sagemaker-xgboost-container`

- **TensorFlow**: `https://github.com/aws/sagemaker-tensorflow-container`

- **PyTorch**: `https://github.com/aws/sagemaker-pytorch-container`

- **Apache MXNet**: `https://github.com/aws/sagemaker-mxnet-container`

- **Chainer**: `https://github.com/aws/sagemaker-chainer-container`

For starters, this lets you understand how these containers are built and how SageMaker trains and predicts with them. You can also build and run them on your local machine for local experimentation. Furthermore, you can customize them (for example, add dependencies), push them to Amazon ECR, and use them with the estimators present in the SageMaker SDK. We'll demonstrate how to do this in this chapter.

The build process is pretty similar from one framework to the next. You'll find detailed instructions in each repository. Let's use TensorFlow as an example and build its container on our local machine. Of course, Docker needs to be running:

1. Clone the `sagemaker-tensorflow-container` repository:

    ```
    $ git clone https://github.com/aws/sagemaker-tensorflow-
    container
    ```

2. In this repository, build the CPU "`base`" image for TensorFlow 1.15.2 with this **Docker** command. Please note that will this take about 15 minutes as the process involves compiling Open MPI (`https://www.open-mpi.org`) and a few more things:

    ```
    $ cd sagemaker-tensorflow-container
    $ docker build -t tensorflow-sagemaker:1.15.2-cpu-py3 -f
    docker/1.15.2/py37/Dockerfile.cpu .
    ```

    TensorFlow 2.x images are managed in a different branch. This is how you would build the CPU "`base`" image for TensorFlow 2.1.0:

    ```
    $ git checkout remotes/origin/tf-2
    $ docker build -t tensorflow-sagemaker:2.1.0-cpu-py3 -f
    docker/2.1.0/py3/Dockerfile.cpu .
    ```

3. Once the image has been built, we can run it interactively and check the versions of TensorFlow and Keras:

    ```
    $ docker run -it tensorflow-sagemaker:1.15.2-cpu-py3
    root@aee4b9004fed:/# python
    >>> import tensorflow
    >>> tensorflow.__version__
    '1.15.2'
    >>> import tensorflow.keras
    >>> tensorflow.keras.__version__
    '2.2.4-tf'
    >>> exit()
    root@9252181601ca:/# exit
    ```

4. Let's imagine that our code needs the `nltk` and `gensim` libraries. All we have to do to add them to this container is edit `Dockerfile.cpu` like so (line 109 in the file):

```
RUN ${PIP} install --no-cache-dir -U \
    nltk \
    gensim \
    numpy==1.17.4 \
```

By building the image again, we will see the libraries being added:

```
---> Running in d9be7bff30e
Collecting nltk
  Downloading nltk-3.5.zip (1.4 MB)
Collecting gensim
  Downloading gensim-3.8.3-cp37-cp37m-manylinux1_x86_64.
whl (24.2 MB)
```

5. Create an Amazon ECR repository and push this image. Please refer to the documentation for details (`https://docs.aws.amazon.com/AmazonECR`):

```
$ aws ecr create-repository --repository-name tensorflow-
sagemaker
$ aws ecr get-login-password | docker login --username
AWS --password-stdin 123456789012.dkr.ecr.eu-west-1.
amazonaws.com
$ docker tag IMAGE_ID 123456789012.dkr.ecr.eu-west-1.
amazonaws.com/tensorflow-sagemaker
$ docker push 123456789012.dkr.ecr.eu-west-1.amazonaws.
com/tensorflow-sagemaker
```

6. The image is now available for training and prediction. All we have to do is pass its name in the `image_uri` parameter into the `TensorFlow` estimator and then it will be used instead of the built-in image (`https://sagemaker.readthedocs.io/en/stable/sagemaker.tensorflow.html`). We'll work with custom containers some more in *Chapter 8, Using Your Algorithms and Code.*

As you can see, you have full visibility and control of framework containers. These containers have another nice property. You can use them with the SageMaker SDK to train and deploy models on your local machine. Let's see how this works.

Training and deploying locally

Local Mode is the ability to train and deploy models with the SageMaker SDK without firing up on-demand managed infrastructure in AWS. You use your local machine instead. In this context, "local" means the machine running the notebook: it could be your laptop, a local server, or a small **Notebook instance**.

> **Note:**
> At the time of writing, Local Mode is not available on SageMaker Studio.

This is an excellent way to quickly experiment and iterate on a small dataset. You won't have to wait for instances to come up, and you won't have to pay for them either!

Let's revisit our previous XGBoost example, highlighting the changes required to use Local Mode:

1. Explicitly set the name of the **IAM** role. `get_execution_role()` does not work on your local machine (it does on a Notebook instance):

   ```
   #role = sagemaker.get_execution_role()
   role = 'arn:aws:iam::123456789012:role/Sagemaker-
   fullaccess'
   ```

2. Load the training and validation datasets from local files. Store the model locally in `/tmp`:

   ```
   training = 'file://training.csv'
   validation = 'file://validation.csv'
   output = 'file:///tmp'
   ```

3. In the `XGBoost` estimator, set `instance_type` to `local`. For local GPU training, we would use `local_gpu`.

4. In `xgb_estimator.deploy()`, set `instance_type` to `local`.

That's all it takes to train on your local machine using the same container you would use at scale on AWS. This container will be pulled once to your local machine and you'll be using it from then on. When you're ready to train at scale, just replace the `local` or `local_gpu` instance type with the appropriate AWS instance type and you're good to go.

> **Note:**
> If you see strange deployment errors, try restarting Docker (`sudo service docker restart`). I found that it doesn't like being interrupted during deployment, which I tend to do a lot when working inside Jupyter Notebooks!

Now, let's see what it takes to run our own code inside these containers. This feature is called **Script Mode**.

Training with script mode

Since your training code runs inside a SageMaker container, it needs to be able to do the following:

- Receive hyperparameters passed to the estimator.
- Read data available in input channels (training, validation, and more).
- Save the trained model in the right place.

Script Mode is how SageMaker makes this possible. The name comes from the way your code is invoked in the container. Looking at the training log for our XGBoost job, we see this:

```
Invoking script with the following command:
python -m xgb-dm --eval-metric auc --max-depth 5
```

Our code is invoked like a plain Python script (hence the name Script Mode). We can see that hyperparameters are passed as command-line arguments, which answers the question of how we should write the script to read them: `argparse`.

Here's the corresponding code snippet in our script:

```
parser = argparse.ArgumentParser()
parser.add_argument('--max-depth', type=int, default=4)
parser.add_argument('--early-stopping-rounds', type=int,
                    default=10)
parser.add_argument('--eval-metric', type=str,
                    default='error')
```

What about the location of the input data and of the saved model? If we look at the log a little more closely, we'll see this:

```
SM_CHANNEL_TRAINING=/opt/ml/input/data/training
SM_CHANNEL_VALIDATION=/opt/ml/input/data/validation
SM_MODEL_DIR=/opt/ml/model
```

These three environment variables define **local paths inside the container**, pointing to the respective locations for the training data, validation data, and the saved model. Does this mean we have to manage data and model copies between S3 and the container? No! SageMaker takes care of all this automatically for us. This is part of the support code present in the container.

Our script only needs to read these variables. I recommend using argparse again, as this will let us pass the paths to our script when we train outside of SageMaker (more on this soon).

Here's the corresponding code snippet in our script:

```
parser.add_argument('--model-dir', type=str,
                    default=os.environ['SM_MODEL_DIR'])
parser.add_argument('--training-dir', type=str,
                    default=os.environ['SM_CHANNEL_TRAINING'])
parser.add_argument('--validation', type=str,
                    default=os.environ['SM_CHANNEL_VALIDATION'])
```

To sum things up, in order to train framework code on SageMaker, we only need to do the following, in order:

1. Use argparse to read hyperparameters passed as command-line arguments. Chances are you're already doing this in your code anyway!

2. Read the SM_CHANNEL_xxx environment variables and load data from there.

3. Read the SM_MODEL_DIR environment variable and save the trained model there.

Now, let's talk about deploying models trained in Script Mode.

Understanding model deployment

In general, your script needs to include the following:

- A function to load the model
- A function to process input data before it's passed to the model
- A function to process predictions before they're returned to the caller

The amount of actual work required depends on the framework and the input format you use.

Deploying with TensorFlow

The TensorFlow container relies on the **TensorFlow Serving** model server for model deployment (`https://www.tensorflow.org/tfx/guide/serving`). For this reason, your training code must save the model in this format.

No model loading function is required. JSON is the default input format, and it also works for `numpy` arrays thanks to serialization. CSV is supported for columnar data.

You can view the container code at `https://github.com/aws/sagemaker-tensorflow-serving-container`.

You can also implement your own preprocessing and postprocessing functions. You'll find more information at `https://sagemaker.readthedocs.io/en/stable/using_tf.html#deploying-from-an-estimator`.

Deploying with Apache MXNet

Likewise, the Apache MXNet container relies on the **Multi-Model Server** (**MMS**) for model deployment (`https://github.com/awslabs/multi-model-server`). It uses the default **MXNet** model format.

Models based on the `Module` API do not require a model loading function. Data can be sent in JSON, CSV, or `numpy` format.

Gluon models do require a model loading function as parameters need to be explicitly initialized. Data can be sent in JSON or `numpy` format.

You can view the container code at `https://github.com/aws/sagemaker-mxnet-serving-container`.

You can also implement your own preprocessing, prediction, and postprocessing functions. You can find more information at `https://sagemaker.readthedocs.io/en/stable/using_mxnet.html`.

Deploying with other frameworks

For XGBoost, scikit-learn, PyTorch, and Chainer, your script needs to provide the following:

- A **mandatory** model_fn() function to load the model. Just like for training, the location of the model to load is passed in the SM_MODEL_DIR environment variable.

- Two optional functions to deserialize and serialize prediction data; that is, input_fn() and output_fn(). JSON, CSV, and numpy are built-in formats. These functions are only required if you need something different.

- An optional predict_fn() function passes deserialized data to the model and returns a prediction. This is only required if you need to preprocess data before predicting it or postprocessing predictions.

For XGBoost and scikit-learn, the model_fn() function is extremely simple and quite generic. Here are a couple of examples that should work in most cases:

```
# Scikit-learn
def model_fn(model_dir):
    clf = joblib.load(os.path.join(model_dir, "model.joblib"))
    return clf


# XGBoost
def model_fn(model_dir):
    model = xgb.Booster()
    model.load_model(os.path.join(model_dir, 'xgb.model'))
    return model
```

For PyTorch and Chainer, things are usually more complicated due to the custom nature of deep learning models, the variety of input parameters, and so on. The examples at https://github.com/awslabs/amazon-sagemaker-examples/tree/master/sagemaker-python-sdk are a good starting point.

SageMaker also lets you import and export models. You can upload an existing model to S3 and deploy it directly on SageMaker. Likewise, you can copy a trained model from S3 and deploy it elsewhere. We'll look at this in detail in *Chapter 11, Deploying Machine Learning Models*.

Now, let's talk about training and deployment dependencies.

Managing dependencies

In many cases, you'll need to add extra source files and extra libraries to the framework's containers. Let's see how we can easily do this.

Adding source files for training

By default, all estimators load the entry point script from the current directory. If you need additional source files for training, estimators let you pass a `source_dir` parameter, which points at the directory storing the files. Please note that the entry point script must be in the same directory.

In the following example, `myscript.py` and all additional source files must be placed in the `src` directory. SageMaker will automatically package the directory and copy it inside the training container:

```
sk = SKLearn(entry_point='myscript.py',
             source_dir='src',
                 . . .
```

Adding libraries for training

You can use different techniques to add libraries that are required for training.

The first technique is to use the `dependencies` parameter. It's available in all estimators, and it lets you list libraries that will be added to the training job. These libraries need to be present locally, in a virtual environment or in a bespoke directory. SageMaker will package them and copy them inside the training container.

In the following example, `myscript.py` needs the `mylib` library. We install it in the `lib` local directory:

```
$ mkdir lib
$ pip install mylib -t lib
```

Then, we pass its location to the estimator:

```
sk = SKLearn(entry_point='myscript.py',
             dependencies=['lib/mylib'],
                 . . .
```

The second technique is to install the necessary libraries in the training script by issuing a pip install command. We used this in *Chapter 6, Training Natural Language Processing Models*, with LDA and NTM. This is useful when you don't want to or cannot modify the SageMaker code that launches the training job:

```
import subprocess, sys
def install(package):
    subprocess.call([sys.executable, "-m",
                     "pip", "install", package])
if __name__=='__main__':
    install('gensim')
    import gensim
    . . .
```

The third technique is to install libraries in the Dockerfile for the container, rebuild the image, and push it to Amazon ECR. If you also need the libraries at prediction time (say, for preprocessing), this is the best option.

Adding libraries for deployment

If you need specific libraries to be available at prediction time, the **only** option is to customize the framework container. You can pass its name to the estimator with the image_uri parameter:

```
sk = SKLearn(entry_point='myscript.py', image_uri=
'123456789012.dkr.ecr.eu-west-1.amazonaws.com/my-sklearn'
. . .
```

We covered a lot of technical topics in this section. Now, let's look at the big picture.

Putting it all together

The typical workflow when working with framework code looks like this:

1. Implement Script Mode in your code; that is, the necessary hyperparameters, input data, and output location.

2. If required, add a model_fn() function to load the model.

3. Test your training code locally, outside of any SageMaker container.

4. Configure the appropriate estimator (XGBoost, TensorFlow, and so on).

5. Train in Local Mode using the estimator, with either the built-in container or a container you've customized.

6. Deploy in Local Mode and test your model.

7. Switch to a managed instance type (say, `ml.m5.large`) for training and deployment.

This logical progression requires little work at each step. It minimizes friction, the risk for mistakes, and frustration. It also optimizes instance time and cost – no need to wait and pay for managed instances if your code crashes immediately because of a silly bug.

Now, let's put this knowledge to work. In the next section, we're going to run a simple scikit-learn example. The purpose is to make sure we understand the workflow we just discussed.

Running your framework code on Amazon SageMaker

We will start from a vanilla Scikit-Learn program and train and save a linear regression model on the Boston Housing dataset, which we already used in *Chapter 4, Training Machine Learning Models*:

```
import pandas as pd
from sklearn.linear_model import LinearRegression
from sklearn.model_selection import train_test_split
from sklearn.metrics import mean_squared_error, r2_score
from sklearn.externals import joblib

data = pd.read_csv('housing.csv')
labels = data[['medv']]
samples = data.drop(['medv'], axis=1)

X_train, X_test, y_train, y_test = train_test_split(
samples, labels, test_size=0.1, random_state=123)

regr = LinearRegression(normalize=True)
regr.fit(X_train, y_train)
y_pred = regr.predict(X_test)

print('Mean squared error: %.2f'
        % mean_squared_error(y_test, y_pred))
print('Coefficient of determination: %.2f'
        % r2_score(y_test, y_pred))
joblib.dump(regr, 'model.joblib')
```

Let's update it so that it runs on SageMaker.

Implementing script mode

Now, we will use the framework to implement script mode, as follows:

1. First, read the hyperparameters as command-line arguments:

```
import argparse

if __name__ == '__main__':
  parser = argparse.ArgumentParser()
  parser.add_argument('--normalize', type=bool,
                       default=False)
  parser.add_argument('--test-size', type=float,
                       default=0.1)
  parser.add_argument('--random-state', type=int,
                       default=123)

  args, _ = parser.parse_known_args()
  normalize = args.normalize
  test_size = args.test_size
  random_state = args.random_state

  data = pd.read_csv('housing.csv')
  labels = data[['medv']]
  samples = data.drop(['medv'], axis=1)
  X_train, X_test, y_train, y_test = train_test_split(
    samples, labels,test_size=test_size,
    random_state=random_state)
  . . .
```

2. Read the input and output paths as command-line arguments. We could decide to remove the splitting code and pass two input channels instead. Let's stick to one channel; that is, `training`:

```
import os

if __name__ == '__main__':
  . . .
  parser.add_argument('--model-dir', type=str,
    default=os.environ['SM_MODEL_DIR'])
  parser.add_argument('--training', type=str,
    default=os.environ['SM_CHANNEL_TRAINING'])
  . . .
  model_dir    = args.model_dir
  training_dir = args.training
  . . .
```

```
filename = os.path.join(training_dir, 'housing.csv')
data = pd.read_csv(filename)
. . .
model = os.path.join(model_dir, 'model.joblib')
dump(regr, model)
```

3. As we're using Scikit-Learn, we need to add `model_fn()` to load the model at deployment time:

```
def model_fn(model_dir):
  model = joblib.load(os.path.join(model_dir, 'model.
joblib'))
  return model
```

With that, we're done. Time to test!

Testing locally

First, we test our script locally, outside of any SageMaker container. I'm using a Notebook instance with the `python3` **conda** environment. You can run this on your local machine as well. Just make sure you have `pandas` and Scikit-Learn installed.

Set the environment variables to empty values as we will pass the paths on the command line:

```
$ source activate python3
$ export SM_CHANNEL_TRAINING=
$ export SM_MODEL_DIR=
$ python sklearn-boston-housing.py --normalize True -test-
ration 0.1 --training . --model-dir .
Mean squared error: 41.82
Coefficient of determination: 0.63
```

Nice. Our code runs fine with command-line arguments. We can use this for local development and debugging, until we're ready to move it to SageMaker Local Mode.

Using Local Mode

1. Configure an `SKLearn` estimator in Local Mode, setting the role according to the setup we're using. Use local paths only:

```
# Use this on a Notebook instance or on SageMaker Studio
role = sagemaker.get_execution_role()
# Use this on a local machine
role = 'arn:aws:iam::0123456789012:role/Sagemaker-
fullaccess'
```

```
sk = SKLearn(entry_point='sklearn-boston-housing.py',
  role=role,
  framework_version='0.20.0',
  instance_count=1,
  instance_type='local',
  output_path=output,
  hyperparameters={'normalize': True, 'test-size': 0.1}
)
```

```
sk.fit({'training':training})
```

2. As expected, we can see how our code is invoked in the training log. Of course, we get the same outcome:

```
/miniconda3/bin/python -m sklearn-boston-housing
--normalize True --test-size 0.1
. . .
Mean squared error: 41.82
Coefficient of determination: 0.63
```

3. Deploy locally and send some CSV samples for prediction:

```
sk_predictor = sk.deploy(initial_instance_count=1,
                         instance_type='local')
```

```
data = pd.read_csv('housing.csv')
payload = data[:10].drop(['medv'], axis=1)
payload = payload.to_csv(header=False, index=False)
```

```
sk_predictor.content_type = 'text/csv'
sk_predictor.accept = 'text/csv'
sk_predictor.serializer =
    sagemaker.serializers.CSVSerializer()
sk_predictor.deserializer =
    sagemaker.deserializers.CSVDeserializer()
```

```
response = sk_predictor.predict(payload)
print(response)
```

By printing the response, we will see the predicted values:

```
[['29.801388899699845'], ['24.990809475886074'],
 ['30.7379654455552'], ['28.786967125316544'],
 ['28.1421501991961'], ['25.301714533101716'],
 ['22.717977231840184'], ['19.302415613883348'],
 ['11.369520911229536'], ['18.785593532977657']]
```

With Local Mode, we can quickly iterate on our model. We're only limited by the compute and storage capabilities of the local machine. When that happens, we can easily move to managed infrastructure.

Using managed infrastructure

When it's time to train at scale and deploy in production, all we have to do is make sure the input data is in S3 and replace the `local` instance type with an actual instance type:

```
sess = sagemaker.Session()
bucket = sess.default_bucket()
prefix = 'sklearn-boston-housing'

training = sess.upload_data(path='housing.csv',
        key_prefix=prefix + "/training")

output = 's3://{}/{}/output/'.format(bucket,prefix)

sk = SKLearn(. . ., instance_type='ml.m5.large')

sk.fit({'training':training})

. . .

sk_predictor = sk.deploy(initial_instance_count=1,
                    instance_type='ml.t2.medium')
```

Since we're using the same container, we can be confident that training and deployment will work as expected. Again, I strongly recommend that you follow this logical progression: local work, Local Mode, and managed infrastructure. It will help you focus on what needs to be done and when.

For the remainder of this chapter, we're going to run additional examples.

Using the built-in frameworks

We've covered XGBoost and Scikit-Learn already. Now, it's time to see how we can use deep learning frameworks. Let's start with TensorFlow and Keras.

Working with TensorFlow and Keras

In this example, we're going to train a simple convolutional neural network on the Fashion-MNIST dataset (`https://github.com/zalandoresearch/fashion-mnist`).

Our code is split in two source files: one for the entry point script (`fmnist.py`, using only TensorFlow 2.x APIs), and one for the model (`model.py`, based on Keras layers). For the sake of brevity, I will only discuss the SageMaker-related steps. You can find the full code in the GitHub repository for this book:

1. `fmnist.py` starts by reading hyperparameters from the command line:

```
import tensorflow as tf
import numpy as np
import argparse, os

from model import FMNISTModel

parser = argparse.ArgumentParser()
parser.add_argument('--epochs', type=int, default=10)
parser.add_argument('--learning-rate', type=float,
                    default=0.01)
parser.add_argument('--batch-size', type=int,
default=128)
```

2. Next, we read the environment variables; that is, the input paths for the training set and the validation set, the output path for the model, and the number of GPUs available on the instance. It's the first time we're using the latter. It comes in handy to adjust the batch size for multi-GPU training as it's common practice to multiply the initial batch's size by the number of GPUs:

```
parser.add_argument('--training', type=str,
default=os.environ['SM_CHANNEL_TRAINING'])
parser.add_argument('--validation', type=str,
default=os.environ['SM_CHANNEL_VALIDATION'])
parser.add_argument('--model-dir', type=str,
default=os.environ['SM_MODEL_DIR'])
parser.add_argument('--gpu-count', type=int,
default=os.environ['SM_NUM_GPUS'])
```

3. Store the arguments in local variables. Then, load the dataset. Each channel provides us with a compressed `numpy` array for storing images and labels:

```
x_train = np.load(os.path.join(training_dir,
        'training.npz'))['image']
```

```
y_train = np.load(os.path.join(training_dir,
        'training.npz'))['label']
x_val = np.load(os.path.join(validation_dir,
        'validation.npz'))['image']
y_val = np.load(os.path.join(validation_dir,
        'validation.npz'))['label']
```

4. Then, prepare the data for training by reshaping the image tensors, normalizing the pixel values, one-hot encoding the image labels, and creating the `tf.data.Dataset` objects that will feed data to the model.

5. Create the model, compile it, and fit it.

6. Once training is complete, save the model in TensorFlow Serving format at the appropriate output location. This step is important as this is the model server that SageMaker uses for TensorFlow models:

```
model.save(os.path.join(model_dir, '1'))
```

We train and deploy the model using the usual workflow:

1. Download the dataset and upload it to S3:

```
import os
import numpy as np
import keras
from keras.datasets import fashion_mnist

(x_train, y_train), (x_val, y_val) = fashion_mnist.load_
data()

os.makedirs("./data", exist_ok = True)
np.savez('./data/training', image=x_train, label=y_train)
np.savez('./data/validation', image=x_val, label=y_val)

prefix = 'tf2-fashion-mnist'

training_input_path = sess.upload_data(
 'data/training.npz', key_prefix=prefix+'/training')

validation_input_path = sess.upload_data(
 'data/validation.npz', key_prefix=prefix+'/validation')
```

2. Configure the `TensorFlow` estimator. Set the `source_dir` parameter so that our model's file is also deployed in the container:

```
from sagemaker.tensorflow import TensorFlow

tf_estimator = TensorFlow(entry_point='fmnist.py',
    source_dir='.',
```

```
role=sagemaker.get_execution_role(),
instance_count=1,
instance_type='ml.p3.2xlarge',
framework_version='2.1.0',
py_version='py3',
hyperparameters={'epochs': 10})
```

3. Train and deploy as usual. We will go straight for managed infrastructure, but the same code will work fine on your local machine in Local Mode:

```
import time
tf_estimator.fit({'training': training_input_path,
                  'validation': validation_input_path})
tf_endpoint_name = 'tf2-fmnist-'+time.strftime("%Y-%m-%d-
%H-%M-%S", time.gmtime())
tf_predictor = tf_estimator.deploy(
                initial_instance_count=1,
                instance_type='ml.m5.large',
                endpoint_name=tf_endpoint_name)
```

4. The validation accuracy should be 91-92%. By loading and displaying a few sample images from the validation dataset, we can predict their labels. The numpy payload is automatically serialized to JSON, which is the default format for prediction data:

```
tf_predictor.content_type = 'application/json'
response = tf_predictor.predict(payload)
prediction = np.array(reponse['predictions'])
predicted_label = prediction.argmax(axis=1)
print('Predicted labels are: {}'.format(predicted_label))
```

The output should look as follows:

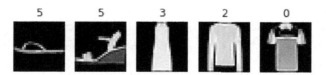

Figure 7.1 – Viewing predicted classes

5. When we're done, we delete the endpoint:

```
tf_predictor.delete_endpoint()
```

As you can see, the combination of Script Mode and built-in containers makes it easy to run TensorFlow on SageMaker. Once you get into the routine, you'll be surprised at how fast you can move your models from your laptop to AWS.

Now, let's take a look at PyTorch.

Working with PyTorch

PyTorch is extremely popular for computer vision, natural language processing, and more.

In this example, we're going to train a **Graph Neural Network (GNN)**. This category of networks works particularly well on graph-structured data, such as social networks, life sciences, and more. In fact, our PyTorch code will use the **Deep Graph Library (DGL)**, an open source library that makes it easier to build and train GNNs with TensorFlow, **PyTorch**, and Apache MXNet (`https://www.dgl.ai/`). DGL is already installed in these containers, so let's get to work directly.

We're going to work with the Zachary Karate Club dataset (`http://konect.cc/networks/ucidata-zachary/`). The following is the graph for this:

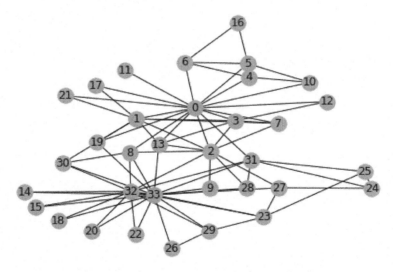

Figure 7.2 – The Zachary Karate Club dataset

Nodes 0 and 33 are teachers, while the other nodes are students. Edges represent ties between these people. As the story goes, the two teachers had an argument and the club needs to be split in two.

The purpose of the training job is to find the "best" split. This can be defined as a semi-supervision classification task. The first teacher (node 0) is assigned class 0, while the second teacher (node 33) is assigned class 1. All the other nodes are unlabeled, and their classes will be computed by a **Graph Convolutional Network**. At the end of the last epoch, we'll retrieve the node classes and split the club accordingly.

The dataset is stored as a pickled Python list containing edges. Here are the first few edges:

```
[('0', '8'), ('1', '17'), ('24', '31'), . . .
```

The SageMaker code is as simple as it gets. We upload the dataset to S3, create a `PyTorch` estimator, and train it:

```python
import sagemaker
from sagemaker.pytorch import PyTorch
sess = sagemaker.Session()
prefix = 'dgl-karate-club'
training_input_path = sess.upload_data('edge_list.pickle',
                                        key_prefix=prefix+'/training')
estimator = PyTorch(role=sagemaker.get_execution_role(),
    entry_point='karate_club_sagemaker.py',
    hyperparameters={'node_count': 34, 'epochs': 30},
    framework_version='1.5.0',
    py_version='py3',
    instance_count=1,
    instance_type='ml.m5.large')
estimator.fit({'training': training_input_path})
```

This hardly needs any explaining at all, does it?

Let's take a look at the abbreviated training script, where we're using Script Mode once again. The full version is available in the GitHub repository for this book:

```python
if __name__ == '__main__':
    parser = argparse.ArgumentParser()
    parser.add_argument('--epochs', type=int, default=30)
    parser.add_argument('--node_count', type=int)
    args, _     = parser.parse_known_args()
    epochs      = args.epochs
    node_count = args.node_count
    training_dir = os.environ['SM_CHANNEL_TRAINING']
    model_dir    = os.environ['SM_MODEL_DIR']
    with open(os.path.join(training_dir, 'edge_list.pickle'),
```

```
'rb') as f:
    edge_list = pickle.load(f)
# Build the graph and the model
. . .
# Train the model
. . .
# Print predicted classes
last_epoch = all_preds[epochs-1].detach().numpy()
predicted_class = np.argmax(last_epoch, axis=-1)
print(predicted_class)
# Save the model
torch.save(net.state_dict(), os.path.join(model_dir,
'karate_club.pt'))
```

The following classes are predicted. Nodes #0 and #1 are class 0, node #2 is class 1, and so on:

```
[0 0 1 0 0 0 0 1 1 0 0 0 0 1 1 0 0 1 0 1 0 1 1 1 1 1 1 1 1
 1 1 1]
```

By plotting them, we can see that the club has been cleanly split:

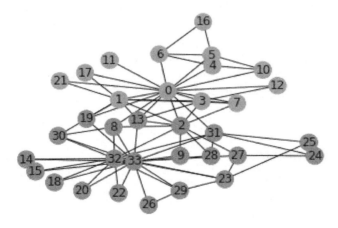

Figure 7.3 – Viewing predicted classes

Once again, the SageMaker code doesn't stand in your way. The workflow and APIs are consistent from one framework to the next, and you can focus on the machine learning problem itself.

To close this chapter, let's look at how SageMaker and Apache Spark can work together.

Working with Apache Spark

In addition to the Python SageMaker SDK that we've been using so far, SageMaker also includes an SDK for Spark (`https://github.com/aws/sagemaker-spark`) This lets you run SageMaker jobs directly from a PySpark or Scala application running on a Spark cluster.

Combining Spark and SageMaker

First, you can decouple the **Extract-Transform-Load (ETL)** step and the machine learning step. Each usually has different infrastructure requirements (instance type, instance count, storage) that need to be the right size both technically and financially. Setting up your Spark cluster just right for ETL and using on-demand infrastructure in SageMaker for training and prediction is a powerful combination.

Second, although SparkMLlib is an amazing library, you may need something else, such as custom algorithms in different languages, or deep learning.

Finally, deploying models for prediction on Spark clusters may not be the best option. SageMaker endpoints should be considered instead, especially since they support the **Mleap** format (`https://mleap-docs.combust.ml`).

In the following example, we'll combine SageMaker and Spark to build a spam detection model. Data will be hosted in S3, with one text file for spam messages and one for non-spam ("ham") messages. We'll use Spark running on an Amazon EMR cluster to preprocess it. Then, we'll train and deploy a model with the XGBoost algorithm that's available in SageMaker. Finally, we'll predict data with it on our Spark cluster. For the sake of language diversity, we'll code with Scala this time.

First of all, we need to build a Spark cluster.

Creating a Spark Cluster

1. Starting from the **Amazon EMR** console at `https://console.aws.amazon.com/elasticmapreduce`, we will create a cluster. All you need to do is give it a name, ask for Spark to be installed, as shown in the following screenshot, select an EC2 key pair, and click on **Create cluster**. You can find additional details at `https://docs.aws.amazon.com/emr/`:

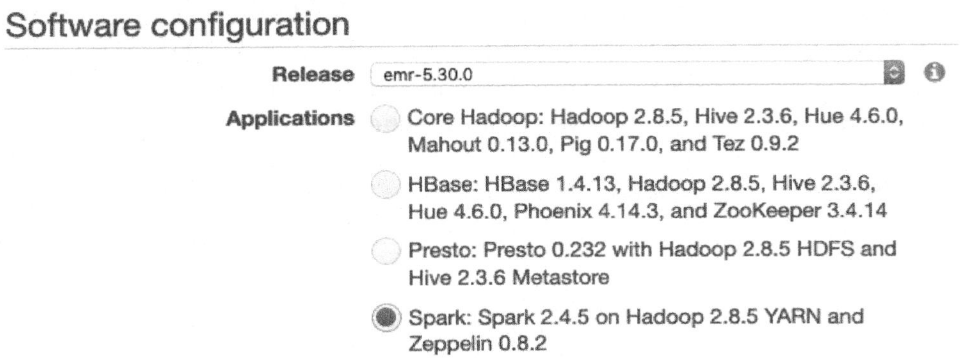

Software configuration

Release   emr-5.30.0

Applications   ○ Core Hadoop: Hadoop 2.8.5, Hive 2.3.6, Hue 4.6.0, Mahout 0.13.0, Pig 0.17.0, and Tez 0.9.2

○ HBase: HBase 1.4.13, Hadoop 2.8.5, Hive 2.3.6, Hue 4.6.0, Phoenix 4.14.3, and ZooKeeper 3.4.14

○ Presto: Presto 0.232 with Hadoop 2.8.5 HDFS and Hive 2.3.6 Metastore

◉ Spark: Spark 2.4.5 on Hadoop 2.8.5 YARN and Zeppelin 0.8.2

Figure 7.4 – Creating a Spark cluster

2. While the cluster is being created, we define our Git repository in the **Notebooks** entry in the left-hand vertical menu, as shown in the following screenshot. Then, we click on **Add repository**:

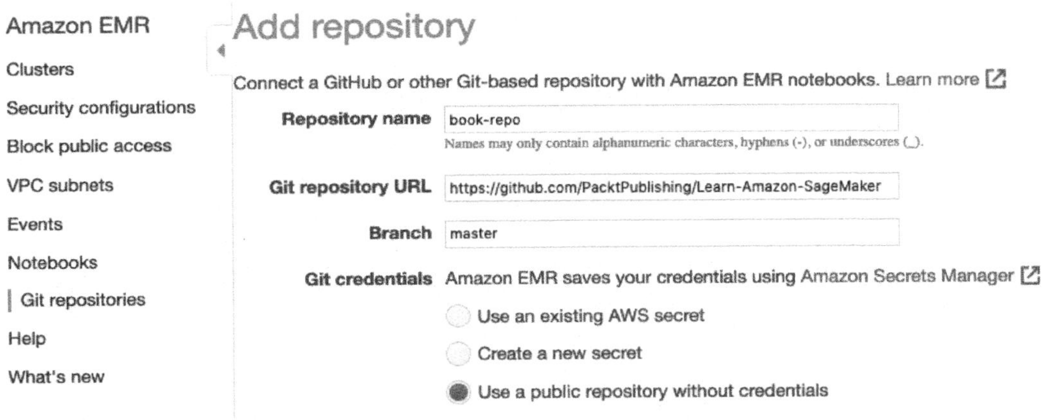

Amazon EMR

Clusters
Security configurations
Block public access
VPC subnets
Events
Notebooks
| Git repositories
Help
What's new

Add repository

Connect a GitHub or other Git-based repository with Amazon EMR notebooks. Learn more [↗]

Repository name   book-repo
Names may only contain alphanumeric characters, hyphens (-), or underscores (_).

Git repository URL   https://github.com/PacktPublishing/Learn-Amazon-SageMaker

Branch   master

Git credentials   Amazon EMR saves your credentials using Amazon Secrets Manager [↗]
○ Use an existing AWS secret
○ Create a new secret
◉ Use a public repository without credentials

Figure 7.5 – Adding a Git repository

3.   Then, we create a Jupyter Notebook connected to the cluster. Starting from the **Notebooks** entry in the left-hand vertical menu, as shown in the following screenshot, we give it a name and select both the EMR cluster and the repository we just created. Then, we click on **Create notebook**:

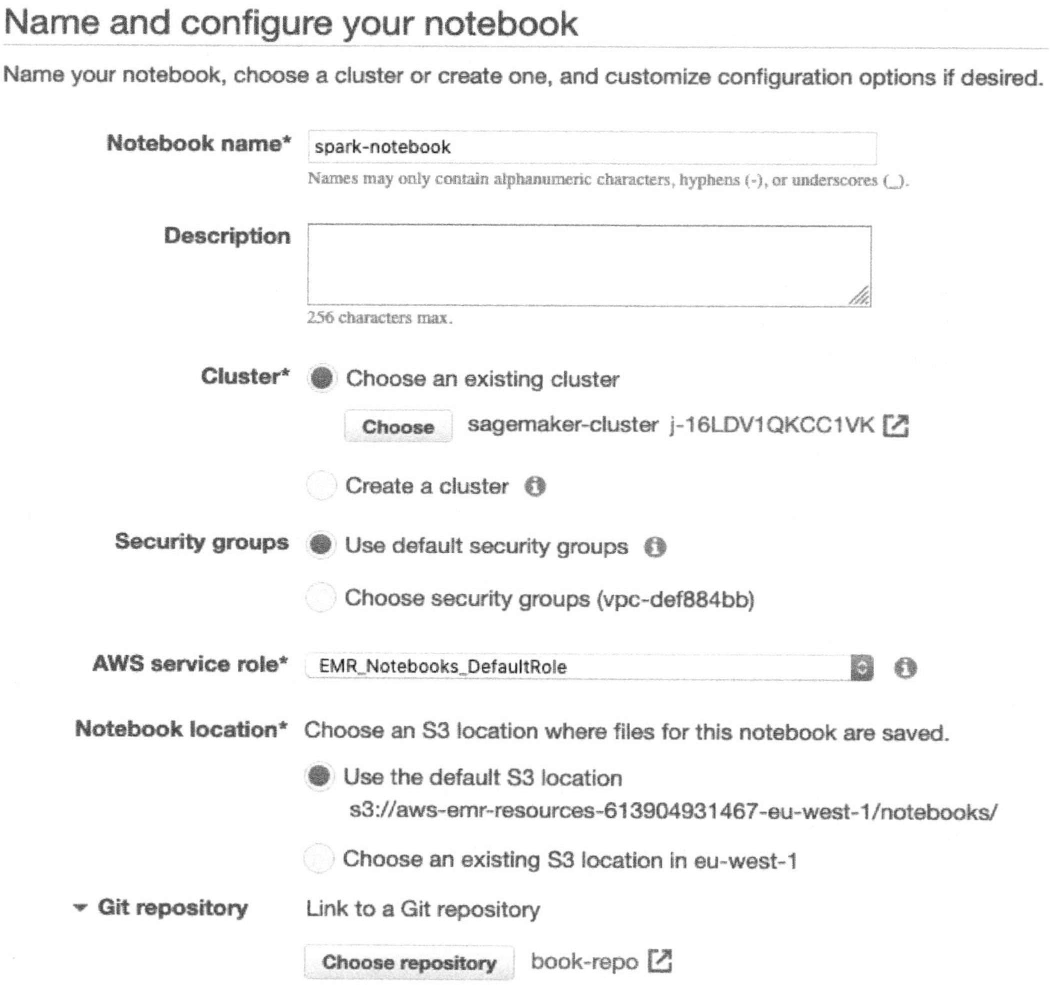

Name and configure your notebook

Name your notebook, choose a cluster or create one, and customize configuration options if desired.

Notebook name*   spark-notebook

Names may only contain alphanumeric characters, hyphens (-), or underscores (_).

Description

256 characters max.

Cluster*   ● Choose an existing cluster

Choose   sagemaker-cluster j-16LDV1QKCC1VK

○ Create a cluster ❶

Security groups   ● Use default security groups ❶

○ Choose security groups (vpc-def884bb)

AWS service role*   EMR_Notebooks_DefaultRole

Notebook location*   Choose an S3 location where files for this notebook are saved.

● Use the default S3 location
s3://aws-emr-resources-613904931467-eu-west-1/notebooks/

○ Choose an existing S3 location in eu-west-1

▼ Git repository   Link to a Git repository

Choose repository   book-repo

Figure 7.6 – Creating a Jupyter Notebook

4.   Once the notebook is ready, we click on **Open in Jupyter**. We'll be taken to the familiar Jupyter interface.

Everything is now ready. Let's write a spam classifier!

Building a spam classification model with Spark and SageMaker

1. First, we need to make sure that our dataset is available in S3. On our local machine, upload the two files to the default SageMaker bucket (feel free to use another bucket):

```
$ aws s3 cp ham s3://sagemaker-eu-west-1-123456789012
$ aws s3 cp spam s3://sagemaker-eu-west-1-123456789012
```

2. Back in the Jupyter Notebook, make sure it's running the Spark kernel. Then, import the necessary objects from Spark MLlib and the SageMaker SDK.

3. Load the data from S3. Convert all the sentences into lowercase. Then, remove all punctuation and numbers and trim any whitespace:

```
val spam = sc.textFile(
"s3://sagemaker-eu-west-1-123456789012/spam")
.map(l => l.toLowerCase())
.map(l => l.replaceAll("[^ a-z]", ""))
.map(l => l.trim())

val ham = sc.textFile(
"s3://sagemaker-eu-west-1-123456789012/ham")
.map(l => l.toLowerCase())
.map(l => l.replaceAll("[^ a-z]", ""))
.map(l => l.trim())
```

4. Then, split the messages into words and hash these words into 200 buckets. This technique is much less sophisticated than the word vectors we used in *Chapter 6, Training Natural Language Processing Models*, but it should do the trick:

```
val tf = new HashingTF(numFeatures = 200)

val spamFeatures = spam.map(
                m => tf.transform(m.split(" ")))
val hamFeatures = ham.map(
                m => tf.transform(m.split(" ")))
```

For example, the following message has one occurrence of a word from bucket 15, one from bucket 83, two words from bucket 96, and two from bucket 188:

```
Array((200,[15,83,96,188],[1.0,1.0,2.0,2.0]))
```

5. We assign a 1 label for spam messages and a 0 label for ham messages:

    ```
    val positiveExamples = spamFeatures.map(
    features => LabeledPoint(1, features))
    val negativeExamples = hamFeatures.map(
    features => LabeledPoint(0, features))
    ```

6. Merge the messages and encode them in **libsvm** format, one of the formats
    supported by **XGBoost**:

    ```
    val data = positiveExamples.union(negativeExamples)
    val data_libsvm = MLUtils.convertVectorColumnsToML(data.
    toDF)
    ```

    The samples now look similar to this:

    ```
    Array([1.0,(200,[2,41,99,146,172,181],[2.0,1.0,1.0,1.0,1.
    0])])
    ```

7. Split the data for training and validation:

    ```
    val Array(trainingData, testData) = data_libsvm.
    randomSplit(Array(0.8, 0.2))
    ```

8. Configure the XGBoost estimator available in the SageMaker SDK. Here, we're
    going to train and deploy in one single step:

    ```
    val roleArn = "arn:aws:iam:YOUR_SAGEMAKER_ROLE"
    ```

    ```
    val xgboost_estimator = new XGBoostSageMakerEstimator(
        trainingInstanceType="ml.m5.large",
        trainingInstanceCount=1,
        endpointInstanceType="ml.t2.medium",
        endpointInitialInstanceCount=1,
        sagemakerRole=IAMRole(roleArn))
    ```

    ```
    xgboost_estimator.setObjective("binary:logistic")
    xgboost_estimator.setNumRound(25)
    ```

9. Fire up a training job and a deployment job on the managed infrastructure, exactly like when we worked with built-in algorithms in *Chapter 4, Training Machine Learning Models*. The SageMaker SDK automatically passes the Spark DataFrame to the training job, so no work is required from our end:

```
val xgboost_model = xgboost_estimator.fit(trainingData_
libsvm)
```

As you would expect, these activities are visible in the SageMaker console (**Training** and **Endpoints**).

10. When deployment is complete, transform the test set and score the model. This automatically invokes the SageMaker endpoint. Once again, we don't need to worry about data movement:

```
val transformedData = xgboost_model.transform(testData_
libsvm)
val accuracy = 1.0 * transformedData.filter($"label"===
$"prediction").count / transformedData.count()
```

The accuracy should be around 97%, which is not too bad!

11. When we're done, delete all SageMaker resources created by the job. This will delete the model, the endpoint, and the endpoint configuration (an object we haven't discussed yet):

```
val cleanup = new SageMakerResourceCleanup(
                    xgboost_model.sagemakerClient)
cleanup.deleteResources(xgboost_model.
getCreatedResources)
```

12. Don't forget to terminate the notebook and the EMR cluster too. You can easily do this in the AWS console.

This example demonstrates how easy it is to combine the respective strengths of Spark and SageMaker. Another way to do this is to build MLlib pipelines with a mix of Spark and SageMaker stages. You'll find examples of this at https://github.com/awslabs/amazon-sagemaker-examples/tree/master/sagemaker-spark.

Summary

Open source frameworks such as Scikit-Learn and TensorFlow have made it simple to write machine learning and deep learning code. They've become immensely popular in the developer community and for good reason. However, managing training and deployment infrastructure still requires a lot of effort and skills that data scientists and machine learning engineers typically do not possess. SageMaker simplifies the whole process. You can go quickly from experimentation to production, without ever worrying about infrastructure.

In this chapter, you learned about the different frameworks available in SageMaker for machine learning and deep learning, as well as how to customize their containers. You also learned how to use Script Mode and Local Mode for fast iteration until you're ready to deploy in production. Finally, you ran several examples, including one that combines Apache Spark and SageMaker.

In the next chapter, you will learn how to use your own custom code on SageMaker, without having to rely on a built-in container.

8
Using Your Algorithms and Code

In the previous chapter, you learned how to train and deploy models with built-in frameworks such as **scikit-learn** or **TensorFlow**. Thanks to **Script Mode**, these frameworks make it easy to use your own code, without having to manage any training or deployment containers.

In some cases, your business or technical environment could make it difficult or even impossible to use these containers. Maybe you need to be in full control of how containers are built. Maybe you'd like to implement your own prediction logic. Maybe you're working with a framework or a language that's not natively supported by SageMaker.

In this chapter, you'll learn how to tailor training and prediction containers to your own needs. You'll also learn how to train and deploy your own custom code, using either the SageMaker SDK directly or command-line open source tools. We'll cover the following topics:

- Understanding how SageMaker invokes your code
- Using the SageMaker Training Toolkit with scikit-learn
- Building a fully custom container for scikit-learn
- Building a fully custom container for R
- Training and deploying with XGBoost and MLflow
- Training and deploying with XGBoost and Sagify

Technical requirements

You will need an AWS account to run examples included in this chapter. If you haven't got one already, please point your browser at `https://aws.amazon.com/getting-started/` to create it. You should also familiarize yourself with the AWS Free Tier (`https://aws.amazon.com/free/`), which lets you use many AWS services for free within certain usage limits.

You will need to install and configure the AWS Command-Line Interface (CLI) for your account (`https://aws.amazon.com/cli/`).

You will need a working Python 3.x environment. Be careful not to use Python 2.7, as it is no longer maintained. Installing the Anaconda distribution (`https://www.anaconda.com/`) is not mandatory but strongly encouraged as it includes many projects that we will need (Jupyter, `pandas`, `numpy`, and more).

You will need a working Docker installation. You'll find installation instructions and documentation at `https://docs.docker.com`.

Code examples included in this book are available on GitHub at `https://github.com/PacktPublishing/Learn-Amazon-SageMaker`. You will need to install a Git client to access them (`https://git-scm.com/`).

Understanding how SageMaker invokes your code

When we worked with built-in algorithms and frameworks, we didn't pay much attention to how SageMaker actually invoked the training and deployment code. After all, that's what "built-in" means: grab what you need off the shelf and get to work.

Of course, things are different if we want to use our own custom code and containers. We need to understand how they interface with SageMaker so that we implement them exactly right.

In this section, we'll discuss this interface in detail. Let's start with the file layout.

Understanding the file layout inside a SageMaker container

To make our life simpler, SageMaker estimators automatically copy hyperparameters and input data inside training containers. Likewise, they automatically copy the trained model from the container to S3. At deployment time, they do the reverse operation, copying the model from S3 into the container.

As you can imagine, this requires a file layout convention:

- Hyperparameters are stored as a JSON dictionary in `/opt/ml/input/config/hyperparameters.json`.
- Input channels are stored in `/opt/ml/input/data/CHANNEL_NAME`.
- The model must be saved in and loaded from `/opt/ml/model`.

Hence, we'll need to use these paths in our custom code. Now, let's see how the training and deployment code is invoked.

Understanding the options for custom training

In *Chapter 7, Extending Machine Learning Services with Built-in Frameworks*, we studied **Script Mode** and how SageMaker uses it to invoke our training script. This feature is enabled by additional Python code present in the framework containers, namely, the SageMaker Training Toolkit (`https://github.com/aws/sagemaker-training-toolkit`).

In a nutshell, this training toolkit copies the entry point script, its hyperparameters, and its dependencies inside the container. By default, it also copies input data inside the container. Then, it invokes the user-provided entry point, the script that you passed to the framework estimator. Curious minds can read the code at `src/sagemaker_training/entry_point.py`.

When it comes to customizing your training code, you have the following options:

- **Customize a framework container, and keep the training toolkit**. You'll have full control over the container itself while still being able to use Script Mode. You'll be able to use the framework estimators. Training code will be identical to what we've done before.

- **Build a fully custom container**. If you want to start from a blank page or don't want any extra code inside your container, this is the way to go. You'll train with the generic `Estimator` module, and Script Mode won't be available. Your training code will be invoked directly (more on this later).

Understanding the options for custom deployment

In the same vein, framework containers include additional Python code for deployment.

The situation is more complex than for training, due to framework particularities:

- **Scikit-learn**, **XGBoost**, and **Chainer**: Deployment is based on a `gunicorn` application installed in the training container. It's inherited from another repository (`https://github.com/aws/sagemaker-containers`), which is now deprecated. At the time of writing, it's not clear what the future will look like.

- **TensorFlow**: Deployment is based on the **TensorFlow Serving** model server, installed in a dedicated container (`https://github.com/aws/sagemaker-tensorflow-serving-container`).

- **Apache MXNet** and **PyTorch**: Both use a dedicated container as the prediction container (`https://github.com/aws/sagemaker-mxnet-serving-container` and `https://github.com/aws/sagemaker-pytorch-serving-container`).
  Deployment is based on the SageMaker Inference Toolkit (`https://github.com/aws/sagemaker-inference-toolkit`), itself based on the **MMS** model server (`https://github.com/awslabs/multi-model-server`).

Again, you have two options:

- **Customize an existing container**. This is a good option if you need full control over the container but don't want to manage the model serving as your deep learning model.

- **Build a fully custom container**. You'll do away with any serving code, and you'll implement your own prediction service instead. The `Flask` and `plumber` libraries are popular choices for Python and R. Your serving code will be invoked directly.

Whether you use a single container for training and deployment or two different containers is up to you. A lot of different factors come into play: who builds the containers, who runs them, and so on. Only you can decide what's the best option for your particular setup.

Now, let's run some examples!

Using the SageMaker training toolkit with scikit-learn

In this example, we're going to build a custom Python container with the SageMaker Training Toolkit. We'll use it to train a `scikit-learn` model on the Boston Housing dataset, using Script Mode and the `SKLearn` estimator.

We need three building blocks:

- The training script: Thanks to Script Mode, we can use exactly the same code as in the `Scikit-Learn` example from *Chapter 7, Extending Machine Learning Services with Built-in Frameworks*.

- We need a `Dockerfile` and Docker commands to build our custom container.

- We also need a `SKLearn` estimator configured to use our custom container.

Let's take care of the container:

1. A `Dockerfile` can get quite complicated. No need for that here! We start from the official Python 3.7 image available on Docker Hub (`https://hub.docker.com/_/python`). We install scikit-learn, `numpy`, `pandas`, `joblib`, and the SageMaker training toolkit:

   ```
   FROM python:3.7
   RUN pip3 install --no-cache scikit-learn numpy pandas
   joblib sagemaker-training
   ```

2. We build the image with the Docker `build` command, tagging it as `sklearn-customer:sklearn`:

   ```
   $ docker build -t sklearn-custom:sklearn -f Dockerfile.
   ```

   You should see the following output, with a different image identifier:

   ```
   Successfully built 84cd12ee647f
   Successfully tagged sklearn-custom:sklearn
   ```

3. Using the AWS CLI, we create a repository in **Amazon ECR** to host this image, and we log in to the repository:

```
$ aws ecr create-repository --repository-name sklearn-
custom
```

```
$ aws ecr get-login-password | docker login --username
AWS
--password-stdin 123456789012.dkr.ecr.eu-west-1.
amazonaws.com/sklearn-custom:latest
```

4. Using the image identifier returned at build, we tag the image with the repository identifier:

```
$ docker tag 84cd12ee647f 123456789012.dkr.ecr.eu-west-1.
amazonaws.com/sklearn-custom:sklearn
```

5. We push the image to the repository:

```
$ docker push 123456789012.dkr.ecr.eu-west-1.amazonaws.
com/sklearn-custom:sklearn
```

The image is now ready for training with a SageMaker estimator:

1. We define an SKLearn estimator, setting the image_uri parameter to the name of the container we just created. We use **Local Mode** for fast training:

```
import sagemaker
from sagemaker.sklearn import SKLearn

session = sagemaker.Session()
output = 'file://.'

sk = SKLearn(
    role=sagemaker.get_execution_role(),
    entry_point='sklearn-boston-housing.py',
    image_name='123456789012.dkr.ecr.eu-west-
                1.amazonaws.com/sklearn-custom:sklearn',
    instance_count=1,
    instance_type='local',
    output_path=output,
    hyperparameters={
        'normalize': True,
        'test-size': 0.1
    }
)
```

2. We set the location of the training channel, and we launch training:

```
training = 'file://.'
sk.fit({'training':training})
```

3. In the training log, we see that our code is still invoked with Script Mode:

```
/usr/local/bin/python -m sklearn-boston-housing
--normalize True --test-size 0.1
```

As you can see, it's easy to customize training containers. Thanks to the SageMaker training toolkit, you can work just as with a built-in framework container. We used `Scikit-Learn` here, and you can do the same with all other frameworks.

However, we cannot use this container for deployment, as it doesn't contain any model serving code. We should add bespoke code to launch a web app, which is exactly what we're going to do in the next example.

Building a fully custom container for scikit-learn

In this example, we're going to build a fully custom container without any AWS code. We'll use it to train a scikit-learn model on the Boston Housing dataset, using a generic `Estimator`. With the same container, we'll deploy the model thanks to a `Flask` web application.

We'll proceed in a logical way, first taking care of the training, then updating the code to handle deployment.

Training with a fully custom container

Since we can't rely on Script Mode anymore, the training code needs to be modified. This is what it looks like, and you'll easily figure out what's happening here:

```
#!/usr/bin/env python
import pandas as pd
import joblib, os, json
if __name__ == '__main__':
    config_dir = '/opt/ml/input/config'
    training_dir = '/opt/ml/input/data/training'
    model_dir = '/opt/ml/model'

    with open(os.path.join(config_dir,
    'hyperparameters.json')) as f:
```

```
        hp = json.load(f)
        normalize = hp['normalize']
        test_size = float(hp['test-size'])
        random_state = int(hp['random-state'])
    filename = os.path.join(training_dir, 'housing.csv')
    data = pd.read_csv(filename)
    # Train model
    . . .
    joblib.dump(regr, os.path.join(model_dir, 'model.joblib'))
```

Using the standard file layout for SageMaker containers, we read hyperparameters from their **JSON** file. Then, we load the dataset, train the model, and save it at the correct location.

There's another very important difference, and we have to dive a bit into Docker to explain it. SageMaker will run the training container as `docker run <IMAGE_ID> train`, passing the `train` argument to the entry point of the container.

If your container has a predefined entry point, the `train` argument will be passed to it, say, `/usr/bin/python train`. If your container doesn't have a predefined entry point, `train` is the actual command that will be run.

To avoid annoying issues, I recommend that your training code ticks the following boxes:

- Name it `train`—no extension, just `train`.
- Make it executable.
- Make sure it's in the `PATH` value.
- The first line of the script should define the path to the interpreter, for example, `#!/usr/bin/env python`.

This should guarantee that your training code is invoked correctly whether your container has a predefined entry point or not.

We'll take care of this in the `Dockerfile`, starting from an official Python image. Note that we're not installing the SageMaker training toolkit any longer:

```
FROM python:3.7
RUN pip3 install --no-cache scikit-learn numpy pandas joblib
COPY sklearn-boston-housing-generic.py /usr/bin/train
RUN chmod 755 /usr/bin/train
```

The name of the script is correct. It's executable, and `/usr/bin` is in the `PATH`.

We should be all set—let's create our custom container, and launch a training job with it:

1. We build and push the image, using a different tag:

    ```
    $ docker build -t sklearn-custom:estimator -f Dockerfile-
    generic .
    $ docker tag <IMAGE_ID> 123456789012.dkr.ecr.eu-west-1.
    amazonaws.com/sklearn-custom:estimator
    $ docker push 123456789012.dkr.ecr.eu-west-1.amazonaws.
    com/sklearn-custom:estimator
    ```

2. We update our notebook code to use the generic `Estimator`:

    ```python
    from sagemaker.estimator import Estimator

    sk = Estimator(
        role=sagemaker.get_execution_role(),
        image_name='123456789012.dkr.ecr.eu-west-
                    1.amazonaws.com/sklearn-custom:estimator',
        instance_count=1,
        instance_type='local',
        output_path=output,
        hyperparameters={
            'normalize': True,
            'test-size': 0.1,
            'random-state': 123
        }
    )
    ```

3. The model artifact is visible in the current directory:

    ```
    %%sh
    tar tvfz model.tar.gz
    ```

    It contains the scikit-learn model we just trained:

    ```
    -rw-r--r-- ec2-user/ec2-user 812 2020-05-20 09:15 model.
    joblib
    ```

Now let's add code to deploy this model.

Deploying a fully custom container

`Flask` is a highly popular web framework for Python (https://palletsprojects.com/p/flask). It's simple and well documented. We're going to use it to build a simple prediction API hosted in our container.

Just like for our training code, SageMaker requires that the deployment script be copied inside the container. The image will be run as `docker run <IMAGE_ID> serve`.

HTTP requests will be sent to port `8080`. The container must provide a `/ping` URL for health checks and an `/invocations` URL for prediction requests. We'll use **CSV** as the input format.

Hence, your deployment code needs to tick the following boxes:

- Name it `serve`—no extension, just `serve`.
- Make it executable.
- Make sure it's in the `PATH`.
- Make sure port `8080` is exposed by the container.
- Provide code to handle the `/ping` and `/invocations` URLs.

Here's the updated `Dockerfile`. We install `Flask`, copy the deployment code, and open port `8080`:

```
FROM python:3.7
RUN pip3 install --no-cache scikit-learn numpy pandas joblib
RUN pip3 install --no-cache flask
COPY sklearn-boston-housing-generic.py /usr/bin/train
COPY sklearn-boston-housing-serve.py /usr/bin/serve
RUN chmod 755 /usr/bin/train /usr/bin/serve
EXPOSE 8080
```

This is how we could implement a simple prediction service with `Flask`:

1. We import the required modules. We load the model from `/opt/ml/model` and initialize the `Flask` application:

```
#!/usr/bin/env python
import joblib, os
import pandas as pd
from io import StringIO

import flask
from flask import Flask, Response
model_dir = '/opt/ml/model'
model = joblib.load(os.path.join(model_dir,
                    'model.joblib'))
app = Flask(__name__)
```

2. We implement the /ping URL for health checks, by simply returning HTTP code 200 (OK):

```
@app.route("/ping", methods=["GET"])
def ping():
    return Response(response="\n", status=200)
```

3. We implement the /invocations URL. If the content type is not text/csv, we return HTTP code 415 (Unsupported Media Type). If it is, we decode the request body and store it in a file-like memory buffer. Then, we read the CSV samples, predict them, and send the results:

```
@app.route("/invocations", methods=["POST"])
def predict():
    if flask.request.content_type == 'text/csv':
        data = flask.request.data.decode('utf-8')
        s = StringIO(data)
        data = pd.read_csv(s, header=None)
        response = model.predict(data)
        response = str(response)

    else:
        return flask.Response(response='CSV data only',
            status=415, mimetype='text/plain')

    return Response(response=response, status=200)
```

4. At startup, the script launches the Flask app on port 8080:

```
if __name__ == "__main__":
    app.run(host="0.0.0.0", port=8080)
```

That's not too difficult, even if you're not yet familiar with Flask.

5. We rebuild and push the image, and we train again with the same estimator. No change is required here.

6. We deploy the model:

```
sk_predictor = sk.deploy(instance_type='local',
                         initial_instance_count=1)
```

> **Reminder**
>
> If you see some weird behavior here (The endpoint not deploying, cryptic error messages, and so on), Docker is probably hosed. `sudo service docker restart` should fix most problems. Cleaning `tmp*` cruft in `/tmp` may also help.

7. We prepare a couple of test samples, set the content type to `text/csv`, and invoke the prediction API:

```
test_samples = ['0.00632, 18.00, 2.310, 0, 0.5380,
6.5750, 65.20, 4.0900, 1,296.0, 15.30, 396.90, 4.98',
'0.02731, 0.00, 7.070, 0, 0.4690, 6.4210, 78.90, 4.9671,
2,242.0, 17.80, 396.90, 9.14']
```

```
sk_predictor.content_type = 'text/csv'
sk_predictor.serializer =
    sagemaker.serializers.CSVSerializer()
```

```
response = sk_predictor.predict(test_samples)
print(response)
```

You should see something similar to this. The API has been successfully invoked:

```
b'[[29.801388899699845], [24.990809475886078]]'
```

8. When we're done, we delete the endpoint:

```
sk_predictor.delete_endpoint()
```

In the next example, we're going to train and deploy a model using the R environment. This will give us an opportunity to step out of the Python world for a bit. As you will see, things are not really different.

Building a fully custom container for R

R is a popular language for data exploration and analysis. In this example, we're going to build a custom container to train and deploy a linear regression model on the Boston Housing dataset.

The overall process is similar to building a custom container for Python. Instead of using `Flask` to build our prediction API, we'll use `plumber` (`https://www.rplumber.io`).

Coding with R and Plumber

Don't worry if you're not familiar with R. This is a really simple example, and I'm sure you'll be able to follow along:

1. We write a function to train our model. It loads the hyperparameters and the dataset from the conventional paths. It normalizes the dataset if we requested it:

```
# train_function.R
library("rjson")
train <- function() {
    hp <- fromJSON(file =
            '/opt/ml/input/config/hyperparameters.json')
    normalize <- hp$normalize
    data <- read.csv(file =
            '/opt/ml/input/data/training/housing.csv',
        header=T)
    if (normalize) {
        data <- as.data.frame(scale(data))
    }
```

It trains a linear regression model, taking all features into account to predict the median house price. Finally, it saves the model in the right place:

```
    model = lm(medv~., data)
    saveRDS(model, '/opt/ml/model/model.rds')
}
```

2. We write a function to serve predictions. Using `plumber` annotations, we define a `/ping` URL for health checks and an `/invocations` URL for predictions:

```
# serve_function.R
#' @get /ping
function() {
  return('')
}


#' @post /invocations
function(req) {
    model <- readRDS('/opt/ml/model/model.rds')
    conn <- textConnection(gsub('\\\\n', '\n',
                                req$postBody))
    data <- read.csv(conn)
    close(conn)
    medv <- predict(model, data)
```

```
        return(medv)
}
```

3. Putting these two pieces together, we write a main function that will serve as
    the entry point for our script. SageMaker will pass either a `train` or `serve`
    command-line argument, and we'll call the corresponding function in our code:

```
library('plumber')
source('train_function.R')
serve <- function() {
    app <- plumb('serve_function.R')
    app$run(host='0.0.0.0', port=8080)}
args <- commandArgs()
if (any(grepl('train', args))) {
    train()
}
if (any(grepl('serve', args))) {
    serve()
}
```

This is all of the R code that we need. Now let's take care of the container.

Building a custom container

We need to build a custom container storing the R runtime, as well as our script. The
`Dockerfile` is as follows:

1. We start from an official R image in **Docker Hub** and add the dependencies
    we need:

```
FROM r-base:latest
RUN R -e "install.packages(c('rjson', 'plumber'),
repos='https://cloud.r-project.org')"
```

2. Then, we copy our code inside the container, and define the main function as its
    explicit entry point:

```
COPY main.R train_function.R serve_function.R /opt/ml/
WORKDIR /opt/ml/
ENTRYPOINT ["/usr/bin/Rscript", "/opt/ml/main.R", "--no-
save"]
```

3. We create a new repository in ECR. Then, we build the image and push it there:

```
$ aws ecr create-repository --repository-name r-custom
$ aws ecr get-login-password | docker login --username AWS
--password-stdin 123456789012.dkr.ecr.eu-west-1.
amazonaws.com/r-custom:latest
$ docker build -t r-custom:latest -f Dockerfile .
$ docker tag <IMAGE_ID> 123456789012.dkr.ecr.eu-west-1.
amazonaws.com/r-custom:latest
$ docker push 123456789012.dkr.ecr.eu-west-1.amazonaws.
com/r-custom:latest
```

We're all set, so let's train and deploy.

Training and deploying a custom container on SageMaker

Jumping into a Jupyter notebook, we use the SageMaker SDK to train and deploy our container:

1. We configure an `Estimator` with our custom container:

```
import sagemaker
from sagemaker.estimator import Estimator

session = sagemaker.Session()
region = session.boto_session.region_name

training = 'file://.'
output = 'file://.'

r_estimator = Estimator(
    role = sagemaker.get_execution_role(),
    image_uri='123456789012.dkr.ecr.eu-west-1.amazonaws.
            com/r-custom:latest',
    instance_count=1,
    instance_type='local',
    output_path=output,
    hyperparameters={'normalize': False}
)

r_estimator.fit({'training':training})
```

2. Once the training job is complete, we deploy the model as usual:

```
r_predictor = r_estimator.deploy
                         (initial_instance_count=1,
                          instance_type='local')
```

3. Finally, we read the full dataset (why not?) and send it to the endpoint:

```
import pandas as pd

data = pd.read_csv('housing.csv')
data.drop(['medv'], axis=1, inplace=True)
data = data.to_csv(index=False)

r_predictor.content_type = 'text/csv'
r_predictor.serializer =
    sagemaker.serializers.CSVSerializer()

response = r_predictor.predict(data)
print(response)
```

The output should look like this:

```
b'[30.0337,25.0568,30.6082,28.6772,27.9288. . .
```

4. When we're done, we delete the endpoint:

```
r_predictor.delete_endpoint()
```

Whether you're using Python, R, or something else, it's reasonably easy to build and deploy your own custom container. Still, you need to build your own little web application, which is something you may neither know how to do nor enjoy doing. Wouldn't it be nice if we had a tool that took care of all of that pesky container and web stuff?

As a matter of fact, there is one: **MLflow**.

Training and deploying with XGBoost and MLflow

MLflow is an open source platform for machine learning (`https://mlflow.org`). It was initiated by Databricks (`https://databricks.com`), who also brought us **Spark**. MLflow has lots of features, including the ability to deploy Python-trained models on SageMaker.

This section is not intended to be an MLflow tutorial. You can find documentation and examples at `https://www.mlflow.org/docs/latest/index.html`.

Installing MLflow

Let's set up a virtual environment for MLflow and install all of the required libraries. At the time of writing, the latest version of MLflow is 1.10, and this is the one we'll use here:

1. We first initialize a new virtual environment on our local machine, named `mlflow-example`. Then, we activate it:

    ```
    $ virtualenv mlflow-example
    $ source mlflow-example/bin/activate
    ```

2. We install MLflow and the libraries required by our training script:

    ```
    $ pip install mlflow gunicorn pandas sklearn xgboost boto3
    ```

3. Finally, we download the Direct Marketing dataset we already used with XGBoost in *Chapter 7, Extending Machine Learning Services with Built-In Framework*:

    ```
    $ wget -N https://sagemaker-sample-data-us-west-2.s3-us-west-2.amazonaws.com/autopilot/direct_marketing/bank-additional.zip
    $ unzip -o bank-additional.zip
    ```

The setup is complete. Let's train the model.

Training a model with MLflow

The training script sets the MLflow experiment for this run so that we may log metadata (hyperparameters, metrics, and so on). Then, it loads the dataset, trains an XGBoost classifier, and logs the model:

```python
# train-xgboost.py
import mlflow.xgboost
import xgboost as xgb
from load_dataset import load_dataset
if __name__ == '__main__':
    mlflow.set_experiment(dm-xgboost')
    with mlflow.start_run(run_name=dm-xgboost-basic') as run:
        x_train, x_test, y_train, y_test = load_dataset(
            'bank-additional/bank-additional-full.csv', ';')
        cls = xgb.XGBClassifier(objective='binary:logistic',
                                eval_metric='auc')
        cls.fit(x_train, y_train)
```

```
        auc = cls.score(x_test, y_test)

        mlflow.log_metric("auc", auc)
        mlflow.xgboost.log_model(cls, "dm-xgboost-model")
        mlflow.end_run()
```

The `load_dataset()` function does what its name implies and logs several parameters:

```
# load_dataset.py

import mlflow
import pandas as pd
from sklearn.model_selection import train_test_split

def load_dataset(path, test_size=0.2, random_state=123):
    data = pd.read_csv(path)
    data = pd.get_dummies(data)
    data = data.drop(['y_no'], axis=1)
    x = data.drop(['y_yes'], axis=1)
    y = data['y_yes']

    mlflow.log_param("dataset_path", path)
    mlflow.log_param("dataset_shape", data.shape)
    mlflow.log_param("test_size", test_size)
    mlflow.log_param("random_state", random_state)
    mlflow.log_param("one_hot_encoding", True)

    return train_test_split(x, y, test_size=test_size,
                            random_state=random_state)
```

Let's train the model and visualize its results in the MLflow web application:

1. Inside the virtual environment we just created, we run the training script just like any Python program:

```
$ python train-xgboost.py
INFO: 'dm-xgboost' does not exist. Creating a new
experiment
AUC  0.91442097596504
```

2. We launch the MLflow web application:

```
$ mlflow ui &
```

3. Pointing our browser at `http://localhost:5000`, we see information on our run, as shown in the following screenshot:

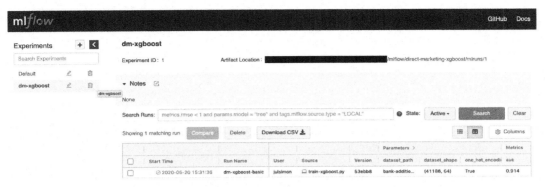

Figure 8.1 Viewing our job in Mlflow

The training was successful. Before we can deploy the model on SageMaker, we must build a SageMaker container. As it turns out, it's the simplest thing.

Building a SageMaker container with MLflow

All it takes is a single command:

```
$ mlflow sagemaker build-and-push-container
```

MLflow will automatically build a Docker container compatible with SageMaker, with all required dependencies. Then, it creates a repository in Amazon ECR named `mlflow-pyfunc` and pushes the image to it. Obviously, this requires your AWS credentials to be properly set up.

Once this command completes, you should see the image in ECR, as shown in the following screenshot:

Figure 8.2 Viewing our container in Mlflow

Our container is now ready for deployment.

Deploying a model locally with MLflow

We will deploy our model using the following steps:

1. We can deploy our model locally with a single command, passing its location and the HTTP port. This fires up a local web application based on `gunicorn`:

    ```
    $ mlflow sagemaker run-local -p 8888 -m
    mlruns/1/8bf1925d313c492a8488d7046c3ae358/artifacts/
    dm-xgboost-model/
    ```

    You should see something similar to this:

    ```
    [2020-07-28 11:38:57 +0000] [512] [INFO] Starting
    gunicorn 20.0.4
    [2020-07-28 11:38:57 +0000] [512] [INFO] Listening at:
    http://127.0.0.1:8000 (512)
    [2020-07-28 11:38:57 +0000] [512] [INFO] Using worker:
    gevent
    [2020-07-28 11:38:57 +0000] [525] [INFO] Booting worker
    with pid: 525
    ```

2. Our prediction code is quite straightforward. We load CSV samples from the dataset, convert them into JSON format, and send them to the endpoint using the `requests` library, a popular Python library for HTTP (`https://requests.readthedocs.io`):

    ```python
    # predict-xgboost-local.py

    import json
    import requests
    from load_dataset import load_dataset

    port = 8888

    if __name__ == '__main__':
        x_train, x_test, y_train, y_test = load_dataset(
            'bank-additional/bank-additional-full.csv')

        input_data = x_test[:10].to_json(orient="split")
        endpoint =
            "http://localhost:{}/invocations".format(port)
        headers = {"Content-type": "application/json;
                    format=pandas-split"}

        prediction = requests.post(endpoint,
        json=json.loads(input_data), headers=headers)

        print(prediction.text)
    ```

3. Running this code in another shell invokes the local model and prints out predictions:

```
$ python predict-xgboost-local.py
[0.00046298891538754106, 0.10499032586812973, . . .
```

4. When we're done, we terminate the local server with *Ctrl + C*.

Now that we're confident that our model works locally, we can deploy it on SageMaker.

Deploying a model on SageMaker with MLflow

This is a one-liner again:

1. We need to pass an application name, the model path, and the name of an **IAM** role allowed to invoke SageMaker endpoints. You can use the same role you've used in previous chapters:

```
$ mlflow sagemaker deploy
-a mlflow-xgb-demo
-m mlruns/1/8bf1925d313c492a8488d7046c3ae358/artifacts/
dm-xgboost-model/
-e arn:aws:iam::123456789012:role/service-role/Sagemaker-
fullaccess
```

2. After a few minutes, the endpoint is in service, and we can see it in the SageMaker console, as shown in the following screenshot:

Figure 8.3 Viewing our endpoint in the SageMaker console

3. We could also use the AWS CLI to list endpoints:

```
$ aws sagemaker list-endpoints
{
  "Endpoints": [
    {
      "EndpointName": "mlflow-xgb-demo",
      "EndpointArn": "arn:aws:sagemaker:eu-west-
                    1:123456789012:endpoint/mlflow-xgb-
```

```
                        demo",
        "CreationTime": 1589985454.032,
        "LastModifiedTime": 1589985825.271,
        "EndpointStatus": "InService"
      }
  ]
}
```

4. We invoke the endpoint with the following code. It loads the test dataset and sends the first 10 samples in JSON format to the endpoint named after our application:

```python
# predict-xgboost.py
import boto3
from load_dataset import load_dataset

app_name = 'mlflow-xgb-demo'
region = 'eu-west-1'

if __name__ == '__main__':
    sm = boto3.client('sagemaker', region_name=region)
    smrt = boto3.client('runtime.sagemaker',
                        region_name=region)

    endpoint = sm.describe_endpoint(EndpointName=
                                              app_name)
    print("Endpoint status: ", endpoint["EndpointStatus"])

    x_train, x_test, y_train, y_test = load_dataset(
        'bank-additional/bank-additional-full.csv')

    input_data = x_test[:10].to_json(orient="split")
    prediction = smrt.invoke_endpoint(
        EndpointName=app_name,
        Body=input_data,
        ContentType='application/json;
                    format=pandas-split')

    prediction =
        prediction['Body'].read().decode("ascii")
    print(prediction)
```

Wait a minute! We are not using the SageMaker SDK. What's going on here?

In this example, we're dealing with an existing endpoint, not an endpoint that we created by fitting an estimator and deploying a predictor. We could still rebuild a predictor using SageMaker SDK, as we'll see in *Chapter 11, Deploying Machine Learning Models.*

Instead, we use our good old friend `boto3`, the AWS SDK for Python. We first invoke the `describe_endpoint()` API to check that the endpoint is in service. Then, we use the `invoke_endpoint()` API to...invoke the endpoint! As you may have guessed, the `list-endpoints` CLI call we ran earlier is based on the `boto3 list_endpoints()` API. For now, we don't need to know more.

We run the prediction code on our local machine, and it produces the following output:

```
$ python3 predict-xgboost.py
Endpoint status:  InService
[0.00046298891538754106, 0.10499032586812973,
0.016391035169363022, . . .
```

5. When we're done, we take down the endpoint with the MLflow CLI. It will clean up all resources created for deployment:

```
$ mlflow sagemaker delete -a mlflow-xgb-demo
```

The development experience with MLflow is pretty simple. It has also plenty of other features you may want to explore.

In the last example of this chapter, we're going to look at another open source tool, purposely built to simplify working with SageMaker models.

Training and deploying with XGBoost and Sagify

Sagify is a CLI tool that minimizes the amount of work required to train and deploy models on SageMaker (`https://github.com/Kenza-AI/sagify`). You write a training function and a prediction function, and Sagify takes care of the rest, both locally and on SageMaker.

> **Note:**
> At the time of writing, Sagify hasn't been updated for SageMaker SDK v2.
> If that's still not the case by the time this book is in your hands, please make sure to install SDK v1 in your virtual environment.

Installing Sagify

You only need to run these steps once. If you need more details, you can find them at `https://kenza-ai.github.io/sagify/#installation`:

1. We create a virtual environment and activate it:

   ```
   $ virtualenv sagify-demo
   $ source sagify-demo/bin/activate
   ```

2. We install the dependencies:

   ```
   $ pip install sagify pandas
   ```

3. We update our local AWS credentials with the SageMaker role in `~/.aws/config`. The file should look similar to this:

   ```
   [default]
   region = eu-west-1
   profile = default
   role_arn=arn:aws:iam::123456789012:role/service-role/
   AmazonSageMaker-ExecutionRole-20200415T163681
   source_profile=default
   ```

4. In the IAM console, we add the ARN of our user to the trust policy for this role. It should look like this:

   ```
   {
     "Version": "2012-10-17",
     "Statement": [
       {
         "Effect": "Allow",
         "Principal": {
           "AWS": "arn:aws:iam::123456789012:user/
                              YOUR_USERNAME",
           "Service": "sagemaker.amazonaws.com"
         },
         "Action": "sts:AssumeRole"
       }
     ]
   }
   ```

The setup is complete. Now, we're going the write our training and prediction code.

Coding our model with Sagify

A little bit of setup is required before we can write our code:

1. First, we initialize a new Sagify project with `sagify init`, as shown in the following screenshot. This creates scaffolding code where'll we add ours:

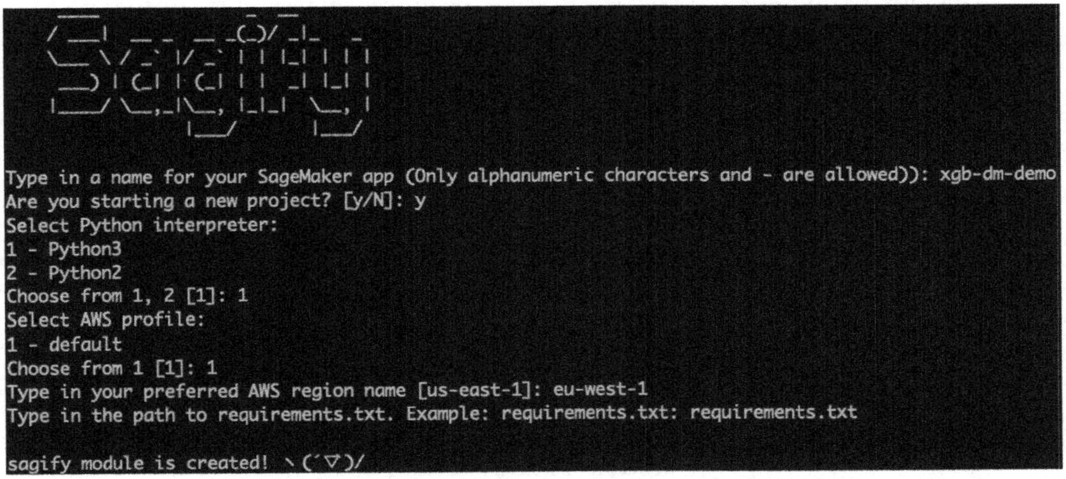

```
Type in a name for your SageMaker app (Only alphanumeric characters and - are allowed)): xgb-dm-demo
Are you starting a new project? [y/N]: y
Select Python interpreter:
1 - Python3
2 - Python2
Choose from 1, 2 [1]: 1
Select AWS profile:
1 - default
Choose from 1 [1]: 1
Type in your preferred AWS region name [us-east-1]: eu-west-1
Type in the path to requirements.txt. Example: requirements.txt: requirements.txt

sagify module is created! ヽ(´▽｀)/
```

Figure 8.4 Creating a new project with Sagify

2. We'll work with the Direct Marketing dataset again, and we just need to copy it to the appropriate location:

```
$ cp bank-additional-full.csv src/sagify_base/local_test/
test_dir/input/data/training
```

3. We define hyperparameters for the training job at `src/sagify_base/local_test/test_dir/input/config/hyperparameters.json`. This is an optional step:

```
{ "test-size": 0.1, "random-state": 123 }
```

4. We replace the skeleton function in `src/sagify_base/training/training.py` with our own training code. First, it reads the hyperparameters:

```
import json, os
import pandas as pd
import xgboost as xgb
from sklearn.model_selection import train_test_split

def train(input_data_path, model_save_path, hyperparams_
path=None):
```

```
with open(hyperparams_path) as f:
    hp = json.load(f)
    test_size =  float(hp['test-size'])
    random_state =  int(hp['random-state'])
```

Then, it loads the dataset, one-hot encodes the categorical features, and splits the data into training and test sets. It also saves the processed test set for further use:

```
data = pd.read_csv(os.path.join(input_data_path,
        'bank-additional-full.csv'))
data = pd.get_dummies(data)
data.drop(['y_no'], axis=1, inplace=True)
x = data.drop(['y_yes'], axis=1)
y = data['y_yes']

x_train, x_test, y_train, y_test = train_test_split(
x, y, test_size=test_size, random_state=random_state)

x_test.to_csv(os.path.join(model_save_path,
                'x_test.csv'),
                index=False,header=False)

y_test.to_csv(os.path.join(model_save_path,
                'y_test.csv'),
                index=False,header=False)
```

Then, it trains the model, saves the metric to a file, and saves the model itself:

```
cls = xgb.XGBClassifier(objective='binary:logistic',
eval_metric='auc')
cls.fit(x_train, y_train)
auc = cls.score(x_test, y_test)

accuracy_report_file_path =
            os.path.join(model_save_path,
                            'report.txt')

with open(accuracy_report_file_path, 'w') as f:
    f.write(str(auc))

cls.save_model(
os.path.join(model_save_path, 'model.joblib'))
```

5. We replace the skeleton code in src/sagify_base/prediction/prediction.py with our own. First, we need a function to load the model—nothing special:

```
def get_model(cls):
    if cls.model is None:
        cls.model = xgb.Booster({'nthread': 4})
        cls.model.load_model(
```

```
        os.path.join(_MODEL_PATH, 'model.joblib'))
        return cls.model
```

We also need a prediction function. It loads the features data from the JSON request, which stores a Python list of CSV samples. It converts it into a `numpy` array then into an XGBoost `DMatrix`. Finally, it predicts the data and returns a JSON answer:

```
def predict(json_input):
    data = json_input['features']
    data = np.array(data)
    data = xgb.DMatrix(data)
    prediction = ModelService.predict(data)
    return {
        "prediction": prediction.tolist()
    }
```

6. The last piece of the puzzle is to create a `requirements.txt` file with the dependencies we need. We place it in the top folder of the project:

```
sklearn
pandas
numpy
boost
```

We're done. Let's build and test this model locally.

Deploying a model locally with Sagify

The Sagify CLI makes it easy to deploy models:

1. First, we build the container that hosts our code:

```
$ sagify build
```

Once it's built, we can see the image on our local machine:

```
REPOSITORY  TAG     IMAGE ID      CREATED        SIZE
xgb-dm-demo latest  e6c4c177d751  7 seconds ago  1.01GB
```

2. We run a local training job:

```
$ sagify local train
```

Once training is complete, the artifacts saved by our training code are available:

```
$ ls src/sagify_base/local_test/test_dir/model
model.joblib  report.txt  x_test.csv  y_test.csv
```

3. We deploy the model locally. This creates a prediction API on port 8080:

```
$ sagify local deploy
```

We can tail the logs from the prediction container:

```
$ docker logs -f `docker ps -q`
Starting the inference server with 6 workers.
[2020-05-21 09:38:34 +0000] [11] [INFO] Starting gunicorn
20.0.4
. . .
[2020-05-21 09:38:35 +0000] [26] [INFO] Booting worker
with pid: 26
```

4. In another shell window, we use `curl` to send a prediction request. It contains the first two samples of the processed test set:

```
$ curl -X POST \
http://localhost:8080/invocations \
-H 'Cache-Control: no-cache' \
-H 'Content-Type: application/json' \
-d '{ "features": [[42,217,4,999,0,1.4,94.465,-
41.8,4.865,5228.1,0,0,0,0,0,0,0,1,0,0,0,0,0,
1,0,0,0,0,0,1,0,0,0,0,1,0,0,1,0,0,1,0,0,0,1,0,0,0,0,1,0,0
,0,0,0,0,1,0,0,0,0,1,0],
[37,93,1,999,0,-3.4,92.431,-
26.9,0.73,5017.5,0,1,0,0,0,0,0,0,0,0,0,0,0,
1,0,0,0,1,0,0,0,0,0,0,1,0,0,0,1,0,0,1,0,1,0,0,0,0,0,0,0,0
,0,1,0,1,0,0,0,0,0,1,0]]
}'
```

We see in the prediction log that it was processed correctly:

```
172.17.0.1 - - [21/May/2020:09:43:49 +0000] "POST /
invocations HTTP/1.1" 200 62 "-" "curl/7.65.3"
```

The `curl` response prints out the predictions:

```
{"prediction":
[0.00044324505142867565, 0.023858681321144104]}%
```

5. When we're done, we end the local deployment with *Ctrl + C*.

Since the model works as expected locally, let's deploy it on SageMaker.

Deploying a model on SageMaker with Sagify

Here too, we'll use the Sagify CLI:

1. We push our container to Amazon ECR:

```
$ sagify push
```

2. We upload the training set to an S3 bucket:

```
$ sagify cloud upload-data -i bank-additional/bank-
additional-full.csv -s s3://jsimon-sagify
```

3. We launch a training job on SageMaker, passing the location of the input data and hyperparameters file, as well as the instance type to use. Of course, you can see this job running in the SageMaker console and in SageMaker Studio:

```
$ sagify cloud train -i s3://jsimon-sagify/data/
-o s3://jsimon-sagify/output/
-e ml.m5.large
-h src/sagify_base/local_test/test_dir/input/config/
hyperparameters.json
```

4. Once training is complete, we deploy the model to an endpoint, passing the location of the model, the instance type, and the instance count:

```
$ sagify cloud deploy -m s3://jsimon-sagify/output/
xgb-dm-demo-2020-05-21-08-43-23-919/output/model.tar.gz
-e ml.t2.medium -n 1
```

5. Once the endpoint is in service, we load the first five samples from the processed test set. We format it according to what the endpoint expects—a JSON string, containing a single key (`features`), followed by a list of lists:

```python
import boto3, json, ast
import pandas as pd

x_test = pd.read_csv('x_test.csv', header=None)

payload = x_test[:5].to_json(orient="values")
payload = {"features": ast.literal_eval(payload) }
payload = json.dumps(payload)
```

The abbreviated payload looks like this. Again, make sure you send a **list of lists**, not a list of strings. This would cause the invocation to fail:

```
{"features": [
   [42, 217, 4, . . . 1, 0],
   [37, 93, 1, . . . 0, 1, 0],
   . . .
]}
```

6. We invoke the endpoint and print out the predictions:

```
endpoint_name = 'xgb-dm-demo-2020-05-21-21-38-35-984'
smrt = boto3.client('runtime.sagemaker')
response = smrt.invoke_endpoint(
    EndpointName=endpoint_name,
    Body=payload,
    ContentType='application/json')
print(response['Body'].read())
```

The output is as follows:

```
b'{"prediction": [0.00044324505142867565,
0.023858681321144104, 0.00967014767229557,
0.0007609269232489169, 0.07970048487186432]}'
```

7. When we're done, we delete the endpoint in the AWS console or with the `delete_endpoint()` API in boto3.

Summary

Built-in frameworks are extremely useful, but sometimes you need something a little—or very—different. Whether you're starting from the built-in containers or starting from scratch, SageMaker lets you build your training and deployment containers exactly the way you want them. Freedom for all!

In this chapter, you learned how to customize Python and R containers both for training and deployment. You saw how you could use them with the SageMaker SDK and its usual workflow. You also learned about two nice open source tools, MLflow and Sagify, and how you can train and deploy models using only a command-line interface.

This concludes our extensive coverage of modeling options on SageMaker: built-in algorithms, built-in frameworks, and custom code. In the next chapter, you'll learn about SageMaker features that help you to scale your training jobs.

Section 3: Diving Deeper on Training

In this section, you will learn advanced training techniques regarding scaling, model optimization, model debugging, and cost optimization.

This section comprises the following chapters:

- *Chapter 9, Scaling Your Training Jobs*
- *Chapter 10, Advanced Training Techniques*

9
Scaling Your Training Jobs

In the four previous chapters, you learned how to train models with built-in algorithms, frameworks, or your own code.

In this chapter, you'll learn how to scale training jobs, allowing them to train on larger datasets while keeping the training time and cost under control. We'll start by discussing when and how to take scaling decisions, thanks to monitoring information and simple guidelines. Then, we'll look at **pipe mode** and **distributed training**, two key techniques for scaling. We'll also discuss storage alternatives to S3 for large-scale training. Finally, we'll launch a large training job on the **ImageNet** dataset.

We'll cover the following topics:

- Understanding when and how to scale
- Streaming datasets with pipe mode
- Distributing training jobs
- Using other storage services
- Training an image classification model on ImageNet

Technical requirements

You will need an AWS account to run examples included in this chapter. If you haven't got one already, please point your browser at https://aws.amazon.com/getting-started/ to create it. You should also familiarize yourself with the AWS Free Tier (https://aws.amazon.com/free/), which lets you use many AWS services for free within certain usage limits.

You will need to install and to configure the AWS Command-Line Interface (CLI) for your account (https://aws.amazon.com/cli/).

You will need a working Python 3.x environment. Be careful not to use Python 2.7, as it is no longer maintained. Installing the Anaconda distribution (https://www.anaconda.com/) is not mandatory but strongly encouraged as it includes many projects that we will need (Jupyter, pandas, numpy, and more).

Code examples included in this book are available on GitHub at https://github.com/PacktPublishing/Learn-Amazon-SageMaker. You will need to install a Git client to access them (https://git-scm.com/).

Understanding when and how to scale

Before we dive into scaling techniques, let's first discuss the monitoring information that we should consider when deciding whether we need to scale and how we should do it.

Understanding what scaling means

Two sources of information are available: the training log and the infrastructure metrics in **Amazon CloudWatch**.

The training log tells us how long the job lasted. In itself, this isn't really useful. How long is *too long*? This feels very subjective, doesn't it? Furthermore, even when training on the same dataset and infrastructure, changing a single hyperparameter can significantly alter training time. Batch size is an example, and there are many more.

When we're concerned about training time, I think we're really trying to answer three questions:

- Is the training time compatible with our business requirements?
- Are we making good use of the infrastructure we're paying for? Did we underprovision or overprovision?
- Could we train faster without spending more money?

Adapting training time to business requirements

Ask yourself this question: what would be the direct impact on your business if your training job ran twice as fast? In many cases, the honest answer should be "none". There is no clear business metric that would be improved.

Sure, some companies run training jobs that last days, even weeks—think autonomous driving or life sciences. For them, any significant reduction in training time means that they get results much faster to analyze them and launch the next iteration.

Some other companies want the freshest models possible, and they retrain every hour. Of course, training time needs to be kept under control to make the deadline.

In both types of companies, scaling is vital. For everyone else, things are not so clear. If your company trains a production model every week or every month, does it really matter whether training reaches the same level of accuracy 30 minutes sooner? Probably not.

Some people would certainly object that they need to train a lot of models all of the time. I'm afraid this is a fallacy. As SageMaker lets you create on-demand infrastructure whenever you need it, training activities will never be capacity-bound. This is the case when you work with physical infrastructure, not with cloud infrastructure. Even if you need to train 1,000 **XGBoost** jobs every day, does it really matter whether each individual job takes 5 minutes instead of 10? Probably not.

Some would retort that "the faster you train, the less it costs". Again, this is a fallacy. The cost of a SageMaker training job is the training time in seconds multiplied by the cost of the instance type and by the number of instances. If you pick a larger instance type, training time will most probably decrease. Will it decrease enough to offset the increased instance cost? Maybe, maybe not. Some training workloads will make good use of the extra infrastructure, and some won't. The only way to know is to run tests and make data-driven decisions.

Right-sizing training infrastructure

SageMaker supports a long list of instance types, which looks like a very nice candy store (`https://aws.amazon.com/sagemaker/pricing/instance-types`). All you have to do is call an API to fire up an 8-GPU instance, more powerful than any server your company would have allowed you to buy. Caveat emptor: don't forget the "pricing" part of the URL!

> **Note:**
>
> If the words "EC2 instance" don't mean much to you, I would definitely recommend reading a bit about Amazon EC2 at `https://docs.aws.amazon.com/AWSEC2/latest/UserGuide/concepts.html`.

Granted, cloud infrastructure doesn't require you to pay a lot of money upfront to buy and host servers. Still, the AWS bill will come at the end of the month. Hence, even using cost optimization techniques such as Managed Spot Training (which we'll discuss in the next chapter), it's critical that you right-size your training infrastructure.

My advice is always the same:

1. Identify business requirements that depend on training time.
2. Start with the smallest reasonable amount of infrastructure.
3. Measure technical metrics and cost.
4. If business requirements are met, did you overprovision? There are two possible answers:
5. a) **Yes**: Scale down and repeat.
6. b) **No**: You're done.
7. If business requirements are not met, identify bottlenecks.
8. Run some tests while scaling up (larger instance types) and scaling out (more instances).
9. Measure technical metrics and cost.
10. Implement the best solution for your business context.
11. Repeat.

Of course, this process is only as good as the people who take part in it. Be critical! "Too slow" is not a data point—it's an opinion.

Deciding when to scale

When it comes to monitoring information, you can rely on two sources:

*   The training log: total training time and the number of samples per second
*   Amazon CloudWatch (`https://aws.amazon.com/cloudwatch`)

As discussed in the previous section, the total training time is not a very useful metric. Unless you have very strict deadlines, it's best to ignore it.

The number of samples per second is more interesting. You can use it to compare your training job to benchmarks available in research papers or blog posts. If someone has managed to train the same model twice as fast on the same GPU, you should be able to do the same. When you get close to that number, you'll also know that there's not a lot of room for improvement and that other scaling techniques should be considered.

First and foremost, you should look at CloudWatch metrics to understand how your training infrastructure is and where potential bottlenecks may lie:

- CPU and GPU utilization of the training container
- Memory utilization of the training container (percentage of total memory available)
- Disk utilization (percentage of total disk available)
- Training throughput (samples per second)

Deciding how to scale

As mentioned earlier, you can either scale up (move to a bigger instance) or scale out (use several instances for distributed training). Let's look at the pros and cons.

Scaling up

Scaling up is simple. You just need to change the instance type. There's no obvious reason to change the format of the dataset. Monitoring stays the same, and there's only one training log to read. Last but not least, training on a single instance is predictable, and very often delivers the best accuracy.

On the downside, your algorithm may not be parallel enough to benefit from the extra computing power. Extra vCPUs and GPUs are only useful if they're put to work. Your network and storage layers must also be fast enough to keep them busy at all times, which may require using alternatives to S3 and **EBS**, generating some extra engineering work. Even if you don't hit any of these problems, there comes a point where there isn't a bigger instance you can use.

> **Note:**
> If the word "EBS" doesn't mean much to you, I would definitely recommend reading a bit about it at `https://docs.aws.amazon.com/AWSEC2/latest/UserGuide/AmazonEBS.html`.

Scaling up with multi-GPU instances

Multi-GPU instances can be used in two configurations:

- **Data parallelism**: The full model is loaded on each GPU. Each training batch is split across all GPUs. When you configure the estimator, you should multiply the batch size by the number of GPUs, to maximize GPU memory utilization. In theory, training on n GPUs is equivalent to training on one GPU with n times the amount of GPU memory. In practice, things are often quite different, as we will see later in this chapter.

- **Model parallelism**: This is useful when a model is too large to fit on a single GPU. Using framework-specific APIs, model developers can assign each layer to a particular GPU. Hence, a training batch will flow across several GPUs to be processed by all layers. To achieve high throughput, this requires a very fast interconnect such as NVIDIA NVLink.

As tempting as multi-GPU instances are, they create specific challenges. An NVIDIA V100 GPU has 5,120 cores and 640 Tensor Cores. It takes a lot of CPU and I/O to keep them 100% busy. Adding more GPUs on the same instance only increases that pressure. You may quickly get to a point where GPUs are stalled, wasting your time and your money on under-utilized infrastructure. Reducing network and storage latency helps, which is why monster instances such as `ml.g4dn.16xlarge` and `ml.p3dn.24xlarge` exist. Still, that level of performance comes literally at a price, and you need to make sure it's really worth it.

You should keep in mind that bigger isn't always better. Although it's very fast, inter-GPU communication introduces some overhead that could be too significant for smaller training jobs. Here too, you should experiment, and find the sweetest spot.

In my experience, getting great performance with multi-GPU instances takes some work. Unless the model is too large to fit on a single GPU or the algorithm doesn't support distributed training, I'd recommend trying first to scale out on single-GPU instances.

Scaling out

Scaling out lets you train on extremely large datasets. Even if your training job doesn't scale linearly, you'll get a noticeable speedup compared to single-instance training. You can use plenty of smaller instances that only process a subset of your dataset, which helps to keep costs under control.

On the downside, datasets need to be prepared in a format that makes them easy to shard across training clusters. As distributed training is pretty chatty, network I/O can also become a bottleneck if you don't pay attention. Still, the main problem is accuracy, which is often lower than for single-instance training. This can be alleviated by asking training instances to synchronize their work periodically, but this is a costly operation that impacts training time.

If you think that scaling is harder than it seems, you're right. Let's try to put all of these notions into practice with a first simple example.

Scaling a BlazingText training job

In *Chapter 6, Training Natural Language Processing Models*, we used **BlazingText** and the Amazon reviews dataset to train a sentiment analysis model. We only trained it on 100,000 reviews at the time. This time, we'll train it on the full dataset: 1.8 million reviews—151 million words. The size of the training set in S3 is 720 MB.

To give BlazingText extra work, we apply the following hyperparameters:

```
bt.set_hyperparameters(mode='supervised', vector_dim=300, word_
ngrams=3, epochs=50)
```

We train on a single `ml.c5.2xlarge` instance. It has 8 vCPUs and 16 GB of RAM and uses Amazon EBS network storage (the `gp2` class, which is SSD-based). This is the case for all training instance types, except those with local **NVMe** storage (`g4dn` and `p3dn`).

The job runs for 2,117 seconds (a little more than 35 minutes), peaking at 4.66 million words per second. CloudWatch metrics are available in the SageMaker console, and you can see them in the following screenshot:

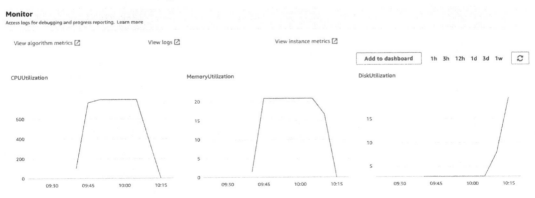

Figure 9.1 Viewing CloudWatch metrics

Memory utilization never exceeds 20%, so we definitely don't need more.

Disk utilization is 2% during the training, going up to 19% when the model is saved (it's about 2.1 GB). We allocated way too much storage to this instance. By default, SageMaker instances get 30 GB of EBS storage, so how much money did we waste here? EBS cost for SageMaker in `eu-west-1` is $0.154 per GB-month, so 30 GB for 2,117 seconds costs 0.154 * 30 * (2117/(24*30*3600)) = $0.00377. That's a ridiculously low amount, but if you train thousands of jobs per month, it will add up. Even if this saves us $10 a year, we should save that! This can easily be done by setting the `volume_size` parameter in all estimators.

Looking at the CPU utilization metric, we see that it plateaus at 792, very close to the maximum possible value of 800 (8 vCPUs at 100% usage). This job is obviously compute-bound.

So, what are our options? If BlazingText supported distributed training in supervised mode (it doesn't), we could have considered scaling out with smaller `ml.c5.xlarge` instances (4 vCPUs and 8 GB of RAM). Why not scale out with `ml.c5.2xlarge`? `ml.c5.xlarge` has more than enough RAM and would let us scale with finer granularity, which is good practice. In other words, we could add capacity in smaller chunks. This is what right-sizing is all about: not too much, not too little—it should be just right.

Anyway, our only choice here is to scale up. Looking at the list of available instances, we could try `ml.c5.4xlarge`. As BlazingText supports GPU acceleration, `ml.g4dn.xlarge` (1 T4 NVIDIA GPU) is also an option. Let's try both, and compare training times and costs.

Here are the results:

Instance type	vCPUs	RAM	Time	Samples per second	Resource utilization	Compute cost (eu-west-1 prices)
ml.c5.2xlarge	8	16	2177	4.66M	CPU: 792% RAM: 20%	(2177/3600) * $0.538 = **$0.325**
ml.c5.4xlarge	16	32	1600 (-26%)	6.64M (+42%)	CPU: 1590% RAM: 9.3%	(1600/3600) * $1.075 = **$0.478** (+47%)
ml.g4dn.xlarge	4	16	964 (-56%)	15.37M (+230%)	CPU: 355% GPU: 72.6% RAM: 21% GPU RAM: 16%	(964/3600) * $0.822 = **$0.220** (-32%)

Table 9.1 – Results of training on various instances

The GPU instance is a clear winner. It's 56% faster and 32% cheaper than our original choice. Blazing indeed! Could we go even further?

GPU memory utilization is low, so there should be room for improvement. Unfortunately, batch size is not a parameter we can set in supervised mode. As the saying goes: "you can't always get what you want".

As GPU utilization is pretty high, maybe adding more GPUs would help. However, BlazingText only supports a single GPU in supervised mode. That rules out trying out `ml.g4dn.12xlarge` and its 4 T4 GPUs.

Another GPU option is `ml.p3.2xlarge`, which hosts a single but more powerful V100 GPU. At $4.627 per hour, it's 5.6 times more expensive. It would have to crush the T4 to make it worth our while. What do you think?

Here are the results:

Instance type	vCPUs	RAM	Time	Samples per second	Resource utilization	Compute cost (eu-west-1 prices)
ml.p3.2xlarge	8	61	816	27.33M	CPU: 745% RAM: 4.5% GPU: 96% GPU RAM : 16.8%	(816/3600) * $4.627 = **$1.049**

Table 9.2 – Result of training on a specific powerful instance

This training job is only 15% faster, but it's more than three times the cost. That's a lot of premium for a modest time saving. The `g4dn` instance is a much more reasonable choice.

This simple example shows you that right-sizing your training infrastructure is not black magic. By following simple rules, looking at a few metrics, and using common sense, you can improve the cost-performance ratio of a training workload. Under the right circumstances, it's even possible to train faster and to reduce costs.

Sometimes, things don't go so well. Let's illustrate this with another example, where we try to scale up a reasonably heavy **Semantic Segmentation** job on multi-GPU instances.

Scaling a Semantic Segmentation training job

In *Chapter 5, Training Computer Vision Models*, we trained the built-in algorithm for Semantic Segmentation on the **Pascal VOC** dataset. Let's see whether we can scale it using multi-GPU instances from the `p3` family. We'll only update the batch size, multiplying it by the number of GPUs present on the instance. All jobs run for 30 epochs.

You can see the results in the following table:

Instance type	GPUs	Batch size	Time	Samples per second	Accuracy (mIOU)	Compute cost (eu-west-1 prices)
ml.p3.2xlarge	1	4	2586	35	0.61	(816/3600) * $4.627 = **$3.23**
ml.p3.8xlarge	4	16	1084 (-58%)	79 (+125%)	0.5238 (-14%)	(1084/3600) * $18.508 = **$5.57**
ml.p3.16xlarge	8	32	1223 (-53%)	80 (+128%)	0.4640 (-24%)	(1223/3600) * $37.016 = **$12.57**

Table 9.3 – Results of scaling semantic segmentation model

Remember what we said earlier about multi-GPU theory: training on n GPUs is equivalent to training on one GPU with n times the amount of GPU memory? So much for theory. We only get a 2x speedup with 4 GPUs, and things are worse with 8. We also see a significant drop in accuracy. We could probably offset it by training longer, but the cost would increase even more.

There is no silver bullet, my friends. Throwing more hardware blindly at a machine learning problem is rarely going to work. Sure, you may get some speedup, but the costs may become too large to make it worthwhile. Again, experimenting and analyzing the results is of paramount importance.

Let's look at some common training challenges and how we could address them. In the process, we'll introduce several SageMaker features that will be covered in the rest of this chapter.

Solving training challenges

"I need lots of storage on training instances".

As discussed in the previous example, most SageMaker training instances use EBS volumes, and you can set their size in the estimator. The maximum size of an EBS volume is 16 TB, so you should have more than enough. If your algorithm needs lots of temporary storage for intermediate results, this is the way to go.

"My dataset is very large, and it takes a long time to copy it to the training instances".

Define "long"! If you're looking for a quick fix, you can use instance types with high network performance, such as instances equipped with the **Elastic Fabric Adapter** (https://aws.amazon.com/hpc/efa). For instance, g4 instances can go up to 50 Gbit/s, and the largest p3 instance goes to 100 Gbits/s.

If that's not enough, and if you're training on a single instance, you should use pipe mode, which streams data from S3 instead of copying it.

If training is distributed, you can switch the **distribution policy** from FullyReplicated to ShardedbyS3Key, which will only distribute a fraction of the dataset to each instance. This can be combined with pipe mode for extra performance.

"*My dataset set is very large, and it doesn't fit in RAM*".

If you want to stick to a single instance, a quick way to solve the problem is to scale up. The ml.r5d.24xlarge and ml.p3dn.24xlarge instances have 768 GB of RAM! If distributed training is an option, then you should use it and shard the dataset.

"*CPU utilization is low*".

Assuming you haven't overprovisioned, the most likely cause is I/O latency (network or storage). The CPU is stalled because it's waiting for data to be fetched from wherever it's stored.

The first thing you should review is the data format. As discussed in previous chapters, there's no escaping **RecordIO** or **TFRecord** files. If you're using other formats (CSV, individual images, and so on), you should start there before tweaking the infrastructure.

If data is copied from S3 to an EBS volume, you can try using an instance with more EBS bandwidth. Numbers are available at https://docs.aws.amazon.com/AWSEC2/latest/UserGuide/ebs-optimized.html.

You can also switch to an instance type with local NVMe storage (g4dn and p3dn). If the problem persists, you should review the code that reads data and passes it to the training algorithm. It probably needs more parallelism.

If data is streamed from S3 with pipe mode, it's unlikely that you've hit the maximum transfer speed of 25 GB/s, but it's worth checking the instance metric in CloudWatch. If you're sure that nothing else could be the cause, you should move to other file storage services, such as **Amazon EFS** and **Amazon FSx for Lustre**.

"*GPU memory utilization is low*".

The GPU doesn't receive enough data from the CPU. You need to increase batch size until memory utilization is close to 100%. If you increase it too much, you'll get an angry `out of memory` error message, such as this one:

```
/opt/brazil-pkg-cache/packages/MXNetECL/MXNetECL-v1.4.1.1457.0/
AL2012/generic-flavor/src/src/storage/./pooled_storage_
manager.h:151: cudaMalloc failed: out of memory
```

When working with a multi-GPU instance in a data-parallel configuration, you should multiply the batch size passed to the estimator by the number of GPUs present on an instance.

When increasing batch size, you have to factor in the number of training samples available. For example, the Pascal VOC dataset that we used for Semantic Segmentation only has 1,464 samples, so it would probably not make sense to increase batch size above 64 or 128.

Finally, batch size has an important effect on job convergence. Very large batches typically slow it down, so you may want to increase the learning rate accordingly.

Sometimes, you'll simply have to accept that GPU memory utilization is low!

"GPU utilization is low".

Maybe your model is simply not large enough to keep the GPU really busy. You should try scaling down on a smaller GPU.

If you're working with a large model, the GPU is probably stalled because the CPU can't feed it fast enough. If you're in control of the data loading code, you should try to add more parallelism, such as additional threads for data loading and preprocessing. If you're not, you should try a larger instance type with more vCPUs. Hopefully, they can be put to good use by the data loading code.

If there's enough parallelism in the data loading code, then slow I/O is likely to be responsible. You should look for a faster alternative (NVMe, EFS, or FSx for Lustre).

"GPU utilization is high".

That's a good place to be! You're efficiently using the infrastructure that you're paying for. As discussed in the previous example, you can try scaling up (more vCPUs or more GPUs), or scaling out (more instances). Combining both can work for highly-parallel workloads such as deep learning.

Now we know a little more about scaling jobs, let's learn about SageMaker features, starting with pipe mode.

Streaming datasets with pipe mode

The default setting of estimators is to copy the dataset to training instances, which is known as File Mode. Instead, pipe mode streams it directly from S3. The name of the feature comes from its use of Unix **named pipes** (also known as **FIFOs**): at the beginning of each epoch, one pipe is created per input channel.

Pipe mode removes the need to copy any data to training instances. Obviously, training jobs start quicker. They generally run faster too, as pipe mode is highly optimized. Another benefit is that you won't have to provision any storage for the dataset on training instances.

Cutting down on training time and storage means that you'll save money. The larger the dataset, the more you'll save. You can find benchmarks at `https://aws.amazon.com/blogs/machine-learning/accelerate-model-training-using-faster-pipe-mode-on-amazon-sagemaker/`.

In practice, you can start experimenting with pipe mode for datasets in the hundreds of megabytes and beyond. In fact, this feature enables you to work with infinitely large datasets. As storage and RAM requirements are no longer coupled to the size of the dataset, there's no practical limit on the amount of data that your algorithm can crunch. Training on petabyte-scale datasets becomes possible.

Using pipe mode with built-in algorithms

The prime candidates for pipe mode are the built-in algorithms, as most of them support it natively:

- **Linear Learner, k-Means, k-Nearest Neighbors, Principal Component Analysis, Random Cut Forest,** and **Neural Topic Modeling**: RecordIO-wrapped protobuf or CSV data

- **Factorization Machines, Latent Dirichlet Allocation**: RecordIO-wrapped protobuf data

- BlazingText (supervised mode): Augmented manifest

- **Image Classification** or **Object Detection**: RecordIO-wrapped protobuf data or augmented manifest

- **Semantic Segmentation:** Augmented manifest

You should already be familiar with **RecordIO-wrapped protobuf**. If not, please revisit *Chapters 4* and *5*, where we covered it in detail. You should split the input dataset into multiple files (100 MB seems to be a sweet spot). This makes it possible to work with an unlimited amount of data regardless of maximum file size, and it can increase I/O performance. The `im2rec` tool has an option to generate multiple list files (`--chunks`). If you have existing list files, you can of course split them yourself.

We looked at the **augmented manifest** format when we discussed datasets annotated by SageMaker Ground Truth in *Chapter 5, Training Computer Vision Models*. For computer vision algorithms, this **JSON Lines** file contains the location of images in S3 and their labeling information. You can learn more at `https://docs.aws.amazon.com/sagemaker/latest/dg/augmented-manifest.html`.

Using pipe mode with other algorithms

As far as built-in frameworks are concerned, **TensorFlow** supports pipe mode thanks to the `PipeModeDataset` class implemented by AWS. Here are some useful resources:

- `https://github.com/aws/sagemaker-tensorflow-extensions`
- `https://github.com/awslabs/amazon-sagemaker-examples/tree/master/sagemaker-python-sdk/tensorflow_script_mode_pipe_mode`
- `https://medium.com/@julsimon/making-amazon-sagemaker-and-tensorflow-work-for-you-893365184233`

For other frameworks and for your own custom code, it's still possible to implement pipe mode inside the training container. A Python example is available at `https://github.com/awslabs/amazon-sagemaker-examples/tree/master/advanced_functionality/pipe_bring_your_own`.

Now, let's run some examples and learn what changes are required to enable pipe mode.

Training factorization machines with pipe mode

We're going to revisit the example we used in *Chapter 4, Training Machine Learning Models*, where we trained a recommendation model on the **MovieLens** dataset. At the time, we used a small version of the dataset, limited to 100,000 reviews. This time, we'll go for the largest version, and we'll convert it into RecordIO format to use pipe mode:

> **Note:**
> Given the size of the dataset, smaller Notebook instances will not suffice.
> `ml.t2.xlarge` and above will be fine.

1. We download and extract the dataset:

```
%%sh
wget http://files.grouplens.org/datasets/movielens/
ml-25m.zip
unzip ml-25m.zip
```

2. This dataset includes 25,000,095 reviews from 162,541 users, on 62,423 movies. Unlike the 100k version, movies are not numbered sequentially. The last movie ID is 209,171, which needlessly increases the number of features. The alternative would be to renumber movies, but let's not do that here:

```
num_users=162541
num_movies=62423
num_ratings=25000095
max_movieid=209171
num_features=num_users+max_movieid
```

3. We load the dataset into a sparse matrix (`lil_matrix` from **SciPy**):

```
X, Y = loadDataset('ml-25m/ratings.csv', num_ratings,
num_features)
```

4. We split the dataset for training and testing:

```
from sklearn.model_selection import train_test_split
X_train, X_test, Y_train, Y_test = train_test_split(X, Y,
test_size=0.05, random_state=59)
```

5. We convert both datasets into RecordIO-wrapped protobuf, and we upload them to S3. Depending on your Notebook instance, this may take 40-45 minutes, so please be patient. The matrix is stored as a single 1.5 GB file:

```
train_data = writeDatasetToProtobuf(X_train, Y_train,
bucket, train_prefix, train_key)
test_data = writeDatasetToProtobuf(X_test, Y_test,
bucket, test_prefix, test_key)
```

6. We configure the two input channels, and we set their input mode to pipe mode:

```
from sagemaker import TrainingInput
s3_train_data = TrainingInput (
    train_data,
    distribution='FullyReplicated',
    content_type='application/x-recordio-protobuf',
    s3_data_type='S3Prefix',
    input_mode='Pipe')
s3_test_data = TrainingInput (
    test_data,
    distribution='FullyReplicated',
    content_type='application/x-recordio-protobuf',
    s3_data_type='S3Prefix',
    input_mode='Pipe')
```

7. We configure an `Estimator` for one `ml.c5.xlarge` instance (4 vCPUs and 8 GB RAM), with 1 GB of EBS storage, the smallest amount possible. This instance costs $0.259 per hour in eu-west-1:

```
from sagemaker import image_uris
region = boto3.Session().region_name
container = image_uris.retrieve('factorization-machines',
region)
fm = sagemaker.estimator.Estimator(
    container,
    role=sagemaker.get_execution_role(),
    instance_count=1,
    instance_type='ml.c5.xlarge',
    output_path=output_prefix,
    volume_size=1)
fm.set_hyperparameters(
    feature_dim=num_features,
    predictor_type='regressor',
    num_factors=64,
    epochs=1)
fm.fit({'train': s3_train_data, 'test': s3_test_data})
```

We get the following results:

Mode	Samples per second	Job duration	Cost
File	87.4K	453s	$0.033
Pipe	96.3K (+10%)	381s (-16%)	$0.027 (-18%)

Table 9.4 – Results after training the model

As you can see, even with a modest 1.5 GB dataset, pipe mode already makes sense. In this example, we saved time both on downloading data and on model training. Given the measly cost of this training job, is it worth spending our precious time optimizing it further? Probably not.

Instead, let's run another example with the Object Detection built-in algorithm. We'll use pipe mode again, and we'll discuss scaling options.

Training Object Detection with pipe mode

In *Chapter 5, Training Computer Vision Models*, we trained the Object Detection algorithm on the Pascal VOC dataset, which we converted into a single RecordIO file. Although it's not necessary here, let's learn how to split this dataset into multiple files:

1. Using a **Notebook instance**, we open a terminal and activate the `conda` environment for **Apache MXNet**. You could use your own virtual environment too:

```
$ source activate mxnet_p36
```

2. We download and extract the Pascal VOC dataset:

```
$ cd /tmp
$ wget http://host.robots.ox.ac.uk/pascal/VOC/voc2012/
VOCtrainval_11-May-2012.tar
$ wget http://host.robots.ox.ac.uk/pascal/VOC/voc2007/
VOCtrainval_06-Nov-2007.tar
$ wget http://host.robots.ox.ac.uk/pascal/VOC/voc2007/
VOCtest_06-Nov-2007.tar
$ tar xf VOCtest_06-Nov-2007.tar
$ tar xf VOCtrainval_06-Nov-2007.tar
$ tar xf VOCtrainval_11-May-2012.tar
```

3. We clone the Apache MXNet repository. We use a built-in script to generate list files and RecordIO files for the training and validation datasets. If we were working with our own dataset, we would just use `im2rec`, as shown in *Chapter 5, Training Computer Vision Models*:

```
$ git clone --single-branch --branch v1.4.x https://
github.com/apache/incubator-mxnet
$ python3 incubator-mxnet/example/ssd/tools/prepare_
dataset.py --dataset pascal --year 2007,2012 --set
trainval --root VOCdevkit --target VOCdevkit/train.lst
$ python3 incubator-mxnet/example/ssd/tools/prepare_
dataset.py --dataset pascal --year 2007 --set test --root
VOCdevkit --target VOCdevkit/val.lst
```

4. We split the list files into 1,000-line chunks. Given the size of Pascal VOC images, the corresponding RecordIO files should be close to 100 MB:

```
$ cd VOCdevkit
$ split -d -l 1000 --additional-suffix=".lst" train.lst
train
$ split -d -l 1000 --additional-suffix=".lst" val.lst val
$ rm train.lst val.lst
$ cd ..
```

5. We use `im2rec` to build the RecordIO chunks: 17 for the training set, and 5 for the validation set, about 85 MB each. Then, we sync them to S3:

```
$ python incubator-mxnet/tools/im2rec.py --num-thread 8
VOCdevkit VOCdevkit
$ mkdir -p input/training input/validation
$ mv VOCdevkit/train??.rec input/training
$ mv VOCdevkit/val??.rec input/validation
$ aws s3 sync input s3://sagemaker-eu-
west-1-123456789012/pascalvoc-split/input
```

Moving back to the notebook, we're ready to train:

1. We update the S3 prefix to `pascalvoc-split`.

2. We set the input mode to pipe mode for both channels:

```
from sagemaker import TrainingInput

train_data = TrainingInput(
    s3_train_data,
    distribution='FullyReplicated',
```

```
        content_type='application/x-recordio',
        s3_data_type='S3Prefix',
        input_mode='Pipe')
validation_data = TrainingInput(
        s3_validation_data,
        distribution='FullyReplicated',
        content_type='application/x-recordio',
        s3_data_type='S3Prefix',
        input_mode='Pipe')
```

3. We launch the training job on an `ml.p3.2xlarge` instance, which hosts an NVIDIA V100 GPU with 16 GB of RAM and costs $4.627 per hour in eu-west-1. As the job starts, we see that no time is spent at all downloading data:

```
2020-05-26 07:42:40 Downloading - Downloading input data
2020-05-26 07:42:40 Training - Downloading the training
image...
```

4. We also see that 7 CPU threads are created to read data and feed it to the GPU. Deep learning is not just about GPUs, it needs fast CPUs too:

```
ImageDetRecordIOParser: pipe:///opt/ml/input/data/train,
use 7 threads for decoding..
```

5. Once the job is complete, we can compare the performance of **file mode** and pipe mode:

Mode	Data download	Images per second	Job duration	Cost
File	41 s	110	5991s	$7.70
Pipe	0 s	138 (+25%)	4963s (-17%)	$6.37 (-17%)

Table 9.5 – Results of training on file and pipe mode

Would you have expected that streaming from S3 could be this much faster than reading block storage from EBS? Given the higher cost of the GPU instance, the cost reduction is quite significant in dollar terms.

Now, let's see zoom in and find out how efficient this job really was.

Scaling our Object Detection job

The following screenshot shows the CloudWatch metrics for our pipe mode job. Please take a minute to observe them, and consider what our next scaling move should be:

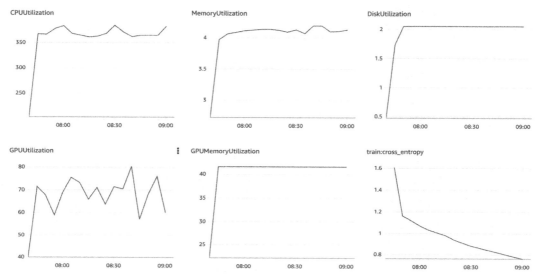

Figure 9.2 Viewing CloudWatch metrics with pipe mode

CPU utilization is medium at 360-380%, about half of the 800% maximum. Memory utilization and disk utilization are very low. GPU utilization is about 70%, and GPU memory utilization is stable at 41.5%.

This instance isn't breaking a sweat! GPU memory isn't even half full. That's not good because we're paying for more than we actually use. The low GPU memory utilization tells us that we should increase batch size and feed more images to the GPU in one go. This looks all the more possible since we have plenty of CPU capacity left to load and prepare images.

Before we jump to conclusions, let's step back and apply our simple scaling process. Unfortunately, at the time of writing, g4dn instances are not available for computer vision built-in algorithms, leaving us with two options: scale down to the less powerful and less expensive ml.p2.xlarge instance or stick with the same instance type and squeeze more performance out of it.

In the spirit of using the smallest instance possible, let's try option 1 first.

Running our Object Detection job on p2

An ml.p2.xlarge instance has 4 vCPUs and 1 NVIDIA K80 GPU with 12 GB of RAM, and it costs $1.361 per hour in eu-west-1. This is 3.4 times less expensive than ml.p3.2xlarge.

Training with a batch size set to 64, we see the following metrics:

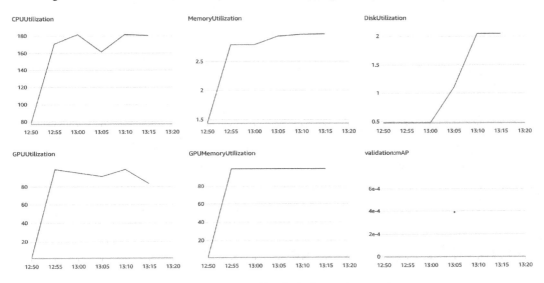

Figure 9.3 Viewing CloudWatch metrics on p2

This is a very busy instance! CPU, memory, and GPU utilization are maxed out. Unfortunately, training speed is much lower at 22 samples per second. Even though this instance is 3.4 times less expensive than the previous p3 instance, it's more than 7 times slower. Not a good deal, but it was worth trying.

Let's go back to the p3 family and tweak.

Tweaking our Object Detection job with p3 instances

The algorithm uses a default batch size of 32. With 41.5% GPU memory usage, we should be able to increase it to 32/0.415 = 77. As data is stored efficiently, there should be a little more room. Let's try 90, and see whether we can get close to 100% GPU memory usage:

```
od.set_hyperparameters(mini_batch_size=90, . . . )
```

After a few minutes of training, we see that GPU memory utilization has jumped to 99.7%. We filled the V100 to the brim this time. CPU and GPU utilization hasn't moved much. It looks like this algorithm isn't large enough to push the V100 into overdrive.

Here are the results:

Mode	Batch size	Data download	Images per second	Job duration	Cost
File	32	41 s	110	5991s	$7.70
Pipe	32	0 s	138 (+25%)	4963s (-17%)	$6.37 (-17%)
Pipe	90	0 s	156 (+42%)	4443s (-26%)	$5.71 (-26%)

Table 9.6 – Results of running the model on the V100 instance

Compared to our initial File Mode job with default batch size, we reduced the total training time by 26%. We also increased images per second by 42%, so the longer the training job, the closer we'd get to that speedup.

Now that we've tried File Mode with EBS and pipe mode with S3, what other storage options do we have? Let's look at Amazon Elastic File System and Amazon FSx for Lustre.

Using other storage services

Two other storage services can be used with SageMaker: **Amazon Elastic File System (EFS)** https://aws.amazon.com/efs) and **Amazon FSx for Lustre** (https://aws.amazon.com/fsx/lustre).

> **Note:**
>
> This section requires a little bit of AWS knowledge on VPCs, subnets, and security groups. If you're not familiar at all with these, I'd recommend reading the following:
>
> https://docs.aws.amazon.com/vpc/latest/userguide/VPC_Subnets.html
> https://docs.aws.amazon.com/vpc/latest/userguide/VPC_SecurityGroups.html

Working with SageMaker and Amazon EFS

EFS is a managed storage service compatiblewith **NFS** v4. It lets you create volumes that can be attached to EC2 instances and SageMaker instances. This is a convenient way to share data, and you can use it to scale I/O for large training jobs.

By default, files are stored in the **Standard** class. You can enable a life cycle policy that automatically moves files that haven't been accessed for a certain time to the **Infrequent Access**, which is slower but more cost-effective.

You can pick one of two throughput modes:

- **Bursting throughput**: Burst credits are accumulated over time, and burst capacity depends on the size of the filesystem: 100 MB/s, plus an extra 100 MB/s for each TB of storage.
- **Provisioned throughput**: You set the expected throughput, from 1 to 1024 MB/s.

You can also pick one of two performance modes:

- **General purpose**: This is fine for most applications.
- **Max I/O**: This is the one to use if tens or hundreds of instances are accessing the volume. Throughput will be maximized at the expense of latency.

Let's set up an EFS volume. Then, we'll mount it on a Notebook instance to copy the **Pascal VOC** dataset from S3. Finally, we'll train it on an Object Detection job. To keep costs reasonable, we won't scale the job, but the overall process would be exactly the same at any scale.

Provisioning an EFS volume

The EFS console makes it extremely simple to create a volume. You can find detailed instructions at `https://docs.aws.amazon.com/efs/latest/ug/getting-started.html`:

1. We set the volume name to `sagemaker-demo`.
2. We select our default **VPC**.
3. We create the volume.

4. Once the volume is ready, you should see something similar to the following screenshot:

Figure 9.4 Creating an EFS volume

The EFS volume is ready to receive data. We're now going to create a new Notebook instance, mount the EFS volume, and copy the Pascal VOC dataset we prepared earlier.

Creating a notebook instance inside a VPC

As EFS volumes live inside a VPC, they can only be accessed by instances located in the same VPC. These instances must also have a **Security Group** that allows inbound NFS traffic:

1. Accordingly, in the EC2 console (`https://console.aws.amazon.com/ec2/#SecurityGroups`), we create a Security Group allowing NFS inbound traffic. The simplest option is to start from the default Security Group for your VPC (it should be called "default"), copy it to a new Security Group, and allow inbound NFS. You can find instructions at `https://aws.amazon.com/premiumsupport/knowledge-center/vpc-copy-security-group-rules/`.

The inbound rules should look like the following screenshot (outbound rules should be left untouched). Don't forget to write down the identifier of this new Security Group (for me, it's sg-09238e6d):

Figure 9.5 Allowing NFS inbound traffic

2. In the VPC console (https://console.aws.amazon.com/vpc/#vpcs:sort=VpcId), we write down the VPC ID of our default VPC. For me, it's vpc-def884bb.

3. Still in the VPC console, we move to the Subnets section (https://console.aws.amazon.com/vpc/#subnets:sort=SubnetId). We write down the subnet IDs and the Availability Zone for all subnets hosted in the default VPC.

    For me, they look like what's shown in the next screenshot:

Figure 9.6 Viewing subnets for the default VPC

4. Moving to the SageMaker console, we create a Notebook instance in the default VPC, selecting the subnet hosted in the eu-west-1a Availability Zone. We also assign it to the Security Group we just created.

The **Network** information for this instance should look like in the next screenshot: `subnet-63715206` is part of the default VPC and is hosted in the eu-west-1a Availability Zone. Security Group `sg-09238e6d` is attached:

Network

Subnet(s)
subnet-63715206

Security Group(s)
sg-09238e6d

Figure 9.7 Notebook instance network settings

Now that the instance is ready, we can mount the EFS volume on it.

Mounting an EFS volume on a notebook instance

We can mount an EFS volume on a notebook instance using the usual Unix `mount` command:

1. Opening a Jupyter terminal on the notebook instance, we first create a mount point:

    ```
    $ mkdir /tmp/efs
    ```

2. In the EFS console, we find the IP address assigned to the volume in the subnet the Notebook instance lives in. As is visible in the next screenshot, mine is `172.31.6.185`:

Figure 9.8 IP addresses for an EFS volume

3. Then, adapting the `mount` command provided by the **Attach** button in the EFS console, we mount the volume on the notebook instance:

```
$ sudo mount -t nfs4
-o nfsvers=4.1,rsize=1048576,wsize=1048576,hard,timeo=600,
retrans=2,noresvport 172.31.6.185:/ /tmp/efs
$ df -h /tmp/efs

Filesystem          Size   Used Avail Use% Mounted on
172.31.6.185:/  8.0E      0  8.0E    0% /tmp/efs
```

4. We copy the Pascal VOC dataset to the EFS volume:

```
$ sudo aws s3 sync s3://sagemaker-eu-west-1-123456789012/
pascalvoc-split/input /tmp/efs/input
```

5. Finally, we unmount the EFS volume. You can also stop or delete the notebook instance if you'd like—we won't need it anymore:

```
$ sudo umount /tmp/efs
```

We're all set. Let's train on this dataset.

Training an Object Detection Model with EFS

The training process is identical, except for the location of input data:

1. Instead of using the `TrainingInput` object to define input channels, we use the `FileSystemInput` object, passing the identifier of our EFS volume and the absolute data path inside the volume:

```
from sagemaker.inputs import FileSystemInput

efs_train_data = FileSystemInput(
                file_system_id='fs-fe36ef34',
                file _system_type='EFS',
                directory_path='/input/train')

efs_validation_data = FileSystemInput(
                file_system_id='fs-fe36ef34',
                file_system_type='EFS',
                directory_path='/input/validation')

data_channels = {'train': efs_train_data,
                'validation': efs_validation_data }
```

2. We configure the `Estimator`, passing the list of subnets for the VPC hosting the EFS volume. SageMaker will launch training instances there so that they may mount the EFS volume. We also pass a Security Group allowing NFS traffic—we reuse the same as for the notebook instance:

```
from sagemaker import image_uris
container = image_uris.retrieve('object-detection',
                                region)
od = sagemaker.estimator.Estimator(
    container,
    role=sagemaker.get_execution_role(),
    instance_count=1,
    instance_type='ml.p3.2xlarge',
    output_path=s3_output_location,
    subnets=['subnet-63715206','subnet-cbf5bdbc',
             'subnet-59395b00'],
    security_group_ids=['sg-09238e6d']
)
```

3. We set hyperparameters (no change here) and train:

```
od.fit(inputs=data_channels)
```

Training lasts about an hour. We don't see any noticeable speedup here, which is to be expected with only one instance.

4. As we don't need the EFS volume anymore, we delete it in the console.

Now, let's see how we can use another storage service, Amazon FSx for Lustre.

Working with SageMaker and Amazon FSx for Lustre

Very large-scale workloads require high throughput and low latency storage, two qualities that Amazon FSx for Lustre possesses. As the name implies, this service is based on the Lustre filesystem (`http://lustre.org`), a popular open source choice for **HPC** applications.

The smallest filesystem you can create is 1.2 TB (like I said, "very large-scale"). We can pick one of two deployment options for FSx filesystems:

- **Persistent**: This should be used for long-term storage that requires high availability.
- **Scratch**: Data is not replicated, and it won't persist if a file server fails. In exchange, we get high burst throughput, making this is a good choice for spiky, short-term jobs.

Optionally, a filesystem can be backed up by an S3 bucket. Objects will be automatically copied from S3 to FSx when they're first accessed.

Just like for EFS, a filesystem lives inside a VPC, and we'll need a Security Group allowing inbound Lustre traffic (ports `988` and `1021-2023`):

1. In the FSx console, we create a filesystem named `sagemaker-demo`, and we select the Scratch deployment type.

2. We set storage capacity to 1.2 TB.

3. In the **Network & security** section, we choose to host in the eu-west-1a subnet of the default VPC, and we assign it the Security Group we just created.

4. In the **Data repository integration** section, we set the import bucket (`s3://sagemaker-eu-west-1-123456789012`) and the prefix (`pascalvoc-split`).

5. On the next screen, we review our choices, as shown in the following screenshot, and we create the filesystem.

    After a few minutes, the filesystem is in service, as shown in the following screenshot:

Figure 9.9 Creating an FSx volume

As the filesystem is backed by an S3 bucket, we don't need to populate it. We can proceed directly to training.

Training an Object Detection model with FSx for Lustre

Now, we will train the model using FSx as follows:

1. Similar to what we just did with EFS, we define input channels with `FileSystemInput`. One difference is that the directory path must start with the name of the filesystem mount point, a random string visible in the console:

```
from sagemaker.inputs import FileSystemInput
fsx_train_data = FileSystemInput(
```

```
      file_system_id='fs-07914cf5a60649dc8',
      file_system_type='FSxLustre',
      directory_path='/bmgbtbmv/pascalvoc-split/input/train')
 fsx_validation_data = FileSystemInput(
      file_system_id='fs-07914cf5a60649dc8',
      file_system_type='FSxLustre',
      directory_path='/bmgbtbmv/pascalvoc-split/input/
                                                validation')
 data_channels = {'train': fsx_train_data,
                  'validation': fsx_validation_data }
```

2. All other steps are identical. Don't forget to update the name of the Security Group passed to the `Estimator`.

3. When we're done training, we delete the FSx filesystem in the console.

Training lasts about an hour. Again, we don't see any noticeable speedup here, which is to be expected with only one instance.

This concludes our exploration of storage options for SageMaker. Summing things up, here are my recommendations:

- First, you should use RecordIO or TFRecord data as much as possible. They're convenient to move around and faster to train on, and they work with both File Mode and pipe mode.

- For development and small-scale production, File Mode is completely fine. Your primary focus should always be your machine learning problem, so don't go chasing seconds. EFS is also an interesting option for collaboration as it makes it easy to share datasets and notebooks.

- If you train with built-in algorithms, pipe mode is a no-brainer, and you should use it at every opportunity. If you train with frameworks or your own code, implementing pipe mode will take some work and is probably not worth the engineering effort unless you're working at a significant scale (hundreds of GBs or more).

- If you have large distributed workloads with tens of instances or more, EFS in Performance Mode is worth trying. Don't go near the mind-blowing FSx for Lustre unless you have insane workloads.

Speaking of distributed workloads, let's see how we can run them on SageMaker.

Distributing training jobs

Distributed training lets you scale training jobs by running them on a cluster of CPU or GPU instances. These may train either on the full dataset or on a fraction of it, depending on the distribution policy that we configure. `FullyReplicated` distributes the full dataset to each instance. `ShardedByS3Key` distributes an equal number of input files to each instance, which is where splitting your dataset into many files comes in handy.

Distributing training for built-in algorithms

Distributed training is available for almost all built-in algorithms. Semantic Segmentation and LDA are notable exceptions.

As built-in algorithms are implemented with Apache MXNet, training instances use its **Key-Value Store** to exchange results. It's set up automatically by SageMaker on one of the training instances. Curious minds can learn more at `https://mxnet.apache.org/api/faq/distributed_training`.

Distributing training for built-in frameworks

You can use distributed training with all frameworks except scikit-learn, which doesn't have native support for it. In particular, **Horovod** (`https://github.com/horovod/horovod`) is available for TensorFlow and **PyTorch**.

Distributed training requires minor changes to your code, which are obviously framework dependent. You can find more information in the framework documentation and at `https://sagemaker.readthedocs.io/en/stable/frameworks/`.

When it comes to SageMaker, the best starting point is one of the sample notebooks, hosted at `https://github.com/awslabs/amazon-sagemaker-examples`:

- **TensorFlow**:

  a) sagemaker-python-sdk/tensorflow_script_mode_horovod

  b) advanced_functionality/distributed_tensorflow_mask_rcnn

- **Keras**: `sagemaker-python-sdk/keras_script_mode_pipe_mode_horovod`

- **PyTorch**: `sagemaker-python-sdk/pytorch_horovod_mnist`

Each framework has its peculiarities, yet everything we discussed in the previous sections stands true. If you want to make the most of your infrastructure, you need to pay attention to batch size, synchronization, and so on. Experiment, monitor, analyze, and iterate!

Distributing training for custom containers

If you're training with your own custom container, you have to implement your own distributed training mechanism. Let's face it: this is going to be a lot of work. SageMaker only helps to provide the name of cluster instances and the name of the container network interface. They are available inside the container in the `/opt/ml/input/config/resourceconfig.json` file.

You can find more information at `https://docs.aws.amazon.com/sagemaker/latest/dg/your-algorithms-training-algo-running-container.html`.

It's time for a distributed training example!

Distributing training for Object Detection

Let's train the Object Detection algorithm on Pascal VOC again. We'll use the version we split into multiple RecordIO files, to shard the dataset across two `ml.p3.2xlarge` instances. Of course, we'll use pipe mode to avoid any copy. We'll also try different synchronization modes, and we'll see how they impact accuracy for a fixed number of epochs:

1. We start from the dataset already present in our default bucket, 17 RecordIO files for training and 5 for validation:

    ```
    bucket = session.default_bucket()
    prefix = 'pascalvoc-split'
    s3_train_data =
    's3://{}/{}/input/train'.format(bucket, prefix)
    s3_validation_data = 's3://{}/{}/input/validation'.
    format(bucket, prefix)
    ```

2. We define input channels in pipe mode, and we ask SageMaker to shard the datasets so that each instance gets half of the data. To avoid always sending the same RecordIO files to an instance, we shuffle them at the beginning of each epoch, using a `ShuffleConfig` object containing a random seed:

    ```
    from sagemaker import TrainingInput
    from sagemaker.session import ShuffleConfig
    train_data = TrainingInput(
                s3_train_data,
                distribution='ShardedByS3Key',
                shuffle_config=ShuffleConfig(59),
                content_type='application/x-recordio',
                s3_data_type='S3Prefix',
    ```

```
                input_mode='Pipe')
validation_data = TrainingInput(
                s3_validation_data,
                distribution='ShardedByS3Key',
                shuffle_config=ShuffleConfig(62),
                content_type='application/x-recordio',
                s3_data_type='S3Prefix',
                input_mode='Pipe')
data_channels = {'train': train_data,
                'validation': validation_data}
```

3. We configure the `Estimator` with two instances and as little storage as possible:

```
from sagemaker import image_uris

region = session.boto_region_name
container = image_uris.retrieve('object-detection',
                                region)

od = sagemaker.estimator.Estimator(
    container,
    role,
    instance_count=2,
    instance_type='ml.p3.2xlarge',
    volume_size=1,
    output_path=s3_output_location)
```

4. We set hyperparameters. We train several times with different synchronization modes: no synchronization; `dist_sync`, which forces training instances to synchronize model parameters at the beginning of each batch; and `dist_async`, which relaxes this constraint:

```
od.set_hyperparameters(
    base_network='resnet-50',
    use_pretrained_model=1,
    num_classes=20,
    epochs=30,
    num_training_samples=16551,
    mini_batch_size=90)
    # kv_store='dist_sync
    # kv_store='dist_async'
od.fit(inputs=data_channels)
```

Each training job lasts about an hour. Here are the results:

Instance count	Input mode	Sync mode	Job duration	Validation mAP	Cost
1	Pipe	-	4443s	0.2453	$5.71
2	Pipe + sharding	No sync	2415s (-46%)	0.0974 (-60%)	$6.20 (+9%)
2	Pipe + sharding	dist_sync	3114s (-30%)	0.2367 (-3.5%)	$8 (+40%)
2	Pipe + sharding	dist_async	3227s (-27%)	0.2285 (-7%)	$8.28 (+45%)

Table 9.7 – Cost analysis of training jobs for various input and sync modes

In the absence of synchronization, each instance trains on half the data, and results are merged at the end of the job. Unsurprisingly, job duration is almost divided by two, and the cost is almost constant. However, accuracy is much worse. The gap would certainly be smaller if we trained for more than 30 epochs, but it's very unlikely that we would close it completely. The following screenshot shows GPU utilization, which is consistently high:

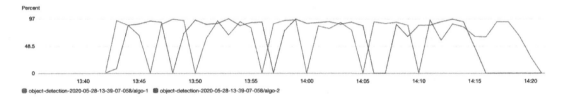

Figure 9.10 GPU utilization with no synchronization

Synchronous training is almost as accurate as single-instance training while achieving a respectable 30% speedup. The cost is higher, and it's up to you to decide whether this extra spend is worth it or not. If it's helping a team of engineers iterate faster, it sure is!

The following screenshot shows GPU utilization. The impact of synchronization is pretty obvious:

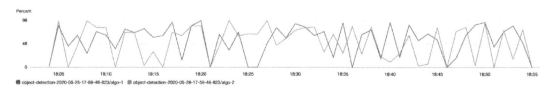

Figure 9.11 GPU utilization with synchronous training

Surprisingly, asynchronous training is slower than synchronous training, and repeated attempts gave the same results. This goes to show the importance of experimentation!

Training an Image Classification model on ImageNet

In *Chapter 5, Training Computer Vision Models*, we trained the Image Classification algorithm on a small dataset with dog and cat images (25,000 training images). This time, let's go for something a little bigger.

We're going to train a ResNet-50 network from scratch on the **ImageNet** dataset, the reference dataset for many computer vision applications (http://www.image-net.org). The 2012 version contains 1,281,167 training images (140 GB) and 50,000 validation images (6.4 GB) from 1,000 classes.

If you want to experiment at a smaller scale, you can work with 5-10% of the dataset. The final accuracy won't be as good, but it doesn't matter for our purposes.

Preparing the ImageNet dataset

This requires a lot of storage: the dataset is 150 GB, so please make sure you have at least 500 GB available to store it in multiple formats. You're also going to need a lot of bandwidth and a lot of patience to download it. Using an EC2 instance in the us-east-1 region, my download took **5 days**:

1. Visit the ImageNet website, register to download the dataset, and accept the conditions. You'll get a username and an access key allowing you to download the dataset.

2. One of the TensorFlow repositories includes a great script that will download the dataset and extract it. Using nohup is essential so that the process continues running even if your session is terminated:

```
$ git clone https://github.com/tensorflow/models.git
$ export IMAGENET_USERNAME=YOUR_USERNAME
$ export IMAGENET_ACCESS_KEY=YOUR_ACCESS_KEY
$ cd models/research/inception/inception/data
$ mv imagenet_2012_validation_synset_labels.txt synsets.txt
$ nohup bash download_imagenet.sh . synsets.txt >& download.log &
```

3. Once this is over (again, downloading will take days), the `imagenet/train` directory contains the training dataset (one folder per class). The `imagenet/validation` directory contains 50,000 images in the same folder. We can use a simple script to organize it with one folder per class:

```
$ wget https://raw.githubusercontent.com/juliensimon/aws/
master/mxnet/imagenet/build_validation_tree.sh
$ chmod 755 build_validation_tree.sh
$ cd imagenet/validation
$ ../../build_validation_tree.sh
$ cd ../..
```

4. We're going to build RecordIO files with the `im2rec` tool present in the Apache MXNet repository. I'm using a notebook instance, so I cloned the repository, and I activated the appropriate `conda` environment:

```
$ wget https://raw.githubusercontent.com/apache/
incubator-mxnet/master/tools/im2rec.py
$ source activate mxnet_p36
```

5. In the `imagenet` directory, we run `im2rec` twice: once to build the list files and once to build the RecordIO files. We create one chunk for each GB of data, and we resize the smaller dimension of images to 224 so that the algorithm won't have to do it:

```
$ cd imagenet
$ python ../incubator-mxnet/tools/im2rec.py --list
--chunks 6 --recursive val validation
$ python ../incubator-mxnet/tools/im2rec.py --num-thread
16 --resize 224 val_ validation

$ python ../incubator-mxnet/tools/im2rec.py --list
--chunks 140 --recursive train train
$ python ../incubator-mxnet/tools/im2rec.py --num-thread
16 --resize 224 train_ train
```

6. Finally, we sync the dataset to S3:

```
$ mkdir -p input/train input/validation
$ mv train_*.rec input/train
$ mv val_*.rec input/validation
$ aws s3 sync input s3://sagemaker-us-
east-1-123456789012/imagenet-split/input/
```

The dataset is now ready for training.

Defining our training job

Now the dataset is ready, we need to think about the configuration of our training job. Specifically, we need to come up with the following:

- An input configuration, defining the location and the properties of the dataset
- Infrastructure requirements to run the training job
- Hyperparameters to configure the algorithm

Let's look at each one of these items in detail.

Defining the input configuration

Given the size of the dataset (150 GB), pipe mode sounds like a great idea. Out of curiosity, I tried training in File Mode. Even with a 100 Gbit/s network interface, it took almost 25 minutes to copy the dataset from S3 to local storage. That wouldn't matter if we trained for days, but that won't be the case here. Pipe mode it is!

Bizarrely, the Image Classification algorithm doesn't support sharding, so we have to use the `FullyReplicated` replication policy. You may wonder why we took care of splitting the dataset into multiple files, then. There are three reasons:

- In general, multiple files create opportunities for more parallelism, making it easier to write code that reads from multiple files.
- We can shuffle the files at the beginning of each epoch, removing any potential bias caused by the order of samples.
- It makes it very easy to work with a fraction of the dataset.

Now that we've defined the input configuration, what about infrastructure requirements?

Defining infrastructure requirements

ImageNet is a large and complex dataset that requires a lot of training to reach good accuracy. It's time to go big and use `ml.p3dn.24xlarge` instances. Each one hosts 8 NVIDIA V100s with 32 GB of GPU memory, twice the amount available on other p3 instances. They also have 96 Intel Skylake cores, 768 GB of RAM, and 1.8TB of local NVMe storage. Although we're not going to use it, the latter is a fantastic storage option for long-running, large-scale jobs. Last but not least, this instance type has 100 Gbits/s networking, a great feature for streaming data from S3 and for inter-instance communication.

For good measure, we're going to use 8 of these instances, for a total of 64 GPUs and 2 TB of GPU memory. Now, at $43.697 per hour per instance, **this is a $350-per-hour training job**.

> **Note:**
>
> You may not want to try this at home or even at work without getting permission. Your service quotas probably don't let you run that much infrastructure anyway, and you would have to get in touch with AWS Support first.
>
> In the next chapter, we're going to talk about Managed Spot Training, a great way to slash training costs. We'll revisit the ImageNet example once we've covered this topic, so you definitely should refrain from training right now!

Setting hyperparameters

The documentation lists the available hyperparameters (`https://docs.aws.amazon.com/sagemaker/latest/dg/IC-Hyperparameter.html`).

We will go for a 50-layer **ResNet** that we'll train for 200 epochs. We stick to the **SGD** optimizer, starting with a high learning rate of 0.5 and halving it every thirty epochs using learning rate scheduling. Accordingly, we set up early stopping with a patience of 30 epochs. In other words, we'll stop training when dividing the learning rate by two doesn't make any difference.

We also use image augmentation, a technique proven to help models to generalize. Here, we ask the data loading code to automatically generate new training images by randomly cropping the images present in the dataset. Quick experiments with other augmentation modes didn't show any improvement.

What about batch size? Given the number of images in the dataset, using the largest batch size possible won't cause any issue. After a bit of experimentation, we find that a batch size of 2,816 (11*256) maximizes GPU memory utilization at 94%.

Training is distributed, and we ask instances to exchange results in synchronous mode. Finally, we decide to display top-3 accuracy during training.

We're now ready to train.

Training on ImageNet

Let's configure the training job:

1. We configure pipe mode on both input channels. Both are fully replicated, and the files of the training channel are shuffled for extra randomness:

```
prefix = 'imagenet-split'

s3_train_path =
's3://{}/{}/input/training/'.format(bucket, prefix)
s3_val_path =
's3://{}/{}/input/validation/'.format(bucket, prefix)
s3_output =
's3://{}/{}/output/'.format(bucket, prefix)

from sagemaker import TrainingInput
from sagemaker.session import ShuffleConfig

train_data = TrainingInput(
    s3_train_path
    distribution='FullyReplicated',
    shuffle_config=ShuffleConfig(59),
    content_type='application/x-recordio',
    s3_data_type='S3Prefix',
    input_mode='Pipe')

validation_data = TrainingInput(
    s3_val_path,
    distribution='FullyReplicated',
    content_type='application/x-recordio',
    s3_data_type='S3Prefix',
    input_mode='Pipe')

s3_channels = {'train': train_data,
               'validation': validation_data}
```

2. We configure the `Estimator` with 8 `ml.p3dn.24xlarge` instances:

```
from sagemaker import image_uris

region_name = boto3.Session().region_name

container = image_uris.retrieve('image-classification',
                                region)

ic = sagemaker.estimator.Estimator(
    container,
    role= sagemaker.get_execution_role(),
    instance_count=8,
    instance_type='ml.p3dn.24xlarge',
    output_path=s3_output)
```

3. We set hyperparameters according to our earlier decisions:

```
ic.set_hyperparameters(
    num_layers=50,
    use_pretrained_model=0,
    num_classes=1000,
    num_training_samples=1281167,
    augmentation_type='crop',
    mini_batch_size=2816,
    epochs=200,
    early_stopping=True,
    early_stopping_patience=30,
    learning_rate=0.5,
    lr_scheduler_factor=0.5,
    lr_scheduler_step='30,60,90,120,150,180',
    kv_store='dist_sync',
    top_k=3)
```

4. We launch training:

```
ic.fit(inputs=s3_channels)
```

Examining results

Training lasts for 17,301 seconds, a little under 5 hours. The cost of the training job is (17,301 / 3,600) * $43.697 * 8 = $1,680. Aren't you glad you refrained from running this notebook? That's a big number. We'll put this in perspective in the next chapter, and we'll slash costs thanks to **Managed Spot Training**.

You can see average per-instance metrics in the following screenshot:

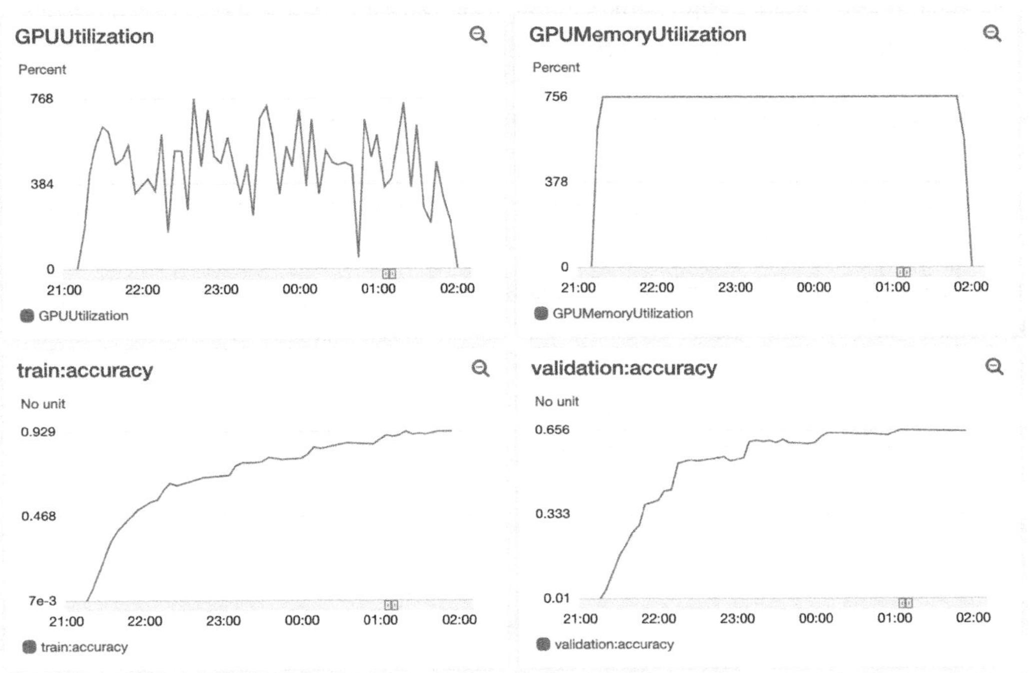

Figure 9.12 Viewing CloudWatch metrics

Average GPU utilization is above 60%, which is consistent with previous ResNet-50 examples. GPU memory utilization is maximal thanks to the large batch size.

Looking at the training log, we see that early stopping was triggered at epoch #150. Hence, the best epoch is #120, with a validation accuracy of 65.77%. As far as training metrics are concerned, top-1 accuracy is 88.7%, and top-3 accuracy is 96.7%.

This is a good result. However, it shows that training from scratch is hard, even with lots of data and infrastructure. In particular, finding optimal hyperparameters feels like a never-ending quest. Did we pick the right learning rate? How does batch size influence accuracy? In the next chapter, we'll take this guessing out of the equation with **Automatic Model Tuning**.

Summary

In this chapter, you learned how and when to scale training jobs. You saw that it definitely takes some careful analysis and experimentation to find the best setup: scaling up versus scaling out, CPU versus GPU versus multi-GPU, and so on. This should help you to make the right decisions for your own workloads and avoid costly mistakes.

You also learned how to achieve significant speedup with techniques such as distributed training, RecordIO, sharding, and pipe mode. Finally, you learned how to set Amazon EFS and Amazon FSx for Lustre for large-scale training jobs.

In the next chapter, we'll cover advanced features for hyperparameter optimization, cost optimization, model debugging, and more.

10
Advanced Training Techniques

In the previous chapter, you learned when and how to scale training jobs using features such as **Pipe Mode** and **distributed training**, as well as alternatives to S3.

In this chapter, we'll conclude our exploration of training techniques. You'll learn how to slash down your training costs with **Managed Spot Training**, how to squeeze every drop of accuracy from your models with **Automatic Model Tuning**, and how to crack models open with **SageMaker Debugger**.

This chapter covers the following topics:

- Optimizing training costs with Managed Spot Training
- Optimizing hyperparameters with Automatic Model Tuning
- Exploring models with SageMaker Debugger

Technical requirements

You will need an AWS account to run the examples included in this chapter. If you haven't got one already, please point your browser at `https://aws.amazon.com/getting-started/` to create it. You should also familiarize yourself with the AWS Free Tier (`https://aws.amazon.com/free/`), which lets you use many AWS services for free within certain usage limits.

You will need to install and to configure the AWS Command-Line Interface (CLI) for your account (`https://aws.amazon.com/cli/`).

You will need a working Python 3.x environment. Be careful not to use Python 2.7, as it is no longer maintained. Installing the Anaconda distribution (`https://www.anaconda.com/`) is not mandatory but strongly encouraged as it includes many projects that we will need (Jupyter, `pandas`, `numpy`, and more).

Code examples included in this book are available on GitHub at `https://github.com/PacktPublishing/Learn-Amazon-SageMaker`. You will need to install a Git client to access them (`https://git-scm.com/`).

Optimizing training costs with Managed Spot Training

In the previous chapter, we trained the **Image Classification** algorithm on the **ImageNet** dataset. The job ran for a little less than 5 hours. At $350 per hour, it cost $1,680. That's a lot of money, but is it really?

Comparing costs

Before you throw your arms up the air yelling "*What is he thinking?*", please consider how much it would cost your organization to own and run this training cluster. A back-of-the-envelope calculation for capital expenditure (servers, storage, GPUs, 100 Gbit/s networking equipment) says at least $1.5M. As far as operational expenditure is concerned, hosting costs won't be cheap, as each equivalent server will require 4-5 kW of power. That's enough to fill one rack at your typical hosting company, so even if high-density racks are available, you'll need several. Add bandwidth, cross connects, and so on: my gut feeling says it would cost about $15K per month (much more in certain parts of the world).

We would need to add hardware support contracts (say, 10% per year, so $150K). We'd also need to add labor costs for daily server maintenance and other hidden costs, but let's ignore them. Depreciating this cluster over 5 years (a very long time for GPUs!), the total monthly cost would be ($1.5M + 60*$15K + 5*$150K)/60 = $52.5. Let's round it to $55K.

Using conservative estimates, this spend is equivalent to 157 hours of training with the large $350-an-hour cluster we've used for our ImageNet example. As we will see later in this chapter, Managed Spot Training routinely delivers savings of 60-70%. So now the spend would be equivalent to 470 hours of ImageNet training per month.

This amounts to 65% usage (470/720) usage month in, month out, and it's very unlikely you'd keep your training cluster that busy. Add downtime, accelerated depreciation caused by hardware innovation, hardware insurance costs, the opportunity cost of not investing $1.5M in other ventures, and so on. The business case for physical infrastructure gets worse by the minute.

Financials matter, but the worst thing is that you'll only have one cluster. What if a potential business opportunity requires another one? Will you spend another $1.5M? If not, will you have to time-share the existing cluster? Of course, only you can decide what's best for your organization. Just make sure that you look at the big picture.

Now, let's see how you can easily enjoy that 70% cost reduction.

Understanding spot instances

At any given time, Amazon EC2 has more capacity than needed. This allows customers to add on-demand capacity to their platforms whenever they need to. On-demand instances may be created explicitly using an API call, or automatically if **Auto Scaling** is configured. Once a customer has acquired an on-demand instance, they will keep it until they decide to release it, either explicitly or automatically.

Spot Instances are a simple way to tap into this unused capacity and to enjoy very significant discounts (50-70% are typical). You can request them in the same way, and they behave the same too. The only difference is that should AWS need the capacity to build on-demand instances, your Spot Instance may be reclaimed. It will receive an interruption notification two minutes before being forcefully terminated.

This isn't as bad as it sounds. In practice, Spot Instances are unlikely to be reclaimed while you use them, and customers routinely keep them for days, if not more. In addition, you can architecture your application for this requirement, for example, running stateless workloads on Spot Instances and relying on managed services for data storage. The cost benefit is too good to pass!

Going to the EC2 console, you can view the price history per instance type in each region in the **Spot Requests** section. For example, the following screenshot shows the spot price of p3.2xlarge for the last 3 months. These are EC2 prices, and the same ratios apply to SageMaker prices:

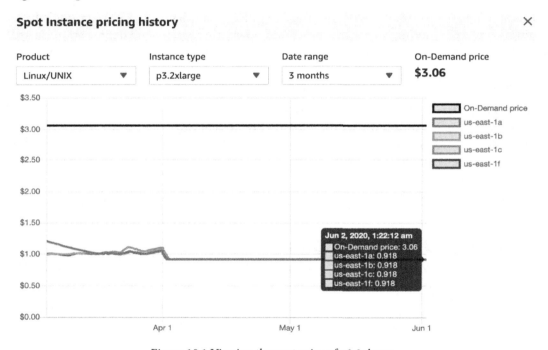

Figure 10.1 Viewing the spot price of p3.2xlarge

As you can see, for the last two months, the spot price has been 70% cheaper than the on-demand price. Discounts vary across instance types, regions, and even availability zones. You can use the describe-spot-price-history API to collect this information programmatically (https://docs.aws.amazon.com/cli/latest/reference/ec2/describe-spot-price-history.html).

Now, let's see what this means for SageMaker.

Understanding Managed Spot Training

Training with spot instances is available in all SageMaker configurations: single-instance training, distributed training, built-in algorithms, frameworks, and your own algorithms.

Setting a couple of estimator parameters is all it takes. You don't need to worry about handling notifications and interruptions. SageMaker will automatically do it for you.

If a training job is interrupted, SageMaker will reobtain adequate spot capacity, and relaunch the training job. If the algorithm uses checkpointing, the latest checkpoint will be loaded, and training will resume from there. If not, the job is restarted from the beginning.

How much work is required to implement checkpointing depends on the algorithm you're using:

- The three built-in algorithms for computer vision support checkpointing, as do XGBoost and Sequence-to-Sequence.

- All other built-in algorithms don't. You can still train them with Spot Instances, however, the maximum running time is limited to 60 minutes to minimize potential waste. If your training job takes longer than 60 minutes, you should try scaling it. If that's not enough, you'll have to use on-demand instances.

- Most frameworks support checkpointing. Some may enable it by default (such as **TensorFlow**), and some don't. Please check the framework documentation for details. Adding checkpointing to your script is generally quite straightforward.

- If you use your own custom code, you need to implement checkpointing.

In the last two cases, you simply have to save checkpoints inside the training container. The default path is /opt/ml/checkpoints, and you can customize it with an estimator parameter. SageMaker will automatically persist these checkpoints to a user-defined S3 path. If your training job is interrupted and relaunched, checkpoints will be copied inside the container at the same location. Your code can then check for their presence and load the appropriate one to resume training.

Please note that checkpointing is available even when you train with on-demand instances. This may come in handy if you'd like to store checkpoints in S3 for further inspection or for incremental training. The only restriction is that checkpointing is not available with **Local Mode**.

Using Managed Spot Training with Object Detection

Switching from on-demand training to Managed Spot Training is very simple. We just have to set the maximum duration of the training job, including any time spent waiting for spot instances to be available.

Let's modify the **Object Detection** training job from *Chapter 9, Scaling Your Training Jobs*. We set an upper bound of 1 hour, plus 1 hour for any spot delay. If either one of these bounds is exceeded, the job will be terminated automatically. This is helpful in killing runaway jobs that last much longer than expected or jobs that are stuck waiting for spot instances:

```
od = sagemaker.estimator.Estimator(
    container,
    role,
    instance_count=2,
    instance_type='ml.p3.2xlarge',
    use_spot_instances=True,
    max_run=3600,                       # 1 hour
    max_wait=7200,                      # 2 hours
    output_path=s3_output)
```

We train with the same configuration as before: Pipe Mode, **sharding**, and dist_sync mode. As the first epoch completes, the training log tells us that checkpointing is active. A new checkpoint is saved automatically each time the validation metric improves:

```
Updating the best model with validation-
mAP=1.615789635726003e-05
Saved checkpoint to "/opt/ml/model/model_algo_1-0000.params"
```

Once the training job is complete, the training log tells us how much we saved:

```
Training seconds: 7166
Billable seconds: 2150
Managed Spot Training savings: 70.0%
```

The job lasts 3,583 seconds, just a bit longer than with on-demand instances. This is normal, as provisioning spot instances may take a few minutes. Applying the 70% discount, the training cost is (7,166/3,600) * $4.627 * 0.3 = $2.76.

Not only is this job 70% cheaper than its on-demand counterpart, but it's also less than half the price of our original single-instance job. This means that we could use even more instances for the same budget. Let's try 4 and 8.

The results are summarized in the following table:

Instance count	EC2 fleet	Input mode	Sync mode	Job duration	Validation mAP	Cost
1	On-demand	Pipe	-	4443s	0.2453	$5.71
2	On-demand	Pipe + sharding	dist_sync	3114s	0.2367	$8
2	Spot	Pipe + sharding	dist_sync	3583s	0.2372	$2.76
4	Spot	Pipe + sharding	dist_sync	2536s	0.2304	$3.91
8	Spot	Pipe + sharding	dist_sync	1983s	0.2081	$6.11

Table 10.1 - Table summarizing spot training result

This goes to show that Managed Spot Training lets you optimize the duration of a job and its cost. Instead of complex capacity planning, you can set a training budget that fits your business requirements, and then grab as much infrastructure as possible.

Let's try another example where we implement checkpointing in Keras.

Using Managed Spot Training and checkpointing with Keras

In this example, we'll build a simple **CNN** to classify the **Fashion-MNIST** dataset. We've already worked with it in *Chapter 7, Extending Machine Learning Services with Built-in Frameworks*, and we'll use **script mode** again. The code will be different, as we'll build a `Sequential` model instead of a custom one.

Checkpointing with Keras

Let's first look at the Keras script itself. For the sake of brevity, only important steps are presented. You can find the full code in the repository for this book. Let's dive into it:

1. Using Script Mode, we store data paths and hyperparameters.

2. Then, we load the dataset and normalize pixel values to the [0,1] range. We also one-hot encode class labels.

3. We build a `Sequential` model: two convolution blocks (`Conv2D` / `BatchNormalization` / `ReLU` / `MaxPooling2D` / `Dropout`), then two fully connected blocks (`Dense` / `BatchNormalization` / `ReLU` / `Dropout`), and finally a `softmax` output layer for the 10 classes in the dataset.

4.   We compile the model, using the **categorical cross-entropy** loss function, and the **Adam** optimizer:

```
model.compile(
    loss=tf.keras.losses.categorical_crossentropy,
    optimizer=tf.keras.optimizers.Adam(),
    metrics=['accuracy'])
```

5.   We define a callback to checkpoint the model each time validation accuracy has increased:

```
from tensorflow.keras.callbacks import ModelCheckpoint
chk_dir = '/opt/ml/checkpoints'
chk_name = 'fmnist-cnn-{epoch:04d}'
checkpointer = ModelCheckpoint(
                    filepath=os.path.join(chk_dir, chk_name),
                    monitor='val_accuracy')
```

6.   We train the model by adding the callback we just created:

```
model.fit(x=x_train, y=y_train,
          validation_data=(x_val, y_val),
          batch_size=batch_size, epochs=epochs,
          callbacks=[checkpointer],
          verbose=1)
```

7.   When training is complete, we save the model, making sure to use the **TensorFlow Serving** format, which is required to deploy on SageMaker:

```
from tensorflow.keras.models import save_model
save_model(model, os.path.join(model_dir, '1'),
           save_format='tf')
```

Now, let's look at our training notebook.

Training with Managed Spot Training and checkpointing

We use the same workflow as before:

1.   We download the Fashion-MNIST dataset and save it to a local directory:

```
import os
import numpy as np
from tensorflow.keras.datasets import fashion_mnist
```

```
(x_train, y_train), (x_val, y_val) = fashion_mnist.load_
data()
os.makedirs("./data", exist_ok = True)
np.savez('./data/training', image=x_train, label=y_train)
np.savez('./data/validation', image=x_val, label=y_val)
```

2. We upload the dataset to S3, and we define the S3 location where SageMaker should copy the checkpoints saved inside the container:

```
import sagemaker
sess = sagemaker.Session()
bucket = sess.default_bucket()
prefix = 'keras2-fashion-mnist'
training_input_path = sess.upload_data(
    'data/training.npz', key_prefix=prefix+'/training')
validation_input_path = sess.upload_data(
    'data/validation.npz', key_prefix=prefix+'/
validation')
output_path = 's3://{}/{}/output/'.format(bucket, prefix)
chk_path = 's3://{}/{}/checkpoints/'.format(bucket,
prefix)
```

3. We configure the `TensorFlow` estimator, enabling Managed Spot Training and passing the S3 output location for checkpoints:

```
from sagemaker.tensorflow import TensorFlow
tf_estimator = TensorFlow(
    entry_point='fmnist-1.py',
    role=sagemaker.get_execution_role(),
    instance_count=1,
    instance_type='ml.p3.2xlarge',
    framework_version='2.1.0',
    py_version='py3',
    hyperparameters={'epochs': 10},
    output_path=output_path,
    use_spot_instances=True,
    max_run=3600,
    max_wait=7200,
    checkpoint_s3_uri=chk_path)
```

4. We launch training as usual:

```
tf_estimator.fit({'training': training_input_path,
                  'validation': validation_input_path})
```

5. In the training log, we see a checkpoint being created every time validation accuracy improves:

```
INFO:tensorflow:Assets written to /opt/ml/checkpoints/
fmnist-cnn-0001/assets
```

While the job is running, we see that checkpoints are also copied to S3:

```
$ aws s3 ls s3://sagemaker-eu-west-1-123456789012/keras2
fashion-mnist/checkpoints/
```
```
PRE fmnist-cnn-0001/
PRE fmnist-cnn-0002/
PRE fmnist-cnn-0003/
PRE fmnist-cnn-0006/
. . .
```

If our spot job gets interrupted, SageMaker will copy its checkpoints inside the container. So, we need to add some logic in our Keras script to load the latest checkpoint if it's available. If it's not, we'll build the model as before and train from scratch.

Resuming training from a checkpoint

This is a pretty simple process—look for checkpoints, and resume training from the latest one:

1. We list the checkpoint directory:

```
import glob
```
```
checkpoints = sorted(glob.glob(
              os.path.join(chk_dir,'fmnist-cnn-*')))
```

2. If checkpoints are present, we find the most recent one, as well as its epoch number. Then, we load the model:

```
from tensorflow.keras.models import load_model
```
```
if checkpoints :
    last_checkpoint = checkpoints[-1]
    last_epoch = int(last_checkpoint.split('-')[-1])
    model = load_model(last_checkpoint)
    print('Loaded checkpoint for epoch ', last_epoch)
```

3. If no checkpoint is present, we build the model as usual:

```
else:
    last_epoch = 0
    model = Sequential()
    . . .
```

4. We compile the model, and we launch training, passing the number of the last epoch:

```
model.fit(x=x_train, y=y_train,
          validation_data=(x_val, y_val),
          batch_size=batch_size,
          epochs=epochs,
          initial_epoch=last_epoch,
          callbacks=[checkpointer],
          verbose=1)
```

How can we test this? There is no way to intentionally cause a spot interruption.

Here's the trick: start a new training job with existing checkpoints in the `checkpoint_s3_uri` path, and increase the number of epochs. This will simulate resuming an interrupted job.

Setting the number of epochs to 20 and keeping the checkpoints in `s3://sagemaker-eu-west-1-123456789012/keras2 fashion-mnist/checkpoints`, we launch the training job again.

In the training log, we see that the latest checkpoint is loaded and that training resumes at epoch 11:

```
Loaded checkpoint for epoch 10
. . .
Epoch 11/20
```

We also see new checkpoints being created as validation accuracy improves, and they're copied to S3:

```
INFO:tensorflow:Assets written to: /opt/ml/checkpoints/fmnist-
cnn-0011/assets
```

As you can see, it's not difficult to set up checkpointing in SageMaker, and you should be able to do the same for other frameworks. Thanks to this, you can enjoy the deep discount provided by Managed Spot Training, without the risk of losing any work if an interruption occurs. Of course, you can use checkpointing on its own, to inspect intermediate training results or for incremental training.

In the next section, we're going to introduce another important feature: Automatic Model Tuning.

Optimizing hyperparameters with Automatic Model Tuning

Hyperparameters have a huge influence on the training outcome. Just like in chaos theory, tiny variations of a single hyperparameter can cause wild swings in accuracy. In most cases, the "why?" evades us, leaving us perplexed about what to try next.

Over the years, several techniques have been devised to try to solve the problem of selecting optimal hyperparameters:

1. **Manual Search**: This means using our best judgment and experience to select the "best" hyperparameters. Let's face it: this doesn't really work, especially with deep learning and its horde of training and network architecture parameters.

2. **Grid Search**: This entails systematically exploring the hyperparameter space, zooming in on hot spots, and repeating the process. This is much better than a manual search. However, this usually requires training hundreds of jobs. Even with scalable infrastructure, the time and dollar budgets can be significant.

3. **Random Search**: This refers to selecting hyperparameters at random. Unintuitive as it sounds, James Bergstra and Yoshua Bengio (of Turing Award fame) proved in 2012 that this technique delivers better models than a grid search with the same compute budget (`http://www.jmlr.org/papers/v13/bergstra12a.html`).

4. **Hyperparameter Optimization (HPO)**: This means using optimization techniques to select hyperparameters, such as **Bayesian Optimization** and **Gaussian Process Regression**. With the same compute budget, HPO typically delivers results with 10x fewer trainings than other techniques.

Understanding Automatic Model Tuning

SageMaker includes an Automatic Model Tuning capability that lets you easily explore hyperparameters ranges and quickly optimize any training metric with a limited number of jobs.

Model tuning supports both **Random Search** and **HPO**. The former is an interesting baseline that helps you to check that the latter is indeed overperforming. You can find a very detailed comparison in this excellent blog post: `https://aws.amazon.com/blogs/machine-learning/amazon-sagemaker-automatic-model-tuning-now-supports-random-search-and-hyperparameter-scaling/`.

Model tuning is completely agnostic to the algorithm you're using. It works with built-in algorithms, and the documentation lists the hyperparameters that can be tuned. It also works with all frameworks and custom containers, and hyperparameters are passed in the same way.

For each hyperparameter that we want to optimize, we have to define the following:

- A name
- A type (parameters can either be an integer, continuous, or categorical)
- A range of values to explore
- A scaling type (linear, logarithmic, or reverse logarithmic, or auto)—this lets us control how a specific parameter range will be explored

We also define the metric we want to optimize for. It can be any numerical value as long as it's visible in the training log and you can pass a regular expression to extract it.

Then, we launch the tuning jobs, passing all of these parameters as well as the number of training jobs to run and their degree of parallelism. With Bayesian optimization, you'll get the best results with sequential jobs (no parallelism), as optimization can be applied after each job. Having said that, running a small number of jobs in parallel is acceptable. Random Search has no restrictions on parallelism as jobs are completely unrelated.

Calling the `deploy()` API on the tuner object deploys the best model. If tuning is still in progress, it will deploy the best model so far, which can be useful for early testing.

Let's run the first example with a built-in algorithm and learn about the Model Tuning API.

Using Automatic Model Tuning with Object Detection

We're going to optimize our **Object Detection** job from *Chapter 9, Scaling Your Training Jobs*. Looking at the documentation, we can see the list of tunable hyperparameters (https://docs.aws.amazon.com/sagemaker/latest/dg/object-detection-tuning.html). Let's try to optimize the learning rate, momentum, and weight decay:

1. We set up the input channels using Pipe Mode. There's no change here.

2. We also configure the estimator as usual, setting up Managed Spot Training to minimize costs. We'll train on a single instance for maximum accuracy:

```
od = sagemaker.estimator.Estimator(
        container,
        role,
        instance_count=1,
        instance_type='ml.p3.2xlarge',
        output_path=s3_output_location,
        use_spot_instances=True,
        max_run=7200,
        max_wait=10800,
        volume_size=1)
```

3. We use the same hyperparameters as in *Chapter 9, Scaling Your Training Jobs*:

```
od.set_hyperparameters(base_network='resnet-50',
                       use_pretrained_model=1,
                       num_classes=20,
                       epochs=30,
                       num_training_samples=16551,
                       mini_batch_size=90)
```

4. We define the three extra hyperparameters we want to tune. We explicitly set logarithmic scaling for the learning rate, to make sure that its different orders of magnitude are explored:

```
from sagemaker.tuner import ContinuousParameter,
hyperparameter_ranges = {
    'learning_rate': ContinuousParameter(0.001, 0.1,
                     scaling_type='Logarithmic'),
    'momentum': ContinuousParameter(0.8, 0.999),
    'weight_decay': ContinuousParameter(0.0001, 0.001)
}
```

5. We set the metric to optimize for:

```
objective_metric_name = 'validation:mAP'
objective_type = 'Maximize'
```

6. We put everything together, using the `HyperparameterTuner` object. We decide to run 30 jobs, with two jobs in parallel. We also enable early stopping to weed out low performing jobs, saving us time and money:

```
from sagemaker.tuner import HyperparameterTuner

tuner = HyperparameterTuner(od,
              objective_metric_name,
              hyperparameter_ranges,
              objective_type=objective_type,
              max_jobs=30,
              max_parallel_jobs=2,
              early_stopping_type='Auto')
```

7. We launch training on the `tuner` object (not on the estimator):

```
tuner.fit(inputs=data_channels)
```

8. While the job is running, we can view intermediate results using SageMaker Experiments:

```
from sagemaker.analytics import
HyperparameterTuningJobAnalytics

exp = HyperparameterTuningJobAnalytics(
   hyperparameter_tuning_job_name=
       tuner.latest_tuning_job.name)

od_jobs = exp.dataframe()
od_jobs.sort_values('FinalObjectiveValue', ascending=0)
```

After a while, you should see something similar to the following screenshot:

	FinalObjectiveValue	TrainingElapsedTimeSeconds	TrainingEndTime	TrainingJobName	TrainingJobStatus	TrainingStartTime	learning_rate	momentu
5	0.610159	4731.0	2020-06-03 20:34:50+00:00	object-detection-200603-1732-008-8ac6877f	Completed	2020-06-03 19:15:59+00:00	0.010305	0.95259
9	0.584129	4433.0	2020-06-03 19:01:50+00:00	object-detection-200603-1732-004-5684ee14	Completed	2020-06-03 17:47:57+00:00	0.011401	0.95664
11	0.557482	4606.0	2020-06-03 18:51:25+00:00	object-detection-200603-1732-002-22adfb41	Completed	2020-06-03 17:34:39+00:00	0.004211	0.97699
3	0.326949	1693.0	2020-06-03 20:05:11+00:00	object-detection-200603-1732-010-6ad971a8	Stopped	2020-06-03 19:36:58+00:00	0.011177	0.97643

Figure 10.2 Viewing our tuning jobs with SageMaker Experiments

This information is also available in SageMaker Studio, in the **Experiments** section.

9. We can also track progress in the **Hyperparameter tuning jobs** section of the SageMaker console, as shown in the following screenshot:

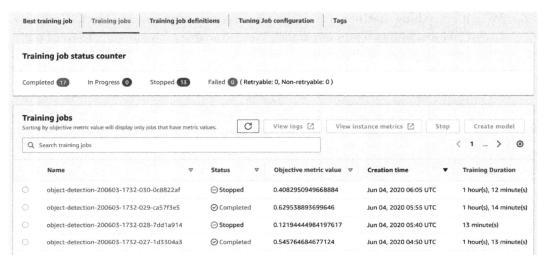

Figure 10.3 Viewing our tuning jobs in the SageMaker console

The job runs for 14 hours (wall time). 17 jobs completed and 13 stopped early. The total training time is 25 hours and 15 minutes. Applying the 70% spot discount, the total cost is 25.25 * $4.627 * 0.3 = $35.

How well did this tuning job do? In *Chapter 9, Scaling Your Training Jobs*, our training job used default hyperparameters and reached a **mAP** accuracy of **0.2453**. Our tuning job hit **0.6315**, as shown in the following screenshot:

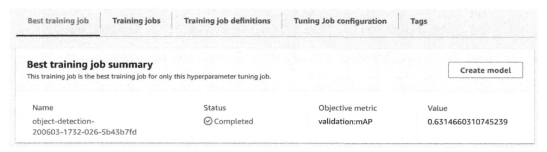

Figure 10.4 Results of our tuning jobs

This very nice score was obtained with the following selection of hyperparameters:

- Learning rate: 0.017193143077332648
- Momentum: 0.8733543185559848
- Weight decay: 0.00010102903446195865

CloudWatch metrics are shown in the next screenshot. The accuracy curve tells me that we could probably train a little longer and get extra accuracy. We could launch a single training job with these hyperparameters and let it run for more epochs:

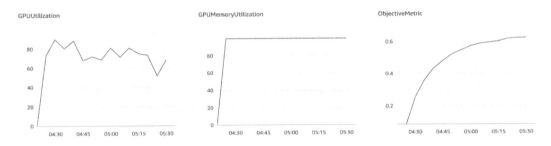

Figure 10.5 Graphs of our results

We could also resume the tuning job using **warm start** and continue exploring the hyperparameter range. We also call `deploy()` on the tuner object and test our model just like any SageMaker model.

As you can see, Automatic Model Tuning is extremely powerful. By running a small number of jobs, we improved our metric by 152%! Cost is negligible compared to the time you would spend experimenting with other techniques.

In fact, running the same tuning job using the random strategy delivers a top accuracy of 0.52. We would certainly need to run many more training jobs to even hope hitting 0.6315.

Let's now try to optimize the **Keras** example we used earlier in this chapter.

Using Automatic Model Tuning with Keras

Automatic Model Tuning can be easily used by any algorithm on SageMaker, which of course includes all frameworks. Let's see how this works with Keras.

Training our simple Keras CNN on the Fashion MNIST dataset for 30 epochs, we get the following results. Hopefully, you should see similar results:

```
loss: 0.0844 - accuracy: 0.9682 - val_loss: 0.2298 - val_
accuracy: 0.9311
```

A result of 93.11% is not bad, but let's see whether we can improve it with Automatic Model Tuning. In the process, we'll also learn how to optimize any metric visible in the training log.

Optimizing on a custom metric

Modifying our training script, we install the `keras-metrics` package (`https://github.com/netrack/keras-metrics`) and add the **precision**, **recall**, and **f1 score** metrics to the training log:

```
import subprocess, sys
def install(package):
    subprocess.call([sys.executable, "-m", "pip", "install",
                        package])
install('keras-metrics')
import keras_metrics
. . .
model.compile(loss=tf.keras.losses.categorical_crossentropy,
            optimizer=tf.keras.optimizers.Adam(),
            metrics=['accuracy',
            keras_metrics.precision(),
            keras_metrics.recall(),
            keras_metrics.f1_score()])
```

After 30 epochs, the metrics now look like this:

```
loss: 0.0869 - accuracy: 0.9678 - precision: 0.9072 - recall:
0.8908 - f1_score: 0.8989 - val_loss: 0.2301 - val_accuracy:
0.9310 - val_precision: 0.9078 - val_recall: 0.8915 - val_f1_
score: 0.8996
```

If we wanted to optimize on the f1 score, we would define the tuner metrics like this:

```
objective_metric_name = 'val_f1'
objective_type = 'Maximize'
metric_definitions = [
    {'Name': 'val_f1', 'Regex': 'val_f1_score: ([0-9\\.]+)'},
]
```

That's all it takes. As long as a metric is visible in the training log, you can use it to tune models.

Optimizing our Keras model

Now, let's run our tuning job:

1. We define the metrics for `HyperparameterTuner` like so, optimizing accuracy and storing the f1 score:

```
objective_metric_name = 'val_acc'
objective_type = 'Maximize'

metric_definitions = [
    {'Name': 'val_f1',
            'Regex': 'val_f1_score: ([0-9\\.]+)'},
    {'Name': 'val_acc',
            'Regex': 'val_accuracy: ([0-9\\.]+)'}
]
```

2. We define the parameters to explore:

```
from sagemaker.tuner import ContinuousParameter,
IntegerParameter

hyperparameter_ranges = {
    'learning_rate': ContinuousParameter(0.001, 0.2,
                        scaling_type='Logarithmic'),
    'batch-size': IntegerParameter(32,512)
}
```

3. We use the same estimator (30 epochs with spot instances), and we define the tuner:

```
tuner = HyperparameterTuner(
    tf_estimator,
    objective_metric_name,
    hyperparameter_ranges,
    metric_definitions=metric_definitions,
    objective_type=objective_type,
```

```
        max_jobs=30,
        max_parallel_jobs=2,
        early_stopping_type='Auto')
```

The tuning job runs for about 2 hours (wall time). The top validation accuracy is 93.41%, a decent improvement over our baseline.

We could certainly do better by training longer. However, the longer we train for, the more overfitting becomes a concern. We can alleviate it with early stopping, which can be implemented with a Keras callback. However, we should make sure that the job reports the metric for the best epoch, not for the last epoch. How can we display this in the training log? With another callback!

Adding callbacks for early stopping

Adding a Keras callback for early stopping is very simple:

1. We add a built-in callback for early stopping, based on validation accuracy:

```
from tensorflow.keras.callbacks import EarlyStopping
early_stopping = EarlyStopping(
    monitor='val_accuracy', min_delta=0.0001,patience=10,
    verbose=1, mode='auto')
```

2. We add a custom callback to store validation accuracy at the end of each epoch, and to display the best one at the end of training:

```
from tensorflow.keras.callbacks import Callback
class LogBestMetric(Callback):
    def on_train_begin(self, logs={}):
        self.val_accuracy = []
    def on_train_end(self, logs={}):
        print("Best val_accuracy:",
                max(self.val_accuracy))
    def on_epoch_end(self, batch, logs={}):
        self.val_accuracy.append(logs.
                            get('val_accuracy'))
best_val_metric = LogBestMetric()
```

3. We add these two callbacks to the training API:

```
model.fit(. . .,
    callbacks=[checkpointer, early_stopping,
            best_val_metric])
```

Testing with a few individual jobs, the last lines of the training log now look like this:

```
Epoch 00048: early stopping
Best val_accuracy: 0.9259
```

4. In the Notebook, we update our metric definition in order to extract the best validation accuracy:

```
objective_metric_name = 'val_acc'
objective_type = 'Maximize'

metric_definitions = [
    {'Name': 'val_acc',
     'Regex': 'Best val_accuracy: ([0-9\\.]+)'}
]
```

Training for 60 epochs this time (about 6 hours, wall time), the top validation accuracy is now at 93.80%. It looks like this is as good as it gets by tweaking the learning rate and the batch size.

Using Automatic Model Tuning for architecture search

Our neural network has plenty more hyperparameters: number of convolution filters, dropout, and so on. Let's try to optimize these as well:

1. We modify our training script to add command-line parameters for the following network parameters, which are used by Keras layers in our model:

```
parser.add_argument('--filters1', type=int, default=64)
parser.add_argument('--filters2', type=int, default=64)
parser.add_argument('--dropout-conv', type=float,
default=0.2)
parser.add_argument('--dropout-fc', type=float,
default=0.2)
```

As you certainly guessed, the parameters let us set values for the number of convolution filters in each layer, the dropout value for convolution layers, and the dropout value for fully connected layers.

2. Accordingly, in the notebook, we define these hyperparameters and their ranges. For the learning rate and the batch size, we use narrow ranges centered on the optimal values discovered by the previous tuning job:

```
from sagemaker.tuner import ContinuousParameter,
                            IntegerParameter
hyperparameter_ranges = {
    learning-rate': ContinuousParameter(0.01, 0.14),
    'batch-size': IntegerParameter(130,160),
    'filters1': IntegerParameter(16,256),
    'filters2': IntegerParameter(16,256),
    'dropout-conv': ContinuousParameter(0.001,0.5,
                    scaling_type='Logarithmic'),
    'dropout-fc': ContinuousParameter(0.001,0.5,
                    scaling_type='Logarithmic')
}
```

3. We launch the tuning job, running 50 jobs, 4 at a time, for 100 epochs this time.

The tuning job runs for about 3 hours, for a total cost of $12.5. Top validation accuracy hits 94.15%. Compared to our baseline, Automatic Model Tuning has improved the accuracy of our model by more than 1%, a very significant gain. If this model is used to predict 1 million samples a day, this translates into over 10,000 additional accurate predictions!

In total, we've spent less than $50. Whatever business metric would be improved by the extra accuracy, it's probably fair to say that this spend would be recouped in no time. As many customers have told me, Automatic Model Tuning pays for itself, and then some.

In *Chapter 2, AutoML with Amazon SageMaker Autopilot*, you may remember that the **Candidate Definition** notebook generated by **SageMake Autopilot** included a model tuning section. Now that we know more about this feature, let's revisit that part of the notebook, and learn about multi-algorithm tuning.

Tuning multiple algorithms

Opening the Candidate Definition notebook, we see that SageMaker AutoPilot configures a multi-algorithm tuning job. Indeed, some candidate pipelines are based on **Linear Learner**, some on **XGBoost**.

Each algorithm has its own estimator, metric, and hyperparameter range. This information is stored in three Python dictionaries, keyed by the estimator name:

```
multi_algo_tuning_parameters = {
  'estimator_dict': {
    'dpp0-xgboost':
    <sagemaker.estimator.Estimator object at 0x7f5d0ec7f310>,
    'dpp2-linear-learner':
    <sagemaker.estimator.Estimator object at 0x7f5d0ec7ff50>
  },
  'hyperparameter_ranges_dict': {
    'dpp0-xgboost': {
      'alpha':
        <sagemaker.parameter.ContinuousParameter
        object at 0x7f5d0ee069d0>,
      'colsample_bytree':
        <sagemaker.parameter.ContinuousParameter
        object at 0x7f5d0ee06950>,
      . . .
    },
    'dpp2-linear-learner': {
      'l1':
        <sagemaker.parameter.ContinuousParameter
        object at 0x7f5d0ee06a50>,
      'learning_rate':
        <sagemaker.parameter.ContinuousParameter
        object at 0x7f5d0ee06a90>,
      . . .
    }
  },
  'objective_metric_name_dict': {
    'dpp0-xgboost':
      'validation:accuracy',
    'dpp2-linear-learner':
      'validation:binary_classification_accuracy'
  }
}
```

These dictionaries are passed to the `create()` API as keyword arguments. The API returns a `HyperparameterTuner` object ready for training:

```
tuner = HyperparameterTuner.create(
  base_tuning_job_name=base_tuning_job_name,
  objective_type='Maximize',
  max_parallel_jobs=7,
  max_jobs=250,
  **multi_algo_tuning_parameters)
```

Input channels have a similar format, and they are passed to the `fit()` API:

```
multi_algo_tuning_inputs = {
  'dpp0-xgboost': {
    'train': <sagemaker.TrainingInput
          object at 0x7f5d0ec7fb90>,
    'validation': <sagemaker.TrainingInput
            object at 0x7f5d0ec7f790>
  },
  'dpp2-linear-learner': {
    'train': <sagemaker.TrainingInput
          object at 0x7f5d0ec7f210>,
    'validation': <sagemaker.TrainingInput
            object at 0x7f5d0ec7fa50>
  }
}
tuner.fit(inputs=multi_algo_tuning_inputs)
```

This concludes our exploration of Automatic Model Tuning, one of the most powerful features in SageMaker. You can find more examples at `https://github.com/awslabs/amazon-sagemaker-examples/tree/master/hyperparameter_tuning`.

Now, let's learn about **SageMaker Debugger** and how it can help us to understand what's happening inside our models.

Exploring models with SageMaker Debugger

SageMaker Debugger lets you configure **debugging rules** for your training job. These rules will inspect its internal state and check for specific unwanted conditions that could be developing during training. SageMaker Debugger includes a long list of **built-in rules** (The loss not decreasing, vanishing gradients, and so on), and you can write your own

Here are some of the built-in rules: `all_zero`, `class_imbalance`, `confusion`, `loss_not_decreasing`, `overfit`, `overtraining`, `similar_across_runs`, `stalled_training_rule`, `tensor_variance`, and `unchanged_tensor`. You can see the full list at `https://docs.aws.amazon.com/sagemaker/latest/dg/debugger-built-in-rules.html`.

In addition, you can save and inspect the model state (gradients, weights, and so on) as well as the training state (metrics, optimizer parameters, and so on). At each training step, the **tensors** storing these values may be saved in near real time in an S3 bucket, making it possible to visualize them while the model is training.

Of course, you can select the tensor **collections** that you'd like to save, how often, and so on. Depending on the framework you use, different collections are available. You can find more information at `https://github.com/awslabs/sagemaker-debugger/blob/master/docs/api.md`. Last but not least, you can save either raw tensor data or tensor reductions to limit the amount of data involved. Reductions include min, max, median, and more.

If you are working with the built-in containers for supported versions of TensorFlow, **PyTorch**, **Apache MXNet**, or the built-in XGBoost algorithm, you can use SageMaker Debugger out of the box, without changing a line of code in your script. Yes, you read that right. All you have to do is add extra parameters to the estimator, as we will do so in the next examples.

With other versions, or with your own containers, minimal modifications are required. You can find the latest information and examples at `https://github.com/awslabs/sagemaker-debugger`.

Debugging rules and saving tensors can be configured on the same training job. For clarity, we'll run two separate examples. First, let's use the XGBoost and Boston Housing example from *Chapter 4, Training Machine Learning Models*.

Debugging an XGBoost job

First, we will configure several built-in rules, train our model, and check the status of all rules:

1. Taking a look at the list of built-in rules, we decide to check for "overtraining" and "overfit". Each rule has extra parameters that we could tweak. We stick to defaults, and we configure the `Estimator` accordingly:

    ```
    from sagemaker.debugger import rule_configs, Rule
    xgb_estimator = Estimator(container,
        role=sagemaker.get_execution_role(),
    ```

```
    instance_count=1,
    instance_type='ml.m5.large',
    output_path='s3://{}/{}/output'.format(bucket, prefix),
    rules=[
      Rule.sagemaker(rule_configs.overtraining()),
      Rule.sagemaker(rule_configs.overfit())
    ]
  )
```

2. We set the hyperparameters and launch training without waiting for the training
    job to complete. The training log won't be visible in the notebook, but it will still be
    available in CloudWatch Logs:

```
xgb_estimator.set_hyperparameters(
  objective='reg:linear', num_round=100)
xgb_estimator.fit(xgb_data, wait=False)
```

3. In addition to the training job, one debugging job per rule is running under the
    hood, and we can check their statuses:

```
description = xgb_estimator.latest_training_job.rule_job_
summary()
for rule in description:
  rule.pop('LastModifiedTime')
  rule.pop('RuleEvaluationJobArn')
  print(rule)
```

This tells us that the debugger jobs are running:

```
{'RuleConfigurationName': 'Overtraining',
 'RuleEvaluationStatus': 'InProgress'}
{'RuleConfigurationName': 'Overfit',
 'RuleEvaluationStatus': 'InProgress'}
```

4. Running the same cell once the training job is complete, we see that no rule
    was triggered:

```
{'RuleConfigurationName': 'Overtraining',
 'RuleEvaluationStatus': 'NoIssuesFound'}
{'RuleConfigurationName': 'Overfit',
 'RuleEvaluationStatus': 'NoIssuesFound'}
```

Had a rule been triggered, we would get an error message, and the training job would be
stopped. Inspecting tensors would help us to understand what went wrong.

Inspecting an XGBoost job

Let's configure a new training job that saves all tensor collections available for XGBoost:

1. We configure the `Estimator`, passing a `DebuggerHookConfig` object.
    We save three tensor collections at each training step: metrics, feature importance,
    and average SHAP values (`https://github.com/slundberg/shap`). These
    values help us to understand how each feature in a data sample contributes to
    increasing or decreasing the predicted value.

    For larger models and datasets, this could generate a lot of data, which would take
    a long time to load and analyze. We would either increase the save interval or save
    tensor reductions:

```
from sagemaker.debugger import DebuggerHookConfig,
CollectionConfig

save_interval = '1'

xgb_estimator = Estimator(container,
    role=role,
    instance_count=1,
    instance_type='ml.m5.large',
    output_path='s3://{}/{}/output'.format(bucket,
                                           prefix),

    debugger_hook_config=DebuggerHookConfig(
      s3_output_path=
        's3://{}/{}/debug'.format(bucket,prefix),
      collection_configs=[
        CollectionConfig(name='metrics',
          parameters={"save_interval": save_interval}),
        CollectionConfig(name='average_shap',
          parameters={"save_interval": save_interval}),
        CollectionConfig(name='feature_importance',
          parameters={"save_interval": save_interval})
      ]
    )
)
```

2. Once the training job has started, we can create a trial and load data that has already been saved. As this job is very short, we see all data within a minute or so:

```
from smdebug.trials import create_trial
s3_output_path = xgb_estimator.latest_job_debugger_
artifacts_path()
trial = create_trial(s3_output_path)
```

3. We can list the name of all tensors that were saved:

```
trial.tensor_names()
['average_shap/f0','average_shap/f1','average_shap/f10',
...
 'feature_importance/cover/f0','feature_importance/cover/
f1',...
 'train-rmse','validation-rmse']
```

4. We can also list the name of all tensors in a given collection:

```
trial.tensor_names(collection="metrics")
['train-rmse', 'validation-rmse']
```

5. For each tensor, we can access training steps and values. Let's use them to plot the two metrics:

```
import matplotlib.pyplot as plt
steps =
  trial.tensor("train-rmse").steps()
train_rmse =
  [trial.tensor('train-rmse').value(s) for s in steps]
val_rmse =
  [trial.tensor('validation-rmse').value(s) for s in
   steps]
plt.title('RMSE over steps')
plt.autoscale()
plt.plot(steps, train_rmse, label='train', color='black')
plt.plot(steps, val_rmse, label='val', color='grey')
plt.legend()
```

6. You can see the result in the following screenshot:

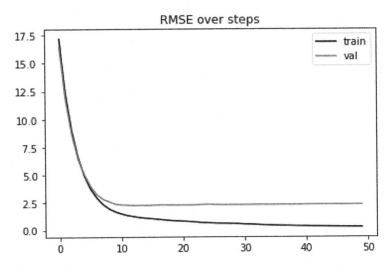

Figure 10.6 Plotting training and validation accuracies over time

7. Using the same reasoning, we write a function that will plot feature information from the `average_shap` and `feature_importance` collections:

```
def plot_features(tensor_prefix):
    num_features = len(dataset.columns)-1
    for i in range(0,num_features):
    feature = tensor_prefix+'/f'+str(i)
    steps = trial.tensor(feature).steps()
    v = [trial.tensor(feature).value(s) for s in steps]
    plt.plot(steps, v, label=dataset.columns[i+1])
    plt.autoscale()
    plt.title(tensor_prefix)
    plt.legend(loc='upper left')
    plt.show()
```

8. We build the `average_shap` plot:

```
plot_features('average_shap')
```

9. You can see this plot in the following screenshot. **dis**, **crim,** and **nox** have the largest average values:

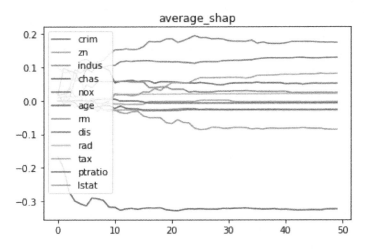

Figure 10.7 Plotting average SHAP values over time

10. We build the `feature_importance/weight` plot:

```
plot_features('feature_importance/weight')
```

You can see it in the following screenshot. **crim**, **age**, and **dis** have the largest weights:

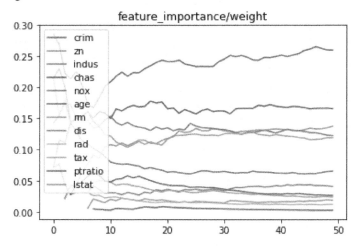

Figure 10.8 Plotting feature weights over time

Now, let's use SageMaker Debugger on our Keras and Fashion-MNIST example.

Debugging and inspecting a Keras job

We can inspect as well as debug a job in Keras using the following steps:

1. The default behavior in TensorFlow 2.x is eager mode, where gradients are not available. Hence, we disable eager mode in our script, which is the only modification required:

```
tf.compat.v1.disable_eager_execution()
```

2. We start from the same estimator. The dataset has 70,000 samples (60,000 for training, plus 10,000 for validation). With 30 epochs and a batch size of 128, our training job will have about 16,400 steps (70,000 * 30 / 128). Saving tensors at each step feels overkill. Let's save them every 100 steps instead:

```
from sagemaker.tensorflow import TensorFlow
from sagemaker.debugger import rule_configs, Rule,
DebuggerHookConfig, CollectionConfig
save_interval = '100'
tf_estimator = TensorFlow(entry_point='fmnist-5.py',
    role=role,
    instance_count=1,
    instance_type='ml.p3.2xlarge',
    framework_version='2.1.0',
    py_version='py3',
    hyperparameters={'epochs': 30},
    output_path=output_path,
    use_spot_instances=True,
    max_run=3600,
    max_wait=7200,
```

3. Looking at the built-in rules available for TensorFlow, we decide to set up "vanishing gradients", "dead ReLU", and "check for input images", a rule that makes sure that input images have been normalized. We need to specify the index of channel information in the input tensor. It's 4 for TensorFlow (batch size, height, width, and channels):

```
    rules=[
Rule.sagemaker(
    rule_configs.poor_weight_initialization()),
Rule.sagemaker(
    rule_configs.dead_relu()),
Rule.sagemaker(
    rule_configs.check_input_images(),
```

```
    rule_parameters={"channel": '3'})
    ],
```

4. Looking at collections available for TensorFlow, we decide to save metrics, losses, outputs, weights, and gradients:

```
debugger_hook_config=DebuggerHookConfig(
    s3_output_path='s3://{}/{}/debug'
            .format(bucket, prefix),
    collection_configs=[
        CollectionConfig(name='metrics',
            parameters={"save_interval":
                        save_interval}),
        CollectionConfig(name='losses',
            parameters={"save_interval":
                        save_interval}),
        CollectionConfig(name='outputs',
            parameters={"save_interval":
                        save_interval}),
        CollectionConfig(name='weights',
            parameters={"save_interval":
                        save_interval}),
        CollectionConfig(name='gradients',
            parameters={"save_interval":
                        save_interval})
    ],
    )
)
```

5. As training starts, we see the rules being launched in the training log:

```
********* Debugger Rule Status *********
*
* PoorWeightInitialization: InProgress
* DeadRelu: InProgress
* CheckInputImages: InProgress
*
******************************************
```

6. When training is complete, we check the status of the debugging rules:

```
description = tf_estimator.latest_training_job.rule_job_
summary()
```

```
for rule in description:
    rule.pop('LastModifiedTime')
```

```
    rule.pop('RuleEvaluationJobArn')
    print(rule)
```

```
{'RuleConfigurationName': 'PoorWeightInitialization',
 'RuleEvaluationStatus': 'NoIssuesFound'}
```

```
{'RuleConfigurationName': 'DeadRelu',
 'RuleEvaluationStatus': 'NoIssuesFound'}
```

```
{'RuleConfigurationName': 'CheckInputImages',
 'RuleEvaluationStatus': 'NoIssuesFound'}
```

7. We create a trial using the same tensors saved in S3:

```
from smdebug.trials import create_trial
```

```
s3_output_path = tf_estimator.latest_job_debugger_
artifacts_path()
```

```
trial = create_trial(s3_output_path)
```

8. Listing the available tensors, we see that our custom metrics have been saved. Let's plot the validation f1 score:

```
import matplotlib.pyplot as plt
```

```
f1 = trial.tensor(val_f1_score)
plt.autoscale()
values = [f1.value(s) for s in f1.steps()]
plt.plot(f1.steps(), values)
```

The graph is visible in the following screenshot:

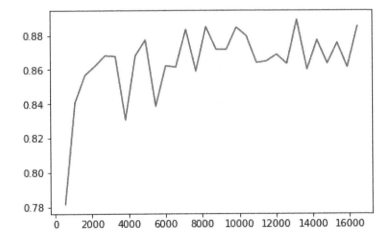

Figure 10.9 Plotting the validation f1 score over time

9. We can also inspect weights and gradients, for example, the filters in the first convolution layer:

```
w = trial.tensor('conv2d/weights/conv2d/kernel:0')
g = trial.tensor('training/Adam/gradients/gradients/
conv2d/Conv2D_grad/Conv2DBackpropFilter:0')
```

```
print(w.value(0).shape)
print(g.value(0).shape)
```

```
(3, 3, 1, 64)
(3, 3, 1, 64)
```

As defined in our training script, the first convolution layer has 64 filters. Each one is 3x3 pixels, with a single channel (2D). Accordingly, the gradients have the same shape.

10. We write a function to plot filter weights and gradients over time:

```
def plot_conv_filter(tensor_name, filter_num, min_
step=0):
    tensor = trial.tensor(tensor_name)
    steps = [s for s in tensor.steps() if s >= min_step]
    plt.autoscale()
    for i in range(0,3):
        for j in range(0,3):
            values = [tensor.value(s)[:,:,0,filter_num][i][j]
                    for s in steps]
            label='({},{})'.format(i,j)
            plt.plot(steps, values, label=label)
    plt.legend(loc='upper left')
    plt.show()
```

11. We plot weights in the last filter of the first convolution layer:

```
plot_conv_filter('conv2d/weights/conv2d/kernel:0', 63)
```

You can see the graph in the following screenshot:

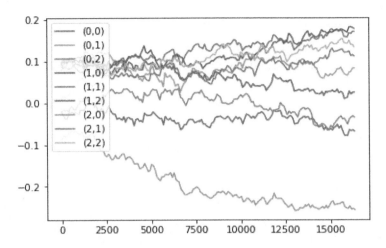

Figure 10.10 Plotting the weights of a convolution filter over time

12. We plot gradients for the last filter of the first convolution layer, looking at the last few steps:

```
plot_conv_filter('conv2d/weights/conv2d/kernel:0', 63)
```

You can see the graph in the following screenshot:

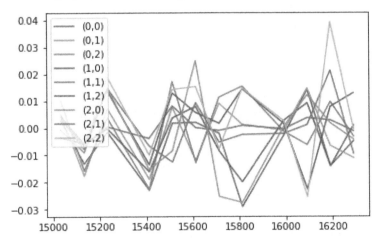

Figure 10.11 Plotting the gradients of a convolution filter over time

As you can see, SageMaker Debugger makes it really easy to inspect training jobs. If you work with the built-in containers that support it, you don't need to modify your code. All configuration takes place in the estimator.

You can find additional examples at `https://github.com/awslabs/amazon-sagemaker-examples`, including some advanced use cases such as real-time visualization and model pruning.

Summary

This chapter concludes our exploration of training techniques. You learned about Managed Spot Training, a simple way to slash training costs by 70% or more. You also saw how checkpointing helps to resume jobs that have been interrupted. Then, you learned about Automatic Model Tuning, a great way to extract more accuracy from your models by exploring hyperparameter ranges. Finally, you learned about SageMaker Debugger, an advanced capability that automatically inspects training jobs for unwanted conditions and saves tensor collections to S3 for inspection and visualization.

In the next chapter, we'll study model deployment in more detail.

Section 4: Managing Models in Production

In this section, you will learn how to deploy machine learning models in a variety of configurations, both with the SDK and with several automation tools. Finally, you will learn how to find the best cost/performance ratio for your prediction infrastructures.

This section comprises the following chapters:

- *Chapter 11, Deploying Machine Learning Models*
- *Chapter 12, Automating Deployment Tasks*
- *Chapter 13, Optimizing Cost and Performance*

11
Deploying Machine Learning Models

In the previous chapters, we've deployed models in the simplest way possible: by configuring an estimator, calling the `fit()` API to train the model, and calling the `deploy()` API to create a real-time endpoint. This is undoubtedly the preferred scenario for development and testing, but it's not the only one.

Models can be imported. For example, you could take an existing model that you trained on your local machine, import it into SageMaker, and deploy it as if you had it trained on SageMaker.

In addition, models can be deployed in different configurations:

- A single model on a real-time endpoint, which is what we've done so far, as well as several model variants in the same endpoint.

- A sequence of up to five models, called an **inference pipeline**.

- An arbitrary number of related models that are loaded on demand on the same endpoint, known as a **multi-model endpoint**. We'll examine this configuration in *Chapter 13, Optimizing Cost and Performance*.

- A single model or an inference pipeline that predicts data in batch mode through a feature known as **batch transform**.

Finally, models can be exported. You can grab a training artifact in S3, extract the model, and deploy it anywhere you like.

In this chapter, we'll cover the following topics:

- Examining model artifacts
- Managing real-time endpoints
- Deploying batch transformers
- Deploying inference pipelines
- Monitoring models with Amazon SageMaker Model Monitor
- Deploying models to container services

Let's get started!

Technical requirements

You will need an AWS account to run the examples included in this chapter. If you haven't got one already, please point your browser to `https://aws.amazon.com/getting-started/` to create one. You should also familiarize yourself with the AWS Free Tier (`https://aws.amazon.com/free/`), which lets you use many AWS services for free within certain usage limits.

You will need to install and configure the AWS Command-Line Interface for your account (`https://aws.amazon.com/cli/`).

You will need a working Python 3.x environment. Be careful not to use Python 2.7, as it is no longer maintained. Installing the Anaconda distribution (`https://www.anaconda.com/`) is not mandatory, but strongly encouraged as it includes many projects that we will need (Jupyter, `pandas`, `numpy`, and more).

The code examples included in this book are available on GitHub at `https://github.com/PacktPublishing/Learn-Amazon-SageMaker`. You will need to install a `git` client to access them (`https://git-scm.com/`).

Examining model artifacts

A model artifact contains one or several files that are produced by a training job that are required for model deployment. The number and the nature of these files depend on the algorithm that was trained. As we've seen many times, the model artifact is stored as a `model.tar.gz` file, at the S3 output location defined in the estimator.

Let's look at some different examples. You can use the artifacts from the jobs we previously trained for this.

Examining artifacts for built-in algorithms

Most built-in algorithms are implemented with **Apache MXNet**, and their artifacts reflect this. For more information on MXNet, please visit `https://mxnet.apache.org/`. Let's get started:

1. Let's start from the artifact for the **Linear Learner** model we trained in *Chapter 4, Training Machine Learning Models*:

```
$ tar xvfz model.tar.gz
x model_algo-1
```

```
$ unzip model_algo-1
archive:  model_algo-1
extracting: additional-params.json
extracting: manifest.json
extracting: mx-mod-symbol.json
extracting: mx-mod-0000.params
```

2. Load the JSON definition of the model (the symbol file):

```
import json
sym_json = json.load(open('mx-mod-symbol.json'))
sym_json_string = json.dumps(sym_json)
```

3. Use the JSON definition to instantiate a new Gluon model. Also, define the name of its input as `data`:

```
import mxnet as mx
from mxnet import gluon
net = gluon.nn.SymbolBlock(
    outputs=mx.sym.load_json(sym_json_string),
    inputs=mx.sym.var('data'))
```

4. By doing this, now, we can easily plot the model:

```
mx.viz.plot_network(
    net(mx.sym.var('data'))[0],
    node_attrs={"shape":"oval","fixedsize":"false"})
```

This creates the following graph:

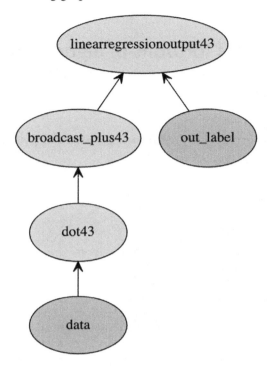

Figure 11.1 – Linear Learner model

5. Then, load the model parameters to learn during training:

```
net.load_parameters('mx-mod-0000.params',
                    allow_missing=True)
net.collect_params().initialize()
```

6. Define a test sample as an MXNet NDArray:

```
test_sample = mx.nd.array([0.00632,18.00,2.310,0,0.5380,6
.5750,65.20,4.0900,1,296.0,15.30,396.90,4.98])
```

7. Forward this through the model and read the output:

```
response = net(test_sample)
print(response)
```

The predicted price of this house is $30,173:

```
array([[30.173424]], dtype=float32)
```

This technique should work with all MXNet-based algorithms. Now, let's take a look at the built-in algorithms for **computer vision**.

Examining artifacts for built-in computer vision algorithms

The three built-in algorithms for computer vision are also based on Apache MXNet. The process is exactly the same:

1. The following is the artifact for the **Image Classification** model we trained on dogs and cats in *Chapter 5, Training Computer Vision Models*:

```
$ tar xvfz model.tar.gz
x image-classification-0010.params
x model-shapes.json
x image-classification-symbol.json
```

2. Load the model and its parameters:

```
import mxnet, json
from mxnet import gluon

sym_json = json.load(
          open('image-classification-symbol.json'))
sym_json_string = json.dumps(sym_json)

net = gluon.nn.SymbolBlock(
    outputs=mx.sym.load_json(sym_json_string),
    inputs=mx.sym.var('data'))

net.load_parameters('image-classification-0010.params',
                    allow_missing=True)
net.collect_params().initialize()
```

3. The input shape is a single 300x300 color image with three channels (red, green, and blue). Accordingly, we create a fake image using random values. We forward it through the model and read the results:

```
test_sample =
    mx.ndarray.random.normal(shape=(1,3,300,300))
response = net(test_sample)
print(response)
```

Funnily enough, this random image is classified as a cat:

```
array([[0.99126923, 0.00873081]], dtype=float32)
```

You can find examples of **Object Detection** models at https://github.com/ aws-samples/amazon-sagemaker-aws-greengrass-custom-object-detection-model/. The process is more involved as the training network needs to be modified for prediction.

If you don't want to use MXNet directly, you could also package and load these models with the Multi Model Server (https://github.com/awslabs/multi-model-server).

Now, let's look at **XGBoost** artifacts.

Examining artifacts for XGBoost

An XGBoost artifact contains a single file – the model itself. However, the format of the model depends on how you're using XGBoost.

Examining artifacts for the built-in XGBoost algorithm

With the built-in algorithm, the model is a pickled file that stores a `Booster` object. Once the artifact has been extracted, we simply unpickle the model and load it:

```
$ tar xvfz model.tar.gz
x xgboost-model
$ python
>>> import pickle
>>> model = pickle.load(open('xgboost-model', 'rb'))
>>> type(model)
<class 'xgboost.core.Booster'>
```

Building a model artifact from an existing model is just as simple:

```
$ python
<train model>
>>> import pickle
>>> pickle.dump(model, open('xgboost-model', 'wb')
$ tar cvfz model.tar.gz xgboost-model
```

Examining artifacts for the built-in XGBoost framework

With the built-in framework, the model is just a saved model. Once the artifact has been extracted, we load the model directly:

```
$ tar xvfz model.tar.gz
x xgb.model
$ python
>>> import xgboost as xgb
>>> bst = xgb.Booster({'nthread': 4})
>>> model = bst.load_model('xgb.model')
>>> type(bst)
<class 'xgboost.core.Booster'>
```

Building a model artifact from an existing model goes like this:

```
$ python
<train model>
>>> import xgboost as xgb
>>> bst = xgb.Booster({'nthread': 4})
<train model>
>>> bst.save_model('xgb.model')
$ tar cvfz model.tar.gz xgb.model
```

Now, let's look at **Scikit-Learn** artifacts.

Examining artifacts for the Scikit-learn framework

Scikit-Learn models are saved and loaded with `joblib` (`https://joblib.readthedocs.io`). This library contains a set of tools that provide lightweight pipelining, but we'll only use it to save models:

```
$ tar xvfz model.tar.gz
x model.joblib
$ python
>>> import joblib
>>> model = joblib.load('model.joblib')
>>> type(model)
<class 'sklearn.linear_model._base.LinearRegression'>
```

Accordingly, you can build a model artifact like so:

```
$ python
>>> from sklearn.linear_model import LinearRegression
>>> regr = LinearRegression()
<train model>
>>> import joblib
>>> joblib.save(regr, 'model.joblib')
$ tar cvfz model.tar.gz model.joblib
```

Finally, let's look at **TensorFlow** artifacts.

Examining artifacts for the TensorFlow framework

TensorFlow and **Keras** models are saved in **TensorFlow Serving** format:

```
$ mkdir /tmp/models
$ tar xvfz model.tar.gz -C /tmp/models
x 1/
x 1/saved_model.pb
x 1/assets/
x 1/variables/
x 1/variables/variables.index
x 1/variables/variables.data-00000-of-00002
x 1/variables/variables.data-00001-of-00002
```

The easiest way to serve such a model is to run the **Docker** image for TensorFlow Serving. You can find more details at `https://www.tensorflow.org/tfx/serving/serving_basic`:

```
$ docker run -t --rm -p 8501:8501
  -v "/tmp/models:/models/fmnist"
  -e MODEL_NAME=fmnist
  tensorflow/serving
```

Building a model artifact from an existing model requires creating a `model.tar.gz` file containing a TensorFlow Serving file tree. Please note that the top folder must be named `1`:

```
$ tar cfz model.tar.gz /tmp/models
```

This process is similar for other frameworks, and you should be able to extract models and build artifacts using the same logic.

Now, let's learn how to deploy models on real-time endpoints.

Managing real-time endpoints

SageMaker endpoints serve real-time predictions using models hosted on fully managed infrastructure. They can be created and managed either with the SageMaker SDK, or with an AWS language SDK such as `boto3`. The latter gives us more flexibility and control. For instance, we can deploy several **Production Variants** on the same endpoint, and also configure **Auto Scaling**.

First, let's look at the SageMaker SDK in greater detail.

Managing endpoints with the SageMaker SDK

The SageMaker SDK lets you work with endpoints in several ways:

- Configure an estimator, train it with `fit()`, deploy an endpoint with `deploy()`, and invoke it with `predict()`.
- Deploy an existing model.
- Invoke an existing endpoint.
- Update an existing endpoint.

We've used the first scenario in many examples so far. Let's look at the other ones.

Deploying an existing model

This is useful when you want to import a model that wasn't trained on SageMaker, or when you want to redeploy a SageMaker model.

In the previous section, we saw what model artifacts look like. In this example, we will start from a TensorFlow Serving artifact and deploy it:

1. The artifact looks like this. Please remember that the top-level directory must be named 1:

    ```
    $ tar tvfz model.tar.gz
    1/
    1/saved_model.pb
    1/assets/
    1/variables/
    1/variables/variables.index
    1/variables/variables.data-00000-of-00002
    1/variables/variables.data-00001-of-00002
    ```

2. Upload the artifact to the default S3 bucket. This is for convenience only; you could upload it anywhere:

    ```
    import sagemaker

    sess = sagemaker.Session()
    prefix = 'byo-tf'
    model_path = sess.upload_data(path='model.tar.gz',
                                  key_prefix=prefix)
    ```

3. Create a SageMaker model from the artifact. As you would expect, the object is framework-specific. You can find more information about how this works for other frameworks at https://sagemaker.readthedocs.io/en/stable/frameworks/:

    ```
    from sagemaker.tensorflow.model import TensorFlowModel

    tf_model = TensorFlowModel(
        model_data=model_path,
        framework_version='2.1.0',
        role=sagemaker.get_execution_role())
    ```

4. This instantly creates a model that we can deploy as usual:

```
import time

tf_endpoint_name = 'keras-tf-fmnist-'
   + time.strftime("%Y-%m-%d-%H-%M-%S", time.gmtime())

tf_predictor = tf_model.deploy(
     initial_instance_count=1,
     instance_type='ml.m5.large',
     endpoint_name=tf_endpoint_name)
```

5. We can then predict as usual:

```
tf_predictor.content_type = 'application/json'
tf_predictor.serializer =
     sagemaker.serializers.JSONSerializer()
tf_predictor.predict(...)
```

Now, let's learn how to invoke an existing endpoint.

Invoking an existing endpoint

This is useful when you want to work with a live endpoint but don't have access to the predictor. All we need to know is the endpoint's name:

1. Build a TensorFlow Serving predictor for the endpoint we deployed in the previous example. Again, the object is framework-specific:

```
from sagemaker.predictor import Predictor

another_predictor = Predictor(
     endpoint_name=tf_endpoint_name,
     content_type =
        sagemaker.serializers.JSONSerializer.CONTENT_TYPE,
     serializer = sagemaker.serializers.JSONSerializer())
```

2. Then, predict it as usual:

```
another_predictor.predict(...)
```

Now, let's learn how to update endpoints.

Updating an existing endpoint

The `deploy()` API lets you update the configuration of an endpoint. We just need to set the `update_endpoint` parameter to `True`. Let's try this on our Keras endpoint:

1. Starting from the same `Model` object, we call `deploy()` again. We set the instance count to 2 and update the endpoint. If we didn't set `update_endpoint`, we would create a new endpoint:

    ```
    tf_predictor = tf_model.deploy(initial_instance_count=2,
                                   instance_type='ml.m5.large',
                                   endpoint_name=tf_endpoint_name,
                                   update_endpoint=True)
    ```

2. The endpoint is updated, as shown in the following screenshot. This update is not disruptive, and you can continue invoking the endpoint:

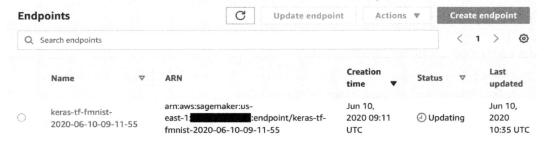

Figure 11.2 – Endpoint being updated

3. Once the update is complete, we will see that the endpoint is now backed by two instances, as shown in the following screenshot:

Variant name ▲	Current weight ▽	Desired weight	Instance type ▽	Elastic Inference	Current instance count ▽	Desired instance count ▽	Instance min - max	Automatic scaling
AllTraffic	1	1	ml.m5.large	-	2	2	-	No

Endpoint runtime settings   Update weights   Update instance count   Configure auto scaling

Figure 11.3 – Endpoint backed by two instances

As you can see, it's very easy to import, deploy, redeploy, and update models with the SageMaker SDK. However, some operations require that we work with lower-level APIs. They're available in the AWS language SDKs, and we'll use our good friend `boto3` to demonstrate them.

Managing endpoints with the boto3 SDK

`Boto3` is the AWS SDK for Python (`https://boto3.amazonaws.com/v1/documentation/api/latest/index.html`). It includes APIs for all AWS services (unless they don't have APIs!). The SageMaker API is available at `https://boto3.amazonaws.com/v1/documentation/api/latest/reference/services/sagemaker.html`.

`Boto3` APIs are service-level APIs, and they give us full control over all service operations. Let's see how they can help us deploy and manage endpoints in ways that the SageMaker SDK doesn't allow.

Deploying endpoints with the boto3 SDK

Deploying an endpoint with `boto3` is a four-step operation:

1. Create one or more models with the `create_model()` API. Alternatively, we could use existing models that have been trained or imported with the SageMaker SDK. For the sake of brevity, we'll do this here.

2. Define one or more Production Variants, listing the infrastructure requirements for each model.

3. Create an **Endpoint Configuration** with the `create_endpoint_config()` API, passing the Production Variants defined previously and assigning each one a weight.

4. Create the endpoint with the `create_endpoint()` API.

    Let's put these APIs to work and deploy an endpoint running two variants of the XGBoost model we trained on the Boston Housing dataset:

5. The two models have already been trained. Their names are `sagemaker-xgboost-2020-06-09-08-33-24-782` and `sagemaker-xgboost-2020-02-24-14-41-35-744`, as visible in the SageMaker console and in SageMaker Studio.

6. Define two Production Variants. Both are backed by a single instance. However, they will receive 9/10th and 1/10th of incoming requests, respectively; that is to say *variant weight / sum of weights*. We could use this setup if we wanted to introduce a new model in production and make sure it worked fine before sending it traffic:

```python
production_variants = [
    { 'VariantName': 'variant-1',
      'ModelName': model_name_1,
      'InitialInstanceCount': 1,
      'InitialVariantWeight': 9,
      'InstanceType': 'ml.t2.medium'},
    { 'VariantName': 'variant-2',
      'ModelName': model_name_2,
      'InitialInstanceCount': 1,
      'InitialVariantWeight': 1,
      'InstanceType': 'ml.t2.medium'}]
```

7. Create an Endpoint Configuration by passing our two production variants and setting optional tags:

```python
import boto3

sm = boto3.client('sagemaker')
endpoint_config_name = 'xgboost-two-models-epc'

response = sm.create_endpoint_config(
    EndpointConfigName=endpoint_config_name,
    ProductionVariants=production_variants,
    Tags=[{'Key': 'Name',
           'Value': endpoint_config_name},
          {'Key': 'Algorithm', 'Value': 'xgboost'}])
```

We can list all Endpoint Configurations with `list_endpoint_configs()` and describe a particular one with the `describe_endpoint_config()` API.

8. Create an endpoint based on this configuration:

```python
endpoint_name = 'xgboost-two-models-ep'

response = sm.create_endpoint(
    EndpointName=endpoint_name,
    EndpointConfigName=endpoint_config_name,
    Tags=[{'Key': 'Name','Value': endpoint_name},
          {'Key': 'Algorithm','Value': 'xgboost'},
          {'Key': 'Environment','Value': 'development'}])
```

We can list all the endpoints with `list_endpoints()` and describe a particular one with the `describe_endpoint()` API.

9. As shown in the following screenshot, the SageMaker console shows us the
Production Variants:

Production variants

Model name	Training job	Variant name	Instance type	Elastic Inference	Initial instance count	Initial weight
sagemaker-xgboost-2020-06-09-08-33-24-782	sagemaker-xgboost-2020-06-09-08-33-24-782	variant-1	ml.t2.medium	-	1	9
sagemaker-xgboost-2020-02-24-14-41-35-744	sagemaker-xgboost-2020-02-24-14-41-35-744	variant-2	ml.t2.medium	-	1	1

Figure 11.4 – Viewing Production Variants

10. Once the endpoint is in service, we can invoke it. Prediction requests will be
forwarded to variants according to their weights:

```
smrt = boto3.Session().client(service_name='runtime.
sagemaker')
response = smrt.invoke_endpoint(EndpointName=endpoint_
name,
                ContentType='text/csv',
                Body=test_sample)
```

11. We can also select the variant that receives the prediction request. This would be
useful for A/B testing, where we need to stick users to a given model:

```
variants = ['variant-1', 'variant-2']
for v in variants:
    response = smrt.invoke_endpoint(
                EndpointName=endpoint_name,
                ContentType='text/csv',
                Body=test_sample,
                TargetVariant=v)
    print(response['Body'].read())
```

This results in the following output:

```
b'[0.0013231043703854084]'
b'[0.001262241625227034]'
```

12. Update the weights, giving equal weights to both variants so that they receive half of the incoming traffic:

```
response = sm.update_endpoint_weights_and_capacities(
    EndpointName=endpoint_name,
    DesiredWeightsAndCapacities=[
        { 'VariantName': 'variant-1',
          'DesiredWeight': 5},
        { 'VariantName': 'variant-2',
          'DesiredWeight': 5}])
```

13. Then, remove one variant entirely and send all traffic to the remaining one. The endpoint stays in service the whole time, and no traffic is lost:

```
production_variants_2 = [
  {'VariantName': 'variant-2',
   'ModelName': model_name_2,
   'InitialInstanceCount': 1,
   'InitialVariantWeight': 1,
   'InstanceType': 'ml.t2.medium'}]
endpoint_config_name_2 = 'xgboost-one-model-epc'
response = sm.create_endpoint_config(
    EndpointConfigName=endpoint_config_name_2,
    ProductionVariants=production_variants_2,
    Tags=[{'Key': 'Name',
           'Value': endpoint_config_name_2},
          {'Key': 'Algorithm','Value': 'xgboost'}])
response = sm.update_endpoint(
    EndpointName=endpoint_name,
    EndpointConfigName=endpoint_config_name_2)
```

14. Finally, clean up by deleting the endpoint and the two endpoint configurations:

```
sm.delete_endpoint(EndpointName=endpoint_name)
sm.delete_endpoint_config(
  EndpointConfigName=endpoint_config_name)
sm.delete_endpoint_config(
  EndpointConfigName=endpoint_config_name_2)
```

As you can see, the boto3 API is more verbose, but it also gives us the flexibility we need for machine learning operations. In the next chapter, we'll learn how to automate these.

Deploying batch transformers

Some use cases don't benefit from a real-time endpoint. For example, you may want to predict 10 GB of data once a week in one go, get the results, and feed them to a downstream application. Batch transformers are a very simple way to get this done.

In this example, we will use the Scikit-Learn script that we trained on the Boston Housing dataset in *Chapter 7, Extending Machine Learning Services with Built-in Frameworks*. Let's get started:

1. Configure the estimator as usual:

```
from sagemaker.sklearn import SKLearn

sk = SKLearn(entry_point='sklearn-boston-housing.py',
    role=sagemaker.get_execution_role(),
    instance_count=1,
    instance_type='ml.m5.large',
    output_path=output,
    hyperparameters={'normalize': True, 'test-size': 0.1})
sk.fit({'training':training})
```

2. Let's predict the training set in batch mode. Remove the target value, save the dataset to a CSV file, and upload it to S3:

```
import pandas as pd

data = pd.read_csv('housing.csv')
data.drop(['medv'], axis=1, inplace=True)
data.to_csv('data.csv', header=False, index=False)

batch_input = sess.upload_data(path='data.csv',
                            key_prefix=prefix +
                                        '/batch')
```

3. Create a transformer object and launch batch processing:

```
sk_transformer = sk.transformer(
                instance_count=1,
                instance_type='ml.m5.large')

sk_transformer.transform(batch_input,
                    content_type='text/csv',
                    wait=True, logs=True)
```

4. In the training log, we can see that SageMaker creates a temporary endpoint and uses it to predict data. For large-scale jobs, we could optimize throughput by mini-batching samples for prediction (using the `strategy` parameter), increase the level of prediction concurrency (`max_concurrent_transforms`), and increase the maximum payload size (`max_payload`).

5. Once the job is complete, the predictions will be available in S3:

```
print(sk_transformer.output_path)
s3://sagemaker-us-east-1-123456789012/sagemaker-scikit-
learn-2020-06-12-08-28-30-978
```

6. Using the AWS CLI, we can easily retrieve these predictions:

```
%%bash -s "$sk_transformer.output_path"
aws s3 cp $1/data.csv.out .
head -1 data.csv.out
[[29.73828574177013], [24.920634119498292], …
```

7. Just like for training, the infrastructure used by the transformer is shut down as soon as the job completes, so there's nothing to clean up.

In the next section, we will look at inference pipelines and how to use them to deploy a sequence of related models.

Deploying inference pipelines

Real-life machine learning scenarios often involve more than one model. For example, you may need to run preprocessing steps on incoming data or reduce its dimensionality with the **PCA** algorithm.

Of course, you could deploy each model to a dedicated endpoint. However, orchestration code would be required to pass prediction requests to each model in sequence. Multiplying endpoints would also introduce additional costs.

Instead, inference pipelines let you deploy up to five models on the same endpoint or for batch transform, and automatically handle the prediction sequence.

Let's say that we wanted to run PCA and then Linear Learner. Building the inference pipeline would look like this:

1. Train the PCA model on the input dataset.

2. Process the training and validation sets with PCA and store the results in S3. Batch Transform is a good way to do this.

3. Train the Linear Learner using the datasets processed by PCA as input.

4. Use the `create_model()` API to create the inference pipeline:

```
response = sagemaker.create_model(
    ModelName='pca-linearlearner-pipeline',
        Containers=[
            {
            'Image': pca_container,
            'ModelDataUrl': pca_model_artifact,
                . . .
            },
            {
            'Image': ll_container,
            'ModelDataUrl': ll_model_artifact,
                . . .
            }
        ],
        ExecutionRoleArn=role
)
```

5. Create the endpoint configuration and the endpoint as usual. We could also use the pipeline with a batch transformer.

You can find a complete example that uses Scikit-Learn and Linear Learner at `https://github.com/awslabs/amazon-sagemaker-examples/tree/master/sagemaker-python-sdk/scikit_learn_inference_pipeline`.

Spark is a very popular choice for data processing, and SageMaker lets you deploy Spark models with the **SparkML** Serving built-in container (`https://github.com/aws/sagemaker-sparkml-serving-container`), which uses the **MLeap** library (`https://github.com/combust/mleap`). Of course, these models can be part of an **inference pipeline**. You can find several examples at `https://github.com/awslabs/amazon-sagemaker-examples/tree/master/advanced_functionality`.

This concludes our discussion on model deployment. In the next section, we'll introduce a SageMaker capability that helps us detect and fix data quality issues that impact prediction quality: **SageMaker Model Monitor**.

Monitoring predictions with Amazon SageMaker Model Monitor

SageMaker Model Monitor has two main features:

- Capturing data sent to an endpoint, as well as predictions returned by the endpoint. This is useful for further analysis, or to replay real-life traffic during the development and testing of new models.

- Comparing incoming traffic to a baseline built from the training set, as well as sending alerts about data quality issues, such missing features, mistyped features, and differences in statistical properties (also known as "data drift").

We'll use the **Linear Learner** example from *Chapter 4, Training Machine Learning Models*, where we trained a model on the Boston Housing dataset. First, we'll add data capture. Then, we'll build a **baseline** and set up a **monitoring schedule** to periodically compare the incoming data to that baseline.

Capturing data

We can set up the data capture process when we deploy an endpoint. We can also enable it on an existing endpoint by using the `update_endpoint` parameter from the `deploy()` API.

At the time of writing, there are certain caveats that you should be aware of:

- You can only send **one sample at a time** if you want to perform model monitoring. Mini-batch predictions will be captured, but they will cause the monitoring job to fail.

- Likewise, data samples and predictions must be **flat, tabular data**. Structured data (such as lists of lists and nested JSON) will be captured, but the model monitoring job will fail to process it. Optionally, you can add a preprocessing script and a postprocessing script to flatten it. You can find more information at `https://docs.aws.amazon.com/sagemaker/latest/dg/model-monitor-pre-and-post-processing.html`.

- The content type and the accept type must be **identical**. You can use either CSV or JSON, but you can't mix them.

Knowing that, let's capture some data!

1. Training takes place as usual. You can find the code in this book's GitHub repository.

2. Create a data capture configuration. Capture 100% of the prediction requests and responses, storing everything in S3:

```
from sagemaker.model_monitor.data_capture_config import
DataCaptureConfig
```

```
capture_path = 's3://{}/{}/capture/'.format(bucket,
prefix)
```

```
ll_predictor = ll.deploy(
    initial_instance_count=1,
    instance_type='ml.t2.medium',
    data_capture_config = DataCaptureConfig(
        enable_capture = True,
        sampling_percentage = 100,
        capture_options = ['REQUEST', 'RESPONSE'],
        destination_s3_uri = capture_path))
```

3. Once the endpoint is in service, we send data for prediction. Within a minute or two, we will see captured data in S3 and then copy it locally:

```
%%bash -s "$capture_path"
aws s3 ls --recursive $1
aws s3 cp --recursive $1 .
```

4. Opening one of the files, we will see samples and predictions, as follows:

```
{"captureData":{"endpointInput":{"observedContentType":
"text/csv","mode":"INPUT","data":"0.00632,18.00,2.310,0,
0.5380,6.5750,65.20,4.0900,1,296.0,15.30,4.98",
"encoding":"CSV"},"endpointOutput":
{"observedContentType":"text/csv; charset=utf-8",
"mode":"OUTPUT","data":"30.4133586884",
"encoding":"CSV"}},"eventMetadata":{"eventId":"8f45e35c
-fa44-40d2-8ed3-1bcab3a596f3","inferenceTime":"2020-07
-30T13:36:30Z"},"eventVersion":"0"}
```

If this was live data, we could use it to test new models later on, in order to compare their performance to existing models.

Now, let's learn how to create a baseline from the training set.

Creating a baseline

SageMaker Model Monitor includes a built-in container we can use to build the baseline, and we can use it directly with the `DefaultModelMonitor` object. You can also bring your own container, in which case you would use the `ModelMonitor` object instead. Let's get started:

1. A baseline can only be built on comma-separated CSV datasets and JSON datasets. Our dataset is space-separated and needs to be converted into a comma-separated CSV. We can then upload it to S3:

```
data.to_csv('housing.csv', sep=',', index=False)
training = sess.upload_data(
    path='housing.csv', key_prefix=prefix + "/baseline")
```

There is a small caveat here: the job building the baseline is a Spark job running in **SageMaker Processing**. Hence, column names need to be Spark-compliant, lest the job fail in cryptic ways. In particular, dots are not allowed in column names. We don't have that problem here, but please keep this in mind.

2. Define the infrastructure requirements, the location of the training set, and its format:

```
from sagemaker.model_monitor import DefaultModelMonitor
from sagemaker.model_monitor.dataset_format import
DatasetFormat
ll_monitor = DefaultModelMonitor(role=role,
    instance_count=1, instance_type='ml.m5.large')
ll_monitor.suggest_baseline(baseline_dataset=training,
    dataset_format=DatasetFormat.csv(header=True))
```

3. As you can guess, this is running as a SageMaker Processing job, and you can find its log in CloudWatch Logs under the `/aws/sagemaker/ProcessingJobs` prefix. Two JSON artifacts are available at its output location: `statistics.json` and `constraints.json`. We can view their content with `pandas`:

```
baseline = ll_monitor.latest_baselining_job
constraints = pd.io.json.json_normalize(
    baseline.suggested_constraints().body_
dict["features"])
schema = pd.io.json.json_normalize(
    baseline.baseline_statistics().body_dict["features"])
```

4. As shown in the following screenshot, the `constraints` file gives us the inferred type of each feature, its completeness in the dataset, and whether it contains negative values or not:

	name	inferred_type	completeness	num_constraints.is_non_negative
0	crim	Fractional	1.0	True
1	zn	Fractional	1.0	True
2	indus	Fractional	1.0	True
3	chas	Integral	1.0	True
4	nox	Fractional	1.0	True

Figure 11.5 – Viewing the inferred schema

5. The `statistics` file adds basic statistics, as shown in the following screenshot:

numerical_statistics.mean	numerical_statistics.sum	numerical_statistics.std_dev	numerical_statistics.min	numerical_statistics.max
3.613524	1828.44292	8.593041	0.00632	88.9762
11.363636	5750.00000	23.299396	0.00000	100.0000
11.136779	5635.21000	6.853571	0.46000	27.7400

Figure 11.6 – Viewing data statistics

It also includes distribution information based on KLL sketches (https://arxiv.org/abs/1603.05346v2), a compact way to define quantiles:

numerical_statistics.distribution.kll.buckets	numerical_statistics.distribution.kll.sketch.parameters.c	numerical_statistics.distribution.kll.sketch.parameters.k	numerical_statistics.distrib
[{'lower_bound': 0.00632, 'upper_bound': 8.903...	0.64	2048.0	[[0.006 0
[{'lower_bound': 0.0, 'upper_bound': 10.0, 'co...	0.64	2048.0	[[18.0, 0.0, 0.0, 0.0, 0.
[{'lower_bound': 0.46, 'upper_bound': 3.187999...	0.64	2048.0	[[2.31, 7.07, 7.07, 2.18,

Figure 11.7 – Viewing the data distribution

Once the baseline has been created, we can set up a monitoring schedule in order to compare incoming traffic to the baseline.

Setting up a monitoring schedule

We simply pass the name of the endpoint, the statistics, the constraints, and the frequency at which the analysis should run. We will go for hourly, which is the shortest frequency allowed:

```
from sagemaker.model_monitor import CronExpressionGenerator
```

```
ll_monitor.create_monitoring_schedule(
    monitor_schedule_name='ll-housing-schedule',
    endpoint_input=ll_predictor.endpoint,
    statistics=ll_monitor.baseline_statistics(),
    constraints=ll_monitor.suggested_constraints(),
    schedule_cron_expression=CronExpressionGenerator.hourly())
```

Here, the analysis will be performed by a built-in container. Optionally, we could provide our own container with bespoke analysis code. You can find more information at https://docs.aws.amazon.com/sagemaker/latest/dg/model-monitor-byoc-containers.html.

Now, let's send some nasty data to the endpoint and see whether SageMaker Model Monitor picks it up.

Sending bad data

Unfortunately, a model may receive incorrect data at times. Maybe it's been corrupted at the source, maybe the application in charge of invoking the endpoint is buggy, and so on. Let's simulate this and see how much impact this has on the quality of the prediction:

1. Starting from a valid sample, we get a correct prediction:

```
test_sample = '0.00632,18.00,2.310,0,0.5380,6.5750,65.20,
4.0900,1,296.0,15.30,4.98'
```

```
ll_predictor.content_type = 'text/csv'
ll_predictor.accept = 'text/csv'
ll_predictor.serializer =
    sagemaker.serializers.CSVSerializer()
ll_predictor.deserializer =
    sagemaker.deserializers.CSVDeserializer()
```

```
response = ll_predictor.predict(test_sample)
print(response)
```

The price of this house is $30,173:

```
[['30.1734218597']]
```

2. Now, let's multiply the first feature by 10,000. Scaling and unit errors are quite frequent in application code:

```
bad_sample_1 = '632.0,18.00,2.310,0,0.5380,6.5750,65.20,4
.0900,1,296.0,15.30,4.98'
response = ll_predictor.predict(bad_sample_1)
print(response)
```

Ouch! The price is negative. Clearly, this is a bogus prediction:

```
[['-35.7245635986']]
```

3. Let's try negating the last feature:

```
bad_sample_2 = '0.00632,18.00,2.310,0,0.5380,6.5750,
65.20,4.0900,1,296.0,15.30,-4.98'
response = ll_predictor.predict(bad_sample_2)
print(response)
```

The prediction is much higher than what it should be. This is a sneakier issue, which means it is harder to detect, which could have serious business consequences:

```
[['34.4245414734']]
```

You should try experimenting with bad data and see which features are the most brittle. All this traffic will be captured by SageMaker Model Monitor. Once the monitoring job has run, you should see entries in its **violation report**.

Examining violation reports

Previously, we created an hourly monitoring job. Don't worry if it takes a little more than 1 hour to see results; job execution is load balanced by the backend, and short delays are likely:

1. We can find more information about our monitoring job in the SageMaker console, in the **Processing jobs** section. We can also call the describe_schedule() API and list executions with the list_executions() API:

```
ll_executions = ll_monitor.list_executions()
print(ll_executions)
```

Here, we can see three executions:

```
[<sagemaker.model_monitor.model_monitoring.
MonitoringExecution at 0x7fdd1d55a6d8>,
<sagemaker.model_monitor.model_monitoring.
```

```
MonitoringExecution at 0x7fdd1d581630>,
<sagemaker.model_monitor.model_monitoring.
MonitoringExecution at 0x7fdce4b1c860>]
```

2. The violations report is stored as a JSON file in S3. We can read it and display it with `pandas`:

```
violations = ll_monitor.latest_monitoring_constraint_
violations()
```

```
violations = pd.io.json.json_normalize(violations.body_
dict["violations"])
```

```
violations
```

This prints out the violations that were detected by the last monitoring job, as shown in the following screenshot:

	feature_name	constraint_check_type	description
0	tax	data_type_check	Data type match requirement is not met. Expect...
1	nox	data_type_check	Data type match requirement is not met. Expect...
2	chas	data_type_check	Data type match requirement is not met. Expect...
3	rad	data_type_check	Data type match requirement is not met. Expect...

Figure 11.8 – Viewing violations

3. Of course, we can also fetch the file in S3 and display its contents:

```
%%bash -s "$report_path"
echo $1
aws s3 ls --recursive $1
aws s3 cp --recursive $1 .
```

Here's a sample entry, warning us that the model received a fractional value for the `"chas"` feature, although it's defined as an integer in the schema:

```
{
    "feature_name" : "chas",
    "constraint_check_type" : "data_type_check",
    "description" :
        "Data type match requirement is not met.
        Expected data type: Integral,
        Expected match: 100.0%.
        Observed: Only 0.0% of data is Integral."
}
```

We could also emit these violations to CloudWatch metrics, and trigger alarms to notify developers of potential data quality issues. You can find more information at `https://docs.aws.amazon.com/sagemaker/latest/dg/model-monitor-interpreting-cloudwatch.html`.

4. When you're done, don't forget to delete the monitoring schedule and the endpoint itself:

```
response = ll_monitor.delete_monitoring_schedule()
ll_predictor.delete_endpoint()
```

As you can see, SageMaker Model Monitor helps you capture both incoming data and predictions, a useful feature for model testing. In addition, you can also perform data quality analysis using a built-in container or your own.

In the next section, we're going to move away from endpoints, and learn how to deploy models to container services.

Deploying models to container services

Previously, we saw how to fetch a model artifact in S3 and how to extract the actual model from it. Knowing this, it's pretty easy to deploy it on a container service, such as **Amazon ECS**, **Amazon EKS**, or **Amazon Fargate**.

Maybe it's company policy to deploy everything in containers, maybe you just like them, or maybe both! Whatever the reason is, you can definitely do it. There's nothing specific to SageMaker here, and the AWS documentation for these services will tell you everything you need to know.

A sample high-level process could look like this:

1. Train a model on SageMaker.

2. When training is complete, grab the artifact and extract the model.

3. Push the model to a Git repository.

4. Write a task definition (for ECS and Fargate) or a pod definition (for EKS). It could use one of the built-in containers or your own. Then, it could run a model server or your own code to clone the model from your Git repository, load it, and serve predictions.

5. Using this definition, run a container on your cluster.

Let's learn how to apply this to Amazon Fargate.

Training on SageMaker and deploying on Amazon Fargate

Amazon Fargate lets you run containers on fully managed infrastructure (https://aws.amazon.com/fargate). There's no need to create and manage clusters, which makes it ideal for users who don't want to get involved with infrastructure details. However, please note that, at the time of writing, Fargate doesn't support GPU containers.

Preparing a model

We will prepare the model using the following steps:

1. First, train a TensorFlow model on Fashion-MNIST. Business as usual!

2. Find the location of the model artifact in S3 and set it as an environment variable:

```
%env model_data {tf_estimator.model_data}
```

3. Download the artifact from S3 and extract it to a local directory:

```
%%sh
aws s3 cp ${model_data} .
mkdir test-models
tar xvfz model.tar.gz -C test-models
```

4. Opening a Terminal, we commit the model to a public Git repository. I'm using one of mine here (https://gitlab.com/juliensimon/test-models); you should replace it with one of yours:

```
<initialize git repository>
$ cd test-models
$ git add model
$ git commit -m "New model"
$ git push
```

Configuring Fargate

Now that the model is available in a repository, we need to configure Fargate. We'll use the command line this time. You could do the same with `boto3` or any other language SDK:

1. `ecs-cli` is a convenient CLI tool used to manage clusters. Let's install it:

    ```
    %%sh
    sudo curl -o /usr/local/bin/ecs-cli https://amazon-ecs-
    cli.s3.amazonaws.com/ecs-cli-linux-amd64-latest
    sudo chmod 755 /usr/local/bin/ecs-cli
    ```

2. Use it to "create" a Fargate cluster. In practice, this isn't creating any infrastructure: we're only defining a cluster name that we'll use to run tasks. Please make sure that your **IAM** role includes the required permission for `ecs:CreateCluster`. If not, please add it before continuing:

    ```
    %%sh
    aws ecs create-cluster --cluster-name fargate-demo
    ecs-cli configure --cluster fargate-demo --region
    eu-west-1
    ```

3. Create a log group in **CloudWatch** where our container will write its output. We only need to do this once:

    ```
    %%sh
    aws logs create-log-group --log-group-name awslogs-tf-ecs
    ```

4. We will need a **Security Group** for our task that opens the two inbound TensorFlow Serving ports (8500 for **gRPC**, 8501 for the **REST** API). If you don't have one already, you can easily create one in the EC2 console. Here, I created one in my default VPC. It looks as follows:

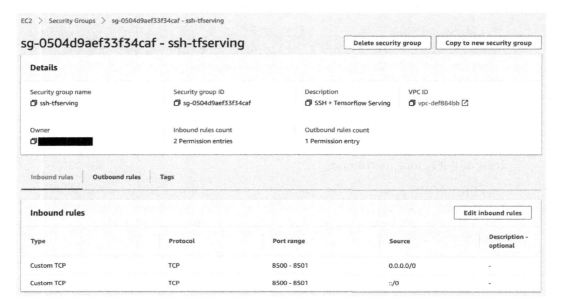

Figure 11.9 – Viewing the Security Group

Defining a task

Now, we need to write a **JSON** file containing a **task definition**: the container image to use, its entry point, and its system and network properties. Let's get started:

1. First, define the amount of CPU and memory that the task is allowed to consume. Unlike ECS and EKS, Fargate only allows a limited set of values, available at https://docs.aws.amazon.com/AmazonECS/latest/developerguide/task-cpu-memory-error.html. We will go for 4 vCPUs and 8 GB of RAM:

```
{
    "requiresCompatibilities": ["FARGATE"],
    "family": "inference-fargate-tf115",
    "memory": "8192",
    "cpu": "4096",
```

2. Next, define the container that will load our model and run predictions. We will use the Deep Learning Container for TensorFlow 1.15.2. You can find the full list at `https://github.com/aws/deep-learning-containers/blob/master/available_images.md`:

```
"containerDefinitions": [{
    "name": "dlc-tf-inference",
    "image": "763104351884.dkr.ecr.eu-west-1.amazonaws.
            com/tensorflow-inference:1.15.2-cpu-py36-
            ubuntu18.04",
    "essential": true,
```

3. Its entry point creates a directory, clones the repository where we pushed the model, and launches TensorFlow Serving:

```
"command": [
    "mkdir -p /test && cd /test && git clone https://
    gitlab.com/juliensimon/test-models.git &&
    tensorflow_model_server --port=8500 --rest_api_
    port=8501 --model_name=1 --model_base_path=/test/
    test-models/model"
],
"entryPoint": ["sh","-c"],
```

4. Accordingly, map the two TensorFlow Serving ports:

```
"portMappings": [
    {
        "hostPort": 8500,
        "protocol": "tcp",
        "containerPort": 8500
    },
    {
        "hostPort": 8501,
        "protocol": "tcp",
        "containerPort": 8501
    }
],
```

5. Define the log configuration that's pointing at the CloudWatch log group we created earlier:

```
"logConfiguration": {
    "logDriver": "awslogs",
```

```
        "options": {
          "awslogs-group": "awslogs-tf-ecs",
          "awslogs-region": "eu-west-1",
          "awslogs-stream-prefix": "inference"
        }
    }
  }],
```

6. Set the networking mode for the container. `awsvpc` is the most flexible option, and it will allow our container to be publicly accessible, as explained at `https://docs.aws.amazon.com/AmazonECS/latest/developerguide/task-networking.html`. It will create an **Elastic Network Interface** in the subnet of our choice:

```
    "networkMode": "awsvpc"
```

7. Finally, define an IAM role for the task. If this is the first time you're working with ECS, you should create this role in the IAM console. You can find instructions for this at `https://docs.aws.amazon.com/AmazonECS/latest/developerguide/task_execution_IAM_role.html`:

```
    "executionRoleArn":
      "arn:aws:iam::123456789012:role/ecsTaskExecutionRole"
  }
```

Running a task

We're now ready to run our task using the Security Group we created earlier and one of the subnets in our default VPC. Let's get started:

1. Launch the task with the `run-task` API, passing the family name of the task definition (not the filename!). Please pay attention to the version number as well as it will automatically increase every time you register a new version of the task definition, so make sure you're using the latest one:

```
%%sh
aws ecs run-task
  --cluster fargate-demo
  --task-definition inference-fargate-tf115:1
  --count 1
  --launch-type FARGATE
  --network-configuration
    "awsvpcConfiguration={subnets=[$SUBNET_ID],
```

```
        securityGroups=[$SECURITY_GROUP_ID],
        assignPublicIp=ENABLED}"
```

2. A few seconds later, we can see our prediction container running (showing the task ID, state, ports, and task definition):

```
%%sh
ecs-cli ps --desired-status RUNNING
a9c9a3a8-8b7c-4dbb-9ec4-d20686ba5aec/dlc-tf-inference
RUNNING
52.49.238.243:8500->8500/tcp, 52.49.238.243:8501->8501/
tcp                                inference-fargate-tf115:1
```

3. Using the public IP address of the container, build a TensorFlow Serving prediction request with 10 sample images and send it to our container:

```
import random, json, requests
inference_task_ip = '52.49.238.243'
inference_url = 'http://' +
                inference_task_ip +
                ':8501/v1/models/1:predict'
indices = random.sample(range(x_val.shape[0] - 1), 10)
images = x_val[indices]/255
labels = y_val[indices]

data = images.reshape(num_samples, 28, 28, 1)
data = json.dumps({"signature_name": "serving_default",
                   "instances": data.tolist()})
headers = {"content-type": "application/json"}
json_response = requests.post(
    inference_url,
    data=data,
    headers=headers)
predictions = json.loads(json_response.text)
['predictions']
predictions = np.array(predictions).argmax(axis=1)

print("Labels     : ", labels)
print("Predictions: ", predictions)
Labels     :  [9 8 8 8 0 8 9 7 1 1]
Predictions:  [9 8 8 8 0 8 9 7 1 1]
```

4. When we're done, we stop the task using the task ARN returned by the `run-task` API and delete the cluster. Of course, you can also use the ECS console:

```sh
%%sh
aws ecs stop-task --cluster fargate-demo --task $TASK_ARN
ecs-cli down --force --cluster fargate-demo
```

The processes for ECS and EKS are extremely similar. You can find simple examples at `https://gitlab.com/juliensimon/dlcontainers`. They should be a good starting point if you wish to build your own workflow.

Kubernetes fans can also use **SageMaker Operators for Kubernetes** and use native tools such as `kubectl` to train and deploy models. A detailed tutorial is available at `https://sagemaker.readthedocs.io/en/stable/workflows/kubernetes/index.html`.

Summary

In this chapter, you learned about model artifacts, what they contain, and how to use them to export models outside of SageMaker. You also learned how to import and deploy existing models, as well as how to manage endpoints in detail, both with the SageMaker SDK and the `boto3` SDK.

Then, we discussed alternative deployment scenarios with SageMaker, using either batch transform or inference pipelines, as well as outside of SageMaker with container services.

Finally, you learned how to use SageMaker Model Monitor to capture endpoint data and monitor data quality.

In the next chapter, we'll discuss automating machine learning workflows with three different AWS services: **AWS CloudFormation**, **AWS CDK**, and **AWS Step Functions**.

12
Automating Machine Learning Workflows

In the previous chapter, you learned how to deploy machine learning models in different configurations, using both the SageMaker SDK and the boto3 SDK. We used their APIs in Jupyter notebooks, the preferred way to experiment and iterate quickly.

However, running notebooks for production tasks is not a good idea. Even if your code has been carefully tested, what about monitoring, logging, creating other AWS resources, handling errors, rolling back, and so on? Doing all of this right would require a lot of extra work and code, opening the possibility for more bugs. A more industrial approach is required.

In this chapter, you'll learn how to automate machine learning workflows with AWS services purposely built to bring repeatability, predictability, and robustness. Complex workflows can be triggered with a few simple APIs, saving you time, effort, and frustration. You'll see how you can preview infrastructure changes before applying them, in order to avoid uncontrolled and potentially destructive operations. Once changes are applied, you'll get full visibility on their progress, and on what has happened. Finally, you'll learn how to clean up all resources involved, without any risk of leaving anything behind. We'll cover the following topics:

- Automating with AWS CloudFormation

- Automating with AWS Cloud Development Kit

- Automating with AWS Step Functions

Technical requirements

You will need an AWS account to run the examples included in this chapter. If you haven't got one already, please point your browser at `https://aws.amazon.com/getting-started/` to create one. You should also familiarize yourself with the AWS Free Tier (`https://aws.amazon.com/free/`), which lets you use many AWS services for free within certain usage limits.

You will need to install and to configure the AWS Command Line Interface for your account (`https://aws.amazon.com/cli/`).

You will need a working Python 3.x environment. Be careful not to use Python 2.7, as it is no longer maintained. Installing the Anaconda distribution (`https://www.anaconda.com/`) is not mandatory, but strongly encouraged as it includes many projects that we will need (Jupyter, `pandas`, `numpy`, and more).

Code examples included in the book are available on GitHub at `https://github.com/PacktPublishing/Learn-Amazon-SageMaker`. You will need to install a Git client to access them (`https://git-scm.com/`).

Automating with AWS CloudFormation

AWS CloudFormation has long been the preferred way to automate infrastructure builds and operations on AWS (`https://aws.amazon.com/cloudformation`). We could certainly write a book on the topic, but we'll stick to basics in this section.

The first step in using **CloudFormation** is to write a template, a **JSON** or **YAML** text file describing the **resources** that you want to build, such as an EC2 instance or an S3 bucket. Resources are available for almost all AWS services, and SageMaker is no exception. If we look at `https://docs.aws.amazon.com/AWSCloudFormation/latest/UserGuide/AWS_SageMaker.html`, we see that we can create **Notebook instances** and deploy endpoints.

A template can (and should) include parameters and outputs. The former help make templates as generic as possible. The latter provide information that can be used by downstream applications, such as instance DNS names or bucket names.

Once you've written your template file, you pass it to CloudFormation to create a **stack**, a collection of AWS resources. CloudFormation will parse the template and create all resources automatically. Dependencies are also managed automatically, and resources will be created in the correct order. If a stack can't be created correctly, CloudFormation will roll it back, deleting resources that have been built so far.

A stack can be updated by applying a newer template revision. CloudFormation will analyze changes, and will create, delete, update or replace resources accordingly. Thanks to **change sets**, you can verify changes before they are performed, and then decide whether to proceed or not.

Of course, a stack can be deleted, and CloudFormation will automatically tear down all its resources, a great way to clean up your builds without leaving any cruft behind.

Let's run a first example, where we deploy a model to a real-time endpoint.

Writing a template

This stack will be equivalent to calling the `boto3` API we studied in *Chapter 11, Deploying Machine Learning Models*: `create_model()`, `create_endpoint_configuration()`, and `create_endpoint()`. Accordingly, we'll define three CloudFormation resources (a model, an endpoint configuration, and an endpoint), and their parameters:

1. Opening a new text file, we first define in the **Parameters** section the input parameters for the stack. Each parameter has a name, a description, and a type. Optionally, we may provide default values:

```
AWSTemplateFormatVersion: 2010-09-09

Parameters:
    ModelName:
        Description: Model name
        Type: String
    ModelDataUrl:
        Description: Location of model artifact
        Type: String
    ContainerImage:
        Description: Container used to deploy the model
        Type: String
    InstanceType:
        Description: Instance type
        Type: String
        Default: ml.m5.large
    InstanceCount:
        Description: Instance count
        Type: String
        Default: 1
    RoleArn:
        Description: Execution Role ARN
        Type: String
```

2. In the **Resources** section, we define a model resource, using the `Ref` built-in function to reference the appropriate input parameters:

```
Resources:
    Model:
        Type: "AWS::SageMaker::Model"
        Properties:
            Containers:
                -
                    Image: !Ref ContainerImage
```

```
              ModelDataUrl: !Ref ModelDataUrl
      ExecutionRoleArn: !Ref RoleArn
      ModelName: !Ref ModelName
```

3. We then define an endpoint configuration resource. We use the `GetAtt` built-in function to get the name of the model resource. Of course, this requires that the model resource already exists, and CloudFormation will make sure that resources are created in the right order:

```
EndpointConfig:
    Type: "AWS::SageMaker::EndpointConfig"
    Properties:
        ProductionVariants:
            -
            ModelName: !GetAtt Model.ModelName
            VariantName: variant-1
            InitialInstanceCount: !Ref InstanceCount
            InstanceType: !Ref InstanceType
            InitialVariantWeight: 1.0
```

4. Finally, we define an endpoint resource. Likewise, we use `GetAtt` to find the name of the endpoint configuration:

```
Endpoint:
    Type: "AWS::SageMaker::Endpoint"
    Properties:
        EndpointConfigName: !GetAtt
        EndpointConfig.EndpointConfigName
```

5. In the **Outputs** section, we return the CloudFormation identifier of the endpoint, as well as its name:

```
Outputs:
    EndpointId:
        Value: !Ref Endpoint
    EndpointName:
        Value: !GetAtt Endpoint.EndpointName
```

Now that the template is complete (`endpoint-one-model.yml`), we can create a stack.

> **Note:**
>
> Please make sure that the IAM role for your user or for your Notebook instance has permission to invoke CloudFormation APIs. If not, please add the `AWSCloudFormationFullAccess` managed policy to the role.

Deploying a model to a real-time endpoint

Let's use the `boto3` API to create a stack deploying a **TensorFlow** model. We'll reuse a model trained with **Keras** on Fashion MNIST:

> **Note:**
>
> For a change, I'm using the us-east-1 region. As our template is completely region-independent, you can use any region that you want. Just make sure that you have trained a model there.

1. We'll need `boto3` clients for SageMaker and CloudFormation:

    ```
    import boto3
    sm = boto3.client('sagemaker')
    cf = boto3.client('cloudformation')
    ```

2. We describe the training job to find the location of its artifact, and its execution role:

    ```
    training_job =
        'tensorflow-training-2020-06-08-07-46-04-367'
    job = sm.describe_training_job(
        TrainingJobName=training_job)
    model_data_url =
        job['ModelArtifacts']['S3ModelArtifacts']
    role_arn = job['RoleArn']
    ```

3. We set the container to use for deployment. In some cases, this is unnecessary, as the same container is used for training and deployment. For **TensorFlow** and other frameworks, SageMaker uses two different containers. You can find more information at `https://github.com/aws/deep-learning-containers/blob/master/available_images.md`:

```
container_image = '763104351884.dkr.ecr.us-east-1.
amazonaws.com/tensorflow-inference:2.1.0-cpu-py36-
ubuntu18.04'
```

4. Then, we read our template, create a new stack, and pass the required parameters:

```
import time
timestamp = time.strftime("%Y-%m-%d-%H-%M-%S", time.
gmtime())
stack_name='endpoint-one-model-'+timestamp
with open('endpoint-one-model.yml', 'r') as f:
  response = cf.create_stack(
      StackName=stack_name,
      TemplateBody=f.read(),
      Parameters=[
          { "ParameterKey":"ModelName",
            "ParameterValue":training_job+
                            '-'+timestamp },
          { "ParameterKey":"ContainerImage",
            "ParameterValue":container_image },
          { "ParameterKey":"ModelDataUrl",
            "ParameterValue":model_data_url },
          { "ParameterKey":"RoleArn",
            "ParameterValue":role_arn }
      ]
  )
```

5. Jumping to the CloudFormation console, we see that the stack is being created, as shown in the following screenshot. Notice that resources are created in the right order: model, endpoint configuration, and endpoint:

Figure 12.1 Viewing stack creation

As we would expect, we also see the endpoint in the SageMaker console, as shown in the next screenshot:

Figure 12.2 Viewing endpoint creation

6. Once the stack creation is complete, we can use its output to find the name of the endpoint:

```
response = cf.describe_stacks(StackName=stack_name)
print(response['Stacks'][0]['StackStatus'])
for o in response['Stacks'][0]['Outputs']:
    if o['OutputKey']=='EndpointName':
        endpoint_name = o['OutputValue']
print(endpoint_name)
```

This prints out the endpoint name, autogenerated by CloudFormation:

```
Endpoint-krBUW6EcTO9d
```

7. We can then test the endpoint as usual. Then, we can delete the stack and its resources:

```
cf.delete_stack(StackName=stack_name)
```

Let's not delete the stack right away. Instead, we're going to use a change set to update it.

Modifying a stack with a change set

Here, we're going to update the number of instances backing the endpoint:

1. We create a new change set using the same template and parameters, except InstanceCount, which we set to 2:

```
response = cf.create_change_set(
    StackName=stack_name,
    ChangeSetName='add-instance',
    UsePreviousTemplate=True,
    Parameters=[
      { "ParameterKey":"InstanceCount",
        "ParameterValue": "2" },
      { "ParameterKey":"ModelName",
        "UsePreviousValue": True },
      { "ParameterKey":"ContainerImage",
        "UsePreviousValue": True },
      { "ParameterKey":"ModelDataUrl",
        "UsePreviousValue": True },
      { "ParameterKey":"RoleArn",
        "UsePreviousValue": True }
    ]
)
```

2. We see details on the change set in the **CloudFormation** console, as shown in the next screenshot. We could also use the `describe_change_set()` API:

Figure 12.3 Viewing a change set

This tells us that the endpoint configuration and the endpoint need to be modified, and possibly replaced. As we already know from *Chapter 11, Deploying Machine Learning Models*, a new endpoint will be created, and applied in a non-disruptive fashion to the existing endpoint.

> **Note:**
>
> When working with CloudFormation, it's critical that you understand the **replacement policy** for your resources. Details are available in the documentation for each resource type.

3. By clicking on the **Execute** button, we execute the change set. We could also use the `execute_change_set()` API. As expected, the endpoint is immediately updated, as shown in the following screenshot:

Figure 12.4 Updating the endpoint

4. Once the update is complete, we see the sequence of events in the CloudFormation console, as shown in the next screenshot. A new endpoint configuration has been created and applied to the endpoint. The previous endpoint configuration has been deleted:

Events (21)

Timestamp	Logical ID	Status	Status reason
2020-06-23 11:13:12 UTC+0200	endpoint-one-model-2020-06-23-08-36-49	⊘ UPDATE_COMPLETE	-
2020-06-23 11:13:12 UTC+0200	EndpointConfig	⊘ DELETE_COMPLETE	-
2020-06-23 11:13:10 UTC+0200	EndpointConfig	⊙ DELETE_IN_PROGRESS	-
2020-06-23 11:13:09 UTC+0200	endpoint-one-model-2020-06-23-08-36-49	⊙ UPDATE_COMPLETE_CLEAN UP_IN_PROGRESS	-
2020-06-23 11:13:06 UTC+0200	Endpoint	⊘ UPDATE_COMPLETE	-
2020-06-23 11:06:26 UTC+0200	Endpoint	⊙ UPDATE_IN_PROGRESS	-
2020-06-23 11:06:22 UTC+0200	EndpointConfig	⊘ UPDATE_COMPLETE	-
2020-06-23 11:06:22 UTC+0200	EndpointConfig	⊙ UPDATE_IN_PROGRESS	Resource creation Initiated
2020-06-23 11:06:20 UTC+0200	EndpointConfig	⊙ UPDATE_IN_PROGRESS	Requested update requires the creation of a new physical resource; hence creating one.
2020-06-23 11:06:09 UTC+0200	endpoint-one-model-2020-06-23-08-36-49	⊙ UPDATE_IN_PROGRESS	User Initiated

Figure 12.5 Updating the stack

5. We can check that the endpoint is now backed by two instances:

```
r = sm.describe_endpoint(EndpointName=endpoint_name)
print r(['ProductionVariants'][0]
['CurrentInstanceCount'])
```

This prints out the number of instances backing the Production Variant:

```
2
```

Let's keep working with change sets and add a second production variant to the endpoint.

Adding a second production variant to the endpoint

Our initial template only defined a single production variant. We'll update it and add another one (endpoint-two-models.yml):

1. In the **Parameters** section, we add entries for a second model:

```
ModelName2:
    Description: Second model name
    Type: String
ModelDataUrl2:
    Description: Location of second model artifact
    Type: String
VariantWeight2:
    Description: Weight of second model
    Type: String
Default: 0.0
```

2. We do the same in the **Resources** section:

```
Model2:
    Type: "AWS::SageMaker::Model"
    Properties:
        Containers:
            -
                Image: !Ref ContainerImage
                ModelDataUrl: !Ref ModelDataUrl2
        ExecutionRoleArn: !Ref RoleArn
        ModelName: !Ref ModelName2
```

3. Moving back to our notebook, we get information on another training job.
    We then create a change set, reading the updated template and passing all
    required parameters:

```
training_job_2 = 'tensorflow-
training-2020-06-08-07-32-18-734'
```

```
job_2=sm.describe_training_job(
        TrainingJobName=training_job_2)
model_data_url_2=
        job_2['ModelArtifacts']['S3ModelArtifacts']
```

```
with open('endpoint-two-models.yml', 'r') as f:
    response = cf.create_change_set(
        StackName=stack_name,
        ChangeSetName='add-model',
        TemplateBody=f.read(),
        Parameters=[
            { "ParameterKey":"ModelName",
              "UsePreviousValue": True },
            { "ParameterKey":"ModelDataUrl",
              "UsePreviousValue": True },
            { "ParameterKey":"ContainerImage",
              "UsePreviousValue": True },
            { "ParameterKey":"RoleArn",
              "UsePreviousValue": True },
            { "ParameterKey":"ModelName2",
              "ParameterValue": training_job_2+'-
                                '+timestamp},
            { "ParameterKey":"ModelDataUrl2",
              "ParameterValue": model_data_url_2 }
        ]
    )
```

4. Looking at the CloudFormation console, we see the changes caused by the change set: create a new model and modify the endpoint configuration and the endpoint:

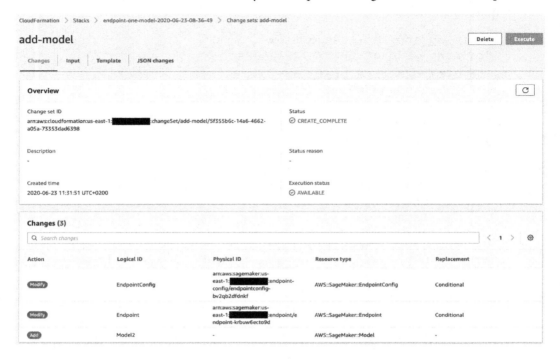

Figure 12.6 Viewing the change set

5. We execute the change set. Once it's complete, we see that the endpoint now supports two production variants. Note that the instance count is back to its initial value, as we defined it as 1 in the updated template:

Figure 12.7 Viewing production variants

The new production variant has a weight of 0, so it won't be used for prediction. Let's see how we can gradually introduce it using **canary deployment**.

Implementing canary deployment

Canary deployment is a popular technique for gradual application deployment (https://martinfowler.com/bliki/CanaryRelease.html), and it can also be used for machine learning models.

Simply put, we'll use a series of stack updates to gradually increase the weight of the second production variant in 10% increments, until it completely replaces the first production variant. We'll also create a **CloudWatch** alarm monitoring the latency of the second production variant; if the alarm is triggered, the change set will be rolled back:

1. We create a CloudWatch alarm monitoring the 60-second average latency of the second production variant. We set the threshold at 50 milliseconds:

```python
cw = boto3.client('cloudwatch')
alarm_name = 'My_endpoint_latency'
response = cw.put_metric_alarm(
    AlarmName=alarm_name,
    ComparisonOperator='GreaterThanThreshold',
    EvaluationPeriods=1,
    MetricName='ModelLatency',
    Namespace='AWS/SageMaker',
    Period=60,
    Statistic='Average',
    Threshold=50000.0,
    AlarmDescription=
        '1-minute average latency exceeds 50ms',
    Dimensions=[
        { 'Name': 'EndpointName',
          'Value': endpoint_name },
        { 'Name': 'VariantName',
          'Value': 'variant-2' }
    ],
    Unit='Microseconds'
)
```

2. We find the ARN of the alarm:

```python
response = cw.describe_alarms(AlarmNames=[alarm_name])
for a in response['MetricAlarms']:
    if a['AlarmName'] == alarm_name:
        alarm_arn = a['AlarmArn']
```

3. Then, we loop over weights and update the stack. Change sets are unnecessary here, as we know exactly what's going to happen from a resource perspective. We set our CloudWatch alarm as a **rollback trigger**, giving it five minutes to go off after each update before moving on to the next:

```python
for w in list(range(10,110,10)):
    response = cf.update_stack(
        StackName=stack_name,
        UsePreviousTemplate=True,
        Parameters=[
            { "ParameterKey":"ModelName",
              "UsePreviousValue": True },
            { "ParameterKey":"ModelDataUrl",
              "UsePreviousValue": True },
            { "ParameterKey":"ContainerImage",
              "UsePreviousValue": True },
            { "ParameterKey":"RoleArn",
              "UsePreviousValue": True },
            { "ParameterKey":"ModelName2",
              "UsePreviousValue": True },
            { "ParameterKey":"ModelDataUrl2",
              "UsePreviousValue": True },
            { "ParameterKey":"VariantWeight",
              "ParameterValue": str(100-w) },
            { "ParameterKey":"VariantWeight2",
              "ParameterValue": str(w) }
        ],
        RollbackConfiguration={
            'RollbackTriggers': [
                { 'Arn': alarm_arn, :
                  'AWS::CloudWatch::Alarm' }
            ],
            'MonitoringTimeInMinutes': 5
        }
    )
    waiter = cf.get_waiter('stack_update_complete')
    waiter.wait(StackName=stack_name)
    print("Sending %d% of traffic to new model" % w)
```

That's all it takes. Pretty cool, don't you think?

This cell will run for a couple of hours, so don't stop it. The next step is to start sending some traffic to the endpoint. For the sake of brevity, I won't include the code, which is identical to the one we used in *Chapter 7, Extending Machine Learning Services with Built-in Frameworks*. You'll find the notebook in the GitHub repository for the book (`ch12/cloudformation/Predict Fashion MNIST images.ipynb`).

Now all we have to do is sit back, have a cup of tea, and enjoy the fact that our model is being deployed safely and automatically. As endpoint updates are seamless, client applications won't notice a thing.

After a couple of hours, deployment is complete. The next screenshot shows invocations for both variants over time. As we can see, traffic was gradually shifted from the first variant to the second one. The glitch at 11:55 was caused by the Python thread sending traffic to the endpoint. Not sure what happened there!

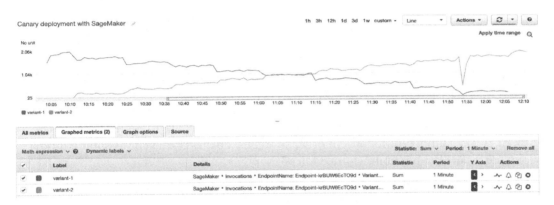

Figure 12.8 Monitoring canary deployment

Latency stayed well under our 50-millisecond limit, and the alarm wasn't triggered, as shown in the next screenshot:

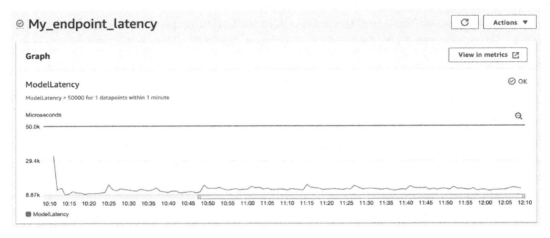

Figure 12.9 Viewing the CloudWatch alarm

This example can serve as a starting point for your own deployments. For example, you could add an alarm monitoring 4xx or 5xx errors. You could also monitor a business metric directly impacted by prediction latency and accuracy, such as click-through rate, conversion rate, and so on. A useful thing to add would be an alarm notification (email, SMS, or even a Lambda function), in order to trigger downstream actions should model deployment fail. The possibilities are endless!

When you're done, **don't forget to delete the stack**, either in the CloudFormation console, or with the delete_stack() API.

Blue-green deployment is another popular technique. Let's see how we can implement it on SageMaker.

Implementing blue-green deployment

Blue-green deployment requires two production environments (https://martinfowler.com/bliki/BlueGreenDeployment.html):

- The live production environment (blue) running version n
- A copy of this environment (green) running version n+1

Let's look at two possible scenarios, which we could implement using the same APIs we've used for canary deployment.

Implementing blue-green deployment with a single endpoint

Starting from an existing endpoint running the current version of the model, we would follow the following steps:

1. Create a new endpoint configuration with two Production Variants: one for the current model and one for the new model. Weights would be set to 1 and 0 respectively.

2. Apply it to the endpoint.

3. Run tests on the new production variant, selecting it explicitly with the `TargetVariant` parameter in `invoke_endpoint()`.

4. When tests are satisfactory, update the weights to 0 and 1. This will seamlessly switch traffic to the new model. If anything goes wrong, revert the weights to 1 and 0.

5. When deployment is complete, update the endpoint to delete the first production variant.

This is a simple and robust solution. However, updating an endpoint takes several minutes, making the whole process not as quick as we may want. Let's see how we can fix this problem by using two endpoints.

Implementing blue-green deployment with two endpoints

Starting from an existing endpoint running the current version of the model, we would implement the following steps:

1. Create a second endpoint running the new version of the model.

2. Run tests on this new endpoint.

3. When the tests are satisfactory, switch all traffic to the new endpoint. This could be achieved in different ways; for example, updating a parameter in your business application, or updating a private DNS entry. If anything goes wrong, revert to the previous setting.

4. When deployment is complete, delete the old endpoint.

This setup is a little more complex, but it lets you switch instantly from one model version to the next, both for deployments and rollbacks.

CloudFormation is a fantastic tool for automation, and any time spent learning it will pay dividends. Yet some AWS users prefer writing code over writing templates, which is why we introduced the **Cloud Development Kit**.

Automating with the AWS Cloud Development Kit

The **Cloud Development Kit (CDK)** is a multi-language SDK that lets you write code to define AWS infrastructure (`https://github.com/aws/aws-cdk`). Using the CDK CLI, you can then provision this infrastructure, using CloudFormation under the hood.

Installing CDK

CDK is natively implemented with **Node.js**, so please make sure that the npm tool is installed on your machine (`https://www.npmjs.com/get-npm`).

Installing CDK is then as simple as this:

```
$ npm i -g aws-cdk
$ cdk --version
1.55.0 (build 48ccf09)
```

Let's create a CDK application and deploy an endpoint.

Creating a CDK application

We'll deploy the same model that we deployed with CloudFormation. I'll use Python, but you could also use JavaScript, TypeScript, Java, and .NET. The API documentation is available at `https://docs.aws.amazon.com/cdk/api/latest/python/`. Let's begin:

1. We create a Python application named `endpoint`:

    ```
    $ mkdir cdk
    $ cd cdk
    $ cdk init --language python --app endpoint
    ```

2. This automatically creates a virtual environment, which we need to activate:

    ```
    $ source .env/bin/activate
    ```

3. This also creates a default `app.py` file for our CDK code, a `cdk.json` file for application configuration, and `requirements.txt` to install dependencies. We'll use the files present in the GitHub repository.

4. In the `requirements.txt` file, we install the CDK package for SageMaker. Each service requires a different package. For example, we would add `aws_cdk.aws_s3` for S3:

```
-e .
aws_cdk.aws_sagemaker
```

5. We then install requirements as usual:

```
$ pip install -r requirements.txt
```

6. In the `cdk.json` file, we store the application context, namely key-value pairs that can be read by the application for configuration (`https://docs.aws.amazon.com/cdk/latest/guide/context.html`):

```
{
  "app": "python3 app.py",
  "context": {
    "role_arn": "arn:aws:iam::123456789012:role/
                 Sagemaker-fullaccess"
    "model_name": "tf2-fmnist",
    "epc_name": "tf2-fmnist-epc",
    "ep_name": "tf2-fmnist-ep",
    "image": "763104351884.dkr.ecr.us-east-1.amazonaws.
             com/tensorflow-inference:2.1-cpu",
    "model_data_url": "s3://sagemaker-us-
        east-1-123456789012/keras2-fashion-mnist/output/
        tensorflow-training-2020-06-08-07-46-04-367/
        output/model.tar.gz"
    "instance_type": "ml.t2.xlarge",
    "instance_count": 1
  }
}
```

This is the preferred way to pass values to your application. You should manage this file with version control in order to keep track of how stacks were built.

7. We can view the context of our application with the `cdk context` command:

```
(.env) (base) → cdk git:(master) ✗ cdk context
Context found in cdk.json:
```

#	Key	Value
1	ep_name	"tf2-fmnist-ep"
2	epc_name	"tf2-fmnist-epc"
3	image	"763104351884.dkr.ecr.eu-west-1.amazonaws.com/tensorflow-inference:2.1-cpu"
4	instance_count	1
5	instance_type	"ml.t2.xlarge"
6	model_data_url	"s3://sagemaker-us-east-1-123456789012/keras2-fashion-mnist/output/tensorflow-training-2020-06-08-07-46-04-367/output/model.tar.gz"
7	model_name	"tf2-fmnist"
8	role_arn	"arn:aws:iam::123456789012:role/Sagemaker-fullaccess"

Figure 12.10 Viewing CDK context

Now, we need to write the actual application.

Writing a CDK application

All code goes in the `app.py` file, which we implement in the following steps:

1. We import the required packages:

```python
import time

from aws_cdk import (
    aws_sagemaker as sagemaker,
    core
)
```

2. We extend the `core.Stack` class to create our own stack:

```python
class SagemakerEndpoint(core.Stack):
  def __init__(self, app: core.App, id: str, **kwargs) ->
  None:
      timestamp = '-'+time.strftime("%Y-%m-%d-%H-%M-%S",
                                    time.gmtime())
      super().__init__(app, id, **kwargs)
```

3. We add a `CfnModel` object, reading the appropriate context values:

```python
        model = sagemaker.CfnModel(
            scope = self,
            id="my_model",
            execution_role_arn=
                self.node.try_get_context("role_arn"),
```

```
containers=[{
  "image":
    self.node.try_get_context("image"),
  "modelDataUrl":
    self.node.try_get_context("model_data_url")
}],
model_name= self.node.try_get_context(
            "model_name")+timestamp
)
```

4. We add a `CfnEndpointConfig` object, using the built-in `get_att()` function to associate it to the model. This creates a dependency that CloudFormation will use to build resources in the right order:

```
epc = sagemaker.CfnEndpointConfig(
    scope=self,
    id="my_epc",
    production_variants=[{
        "modelName": core.Fn.get_att(
                        model.logical_id,
                        'ModelName'
                     ).to_string(),
        "variantName": "variant-1",
        "initialVariantWeight": 1.0,
        "initialInstanceCount": 1,
        "instanceType":
            self.node.try_get_context(
            "instance_type")
    }],
    endpoint_config_name=
        self.node.try_get_context("epc_name")
        +timestamp
)
```

5. We add a `CfnEndpoint` object, using the built-in `get_att()` function to associate it with the endpoint configuration:

```
ep = sagemaker.CfnEndpoint(
    scope=self,
    id="my_ep",
    endpoint_config_name=
        core.Fn.get_att(
            epc.logical_id,
            'EndpointConfigName'
```

```
                    ).to_string(),
            endpoint_name=
                self.node.try_get_context("ep_name")
                +timestamp
        )
```

6. Finally, we instantiate the application:

```
app = core.App()
SagemakerEndpoint(
    app,
    "SagemakerEndpoint",
    env={'region': 'us-east-1'}
)
app.synth()
```

Our code is complete!

Deploying a CDK application

We can now deploy the endpoint:

1. We can list the available stacks:

```
$ cdk list
SagemakerEndpoint
```

2. We can also see the actual CloudFormation template. It should be extremely similar to the template we wrote in the previous section:

```
$ cdk synth SagemakerEndpoint
```

3. Deploying the stack is equally simple:

```
$ cdk deploy SagemakerEndpoint
SagemakerEndpoint: deploying..
SagemakerEndpoint: creating CloudFormation changeset...
SagemakerEndpoint
```

4. Looking at CloudFormation, we see that the stack is created using a change set. The SageMaker console also tells us that the endpoint is in service.

5. Editing `app.py`, we set the initial instance count to 2. We then ask CDK to deploy the stack, but without executing the change set. This will allow us to review it in the CloudFormation console:

```
$ cdk deploy --no-execute SagemakerEndpoint
SagemakerEndpoint: deploying...
SagemakerEndpoint: creating CloudFormation changeset...
Changeset CDK-7b21a26b-2bf7-4ce3-af74-21fd78dc5d0a
created and waiting in review for manual execution
(--no-execute)
SagemakerEndpoint
```

6. If we're happy with the change set, we can execute it in the console, or run the previous command again without `--no-execute`. As expected, and as shown in the next screenshot, the endpoint is updated:

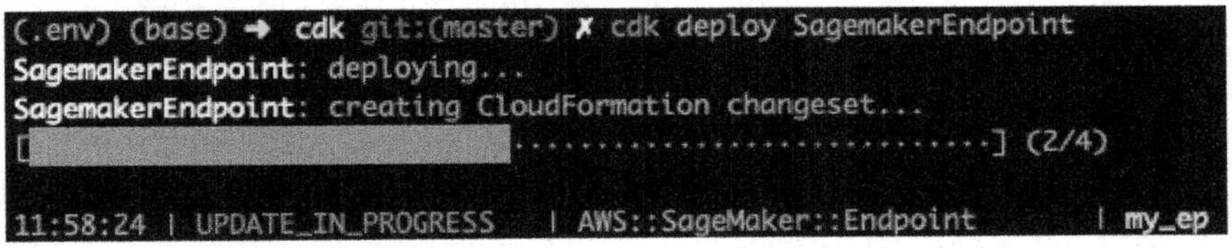

Figure 12.11 Updating the endpoint

7. When we're done, we can destroy the stack:

```
$ cdk destroy SagemakerEndpoint
```

As you can see, the CDK is an interesting alternative to writing templates directly, while still benefiting from the rigor and the robustness of CloudFormation.

One thing we haven't done yet is automate an end-to-end workflow, from training to deployment. Let's do this with **AWS Step Functions**.

Automating with AWS Step Functions

AWS Step Functions let you define and run workflows based on **state machines** (https://aws.amazon.com/step-functions/). A state machine is a combination of steps, which can be sequential, parallel, or conditional. Each step receives an input from its predecessor, performs an operation, and passes the output to its successor. Step Functions are integrated with many AWS services, such as Lambda, DynamoDB, and SageMaker, and you can easily use them in your workflows.

State machines can be defined using JSON and the **Amazon States Language**, and you can visualize them in the service console. State machine execution is fully managed, so you don't need to provision any infrastructure to run.

When it comes to SageMaker, Step Functions has a dedicated Python SDK, named the **Data Science SDK** (`https://github.com/aws/aws-step-functions-data-science-sdk-python`). In my humble opinion, this is a confusing name, as the SDK has nothing to do with data science. Anyway, it makes it extremely easy to build end-to-end workflows with SageMaker.

Let's run an example where we automate training and deployment for a Scikit-Learn model trained on the Boston Housing dataset.

> **Note:**
> At the time of writing, the Data Science SDK hasn't been updated for SageMaker SDK v2. Thus, the following code runs with SDK v1 (`sdkv1/ch12/step_functions` in the repository). I'll push code to `sdkv2/ch12/step_functions` once the updated SDK is available.

Setting up permissions

First, please make sure that the IAM role for your user or for your Notebook instance has permission to invoke Step Functions APIs. If not, please add the `AWSStepFunctionsFullAccess` managed policy to the role.

Then, we need to create a service role for Step Functions, allowing it to invoke AWS APIs on our behalf:

1. Starting from the IAM console (`https://console.aws.amazon.com/iam/home#/roles`), we click on **Create role**.

2. We select **AWS service** and **Step Functions**.

3. We click through the next screens until we can enter the role name. Let's call it `StepFunctionsWorkflowExecutionRole`, and click on **Create role**.

4. Selecting this role, we click on its **Permission** tab, then on **Add inline policy**.

5. Selecting the JSON tab, we replace the empty policy with the content of the `ch12/step_functions/service-role-policy.json` file, and we click on **Review policy**.

6. We name the policy StepFunctionsWorkflowExecutionPolicy and click on **Create policy**.

7. We write down the ARN on the role, and we close the IAM console.

Setup is now complete; let's create a workflow.

Implementing our first workflow

In this workflow, we'll go through the following step sequence: train the model, create it, use it for a batch transform, create an endpoint configuration, and deploy the model to an endpoint:

1. We upload the training set to S3, as well as a test set where we removed the target attribute. We'll use the latter for a batch transform:

```python
import sagemaker
import pandas as pd

sess = sagemaker.Session()
bucket = sess.default_bucket()
prefix = 'sklearn-boston-housing-stepfunc'

training_data = sess.upload_data(
    path='housing.csv',
    key_prefix=prefix + "/training")

data = pd.read_csv('housing.csv')
data.drop(['medv'], axis=1, inplace=True)
data.to_csv('test.csv', index=False, header=False)
batch_data = sess.upload_data(
    path='test.csv',
    key_prefix=prefix + "/batch")
```

2. We configure our estimator as usual:

```python
from sagemaker.sklearn import SKLearn

output = 's3://{}/{}/output/'.format(bucket,prefix)

sk = SKLearn(
    entry_point='sklearn-boston-housing.py',
    role=sagemaker.get_execution_role(),
    train_instance_count=1,
    train_instance_type='ml.m5.large',
    output_path=output,
    hyperparameters={
        'normalize': True,
        'test-size': 0.1
```

```
        }
    )
```

3. We also define the transformer that we'll use for the batch transform:

```
sk_transformer = sk.transformer(
    instance_count=1,
    instance_type='ml.m5.large')
```

4. We import the Step Functions objects required by the workflow. You can find API documentation at https://aws-step-functions-data-science-sdk.readthedocs.io/en/latest/:

```
import stepfunctions
from stepfunctions import steps
from stepfunctions.steps import TrainingStep, ModelStep,
TransformStep
from stepfunctions.inputs import ExecutionInput
from stepfunctions.workflow import Workflow
```

5. We define the input of the workflow. We'll pass it a training job name, a model name, and an endpoint name:

```
execution_input = ExecutionInput(schema={
    'JobName': str,
    'ModelName': str,
    'EndpointName': str}
)
```

6. The first step of the workflow is the training step. We pass it the estimator, the location of the dataset in S3, and a training job name:

```
from sagemaker import s3_input

training_step = TrainingStep(
  'Train Scikit-Learn on the Boston Housing dataset',
  estimator=sk,
  data={'training':
        s3_input(training_data, content_type='text/csv')},
  job_name=execution_input['JobName']
)
```

7. The next step is the model creation step. We pass it the location of the model trained in the previous step, and a model name:

```
model_step = ModelStep(
    'Create the model in SageMaker',
    model=training_step.get_expected_model(),
    model_name=execution_input['ModelName']
)
```

8. The next step is running a batch transform on the test dataset. We pass the transformer object, the location of the test dataset in S3, and its content type:

```
transform_step = TransformStep(
    'Transform the dataset in batch mode',
    transformer=sk_transformer,
    job_name=execution_input['JobName'],
    model_name=execution_input['ModelName'],
    data=batch_data,
    content_type='text/csv'
)
```

9. The next step is creating the endpoint configuration:

```
endpoint_config_step = EndpointConfigStep(
    "Create an endpoint configuration for the model",
    endpoint_config_name=execution_input['ModelName'],
    model_name=execution_input['ModelName'],
    initial_instance_count=1,
    instance_type='ml.m5.large'
)
```

10. The last step is creating the endpoint:

```
endpoint_step = EndpointStep(
    "Create an endpoint hosting the model",
    endpoint_name=execution_input['EndpointName'],
    endpoint_config_name=execution_input['ModelName']
)
```

11. Now that all steps have been defined, we chain them in sequential order:

```
workflow_definition = Chain([
    training_step,
    model_step,
    transform_step,
    endpoint_config_step,
    endpoint_step
])
```

12. We now build our workflow, using the workflow definition and the input definition:

```
import time

timestamp = time.strftime("%Y-%m-%d-%H-%M-%S", time.gmtime())

workflow_execution_role = "arn:aws:iam::0123456789012:role/
StepFunctionsWorkflowExecutionRole"

workflow = Workflow(
    name='sklearn-boston-housing-workflow1-{}'
        .format(timestamp),
    definition=workflow_definition,
    role=workflow_execution_role,
    execution_input=execution_input
)
```

13. We can visualize the state machine, an easy way to check that we built it as expected, as shown in the next screenshot:

```
workflow.render_graph(portrait=True)
```

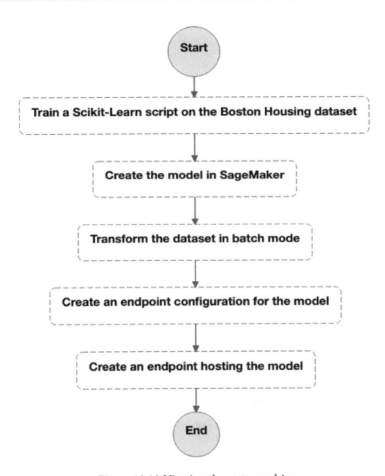

Figure 12.12 Viewing the state machine

14. We create the workflow:

```
workflow.create()
```

15. The workflow is visible in the Step Functions console, as shown in the following screenshot. We can see both its graphical representation and its JSON definition based on the Amazon States Languages. We could edit the workflow as well if needed:

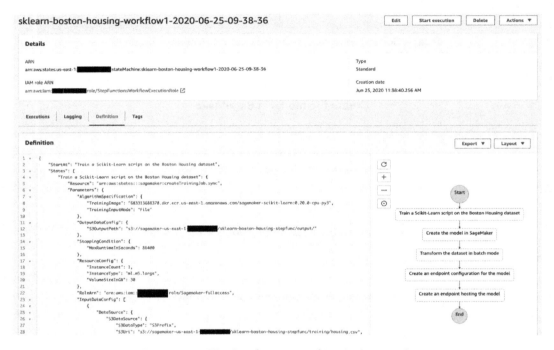

Figure 12.13 Viewing the state machine in the console

16. We run the workflow:

```
execution = workflow.execute(
 inputs={
   'JobName': 'sklearn-boston-housing-{}'
              .format(timestamp),
   'ModelName': 'sklearn-boston-housing-{}'
                .format(timestamp),
   'EndpointName': 'sklearn-boston-housing-{}'
                   .format(timestamp)

 }
)
```

17. We can track its progress with `render_progress()` and the `list_events()` API. We can also see it in the console, as shown in the next screenshot. Note that we also see the input and output of each step, a great way to troubleshoot problems:

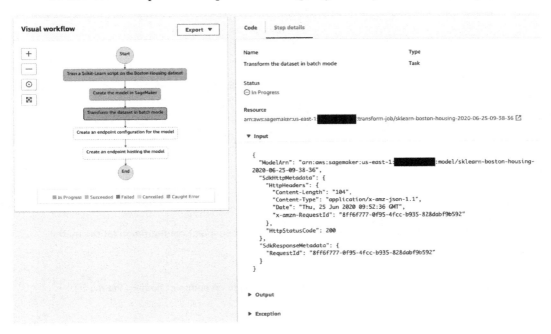

Figure 12.14 Running the state machine

18. When the workflow is complete, you can test the endpoint as usual. **Don't forget to delete it in the SageMaker console when you're done**.

This example shows how simple it is to build a SageMaker workflow with this SDK. Still, we could improve it by running batch transform and endpoint creation in parallel.

Adding parallel execution to a workflow

The next screenshot shows the workflow we're going to build. The steps themselves are exactly the same. We're only going to modify the way they're chained:

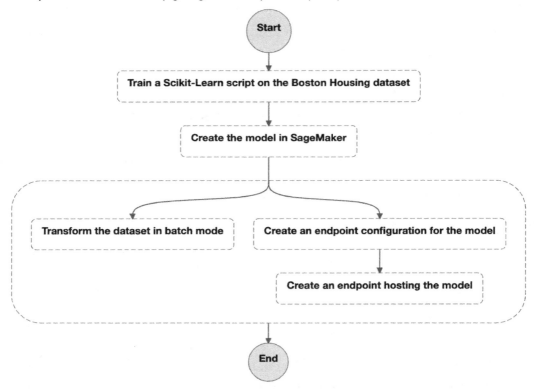

Figure 12.15 Viewing the parallel state machine

1. Our workflow has two branches, one for batch transform and one for the endpoint:

```
batch_branch = Chain([
  transform_step
])
```

```
endpoint_branch = Chain([
  endpoint_config_step,
  endpoint_step
])
```

2. We create a `Parallel` step in order to allow parallel execution of these two branches:

```
parallel_step = Parallel('Parallel execution')
parallel_step.add_branch(batch_branch)
parallel_step.add_branch(endpoint_branch)
```

3. We put everything together:

```
workflow_definition = Chain([
    training_step,
    model_step,
    parallel_step
])
```

That's it! We can now create and run this workflow just like in the previous example.

Looking at the Step Functions console, we see that the workflow does run the two branches in parallel. There is a minor problem, however. The endpoint creation step is shown as complete, although the endpoint is still being created. You can see in the SageMaker console that the endpoint is listed as **Creating**. This could cause a problem if a client application tried to invoke the endpoint right after the workflow completes.

Let's improve this by adding an extra step, waiting for the endpoint to be in service. We can easily do this with a Lambda function.

Adding a Lambda function to a workflow

If you've never looked at **AWS Lambda**, you're missing out: `https://aws.amazon.com/lambda`. Lambda is at the core of serverless architectures, where you can write and deploy short functions running on fully managed infrastructure, and interacting with fully managed services such as S3 or DynamoDB. These functions can be triggered by all sorts of AWS events, and they can also be invoked on demand.

Setting up permissions

Creating a Lambda function is simple. The only prerequisite is to create an **execution role**, an IAM role that gives the function permission to invoke other AWS services. Here, we only need permission for the `DescribeEndpoint` API, as well as permission to create a log in CloudWatch. Let's use the `boto3` API for this. You can find more information at `https://docs.aws.amazon.com/lambda/latest/dg/lambda-permissions.html`:

1. We first define a **trust policy** for the role, allowing it to be assumed by the Lambda service:

    ```
    {
      "Version": "2012-10-17",
      "Statement": [{
        "Effect": "Allow",
        "Principal": {
          "Service": "lambda.amazonaws.com"
        },
        "Action": "sts:AssumeRole"
      }]
    }
    ```

2. We create a role and attach the trust policy to it:

    ```
    iam = boto3.client('iam')
    with open('trust-policy.json') as f:
        policy = f.read()
        role_name = 'lambda-role-sagemaker-describe-endpoint'
    response = iam.create_role(
        RoleName=role_name,
        AssumeRolePolicyDocument=policy,
        Description='Allow function to invoke all SageMaker
    APIs'
    )
    role_arn = response['Role']['Arn']
    ```

3. We define a policy listing the APIs that are allowed:

```json
{
  "Version": "2012-10-17",
  "Statement": [
    {
      "Effect": "Allow",
      "Action": "sagemaker:DescribeEndpoint",
      "Resource": "*"
    },
    {
      "Effect": "Allow",
      "Action": [
          "logs:CreateLogGroup",
          "logs:CreateLogStream",
          "logs:PutLogEvents"
      ],
      "Resource": "*"
    }
  ]
}
```

4. We create the policy and add it to the role:

```python
with open('policy.json') as f:
    policy = f.read()
```

```python
policy_name = 'Sagemaker-describe-endpoint'
```

```python
response = iam.create_policy(
    PolicyName=policy_name,
    PolicyDocument=policy,
    Description='Allow the DescribeEndpoint API'
)
```

```python
policy_arn = response['Policy']['Arn']
```

```python
response = iam.attach_role_policy(
    RoleName=role_name,
    PolicyArn=policy_arn
)
```

The IAM setup is complete.

Writing a Lambda function

We can now write a short Lambda function. It receives a JSON event as input, which stores the ARN of the endpoint being created by the EndpointStep step. It simply extracts the endpoint name from the ARN, creates a boto3 waiter, and waits until the endpoint is in service. The following screenshot shows the code in the Lambda console:

Figure 12.16 Our Lambda function

Let's deploy this function:

1. We create a deployment package for the Lambda function and upload it to S3:

```
$ zip -9 lambda.zip lambda.py
$ aws s3 cp lambda.zip s3://my-bucket
```

2. We create the function with a timeout of 15 minutes, the longest possible run time for a Lambda function. Endpoints are typically deployed in less than 10 minutes, so this should be more than enough:

```
lambda_client = boto3.client('lambda')

response = lambda_client.create_function(
    FunctionName='sagemaker-wait-for-endpoint',
    Role=role_arn,
    Runtime='python3.6',
```

```
        Handler='lambda.lambda_handler',
        Code={
            'S3Bucket': bucket_name,
            'S3Key': 'lambda.zip'
        },
        Description='Wait for endpoint to be in service',
        Timeout=900,
        MemorySize=128
    )
```

3. Now that the Lambda function has been created, we can easily add it to the existing workflow. We define a `LambdaStep` and add it to the endpoint branch. Its payload is the endpoint ARN, extracted from the output of the `EndpointStep`:

```
lambda_step = LambdaStep(
    'Wait for endpoint to be in service',
    parameters={
        'FunctionName': 'sagemaker-wait-for-endpoint',
        'Payload': {"EndpointArn.$": "$.EndpointArn"}
    },
    timeout_seconds=900
)
```

```
endpoint_branch = steps.Chain([
    endpoint_config_step,
    endpoint_step,
    lambda_step
])
```

4. Running the workflow again, we see in the following screenshot that this new step receives the endpoint ARN as input and waits for the endpoint to be in service:

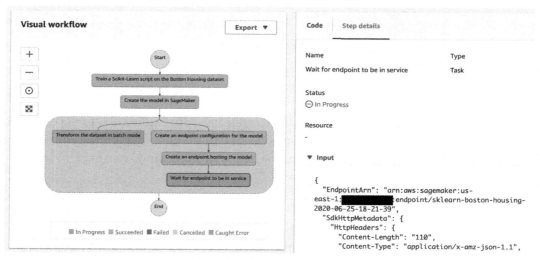

Figure 12.17 Running the state machine with Lambda

5. Once the workflow is complete, we can check the execution time of the function in its CloudWatch log. As shown in the following screenshot, it ran for 394 seconds, about 6.5 minutes:

	Timestamp	Message
		There are older events to load. *Load more.*
▶	2020-06-25T20:26:53.268+02:00	START RequestId: a415b063-3361-4815-b6ea-099d01a53429 Version: $LATEST
▶	2020-06-25T20:26:53.268+02:00	{'EndpointArn': 'arn:aws:sagemaker:us-east-1:████:endpoint/sklearn-boston-housing-2020-06-25-18-21-39'}
▶	2020-06-25T20:33:27.490+02:00	END RequestId: a415b063-3361-4815-b6ea-099d01a53429
▶	2020-06-25T20:33:27.490+02:00	REPORT RequestId: a415b063-3361-4815-b6ea-099d01a53429 Duration: 394218.60 ms Billed Duration: 394300 ms Memory Size: 128 MB

Figure 12.18 Viewing the Lambda log

Now, client applications notified of the completion of the workflow could safely invoke the endpoint.

There are many other ways you can use Lambda functions with SageMaker: extract training metrics, run test sets on an endpoint, and more. The possibilities are endless.

Summary

In this chapter, you first learned how to deploy and update endpoints with AWS CloudFormation. You also saw how it can be used to implement canary deployment and blue-green deployment.

Then, you learned about the AWS CDK, an SDK specifically built to easily generate and deploy CloudFormation templates using a variety of programming languages.

Finally, you built a complete end-to-end workflow with AWS Step Functions, and you saw how to implement parallel execution and how to call Lambda functions.

In the next and final chapter, you'll learn about additional SageMaker capabilities that help you optimize the cost and performance of predictions.

13
Optimizing Prediction Cost and Performance

In the previous chapter, you learned how to automate training and deployment workflows.

In this final chapter, we'll focus on optimizing cost and performance for prediction infrastructure, which typically accounts for 90% of the machine learning spend by AWS customers. This number may come as a surprise, until we realize that the model built by a single training job may end on multiple endpoints running 24/7 at large scale.

Hence, great care must be taken to optimize your prediction infrastructure so as to ensure that you get the most bang for your buck!

This chapter has the following topics:

- Autoscaling an endpoint
- Deploying a multi-model endpoint
- Deploying a model with Amazon Elastic Inference
- Compiling models with Amazon SageMaker Neo

Technical requirements

You will need an AWS account to run examples included in this chapter. If you haven't got one already, please point your browser at `https://aws.amazon.com/getting-started/` to create it. You should also familiarize yourself with the AWS Free Tier (`https://aws.amazon.com/free/`), which lets you use many AWS services for free within certain usage limits.

You will need to install and to configure the AWS CLI for your account (`https://aws.amazon.com/cli/`).

You will need a working Python 3.x environment. Be careful not to use Python 2.7, as it is no longer maintained. Installing the Anaconda distribution (`https://www.anaconda.com/`) is not mandatory but strongly encouraged as it includes many projects that we will need (Jupyter, `pandas`, `numpy`, and more).

Code examples included in the book are available on GitHub at `https://github.com/PacktPublishing/Learn-Amazon-SageMaker`. You will need to install a Git client to access them (`https://git-scm.com/`).

Autoscaling an endpoint

Autoscaling has long been the most important technique in adjusting infrastructure size to incoming traffic, and it's available for SageMaker endpoints. However, it's based on **Application Autoscaling**, and not on **EC2 Autoscaling** (`https://docs.aws.amazon.com/autoscaling/application/userguide/what-is-application-auto-scaling.html`), although the concepts are extremely similar.

Let's set up autoscaling for the **XGBoost** model we trained on the Boston Housing dataset:

1. We first create an **Endpoint Configuration**, and we use it to build the endpoint. Here, we use the m5 instance family: t2 and t3 are not recommended for autoscaling as their burstable behavior makes it harder to measure their real load:

```
model_name = 'sagemaker-xgboost-2020-06-09-08-33-24-782'
endpoint_config_name = 'xgboost-one-model-epc'
endpoint_name = 'xgboost-one-model-ep'
production_variants = [{
    'VariantName': 'variant-1',
    'ModelName': model_name,
    'InitialInstanceCount': 2,
    'InitialVariantWeight': 1,
    'InstanceType': 'ml.m5.large'}]
sm.create_endpoint_config(
```

```
            EndpointConfigName=endpoint_config_name,
            ProductionVariants=production_variants)
sm.create_endpoint(
        EndpointName=endpoint_name,
        EndpointConfigName=endpoint_config_name)
```

2. Once the endpoint is in service, we define the target value that we want to scale on, namely, the number of instances backing the endpoint:

```
app = boto3.client('application-autoscaling')
app.register_scalable_target(
  ServiceNamespace='sagemaker',
  ResourceId=
      'endpoint/xgboost-one-model-ep/variant/variant-1',
  ScalableDimension=
      'sagemaker:variant:DesiredInstanceCount',
  MinCapacity=2,
  MaxCapacity=10)
```

3. Then, we apply a scaling policy for this target value:

```
policy_name = 'xgboost-scaling-policy'
app.put_scaling_policy(
  PolicyName=policy_name,
  ServiceNamespace='sagemaker',
  ResourceId=
     'endpoint/xgboost-one-model-ep/variant/variant-1',
  ScalableDimension=
     'sagemaker:variant:DesiredInstanceCount',
  PolicyType='TargetTrackingScaling',
```

4. We use the only built-in metric available in SageMaker, `SageMakerVariantInvocationsPerInstance`. We could also define a custom metric if we wanted to. We set the metric threshold at 1,000 invocations per minute. This is a bit of an arbitrary value. In real life, we would run a load test on a single instance, and monitor model latency in order to find the actual value that ought to trigger autoscaling. You can find more information at `https://docs.aws.amazon.com/sagemaker/latest/dg/endpoint-scaling-loadtest.html`. We also define a 60-second cooldown for scaling in and out, a good practice for smoothing out transient traffic drops and peaks:

```
TargetTrackingScalingPolicyConfiguration={
    'TargetValue': 1000.0,
```

```
    'PredefinedMetricSpecification': {
        'PredefinedMetricType':
        'SageMakerVariantInvocationsPerInstance'
    },
    'ScaleInCooldown': 60,
    'ScaleOutCooldown': 60
}
)
```

5. As shown in the following screenshot, autoscaling is now configured on
    the endpoint:

Figure 13.1 – Viewing autoscaling

6. Using an infinite loop, we send some traffic to the endpoint:

```
test_sample = '0.00632, 18.00, 2.310, 0, 0.5380, 6.5750,
65.20, 4.0900, 1, 296.0, 15.30, 396.90, 4.98'

smrt=boto3.Session().client(service_name='runtime.
sagemaker')

while True:
    smrt.invoke_endpoint(EndpointName=endpoint_name,
                         ContentType='text/csv',
                         Body=test_sample)
```

7. Looking at the **CloudWatch** metrics for the endpoints, as shown in the following
    screenshot, we see that invocations per instance exceed the threshold we defined:
    1.42k versus 1k:

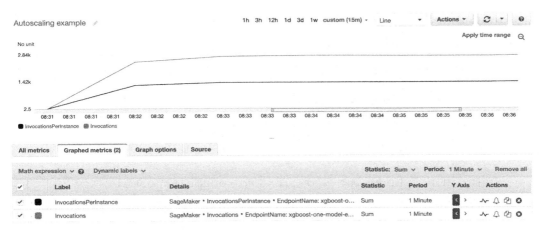

Figure 13.2: Viewing CloudWatch metrics

8. Autoscaling quickly kicks in and decides to add another instance, as visible in the following screenshot. If the load was even higher, it could decide to add several instances at once:

Endpoint runtime settings

Variant name ▲	Current weight ▽	Desired weight	Instance type ▽	Elastic Inference	Current instance count ▽	Desired instance count ▽	Instance min - max	Automatic scaling
variant-1	1	1	ml.m5.large	-	2	3	n/a	n/a

Figure 13.3: Viewing autoscaling

9. A few minutes later, the extra instance is in service, and invocations per instance are now below the threshold (935 versus 1,000):

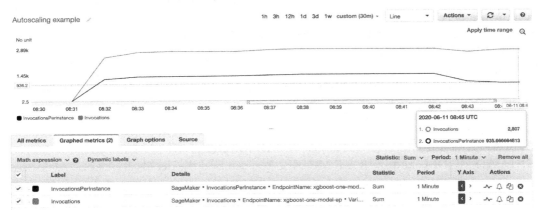

Figure 13.4: Viewing CloudWatch metrics

A similar process takes place when traffic decreases.

10. Once we're finished, we delete everything:

```
app.delete_scaling_policy(
  PolicyName=policy_name,
  ServiceNamespace='sagemaker',
  ScalableDimension=
        'sagemaker:variant:DesiredInstanceCount',
  ResourceId='endpoint/xgboost-one-model-ep/variant
  /variant-1')
```
```
sm.delete_endpoint(EndpointName=endpoint_name)
```
```
sm.delete_endpoint_config(
  EndpointConfigName=endpoint_config_name)
```

Setting up autoscaling is easy. It helps you automatically adapt your prediction infrastructure and the associated costs to changing business conditions.

Now, let's study another technique that you'll find extremely useful when you're dealing with a very large number of models: **multi-model endpoints**.

Deploying a multi-model endpoint

Multi-model endpoints are useful when you're dealing with a large number of models that it wouldn't make sense to deploy to individual endpoints. For example, imagine an SaaS company building a regression model for each one of their 10,000 customers. Surely they wouldn't want to manage (and pay for) 10,000 endpoints!

Understanding multi-model endpoints

A multi-model endpoint can serve CPU-based predictions from an arbitrary number of models stored in S3 (GPUs are not supported at the time of writing). The path of the model artifact to use is passed in each prediction request. Models are loaded and unloaded dynamically, according to usage and to the amount of memory available on the endpoint. Models can also be added to, or removed, from the endpoint by simply copying or deleting artifacts in S3.

In order to serve multiple models, your inference container must implement a specific set of APIs that the endpoint will invoke: LOAD MODEL, LIST MODEL, GET MODEL, UNLOAD MODEL, and INVOKE MODEL. You can find the details at https://docs.aws.amazon.com/sagemaker/latest/dg/mms-container-apis.html.

At the time of writing, the latest built-in containers for **Scikit-Learn, XGBoost, Apache MXNet**, and **PyTorch** natively support these APIs. For other algorithms and frameworks, your best option is to build a custom container that includes the **SageMaker Inference Toolkit**, as it already implements the required APIs (`https://github.com/aws/sagemaker-inference-toolkit`).

This toolkit is based on the multi-model server (`https://github.com/awslabs/multi-model-server`), which you could also use directly from the CLI to serve predictions from multiple models. You can find more information at `https://docs.aws.amazon.com/sagemaker/latest/dg/build-multi-model-build-container.html`.

Building a multi-model endpoint with Scikit-Learn

Let's build a multi-model endpoint with **Scikit-Learn**, hosting models trained on the Boston Housing dataset. This is only supported for Scikit-Learn 0.23-1 and above:

> **Note:**
> If, for some reason, you can't use this version, the GitHub repository for this book also includes an example with a custom container for version 0.20.0.
> It's based on the mme branch of the Scikit-Learn container. I can't guarantee it will keep working forever, but it should get you started in the right direction.

1. We upload the dataset to S3:

```
import sagemaker, boto3

sess = sagemaker.Session()
bucket = sess.default_bucket()

prefix = 'sklearn-boston-housing-mme'
training = sess.upload_data(path='housing.csv',
                            key_prefix=prefix +
                            '/training')
output = 's3://{}/{}/output/'.format(bucket,prefix)
```

2. We train three models with a different test size, storing their names in a dictionary. Here, we use the latest version of Scikit-Learn, the first one to support multi-model endpoints:

```
from sagemaker.sklearn import SKLearn

jobs = {}
for test_size in [0.2, 0.1, 0.05]:
    sk = SKLearn(entry_point=
```

```
                        'sklearn-boston-housing-v2.py',
              role=sagemaker.get_execution_role(),
              framework_version='0.23-1',
              instance_count=1,
              instance_type='ml.m5.large',
              output_path=output,
              hyperparameters={ 'normalize': True,
                                'test-size': test_size }
    )
    sk.fit({'training':training}, wait=False)
    jobs[sk.latest_training_job.name] = {}
    jobs[sk.latest_training_job.name]['test-size'] =
        test_size
```

3. We find the S3 URI of the model artifact along with its prefix:

```
import boto3

sm = boto3.client('sagemaker')

for j in jobs.keys():
    job = sm.describe_training_job(TrainingJobName=j)
    jobs[j]['artifact'] =
        job['ModelArtifacts']['S3ModelArtifacts']
    jobs[j]['key'] = '/'.join(
        job['ModelArtifacts']['S3ModelArtifacts']
        .split('/')[3:])
```

4. We delete any previous model stored in S3:

```
%%sh -s "$bucket" "$prefix"
aws s3 rm --recursive s3://$1/$2/models
```

5. We copy the three model artifacts to this location:

```
s3 = boto3.client('s3')

for j in jobs.keys():
    copy_source = { 'Bucket': bucket,
                    'Key': jobs[j]['key'] }
    s3.copy_object(CopySource=copy_source, Bucket=bucket,
                   Key=prefix+'/models/'+j+'.tar.gz')

response = s3.list_objects(Bucket=bucket,
                           Prefix=prefix+'/models/')
for o in response['Contents']:
    print(o['Key'])
```

This lists the model artifacts:

```
sklearn-boston-housing-mme/models/sagemaker-scikit-
learn-2020-06-15-15-45-41-752.tar.gz
```

```
sklearn-boston-housing-mme/models/sagemaker-scikit-
learn-2020-06-15-15-45-42-385.tar.gz
```

```
sklearn-boston-housing-mme/models/sagemaker-scikit-
learn-2020-06-15-15-45-42-794.tar.gz
```

6. We define the name of the script, and the S3 location where we'll upload the code archive. Here, I'm passing the training script, which includes a `model_fn()` function to load the model. This is the only function that will be used to serve predictions:

```
script = 'sklearn-boston-housing-v2.py'
script_archive = 's3://{}/{}/source/source.tar.gz'.
                    format(bucket, prefix)
```

7. We create the code archive, and we upload it to S3:

```
%%sh -s "$script" "$script_archive"
tar cvfz source.tar.gz $1
aws s3 cp source.tar.gz $2
```

8. We create the multi-model endpoint with the `create_model()` API and we set the `Mode` parameter accordingly:

```
import time
model_name = prefix+'-'+time.strftime("%Y-%m-%d-%H-
%M-%S", time.gmtime())
response = sm.create_model(
  ModelName = model_name,
  ExecutionRoleArn = role,
  Containers = [{
    'Image': sk.image_uri,
    'ModelDataUrl': 's3://{}/{}/models/'.format(bucket,
                      prefix),
    'Mode': 'MultiModel',
    'Environment': {
        'SAGEMAKER_PROGRAM' : script,
        'SAGEMAKER_SUBMIT_DIRECTORY' : script_archive
    }
  }]
)
```

9. We create the endpoint configuration as usual:

```
epc_name = prefix+'-epc'+time.strftime("%Y-%m-%d-%H-
%M-%S", time.gmtime())
```

```
response = sm.create_endpoint_config(
    EndpointConfigName = epc_name,
    ProductionVariants=[{
        'InstanceType': 'ml.m5.large',
        'InitialInstanceCount': 1,
        'InitialVariantWeight': 1,
        'ModelName': model_name,
        'VariantName': 'variant-1'}]
)
```

10. We create the endpoint as usual:

```
ep_name = prefix+'-ep'+time.strftime("%Y-%m-%d-%H-%M-%S",
time.gmtime())
```

```
response = sm.create_endpoint(
    EndpointName=ep_name,
    EndpointConfigName=epc_name)
```

11. Once the endpoint is in service, we load samples from the dataset and convert them to a numpy array:

```
import pandas as pd
import numpy as np
from io import BytesIO
```

```
data = pd.read_csv('housing.csv')
payload = data[:10].drop(['medv'], axis=1)
buffer = BytesIO()
np.save(buffer, payload.values)
```

12. We predict these samples with all three models, passing the name of the model to use for each prediction request; for example, sagemaker-scikit-learn-2020-06-15-15-45-41-752.tar.gz:

```
smrt = boto3.client('runtime.sagemaker')
for j in jobs.keys():
    model_name=j+'.tar.gz'
    response = smrt.invoke_endpoint(
        EndpointName=ep_name,
        TargetModel=model_name,
        Body=buffer.getvalue(),
```

```
                    ContentType='application/x-npy')
        print(response['Body'].read())
```

13. We could train more models, copy their artifacts to the same S3 location, and use them directly without recreating the endpoint. We could also delete those models we don't need.

14. Once we're finished, we delete everything:

```
    sm.delete_endpoint(EndpointName=ep_name)
    sm.delete_endpoint_config(EndpointConfigName=epc_name)
    sm.delete_model(ModelName=prefix)
```

As you can see, multi-model endpoints are a great way to serve as many models as you'd like from a single endpoint, and setting them up isn't difficult.

In the next section, we're going to study another cost optimization technique that can help you save a lot of money on GPU prediction: **Amazon Elastic Inference**.

Deploying a model with Amazon Elastic Inference

When deploying a model, you have to decide whether it should run on a CPU instance, or on a GPU instance. In some cases, there isn't much of a debate. For example, some algorithms simply don't benefit from GPU acceleration, so they should be deployed to CPU instances. At the other end of the spectrum, complex deep learning models for Computer Vision or Natural Language Processing run best on GPUs.

In many cases, the situation is not that clear-cut. First, you should know what the maximum predicted latency is for your application. If you're predicting click-through rate for a real-time ad tech application, every millisecond counts. If you're predicting customer churn in a back-office application, not so much.

In addition, even models that could benefit from GPU acceleration may not be large and complex enough to fully utilize the thousands of cores available on a modern GPU. In such scenarios, you're stuck between a rock and a hard place: deploying on CPU would be a little slow for your needs, and deploying on GPU wouldn't be cost effective.

This is the problem that Amazon Elastic Inference aims to solve (https://aws.amazon.com/machine-learning/elastic-inference/). It lets you attach fractional GPU acceleration to any EC2 instance, including notebook instances and endpoint instances. **Accelerators** come in three different sizes (medium, large, and extra large), which let you find the best cost-performance ratio for your application.

Elastic Inference is available for TensorFlow, PyTorch, and Apache MXNet. You can use it in your own code running on EC2 instances, thanks to AWS extensions available in the **Deep Learning AMI**. You can also use it with **Deep Learning Containers**. More information is available at `https://docs.aws.amazon.com/elastic-inference/latest/developerguide/working-with-ei.html`.

Of course, **Elastic Inference** is available on SageMaker. You can attach an accelerator to a **Notebook Instance** at creation time, and work with the built-in **conda** environments. You can also attach an accelerator to an endpoint, and we'll show you how to do this in the next example.

Deploying a model with AWS

Let's reuse the **Image Classification** model we trained on dog and cat images in *Chapter 5, Training Computer Vision Models*. This is based on an 18-layer ResNet model, which is pretty small as far as convolution neural networks are concerned:

1. Once the model has been trained, we deploy it as usual on two endpoints: one backed by an `ml.c5.large` instance, and another one backed by an `ml.g4dn.xlarge` instance, the most cost-effective GPU instance available on SageMaker:

```
import time
endpoint_name = 'c5-'+time.strftime("%Y-%m-%d-%H-%M-%S",
                                    time.gmtime())
c5_predictor = ic.deploy(initial_instance_count=1,
                         instance_type='ml.c5.large',
                         endpoint_name=endpoint_name,
                         wait=False)
endpoint_name = 'g4-'+time.strftime("%Y-%m-%d-%H-%M-%S",
                                    time.gmtime())
g4_predictor = ic.deploy(initial_instance_count=1,
                         instance_type='ml.g4dn.xlarge',
                         endpoint_name=endpoint_name,
                         wait=False)
```

2. We then download a test image, predict it 1,000 times, and measure the total time this took:

```
with open(file_name, 'rb') as f:
    payload = f.read()
    payload = bytearray(payload)
def predict_images(predictor, iterations=1000):
    total = 0
```

```
    predictor.content_type = 'application/x-image'
    for i in range(0, iterations):
        tick = time.time()
        response = predictor.predict(payload)
        tock = time.time()
        total += tock-tick
    return total/iterations
```

```
predict_images(c5_predictor)
predict_images(g4_predictor)
```

3. The results are shown in the next table. We also compute images per second per dollar, which takes the instance cost into account (based on eu-west-1 prices).

Instance type	Acceleration	Cost	Time	Images/s	Images/s/$
ml.c5.large	none	$0.134	44.87ms	22.3	166
ml.g4dn.xlarge	1 NIVIDIA T4 GPU	$0.821	11.16ms	89.6	109

Table 13.1: Cost analysis for computing images

Unsurprisingly, the GPU instance is about four times faster. Yet, the CPU instance is more cost effective, as it's over six times less expensive. Putting it another way, you could run your endpoint with six CPU instances instead of one GPU instance, and get more throughput for the same cost. This shows why it's so important to understand the latency requirement of your application. Fast and slow are relative concepts!

4. We then deploy the same model on three more endpoints backed by ml.c5. large instances accelerated by a medium, large, and extra-large **Elastic Inference Accelerator**. All it takes is an extra parameter in the deploy() API. Here's the code for the medium endpoint:

```
endpoint_name = 'c5-medium-'
    +time.strftime("%Y-%m-%d-%H-%M-%S", time.gmtime())
```

```
c5_medium_predictor = ic.deploy(
    initial_instance_count=1,
    instance_type='ml.c5.large',
    accelerator_type='ml.eia2.medium',
    endpoint_name=endpoint_name,
    wait=False)
```

```
predict_images(c5_medium_predictor)
```

You can see the results in the following table:

Instance type	Acceleration	Cost	Time	Images/s	Images/s/$
ml.c5.large + ml.eia2.medium	1 FP-32 TFLOPS 8 FP-16 TFLOPS	$0.315	26.34ms	38	120
ml.c5.large + ml.eia2.large	2 FP-32 TFLOPS 16 FP-16 TFLOPS	$0.496	23.5ms	42.6	86
ml.c5.large + ml.eia2.xlarge	4 FP-32 TFLOPS 32 FP-16 TFLOPS	$0.657	20.3ms	49.3	75

Table 13.2: Cost analysis for computing images in accelerator instances

With a medium accelerator, predictions are almost twice as fast than on a CPU, and 2.6 times more cost effective than on a GPU. This creates a third and a very interesting option halfway between the CPU and GPU instance, giving you more freedom to choose the right cost-performance ratio for your application. Here, the large and extra-large accelerators don't look very compelling, probably because our model is too small to fully utilize them.

5. Attentive readers will have noticed that the previous tables include TeraFLOP values for both 32-bit and 16-bit floating-point values. Indeed, either one of these data types may be used to store model parameters. Looking at the documentation for the image classification algorithm, we see that we can actually select a data type with the precision_dtype parameter, and that the default value is float32. This begs the question: would the results differ if we trained our model in float16 mode? There's only one way to know, isn't there?

```
ic.set_hyperparameters(
    num_layers=18,
    use_pretrained_model=0,
    num_classes=2
    num_training_samples=22500,
    mini_batch_size=128,
    precision_dtype='float16',
    epochs=10)
```

6. Training again, we hit the same level of accuracy as in `float32` mode. Deploying benchmarking again, we get the following results:

Instance type	Acceleration	Cost	Time	Images/s	Images/s/$
`ml.c5.large`	None	$0.134	44.19ms	22.6	168
`ml.g4dn.xlarge`	1 NIVIDIA T4 GPU	$0.821	10.45ms	95.7	117
`ml.c5.large +` `ml.eia2.medium`	1 FP-32 TFLOPS 8 FP-16 TFLOPS	$0.315	20.32ms	49.2	156
`ml.c5.large +` `ml.eia2.large`	2 FP-32 TFLOPS 16 FP-16 TFLOPS	$0.496	21.85ms	45.8	92
`ml.c5.large +` `ml.eia2.xlarge`	4 FP-32 TFLOPS 32 FP-16 TFLOPS	$0.657	20.45ms	48.9	74

Table 13.3: Cost analysis for computing in float16 mode

No meaningful difference is visible on the CPU instance. The GPU instance is about 6% faster. However, the medium accelerator steals the show as its predictions are now 23% faster. From a throughput perspective, it's almost as cost effective as the naked CPU instance, while predicting twice as fast.

Oddly enough, the large accelerator is slower. I ran multiple tests with the same results. Go figure! Just like in the previous example, the extra-large accelerator doesn't improve prediction speed.

In this last example, switching a single endpoint instance from `ml.g4dn.xlarge` to `ml.c5.large+ml.eia2.medium` would save you ($0.821-$0.315) * 24 * 30 = $364 dollars per month. That's serious money!

As you can see, Amazon Elastic Inference is extremely easy to use, and it gives you additional deployment options. Once you've defined the prediction latency requirement for your application, you can quickly experiment, and find the best cost-performance ratio.

Now, let's talk about another SageMaker capability that lets you compile models for a specific hardware architecture: **Amazon Neo**.

Compiling models with Amazon SageMaker Neo

Embedded software developers have long learned how to write highly optimized code that both runs fast and uses hardware resources frugally. In theory, the same techniques could also be applied to optimize machine learning predictions. In practice, this is a daunting task given the complexity of machine learning libraries and models.

This is the problem that Amazon Neo aims to solve.

Understanding Amazon Neo

Amazon Neo has two components: a model compiler that optimizes models for the underlying hardware, and a small runtime named the **Deep Learning Runtime** (**DLR**), used to load optimized models and run predictions (`https://aws.amazon.com/sagemaker/neo`).

Amazon Neo can compile models trained with:

- **Two built-in algorithms**: XGBoost, and Image Classification.
- **Built-in frameworks**: TensorFlow/Keras, PyTorch, Apache MXNet/Gluon, as well as models in **ONNX** format. Many operators are supported, and you can find the full list at `https://aws.amazon.com/releasenotes/sagemaker-neo-supported-frameworks-and-operators`.

Training takes place as usual, using your estimator of choice. Then, using the `compile_model()` API, we can easily compile the model for one of these hardware targets:

- Amazon EC2 instances of the following families: `c4`, `c5`, `m4`, `m5`, `p2`, `p3`, and `inf1` (which we'll discuss later in this chapter), as well as Lambda
- AI-powered cameras: AWS DeepLens, Acer aiSage
- NVIDIA Jetson platforms: TX1, TX2, Nano, and Xavier
- Rapsberry Pi
- System-on-chip platform from Rockchip, Qualcomm, Ambarella, and more

Model compilation performs both architecture optimizations (such as fusing layers), and code optimizations (replacing machine learning operators with hardware-optimized versions). The resulting artifact is stored in S3, and contains both the original model and its optimized form.

The DLR is then used to load the model, and predict with it. Of course, it can be used in a standalone fashion, for example, on a Raspberry Pi. You can find installation instructions at `https://neo-ai-dlr.readthedocs.io`. As the DLR is open source (`https://github.com/neo-ai/neo-ai-dlr`), you can also build it from source and, why not, customize it for your own hardware platform!

When it comes to using the DLR with SageMaker, things are much simpler. SageMaker provides built-in containers with Neo support, and these are the ones you should use to deploy models compiled with Neo (as already mentioned, the training container remains unchanged). You can find a list of Neo-enabled containers at `https://docs.aws.amazon.com/sagemaker/latest/dg/neo-deployment-hosting-services-cli.html`.

Last but not least, one of the benefits of the DLR is its small size. For example, the Python package for p2 and p3 instances is only 5.4 MB in size, orders of magnitude smaller than your typical deep learning library and its dependencies. This is obviously critical for embedded environments, and it's also welcome on SageMaker as containers will be smaller, too.

Let's reuse our image classification example, and see whether Neo can speed it up.

Compiling and deploying an image classification model on SageMaker

In order to give Neo a little more work, we train a 50-layer ResNet this time. Then, we'll compile it, we'll deploy it to an endpoint, and we'll compare it with the vanilla model:

1. Setting `num_layers` to 50, we train the model for 30 epochs. Then, we deploy it to an `ml.c5.4xlarge` instance as usual:

    ```
    ic_predictor = ic.deploy(initial_instance_count=1,
                             instance_type='ml.c5.4xlarge',
                             endpoint_name=ic_endpoint_name)
    ```

2. We compile the model with Neo, targeting the EC2 c5 instance family. We also define the input shape of the model: 1 image, 3 channels (red, green, blue), 224 x 224 pixels (the default value for the image classification algorithm). As built-in algorithms are implemented with Apache MXNet, we set the framework accordingly:

    ```
    output_path = 's3://{}/{}/output-neo/'
                  .format(bucket, prefix)
    ic_neo_model = ic.compile_model(
    ```

```
        target_instance_family='ml_c5',
        input_shape={'data':[1, 3, 224, 224]},
        role=role,
        framework='mxnet',
        framework_version='1.5.1',
        output_path=output_path)
```

3. We then deploy the compiled model as usual, explicitly setting the prediction container to the Neo-enabled version of image classification:

```
ic_neo_model.image = get_image_uri(
        session.boto_region_name,
        'image-classification-neo',
        repo_version='latest')
```

```
ic_neo_predictor = ic_neo_model.deploy(
        endpoint_name=ic_neo_endpoint_name,
        initial_instance_count=1,
        instance_type='ml.c5.4xlarge')
```

4. Downloading a test image, and using the same benchmarking function that we used for Amazon Elastic Inference, we measure the time required to predict 1,000 images:

```
predict_images(ic_predictor)
predict_images(ic_neo_predictor)
```

Prediction with the vanilla model takes 87 seconds. Prediction with the Neo-optimized model takes 28.5 seconds, 3 times faster! That compilation step sure paid off. You'll also be happy to learn that compiling Neo models is free of charge, so there's really no reason not to try it.

Let's take a look at these compiled models.

Exploring models compiled with Neo

Looking at the output location passed to the `compile_model()` API, we see the model artifact generated by Neo:

```
$ aws s3 ls s3://sagemaker-eu-west-1-123456789012/dogscats/
output-neo/
model-ml_c5.tar.gz
```

Copying it locally and extracting it, we see that it contains both the original model, and its compiled version:

```
$ aws s3 cp s3://sagemaker-eu-west-1-123456789012/dogscats/
output-neo/model-ml_c5.tar.gz .
$ tar xvfz model-ml_c5.tar.gz
compiled.meta
model-shapes.json
compiled.params
compiled_model.json
compiled.so
```

In particular, the `compiled.so` file is a native file containing hardware-optimized versions of the model operators:

```
$ file compiled.so
compiled.so: ELF 64-bit LSB shared object, x86-64
$ nm compiled.so | grep conv | head -3
0000000000005880 T fused_nn_contrib_conv2d_NCHWc
00000000000347a0 T fused_nn_contrib_conv2d_NCHWc_1
0000000000032630 T fused_nn_contrib_conv2d_NCHWc_2
```

We could look at the assembly code for these, but something tells me that most of you wouldn't particularly enjoy it. Joking aside, this is completely unnecessary. All we need to know is how to compile and deploy models with Neo.

Now, how about we deploy our model to a **Raspberry Pi**?

Deploying an image classification model on a Raspberry Pi

The Raspberry Pi is a fantastic device, and despite its limited compute and memory capabilities, it's well capable of predicting images with complex deep learning models. Here, I'm using a Raspberry Pi 3b, with a 1.2 GHz quad-core ARM processor and 1 GB of memory. That's definitely not much, yet it could run a vanilla Apache MXNet model.

Inexplicably, there is no pre-packaged version of MXNet for Raspberry Pi, and building it from source is a painstakingly long and unpredictable process (I'm looking at you, OOM errors). Fortunately, thanks to the DLR, we can do away with all of it!

1. In our SageMaker notebook, we compile the model for the Raspberry Pi:

```
output_path = 's3://{}/{}/output-neo/'
              .format(bucket, prefix)
```

```
ic_neo_model = ic.compile_model(
    target_instance_family='rasp3b',
    input_shape={'data':[1, 3, 224, 224]},
    role=role,
    framework='mxnet',
    framework_version='1.5.1',
    output_path=output_path)
```

2. On our local machine, we fetch the compiled model artifact from S3 and copy it to the Raspberry Pi:

```
$ aws s3 cp s3://sagemaker-eu-west-1-123456789012/
dogscats/output-neo/model-rasp3b.tar.gz .
$ scp model-rasp3b.tar.gz pi@raspberrypi:~
```

3. Moving to the Raspberry Pi, we extract the compiled model to the `resnet50` directory:

```
$ mkdir resnet50
$ tar xvfz model-rasp3b.tar.gz -C resnet50
```

4. Installing the DLR is very easy. We download the package and use `pip` to install it:

```
$ wget https://neo-ai-dlr-release.s3-us-west-2.amazonaws.
com/v1.2.0/pi-armv71-raspbian4.14.71-glibc2_24-
libstdcpp3_4/dlr-1.2.0-py2.py3-none-any.whl
$ pip3 install dlr-1.2.0-py2.py3-none-any.whl
```

5. We first write a function that loads an image from a file, resizes it to 224 x 224 pixels, and shapes it as a (`1, 3, 224, 224`) numpy array, the correct input shape of our model:

```
import numpy as np
from PIL import Image

def process_image(filename):
    image = Image.open(filename)
    image = image.resize((224,224))
    image = np.asarray(image)          # (224,224,3)
    image = np.moveaxis(image, 2, 0).  # (3,224,224)
    image = image[np.newaxis, :].      # (1,3,224,224)
    return image
```

6. Then, we import the DLR, and load the compiled model from the `resnet50` directory:

```
from dlr import DLRModel
model = DLRModel('resnet50')
```

7. Then, we load a dog image … or an image of a cat. Your choice!

```
image = process_image('dog.jpg')
#image = process_image('cat.png')
input_data = {'data': image}
```

8. Finally, we predict the image 100 times, printing the prediction to defeat any lazy evaluation that MXNet could implement:

```
import time
total = 0
for i in range(0,100):
    tick = time.time()
    out = model.run(input_data)
    print(out[0])
    tock = time.time()
    total+= tock-tick
print(total)
```

The dog and cat images, visible in the next images, are respectively predicted as [2.554065e-09 1.000000e+00] and [9.9967313e-01 3.2689856e-04], which is very nice given the validation accuracy of our model (about 84%):

Figure 13.5: Test images (source: Wikimedia)

Prediction time is about 1.2 seconds per image, which is slow but certainly good enough for plenty of embedded applications. Predicting with the vanilla model takes about 6-7 seconds, so the speedup is very significant.

As you can see, compiling models is a very effective technique. In the next section, we're going to focus on one of Neo's targets, **AWS Inferentia**,

Deploying models on AWS Inferentia

AWS Inferentia is a custom chip designed specifically for high throughput and low-cost prediction (`https://aws.amazon.com/machine-learning/inferentia`). Inferentia chips are hosted on **EC2 inf1** instances. These come in different sizes, with 1, 4, or 16 chips. Each chip contains four **NeuronCores**, implementing high-performance matrix multiply engines that speed up typical deep learning operations such as convolution. NeuronCores also contain large caches that save external memory accesses.

In order to run on Inferentia, models need to be compiled and deployed with the Neuron SDK (`https://github.com/aws/aws-neuron-sdk`). This SDK lets you work with TensorFlow, PyTorch, and Apache MXNet models.

You can work with the Neuron SDK on EC2 instances, compiling and deploying models yourself. Once again, SageMaker simplifies the whole process, as inf1 instances are part of the target architectures that Neo can compile models for.

You can find an example at `https://github.com/awslabs/amazon-sagemaker-examples/tree/master/sagemaker_neo_compilation_jobs/deploy_tensorflow_model_on_Inf1_instance`.

To close this chapter, let's sum up all the cost optimization techniques we discussed throughout the book.

Building a cost optimization checklist

You should constantly pay attention to cost, even in the early stages of your machine learning project. Even if you're not paying the AWS bill, someone is, and I'm sure quite you'll quickly find out who that person is if you spend too much.

Regularly going through the following checklist will help you spend as little as possible, get the most machine learning happy bang for your buck, and hopefully keep the Finance team off your back!

Optimizing costs for data preparation

With so much focus on optimizing training and deployment, it's easy to overlook data preparation. Yet, this critical piece of the machine learning workflow can incur very significant costs.

> **Tip #1**
> Resist the urge to build ad hoc ETL tools running on instance-based services.

Obviously, your workflows will require data to be processed in a custom fashion, for example, to apply domain-specific feature engineering. Working with a managed service such as **Amazon Glue, Amazon Athena**, or **Amazon SageMaker Processing**, you will never have to provision any infrastructure, and you will only pay for what you really use.

As a second choice, **Amazon EMR** is a fine service, provided that you understand how to optimize its own cost. As much as possible, you should avoid running long-lived, low-usage clusters. Instead, you should run transient clusters, and rely massively on **Spot Instances** for task nodes. You can find more information here:

- `https://docs.aws.amazon.com/emr/latest/ManagementGuide/emr-plan-longrunning-transient.html`
- `https://docs.aws.amazon.com/emr/latest/ManagementGuide/emr-instance-purchasing-options.html`

The same advice applies to **Amazon EC2** instances.

> **Tip #2**
> Use SageMaker Ground Truth and automatic labeling to cut down on data labeling costs.

If you need to label large unstructured datasets, enabling automatic labeling in **SageMaker Ground Truth** can save you a significant amount of time and money compared to labeling everything manually. You can read about it at `https://docs.aws.amazon.com/sagemaker/latest/dg/sms-automated-labeling.html`.

Optimizing costs for experimentation

Experimentation is another area that is often overlooked, and you should apply the following tips to minimize the related spend.

> **Tip #3**
>
> You don't have to use notebook instances.

As explained in *Chapter 1, Introducing Amazon SageMaker*, you can easily work with the SageMaker SDK on your local machine, or on a local development server.

> **Tip #4**
>
> Stop notebook instances when you don't need them.

This sounds like an obvious one, but are you really doing it? There's really no reason to run idle notebook instances: commit your work, stop them, and then restart them when you need them again. Storage is persisted and you can also use a **Lifecycle Configuration** to automate package installation or repository synchronization. You can read more about this at `https://docs.aws.amazon.com/sagemaker/latest/dg/notebook-lifecycle-config.html`.

> **Tip #5**
>
> Experiment at small scale, and with notebook instances of the correct size.

Do you really need the full dataset to start visualizing data and evaluating algorithms? Probably not. By working on a small fraction of your dataset, you'll be able to use smaller notebook instances. Here's an example: imagine 5 developers working 10 hours a day on their own `ml.c5.2xlarge` notebook instance. The daily cost is 5*10*$0.557=$27.85.

Right-sizing to `ml.t3.xlarge` (less RAM, burstable behavior), the daily cost would be reduced to 5*10*$0.233=$11.65. You would save $486 per month, which you could certainly spend on more experimentation, more training, more **Automatic Model Tuning**, and suchlike.

If you need to perform large-scale cleaning and processing, please take the time to migrate that work to a managed service (see Tip #1). Instead of working all day long with a humongous notebook instance. Don't say "Me? Never!". I know you're doing it!

> **Tip #6**
>
> Use Local Mode.

We saw in *Chapter 7, Extending Machine Learning Services with Built-in Frameworks*, how to use **Local Mode** to avoid firing up managed infrastructure in the AWS Cloud. This is a great technique to quickly iterate at no cost in the experimentation phase!

Optimizing costs for model training

There are many techniques you can use, and we've already discussed most of them.

> **Tip #7**
>
> Don't train on notebook instances.

I'm going to repeat myself here, but it's an important point. Unfortunately, this antipattern seems to be pretty common. People pick a large notebook instance (say, `ml.p3.2xlarge`, $4.284 per hour), fire up a large job, leave it running, forget about it, and end up paying good money for an instance sitting idle for hours once the job is complete.

Instead, please run your training jobs on managed instances. Thanks to **Distributed Training**, you'll get your results much quicker, and as instances are terminated as soon as training is complete, you will never overpay for training.

As a bonus, you won't be at the mercy of a clean-up script (or an overzealous admin) killing all notebook instances in the middle of the night ("because they're doing nothing, right?").

> **Tip #8**
>
> Pack your dataset in RecordIO / TFRecord files.

This makes it easier and faster to move your dataset around and distribute it to training instances. We discussed this at length in *Chapter 5, Training Computer Vision Models*, and *Chapter 6, Training Natural Language Processing*.

> **Tip #9**
>
> Use Pipe Mode.

Pipe Mode streams your dataset directly from Amazon S3 to your training instances. No copying is involved, which saves on start up time. We discussed this feature in detail in *Chapter 9, Scaling Your Training Jobs.*

> **Tip #10**
> Right-size training instances.

We saw how to do this in *Chapter 9, Scaling Your Training Jobs.* One word: **CloudWatch**.

> **Tip #11**
> Use Managed Spot Training.

We covered this in great detail in *Chapter 10, Advanced Training Techniques.* If that didn't convince you, nothing will! Seriously, there are very few instances when **Managed Spot Training** should not be used, and it should be a default setting in your notebooks.

> **Tip #12**
> Use AWS-provided versions of TensorFlow, Apache MXNet, and so on.

We have entire teams dedicated to extracting the last bit of performance from deep learning libraries on AWS. No offense, but if you think you can `pip install` and go faster, your time is probably better invested elsewhere. You can find more information at the following links:

- `https://aws.amazon.com/blogs/machine-learning/faster-training-with-optimized-tensorflow-1-6-on-amazon-ec2-c5-and-p3-instances/`

- `https://aws.amazon.com/about-aws/whats-new/2018/11/tensorflow-scalability-to-256-gpus/`

- `https://aws.amazon.com/blogs/machine-learning/amazon-web-services-achieves-fastest-training-times-for-bert-and-mask-r-cnn/`

Optimizing costs for model deployment

This very chapter was dedicated to several of these techniques. I'll add a few more ideas to cut costs even further.

> **Tip #13**
> Use batch transform if you don't need online predictions.

Some applications don't require a live endpoint. They are perfectly fine with **Batch Transform**, which we studied in *Chapter 11, Deploying Machine Learning Models*. The extra benefit is that the underlying instances are terminated automatically when the batch job is done, meaning that you will never overpay for prediction because you left an endpoint running for a week for no good reason.

> **Tip #14**
> Delete unnecessary endpoints.

This requires no explanation, and I have written "Delete the endpoint when you're done" tens of times in this book already. Yet, this is still a common mistake.

> **Tip #15**
> Right-size endpoints, and use autoscaling.

> **Tip #16**
> Use a multi-model endpoint to consolidate models.

> **Tip #17**
> Compile models with Amazon Neo to use fewer hardware resources.

> **Tip #18**
> At large scale, use AWS Inferentia instead of GPU instances.

And, of course, the mother of all tips for all things AWS, which is why we dedicated a full chapter to it – *Chapter 12, Automating Machine Learning Workflows*:

> **Tip #19**
> Automate, automate, automate!

Equipped with this checklist, not only will you slash your machine learning budget, but you will also build more robust and more agile workflows. Rome wasn't built in a day, so please take your time, use common sense, apply the techniques that matter most right now, and iterate.

Summary

In this final chapter, you learned different techniques that help to reduce prediction costs with SageMaker. First, you saw how to use autoscaling to scale prediction infrastructure according to incoming traffic. Then, you learned how to deploy an arbitrary number of models on the same endpoint, thanks to multi-model endpoints.

We also worked with Amazon Elastic Inference, which allows you to add fractional GPU acceleration to a CPU-based instance, and to find the right cost-performance ratio for your application. We then moved on to Amazon SageMaker Neo, an innovative capability that compiles models for a given hardware architecture, both for EC2 instances and embedded devices. Finally, we built a cost optimization checklist that will come in handy in your upcoming SageMaker projects.

You've made it to the end. Congratulations! You now know a lot about SageMaker. Now, go grab a dataset, build cool stuff, and let me know about it!

Other Books You May Enjoy

If you enjoyed this book, you may be interested in these other books by Packt:

Mastering Machine Learning on AWS

Saket Mengle, Maximo Gurmendez

ISBN: 978-1-78934-979-5

- Manage AI workflows by using AWS cloud to deploy services that feed smart data products
- Use SageMaker services to create recommendation models
- Scale model training and deployment using Apache Spark on EMR
- Understand how to cluster big data through EMR and seamlessly integrate it with SageMaker
- Build deep learning models on AWS using TensorFlow and deploy them as services

Hands-On Artificial Intelligence on Amazon Web Services

Subhashini Tripuraneni, Charles Song

ISBN: 978-1-78953-414-6

- Gain useful insights into different machine and deep learning models
- Build and deploy robust deep learning systems to production
- Train machine and deep learning models with diverse infrastructure specifications
- Scale AI apps without dealing with the complexity of managing the underlying infrastructure
- Monitor and Manage AI experiments efficiently
- Create AI apps using AWS pre-trained AI services

Leave a review - let other readers know what you think

Please share your thoughts on this book with others by leaving a review on the site that you bought it from. If you purchased the book from Amazon, please leave us an honest review on this book's Amazon page. This is vital so that other potential readers can see and use your unbiased opinion to make purchasing decisions, we can understand what our customers think about our products, and our authors can see your feedback on the title that they have worked with Packt to create. It will only take a few minutes of your time, but is valuable to other potential customers, our authors, and Packt. Thank you!

Index

C

T

Made in the USA
Las Vegas, NV
22 June 2021